Shobha De

Critical Studies

Series in Indian Writing

General Editor: R.K. Dhawan

Shobha De

Critical Studies

Edited by

Jaydipsinh Dodiya

Prestige

an international publishing house

Published by
Prestige Books
New Delhi 110 058
Ph. 011-25507139
email: prestigebooks@gmail.com
website: asiabookclub.com

Associate Office
60/29-45 Parramatta Road,
Concord, NSW 2137
Australia

ISBN: 81-7551-079-X
Edition 2011
Rs. 700

Printed at Mehra Offset Press, New Delhi 110 002

Contents

Comparative Studies

Socialite Evenings

Starry Nights

Sisters

Strange Obsession

Small Betrayals

Shooting from the Hip

Selective Memory

PREFACE

Shobha De, by common consent, is the most popular Indian woman writer today. Most of her books are bestsellers as she truthfully projects the image of the upper class woman of contemporary India. It is quite befitting that a critical evaluation of her work be made. The present book purports to be a pioneering attempt to assess her contribution to the Indian literary scene.

I cannot close these prefatory remarks without thanking the people who made this project possible. I put on record my sincere gratitude to Mr. Kalpakbhai Trivedi, former Pro-Vice-Chancellor of Saurashtra University, Professor A.K. Singh, Professor Rupsinhji Solanki, Professor Kamlesh Joshipura and Dr. Hastuben Sedani for their constant encouragement. I discussed the framework and scope of the book with Dr. Suman Bala, University of Delhi, and gained from her advice. Last but not the least, I must acknowledge my gratitude to my wife Mrs. Jignasha Dodiya, son Kuldeep and daughter Bhargavi without whose support and cooperation, this book would not have seen the light of the day.

JAYDIPSINH DODIYA

Saurashtra University
Rajkot

for

Hon. Dipchandbhai Gardi

President

Shardagram Education Trust

Mangrol

The Fiction of Shobha De: An Introduction

JAYDIPSINH DODIYA and R.K. DHAWAN

Shobha De is one of the most eminent and popular Indian novelists of our time; she is India's best-selling author. She was born in Maharashtra in 1948 and was educated in Delhi and Bombay. She graduated from St. Xavier's College, Bombay, with a degree in Psychology. She began a career in journalism in 1970 in the course of which she founded and edited three popular magazines *Stardust, Society* and *Celebrity* and was consulting Editor to *Sunday* and *Megacity*. She earned both name and fame while working as a free-lance writer and columnist for several leading newspapers and magazines. She is mother of six children. At present she lives in Bombay with her family. Even at the age of fifty-one, she is quite youthful, energetic and active.

Shobha De is the author of twelve books. In 1988, she wrote her first novel—the best-selling *Socialite Evenings* and in 1990 she published *Starry Nights*. Her other works are *Sisters, Sultry Days, Strange Obsession, Snapshots, Second Thoughts, Uncertain Liaisons* (co-authored with Khushwant Singh), *Shooting from the Hip, Small Betrayals, Surviving Men* and *Selective Memory: Stories from My Life*.

Shobha De as a writer is gifted with extraordinary ability to discuss very sensitive aspects of human life tactfully. The way she narrates each and every aspect of human relationship in general and man-woman relationship in particular, is really wonderful. The orthodox people in India criticise her for her open discussion of sexual matters. But her fiction has got tremendous response not only from several European countries but all over the world. All classes of people read and enjoy her fiction. It is no less an achievement. In fact, as a writer she differs considerably from other Indian women novelists writing in English. She is a writer who believes in very frank narration of incidents and absolute open-heartedness. We don't find anything reserved in her fiction from narrative point of view. In my opinion, she is the last person to care for what orthodox readers say about the subject-matter of her fiction. As a creative writer, she is becoming immensely popular day by day. Most of the readers enjoy her extraordinary narrative technique as well as her subject-matter.

One of the major reasons of Shobha De's popularity as a writer is her intimate understanding of the psyche of woman and her problems. Her treatment of the contemporary urban woman's position and the challenges she faces is not without significance. Says Shobha De: "I did write with a great deal of empathy toward women. Without waving the feminist flag, I feel very strongly about the woman's situation." Largely speaking, Indian fiction depicts three kinds of women: first, the poor women, belonging mostly to the rural class, portrayed by writers like Kamala Markandaya and R.K. Narayan; secondly, the middle class women, especially the educated and employed, depicted by writers like Nayantara Sahgal and Shashi Deshpande; and thirdly, the neo-rich aristocrat women depicted by writers like Namita Gokhale and Shobha De.

Shobha De has been many things to many people: super model, celebrity journalist and best-selling author. Her enigmatic personality has held her admirers under some kind of a spell. The present book attempts to make an inquiry into the nature and content of her fictional writings. During the period of last ten years since she started writing fiction, she has received a mixed response: her detractors dub her as the princess of pornography whileas her admirers extol her as a kind of queen among storytellers having irresistible appeal to the readers. Her novels, says R.S. Pathak in "Feminist Concerns in Shobha De's Works," seem to be the modern version of picaresque novels of the eighteenth century. The picaro in this case is a woman but she, too, is avid of experiences, in search of which she goes from place to place.

Thematically, Shobha De's novels are highly complex. They offer sufficient stuff to the critics to interpret them in varied ways. Sarbani Sen discusses the domain of cultural politics in De's fiction. Shobha De gives vivid picture of the society and culture of the high society of contemporary India. Eminent Italian scholar Alessandro Monti evaluates the fiction of Shobha De in terms of 'the making of modern India.'

Shobha De has been refereed to in the most number of multilingual gossip columns; she was a clue in a noted crossword puzzle; she is undoubtedly the most reactionary novelist (her first three novels have been chosen by the reputed School of Oriental and African Studies of London as course material); and she was the first person to popularize the now much read and heard Indian Esperanto: Hinglish. If De has been selected, it means that she is being taken more seriously. It is also because her fiction portrays the contemporary reality more distinctively than that of other writers.

Shobha De is essentially a feminist writer. Like Nayantara Sahgal and Shashi Deshpande, she concentrates on women's problems and gives a new approach to them. She is a modern novelist who recognizes the displacement and marginalization of women and attempts to turn this pattern upside down through her writings. She constantly tries to shatter patriarchal hegemony and raises a voice of protest against male dominance. For this, she explores the world of urban women in India. In "Two Aspects of Feminism. The Expressive and the Explosive in Shobha De," Sanjay Kumar discusses the women's role to challenge and protest in Shobha De's novels *Sisters* and *Strange Obsession*. According to Pushp Lata, Shobha De's female protagonists are remarkable when measured against men. The man-woman's complementary image has been completely shattered in her novels. This is her viewpoint in her article "A Protest against the Patriarchal in Shobha De's Works."

II

Socialite Evenings, the first novel of Shobha De, is about the journey of a prominent Bombay socialite Karuna, from a gauche middle class girl to a self-sufficient woman. Making a feminist approach, S.P. Swain analyzes the novel which gives us the picture of the marginalization of the Indian women at the hands of their husbands. Subhash Chandra discusses *Socialite Evenings* as a novel that presents the institutions of family and marriage existing in the wealthy class of the Indian society. According to him, this portrayal is authentic, being an inside story, because the narrator (the writer) herself belongs to this class. Pramod Nayar, on the other hand, considers *Socialite Evenings* as a romantic tale, suffused with feminist traits. Urbashi Barat is of the view that the most ubiquitous and enduring theme in the novel is the search for identity and selfhood. She analyzes in detail *Socialite Evenings* as a version of Kunstlerroman.

G. Sheela Swarupa Rani says that Karuna has a quest to find about herself which springs from her discontent with her own life which doesn't come up to her expectations. For Inna Walter, *Socialite Evenings* is essentially a story of the modern New Woman, named Karuna in the novel, who is independent in every way. It is an initiation tale from innocence to experience, in the style of Bharati Mukherjee's *Wife* and *Jasmine*.

In order to highlight the status of women, Shobha De gives a negative portrayal of men in some of her novels. In his article on Gloria Naylor and Shobha De, Subhash Chandra makes a comparative study of the image of man in their novels *The Women of Brewster Place* and *Socialite Evenings* respectively. In *Socialite Evenings*, the picture of man as husband is determined by the dictates of the feminist ideology. While the women in the novel go around indulging in promiscuous sex, the husbands are made to tolerate or ignore it. In her article "From Purdah to Popular Culture," Bhargavi Rao compares feminine sensibility as embedded in Anees Jung's *Unveiling India* and Shobha De's *Socialite Evenings*.

III

Shobha De's second novel, *Starry Nights*, took the reading public by storm for its frank and candid expression of love and lust. It is the story of a film star Aasha Rani, who comes from a small-town background to the tinsel world of Bombay and after struggling for sometime she becomes a star. In acquiring this stature, she does not hesitate to adopt any method including semi-nudity and free sex. Sandhyarani Dash focuses on the character of Aasha Rani and takes into account various factors that lead to her explorations vis-a-vis her sexploitations in a male-dominated society. Geeta Barua considers the novel as a story of the rise and fall of a star, the protagonist Aasha Rani.

Shobha De, in the opinion of Nisha Trivedi, realistically presents in her fiction the models of different types of women before us. These women are strong in character and take bold decisions to survive in society. This is true of Aasha Rani who struggles, survives and achieves success. Sudhir Kumar takes a feminist approach to the novel and interprets it in the light of the contemporary feminist critical theories put forth by M. Gilbert and Susan Gubar. Prabhat Kumar Pandeya discusses the theme of lesbianism in the novel and argues that this trait of Aasha Rani has a bearing on her character.

IV

Shobha De's third novel *Sisters*, published in 1992, draws our attention neither to the aristocrats of high social circles nor to the glamorous world of Bombay film industry, but to the fabulous and intriguing corporate world of business tycoons. Analyzing the novel, Neena Arora finds the novel perfect for a super-hit Hindi formula film with well-measured doses of suspense, romance, imported locales and sex. Another critic, E. Satyanarayana, finds the novel dealing with the psychic conflict of a liberated woman protagonist who is caught between a personal self and a societal self.

V

Not all writings of Shobha De are 'aberrations.' On the title page of her third novel, *Sultry Days*, she writes: "Finally a book by me, that they [her children] can read." In this novel, Shobha De returns to the mainstream new woman, says Sharad Shrivastava in his article on the novel. Nisha, the narrator, is attracted to Deb because he is a mixture of opposites. However, she sees through Deb's psuedo-commitments and in the process discovers her own commitments. Indira Bhatt makes a comparative study of *Sultry Days* with Gita Mehta's *A River Sutra* in terms of the theme of orientalism. Whileas Shobha De depicts the modern life-style of neo-rich people, Gita Mehta selects aspects of traditional spiritual heritage of Indian society.

VI

Shobha De's next novel, *Strange Obsession*, acquired popularity for depicting lesbian relationship. The story revolves around the life and lustful relationship of two young women, Amrita and Meenakshi. Both the scholars Neelam Tikkha and Gajendra Kumar deal with the philosophy of lesbianism and its practice in the novel.

VII

Shobha De's novel *Snapshots* is essentially a feminist work. It unveils the life of six girls of Santa Maria High School. Examining the novel, Urbashi Barat finds Shobha De using the popular narrative technique of exploring the lives of individuals within a closed environment from shifting points of view, so that there is no one protagonist and the different stories of different characters make up a mosaic that represents the novelist's vision of life. Madhumalati Adhikari discusses at length the equation of power in the novel. Her analysis indicates that Shobha De, like all feminist writers, is deeply concerned with the alignment of power that exerts physical, political, social and economic control over women in order to fragment her. In another article, she discusses the novel as a postcolonial text, as one that "embodies the spirit of postcolonial literature that concretizes the adventures of powerful, emancipated new woman."

VIII

Second Thoughts deals with the story of a young middle class Bengali girl, Maya, who marries a Bombay-based foreign-returned Bengali boy. The young bride is more fascinated and in love with Bombay than at the prospect of having married Ranjan. Once in Bombay after her marriage, her disillusionment begins. On second thoughts, she learns to survive the sultriness of not only Bombay but also her marriage. Alka Saxena analyzes the novel at length and shows how it offers a slice of urban life. Similarly, Jaydipsinh Dodiya finds the novel an explosive tale of love and betrayal that exposes the hollowness of Indian marriage system. G.D. Barche lends a new dimension to the novel by comparing it to the Biblical story of Adam and Eve. He is of the view that in delineating the lives of Maya and Ranjan, Shobha De has reproduced and restructured the myth of Fall.

IX

In *Small Betrayals* and *Shooting from the Hip*, Shobha De ventures to experiment with other genres of literature. In the former she handles the technique of short story whileas in the latter she deals with essay writing of which she has been a past master as a journalist. Madhumalati Adhikari discusses at length the stories collected in the volume *Small Betrayals* and finds that Shobha De has explored in these the average experiences of betrayal in its infinite variety. *Shooting from the Hip* presents Shobha De as a versatile writer as she touches upon different areas like politics, media, food, festivals, films, books and personalities. She gives absorbing profiles of Khushwant Singh, Vikram Seth, R.K. Laxman, J.R.D. Tata, Amitabh Bachchan, Benazir Bhutto, Asha Bhonsle. "On her observations on travel, food and films," says the critic K.V. Surendran, "she is straightforward and original."

X

The publication of the latest work, *Selective Memory* (Penguin 1998) is a landmark in the literary career of Shobha De. Subtitled as "Stories from My Life," it is a heartening change for the readers of Shobha De. It gives them an ample opportunity to know the author more intimately. It is written at a time in her life that is appropriate to take stock of things as anybody would feel at fifty. Shobha De describes how she was persuaded to write her autobiography by David Davidar when she was nearing the "mid-point age." While she has been honest in giving expression to her perceptions and feelings, she deliberately chooses what she wishes to reveal of her past. Much has therefore been left out which she would not like to share with others. The noted critic Urbashi Barat points out that Shobha De's focus on certain parts of her life is quite in the tradition of autobiography.

Though Shobha De does not reveal all the secrets of her hectic colourful life, *Selective Memory* serves as an excellent source to understand the author and her life. An unbiased reading of the autobiography gives us an authentic picture of the middle-class Maharashtrian woman and her various roles as a model, columnist, and writer. In his scholarly paper on *Selective Memory*, N.P. Singh focuses on the theme of generation gap embedded in the text of the narrative from the beginning to the end.

Shobha De's handling of the mode of autobiography is superb. In this epic first person narrative, points out Chittaranjan Misra in his article "Shobha De on Shobha De," the writer talks about the art of autobiography like a self-conscious narrator. She reconstructs the images of the self in the irrevocable past.

The real beauty of an autobiography is constituted in the image of the self that emerges through the writing. So, self must be placed at the central position. In *Selective Memory*, according to the critic P.S. Kasture, Shobha De is successful in keeping constant focus on her self without violating the sanctity of other selves.

The book has added in great measure to the literary success of the author. In her article "*Selective Memory*: A Reflective Response," Nirmala C. Prakash says that prior to the publication of this work, Shobha De had never been considered a serious writer. After reading the book, one is bound to shake off the image of the writer as one who has no substance in her writings and caters to the appeasement of male psychology. There emerges in the book the image of a person who is deeply conventional, highly devoted, a skilful storyteller and a shrewd judge of people.

The De Debate: Cultural Politics and De's Novels

SARBANI SEN

Ours is a complex, confusing and complicated world. A maze wherein powerflows, powerlines and powergames dangerously collide and fractitiously contend with each other. In the contest to dominate and exploit, in the effort to snatch the maximum share of magnificent world cheesecake there are very many powers and as many ruthless chessplayers. Not surprisingly, therefore, India and other ex-colonies like her find themselves after Independence to be in the iron grip of a newer, more sophisticated and more dangerous colonialism-neo-colonialism.

Colonialism according to the *International Relations Dictionary* is "the rule of an area and its people by an external soverignty [that] advances the military security, economic advantage and international prestige of the imperial powers."[1] New-colonialism on the other hand is described by Cohen as "a complex of economic, political and military relations of the more economically developed lands on the less. . . . It is the network of means of control exercised by one economy on the other."[2] In this urge to exercise power without responsibility or as Alexander Deconde puts it, "Colonise through the backdoor,"[3] it becomes important if not mandatory to generate the same psychology of dependence that O. Manoni[4] defined as an attribute of colonialism. Though economic power is what neo-colonial news centres in Anglo-America are really looking for, it becomes as necessary for these interests to control and manpulate culture. In the effort to create the right clients, namely "Clients willing to adjust their laws and politics to the requirements of big business,"[5] it is expedient to use the tool of culture. To quote Evans in this context, "they first introduce the wares and even more important, by trying to convince the people to consume them, the multinational firms (through whom neo-colonialism is concretised) . . . help to shape the cultural life of the less developed countries."[6]

America's CIA Manual puts it thus, "The human being should be considered the primary objective in a political war. And the human being has the most critical point in his mind. Once his mind has been reached, the political animal has been decapitated without receiving bullets."[7] Since America, who with England constitutes the main players in the neo-colonial power arena, finds it essential to reach the mind, she uses the mass media—T.V. radio and the print medium. In a manner reminiscent of British or French colonial cultural imposition, Anglo-American neo-colonialism propagates, rather thrusts down their neo-colonies, images of themselves—images of glamour, glitz and glory, images that cannot coexist with the neo-colonies' own native cultural ethos. Using the baits of fame, money and status to entrap their nature stooges to carry out their gameplan, this coca-cola imperialism creates conditions that are as extremely as extensively dangerous, for it not only subverts indigenous culture but also hits where it hurts the most—the soul. This situation is not very different from what the poet Graham Fielder had described so succinctly:

> It is the white man's burden
> As everybody knows
> To teach the Black to feel ashamed
> And then to sell him clothes.[8]

It is against this background and knowledge that Shobha De needs to be viewed. Born in 1948, the glamorous novelist and journalist is a product of this powered and loaded cultural field. Writing for a public created by and inhabiting the post-MTV world, Shobha De has poised herself prettily on the edge of success, acquired on the neo-coloniser's terms, acquired by being co-opted. Fame and success that have come to her also because like her journalistic writings, her novels are read. If they tick with the masses, it is perhaps becuase they find in it a portrayal of contemporary reality or more appropriately what they think reality is. This is a fact that cannot and ought not to the ignored. As critical opinion has it, there is in De "much that is amusing, outrageous, thought-provoking, even shocking."[9] "Rarely does one see an Indian author writing with such frankness and obvious feeling"[10] "Slaughter(ing) Macho males with vengeance and rattle poison(ing) her gender with disdain and disregard . . . (She is) scintillating . . . and ruthless . . . demolish(ing) civilizations."[11]

No wonder then that De has aroused a veritable storm and that a fiery debate rages around her. A debate where the camps are sharply divided, ranging in approach from being fanatically adoring to relentlessly severe. If one section of critics dismiss her as the princess of pornography, the other group extols her as a kind of queen among storytellers with the right to have an adulating world at her beaufiful feet. What has added fuel to the raging fire is that three of her novels have been chosen by the reputed school of Oriental and African studies, London as course material. If De has been selected, De the supposed writer of quickie bestsellers, it means that she is being taken seriously. And since neocolonial cultural politics has made us dependent and hungry for "phoren" approval, it means that De has arrived as a novelist. And how.

The question that requires analysis is whether De deserves the recognition she is getting or is she merely being rewarded for allowing herself to be co-opted. Is she really, as Paul Roberts puts it, "a good writer, enigmatic, straightforward, crude, erudite, girlish, wise,"[12] or is she merely drawing the kind of India the Euro-American neo-colonial powers desire to see? Or desire to convert India into? Is De's Bombay of *Starry Nights, Sisters* and the just released *Small Betrayals*, Bombay or a xerox copy if not a poorer version of downtown London or Big Apple, New York?

Shobha De's *Sisters* published in 1992 and set in Bombay is the engrossing tale of two beautiful, wealthy and warring sisters. Inhabiting the corrupt world of big business, the "women play for very high stakes and are driven by ambition, lust, greed and hate."[13] What is unmistakable about the novel is that in spite of the Indian names and setting, it is unmistakably American in inspiration. It has all the spicy ingredients that go into the cooking of the piping hot American bestseller—a pair of amazingly beautiful, ruthlessly ambitious, filthily rich, single, young and glamorous ladies dazzling with diamonds and oozing oomph, who hate and love each other with equal ferocity. It needs no critical acumen to see that De is producing a desi version of an American bestseller, where the Indian ambience is merely an exoticising on an unmistakably American cake. However unlike photocopies, De sells, managing to create a public eager to lap in the supposed new Indian reality. This is not to say that Indian women cannot be ambitious, glamorous or believers in free sex. Or to deny that the number of "liberated" Westernized women ready for a good lie is rising. Yes, De might be turning the spotlight on the new morality that has finally set in, and on the new neo-colonial generation who recognize no inhibitions or age-old cultural bonds on their behaviour and lives in the mad race to ape the West. The internalization of the American ethos by the neo-colonial generation may signify the success of the Anglo-American neo-colonial experiment but the valorisation by Shobha De of this miniscule even if gradually expanding minority bespeaks volumes on where Shobha De's sympathies lie.

The same could be said of *Starry Nights* (1991) "a pulsating account of survival and success in the ruthless world of Hindi films."[14] The constant reiteration in it of physical couplings may be in keeping with the public secret of Bollywood's casting couch but it is the Americanized attitude to the body and the un-Indian amorality signified therein that is noteworthy. What one needs to remember however is that much of India's manners and many of her morals flow in from Bollywood. Given the reach of the cinema as also the other arms of the Indian media-print, TV, Cable and radio—it is not in the least surprising that cultural imperialist forces and their Indian adherents like De should subvert these forms and use them to peg their ideas on. The images that beam down at us from magazine covers, TV screens or celluloid films is more often than not, Westernized, decultured. Being essentially a media person with undoubted exposure and inside knowledge of Bollywood's dark secrets, De is not unacquainted with these undercurrents. Yet, she chooses because it suits her to glamourize the Bollywood world, with its ugly gossip, hot scandals and sexual orgies. The authorial point of view almost seems to condone Aasha Rani's many relationships with a multitude of men and occasionally women or her connections with blue films and underworld dons. This novel like the earlier one has a pair of warring star sisters—one of De's overused yet surefire formula for selling success—who at the end, reunite and predictably so.

What is less predictable is De's latest offering hot from the printing press—*Small Betrayals* (1995). A collection of short, happy stories, it delineates the shattering of the great Indian dream. The tales show how our own lives are not in our own hands, how we are betrayed everytime, how in postcolonial India, there is no affection, no understanding, no connecting. Instead there are marital breakups, sexual dissatisfaction and communal riots. Neo-colonial designs have come to fruition here. Adding to the interest value of this book is De's sharp eye for detail, her piercingly accurate characterization, her "perceptive insight of the secret depths of the human psyche."[15] Here at last are "easily recognizable everyday people, their lives and souls laid bare . . . each story encompass(ing) its own exquisite world of passion, romance, fantasy and inevitably hard reality."[16] The reality of the great Indian betrayal. To neo-colonialism. Significantly this book has not been prescribed by the S.O.A.S.

Viewing Shobha De thus as a willing tool to further neo-colonial interests is not to lend seriousness to a flimsy writer of flimsier bestsellers using sex to boost up sales. Rather sensitiveness to this angle would highlight De's conscious unconscious cooptation, that she is selling the India neo-colonial forces want to see in order to make a quick buck. It would throw light also on the cultural politics behind the lionising of Shobha De abroad. Awareness of neo-colonial cultural-manoeuvres that have created a public for the likes of De even if destined to succeed in our unipolar world and a post-Manmohanomics resistance. India might at least make us mentally cognizant of the play of forces of cultural politics that have penetrated into every little aspect of Indian life including the world of her bestsellers and their reputation abroad. Whether we choose to recognize it or not, the reality is that neo-colonialism has altered the cultural situation, and altered it almost irrevocably. What the Indian intellectual will or will not do about it, though, only Father Time can tell.

NOTES

1. Jack C. Plane and Roy Otan, *The International Relations Dictionary* (Santa Barbara, California: ABC—CUO, 1988), p. 26.
2. Benjamin J. Cohen, *The Question of Imperialism* (New York: Basic Books, 1973), p. 11.
3. Edward M. Bennet, "Colonialism," *Encyclopaedia of American Foreign Policy*, ed. Alexander Deeonde (New York: Scribners, 1978), i, p. 137

4. O. Manoni, *Preopero and Caliban: The Psychology of Colonization* (New York: Fredrick A. Prager, 1956), p. 25.
5. Estes Kefauver, *In a Few Hands* (Harmondsworth: Penguin, 1956), p. 200.
6. Peter Evans, "Shoes, OPIC and the Unique Persuasion and Multinational Corporations and U.S.-Brazilian Relations," *Capitalism and the State in U.S.-Latin America Relations*, ed. Richard R. Fagen (Stanford: Stanford University Press, 1979), p. 300.
7. Qtd. Howard H. Frederick, "Electronic Penetration," *Reagan Versus the Sandinistas: The Undeclared War on Nicaragua*, ed. Thomas Walker (Colorado: Westview Press, 1987), p. 123.
8. Marcus Linea:, *Zapping the Third World: The Disaster of Development Aid* (London: Pluto Press, 1985), p. 210.
9. *The Hindustan Times*, qtd. *Small Betrayals* (New Delhi: UBSPD, 1995).
10. *Business Standard, ibid.*
11. *The Tribune, ibid.*
12. Paul W. Roberts, *The Toronto Review, ibid.*
13. Shobha De, *Sisters* (New Delhi: Penguin, 1992).
14. Shobha De, *Starry Nights* (New Delhi: Penguin, 1991).
15. Title Page, Shobha De, *Small Betrayals*.
16. *Ibid.*

Shakti Unleashed in Muppyland: Shobha De and the Making of Modern India

ALESSANDRO MONTI

> What is a Maharashtrian Yuppy known as? The answer is too damn obvious—a "Muppy," naturally.
>
> Shobha De, "Muppies!"

In her depiction of Bollywood (the Bombay filmi industry) and of the demimonde that revolves around it, Shobha De stresses certain controversial features of social and human conduct, whose disruptive rules break down with insistent perversity all decent communal ethos.

As a rule, Indian critics tend to highlight some of Shobha De's novels (especially, *Socialite Evenings*, 1989) as though they were a saucy stage show, dramatizing rampant sexual licence (in the form of adultery, homosexuality or lesbianism or general unshamed promiscuity) along with a propensity to corruption and shady dealings, these embarrassing facets being the hallmark of the new India.

However, given the unstructured quality of her contemporary chronicle, such a black agenda has its lighter side.[1] It is less a matter of deploying a systematic view of the changes in modern India or of tackling the gender issue than of trying one's hand at a form of sophisticated gossip, strongly reminiscent of the nineteenth century Anglo-Indian "gup-gup."

Her discourse simply replaces the colonial "station" or the "heavenly" Simla with Bombay, the modern Asiatic metropolis, culturally on a par with Western counterparts like London or New York. As a matter of fact, Shobha De popularizes a line of argument already suggested by Salman Rushdie in his collected essays, *Imaginary Homelands* (1991), in which he writes that "given the international and increasingly homogeneous nature of metropolitan culture, the journey from, for example, rural America to New York City is a more extreme act of migration than a move from, say, Bombay."[2]

Such a sense of continuity between West and East is conveyed by the topical word "socialite," in one of Shobha De's most notorious novels, the aforementioned *Socialite Evenings*. The use of the word "socialite" goes back to the "roaring" or, rather, "naughty" thirties, first appearing in an essay by Wyndham Lewis (collected in the miscellaneous volume *Press Gang*, 1937), "apropos of the wealthy, lissom Mayfair film amateur, socialite, dress designer, surrealist."[3]

Since the composite picture that Shobha De draws in her novel in certain respects circumscribes the social and human setting within which the narrative action takes place, it makes sense to turn to a provocative and stimulating suggestion voiced by Gayatri Chakravorty Spivak in an interview, positing the notion of India as a metonym for select slices of "socialized" population, immediately locatable as part of a circuit.[4]

The network of circuits Gayatri Spivak speaks of is somewhat similar in its role and function to the structure advocated by V.S. Naipaul in *India—a Million Mutinies Now* (1990) for the so-called "in-groupings," these being relatively small social units which are trying hard to organize and fit themselves into the updated varieties of the traditional divisions and subdivisions that rule the Hindu world. At the top of the social ladder, such groups belong to the fringes of monied power, of which they are both the mundane "ragtag and bobtail" appendix and the mongrel labour force that is also available for sexual exploitation, within the Bollywood system.

To equate the "socialite" milieu with the Bollywood world (or underworld) posits a deregulative metonym, which disrupts the measure of a common civilized space, such as that yielded by the notion of a "socialized" community. This safe measure is heavily discounted in the novel *Starry Nights* (1991), with its derogatory sequences of "sthalas" (places) devoted either to wholesale corruption or to temporary escapes from the Bollywood hell. The inverted epiphany sketched by Shobha De ranges from the luxurious bedchamber of the ambiguous and powerful Sheth Amirchand, a politician who is the don of Bombay's underworld, to Dubai, a fallen paradise for neurotic shoppers and updated Eastern mobsters, or "goondas."

The unsavoury touches in the human and social landscape draw attention both to the liminal quality of the "socialite" circuit, whose members are bent on pleasure, and the nefarious activities of the "socialized capital," craftily devising destructive strategies of power and control. Once again, *Starry Nights* makes a valuable test-case, spotlighting as it does the career of the filmi star Aasha Rani, who whores her way to ephemeral stardom. The pressures the filmi milieu exacts on the heroine of *Starry Nights* are toned down to a more intimate quest for self-expression and identity in *Socialite Evenings*. Actually, the novel might be easily viewed as a sort of subdued feminist manifesto, at a crossroads between the "socialite" lure and the unredeemed nostalgia for a lost way of life.

A war cry in Shobha De's essays summarizes the issue here at hand, "Putting the sati-savitri act together in our confused times hasn't been a cake-walk. Plus, who really wants to prove her untainted character to a boring Rama, when there might be a devastating Ravana around?"[5] The naughty wording of the sentence, making irresistible fun of the respectable Hindu wife who is identified with the devoted Sati/Savitri type, deploys a series of clever puns. The name of the idealized "pativrata" Sita is switched into the contiguous "Sati," both the first spouse of Siva, who sacrifices herself so as to remove an offence against the God, and the title given to a widow sanctified by being burned alive. However, Sita and Sati share the same rite of female purification through burning, since Sita must submit herself to the ordeal by fire, after Rama has rescued her from the clutches of Ravana, the demon-king of Sri Lanka.

A further sense of transgression is given by the uncapitalized words "sati" and "savitri," whereas "Rama" and "Ravana" are correctly given in capitals. An Indian writer expatriated to Canada, M.G. Vassanji, adopts a similar device in *No New Land*, 1991. In his novel, an Indian migrant living in Toronto speaks of a Canadian woman he has sexual relations with as a "gauri," a "deshi" variant for a vamp.[6] In both De's and Vassanji's texts, the refusal to capitalize defuses the derogative innuendos suggested by the proper spelling of the three names as Sati, Savitri and Gauri, which in their correct form all posit a role of feminine sacrificial devotion to a husband.

In relation to the "pativrata," the unconventional use of "sati" and "savitri" acts as a medium of defilement, recounting as it does the issue of gender in terms of discursive displacement. By deflecting the usual iconic role of the Hindu married woman into an overt figure of sexual transgression, the writer unsentimentalizes the male character, replacing the "boring" Rama with the more "interesting" Ravana. Such a beckoning change in lexicon is shockingly clothed in the easy language of slang, the measure of the dominant Hindu patriarchal ideology being here deconstituted as the impossibility of seeing the traditional marriage as it were a mere "cake-walk."

This discursive strategy mobilizes the figure of the mythical female, thus forcing the traditional disciplinary thrust into an unmistakable plea for a deregulated behaviour. A comprehensive pattern for the proairetic organization of the discourse might be found in the Bengali "bhadralok" comedy of the nineteenth century. Bankim Chandra Chatterjee's novella *Indira* (1873, revised and enlarged in 1893) depicts a corrective version of Sita's misfortunes, the heroine being kidnapped by a gang of "dacoits," while on the way to her husband. As in the case of Sita, she loses both caste and bridal identity, and has to submit herself to the "vrata" of banishment.

However, Bankim Chandra highlights a role of seduction for Indira, who plays in disguise the "mohini" with her husband, a "socialized" character in perspective, given his shady dealings with the English or his propensity to be enticed by women. The inverted paradigm in which sita becomes mohini and Rama Ravana entails a further (but unexchangeable) excess, whose distancing shift foregrounds the body of the woman as an object of female desire and knowledge, escaping as it were the circuit of marriage and childbirth.

The Bengali "antapur" in which the two women Indira and Subhashini interact and plot might be viewed as an incipient site of feminine "jouissance," marking the already shifting line between the ambiguous shadows of the "zanana" and the uncaring promiscuity of the contemporary "socialite" milieu. The situation acts as a prelude to the quasi-lesbian infringement in *Socialite Evenings* (last section of chapter 8), in which the high-class whore Nisha grotesquely exposes her excessive body. Despite its intimations of forbidden intimacy, the "overflowing" sexual tension of the passage soon yields to parody and estrangement.

The naked body of Nisha (or rather, its anatomical close up) is viewed as it were an object of otherness and depersonalizing reification.

shattering the unity of the self. Her body is marked as an "extravagant" assemblage of erogeneous zones with different price tags,

> Nisha's "perfect" body—I must admit it looked pretty grotesque to me, with bulbous breasts and a small ass. If there was one feature that was indeed perfect—it was her navel. But, as she sardonically pointed out to me, 'It is cute, *yaar*. But what use is it to me?' She had a point.[7]

Nisha's "exorbitance" serves as a foil for the myth of the goddess Sati, whose scattered and labelled body construes the Indian landscape as a grid of sacred sites, these being the fragmented icons of a divine body, offered to the reconstituting gaze of the devotee. The ritual act of viewing the Goddess through the scattered parts of her body brackets as well the pornographic extravaganza of *Strange Obsession*, 1992.

The case of the insane woman known as Minx, with her obsessive and voyeuristic passion for the supermodel Amrita, releases the impulse to telescope the fetishized object, either of love in the novel or of worship in the real life, into a victim to be destroyed. It is less a matter of constructing a high comedy in the "adirasa" mood, than of epitomizing the processes which sacralize the female body through evoking the loss of a pristine wholeness, concerning primarily the status of Hindu wife. In a similar vein, her refusal to survive as a star distances the heroine of *Starry Nights* from her fascinating body, as if she were mimicking the Sita/Sati pattern of self-imposed exile or death. Only by disavowing her polluting filmi career can she share again a communal female identity as a virtual "pativrata."

Aasha Rani's painful return to type qualifies the frivolous overtones of the fashionable "deshi" discourse, that forms the pattern of the "socialite" group in *Socialite Evenings* as well as that of the writer herself in the essay "The Convertible Culture."[8] However, the transition from what is "phoren" back to a "deshi" style of life updates the lexical medium into the more glamorous language of advertisement and fashionable ethnicity. Whereas the old-fashioned use in Indian English could take advantage of such peculiar idioms as "suitings" instead of "suits," to indicate its vocation of miscegenating freely between the two cultures, the return to tradition advocated by the mundane characters of *Socialite Evenings* deploys a new model of hybridization, interbreeding as it were the untranslatable glamour of the East with the promotional lingo of the West.

It is relevant to the present discussion the lavish use of ethnic sartorial idioms in *Socialite Evenings*, such as "heavily embroidered *lehenga*" or "*zary*-bordered *angavastram*." (10) I corroborate my point by quoting a few captions from an advertisement, whose flamboyant language promotes a deluxe sari shop in Bangalore. At "Saree Kemp" customers can find "futuristic and fusion" saris, such as "Agnika, a flaming shamoy with Parsi border" (actually, a red sari, presumably named after Agni, the god of fire), or "Artika, a fusion of Patola and Sambalpuri," or "Mahika, a dewy crepe-and-zari ghagra choli," and so on.

The language of advertising and the "socialite" style transpose the rich variety and multiplicity that characterize the culture of India into a high-flown extravagance of language, so as to continuously defer the process of comprehension of the text to a sophisticated and hybridized mercantile rhetoric. A Taj Mahal of the new India devoted to consumerism, the Bangalore Kemp chain of "kidswear, salwar kameez, saris and men" stores, with their crowds of manikins representing either ethnic glamour in dressing or slightly outdated "phoren" fashion, highlights the travesty Shobha De's "muppies" (or, rather "muppets") are obliged to display as a precarious mark of their divided lives.

Such a sign of mimicry is derisively defused by a scathing remark in *Starry Nights*, whereby a debutante Aasha Rani is mocked off as "another Southie idli," because of her hideous candy-pink sari, the implication being that you can have her as easily as you can have an idli. The reference to food de-indexes the ethnic paradigm, since it equates the "socialite" milieu with a fast food dedicated to sexual gluttony against sari-clad women.

NOTES

1. Shobha De, "Treat this volume as an unstructured chronicle of our times," "Author's Note," p. xii, in *Shooting from the Hip* (1994; New Delhi: UBS, 1995).
2. Salman Rushdie, "Gunter Grass," in *Imaginary Homelands* (London:

Granta Books, 1991), p. 278.

3. The volume is edited by Russell Leonard, and a Leonard Daintee is speaking. The full title of the volume (a collection of parodies) is *Press Gang! Crazy World Cronicle.*
4. Gayatri Chakravorty Spivak, "Postmarked Calcutta, India," in *The Post-Colonial Critic*, ed. Sarah Harasym (New York and London: Routledge, 1990), pp. 80-81.
5. Shobha De, "The Mirage of Womancipation," in *Shooting from the Hip*, p. 111. For a dictionary definition of "cake walking," "a couple dance, in which a man and a woman strutted, stepping highly to a lively music, around the ballroom, the best couple being presented with a highly decorated cake." It was in vogue at the turn of the century.
6. M.G. Vassanji, *No New Land* (Toronto: McLelland and Stewart, 1991), p. 108.
7. Shobha De, *Socialite Evenings* (1989; New Delhi: Penguin India, 1993), p. 105.
8. Shobha De, "The Convertible Culture," in *Shooting from the Hip*, pp. 13-18.

Feminist Concerns in Shobha De's Work: A Study in Attitudes

R.S. PATHAK

In 1928, Virginia Woolf delivered a modest lecture called *A Room of One's Own*. No body could have foreseen at that time that one day it would give rise to a new thinking on issues pertaining to the status and role of women. Talking about women's relationships, Virginia Woolf says that they are "too simple" and that "So much has been left out, unattempted."[1] While books like Simone de Beauvoir's *The Second Sex* (1949-50) nurtured the feminist ideology, it was in the seventies and eighties of the present century that various issues touching women were considered systematically. A positive sense of feminine identity has found recognition now, and women are stepping out of the rigid sex roles assigned to them traditionally. They are busy, in the Western world and the urban patches in India, with "self-actualizing, whose identities are not dependent on men."[2] Conscious of the evils originating from patriarchy, they would not endorse the wisdom of Tennysonian separation of roles and spheres of activity: "Man for the field and woman for the hearth:/Man for the sword and for the needle she." (*The Princess,* V, 427) Indian women novelists have concentrated on women's problems in their work and have given vent to a new approach to and consciousness of the emerging phenomenon. What was just a beginning in writers like Anita Desai has assumed a strident posture in Shobha De and others.

Shobha De burst upon the literary scene with her best-seller *Socialite Evenings* in 1988, which was followed by *Starry Nights* in 1990, *Sisters* and *Strange Obsession* in 1992, *Sultry Days* in 1994, *Snapshots* in 1995, and *Second Thoughts* in 1996. The popularity of Shobha De's novels is due to their contents, her mastery over the art of story telling, and her use of the language. In fact, her novels seem to be the modern version of picaresque novels of the eighteenth century. The picaro in this case is a woman, but she, too, is avid of experiences, in search of which she goes from place to place. Shobha De began her career as a journalist in 1970 in the course of which she founded and edited three popular magazines—*Stardust, Society* and *Celebrity* and acted as Consulting Editor to *Sunday* and *Megacity*. It may be partly on account of her experience as a journalist that she is able to say things interestingly and with a courage of conviction in a language uniquely her own. Her novels also owe their incomparable popularity to her intimate understanding of the psyche for women and their problems.

Shobha De claims to be "a pioneer" in the field of "popular fiction" writing. She also claims to be "among the first to explore the world of the urban woman in India."[3] Through her novels and essays, De has tried to shatter patriarchal hegemony. Woman's significant difference underlies her sexuality, and it is from her sexuality that most of her problems arise. As Alice Jardine puts it, "The putting into discourse of 'woman' as that *process* diagnosed . . . is intrinsic to modernity; indeed, the valorization of the feminine, woman, and her obligatory, that is historical, connotations, as somehow intrinsic to new and necessary modes of thinking, writing, and speaking."[4] Any sensible analysis of a literary work from feminist point of view will do well to bear this fact in mind. It is this factor that lends authenticity to Shobha De's treatment of women's problems.

Shobha De's fictional world has aroused curiosity and interest on the one hand and downright rejection and denunciation on the other. The works of this "high priestess of gossip and innuendo"[5] have been regarded as "equivalent of Hindi films with their peephole voyeurism."[6] When first published, Shobha De's novels evoked hostile reviews. *Socialite Evenings,* for example, was branded as a "high society potpouri, bland and banal," bristling with orgy-laced parties and "voyeuristic servings of souped-up, four-wheel-drive-sex-in-all-directions."[7] Another reviewer found it "choked with listless lust" and criticized its "witless dialogue."[8] *Starry Nights*, which with its brazen portrayal of sex and 'sexploitation' steals a march over the earlier novel, was described as "confession of a man-eater."[9] Despite their titillating details, what Shobha De's novels indicate is the arrival of a new Indian woman eager to defy rebelliously against the well-entrenched moral orthodoxy of the patriarchal social system. Her novels are not just a series of "bodice ripper."[10] To David Davidar, they are serious attempts at "discovering India through Indian eyes."[11] One may not like everything in De's fiction, but her treatment of the contemporary urban Indian woman's challenges, predicament, values and life-style is surely not without significance. De herself would consider the treatment of the Woman Question as the most significant contribution made by her work. She once said: "I write with a great deal of empathy towards women. Without waving the feminist flag, I feel very strongly about the woman's situation."[12] The present paper aims at considering Shobha De's treatment of feminist issues as found in her novels with particular reference to *Snapshots.*

II

Shobha De's explosive novel called *Snapshots* presents 'snapshots' from the life of six women who were friends at school—"the 'girls' from Santa Maria High School, leading predictable, mundane lives of domesticity and imagined bliss."[13] These friends had drifted away in due course and "disintegrated through marriages, transfers and unshared interests." (11) One of them residing in London is called upon to write, direct and produce a "bold and meaty" serial on "the exciting world of the Nineties' Indian urban women," for which she needs "authentic voices." (222) The get-together of these 'Sisters of the Subcontinent' at the house of one of them, Reema, begins well. Despite their problems and initial resistance, they all attend it. There is so much to catch on and memories start to surface—some happy, others bittersweet and some downright poisonous. As Swati, the spirit behind this get-together, tells them:

> We aren't here just to chit-chat. I want to know everything about everybody from the time we left school. Every single dirty detail. What happened to all the boyfriends? Where did the school crushes go? And the breathless infatuations? (90)

Infidelity, incest, rape, lies and even death and the evil that lurks beneath the apparently placid everyday lives of these six women form the substance of the novel appropriately called *Snapshots*. These women represent different kinds of urban women in India, but are hardly better than "schoolgirls playing adult games." (181) Forced to confront dark secrets that they thought lay buried deep in the past, these women begin to turn against one another and the mood of the party turns nightmarish, ending with the suicide of one of them. It is through their behaviour and conversation that Shobha De throws significant light on the predicament of women in India.

III

The cardinal issue thrashed by Shobha De in her novels relates to power, the desire to dictate and direct action and thinking of others, which is uppermost in human psychology. Hobbes is not the only one to talk about mortals obsessed with "a perpetual and restless desire of power after power that ceases only in death." Shobha De writes:

> Eventually, every relationship is a power struggle either on an overt or subliminal level. . . . Control over the situation has been a male prerogative over the centuries. Women's destinies have been determined largely in that context alone. . . . It is time they were made aware of their own potential and power. Shakti needs to be harnessed, directed and explored for the furtherance of overall human development. The very concept of the sexes locked in eternal battle is negative and destructive. . . . When one talks of shakti unleashed, one also remembers the two connotations of shakti—the destructive avtaar is as potent as the creative one. It is in maintaining the state of equilibrium between these two opposing forces that can lead to creative and dynamic harmony. . . . Men will have to come to terms with woman power.[14]

Shobha De's novels have emphasized the value of equivalence of power. Whenever this balance collapses, there is tension in society and double-dealings and hypocrisy predominate. The novelist can easily visualize a change in this respect taking place in the contemporary society, but men, she says, are not willing to accept it and "many men expressed their anxiety over the changed power equation."[15]

Significantly enough, the term 'power' and its synonyms have been reiteratively used in *Snapshots*. Who would know about the power game better than Champabai, a brothel-owner, who says to Rashmi:

> Never give yourself to any man for free. You know why? Men don't value anything they get so easily. That's why we are here: to satisfy their lust, not for sex but power. Power over women. Power over us—you and me. If they buy your sex, pay for you, they feel like kings. Give it to them with love for nothing and they'll kick you in the gut. (43)

In an affair with her husband's brother, Reema is said "to have invested [her] all into this crazy arrangement. . . . He has the power. You don't." (116) A perfect rake like Balbir asks these six women to be honest with themselves and tell him: "Do you fuck because you enjoy fucking? Or is it power-play?" (162) It is "powerful" people like Juan Mendonca who can play politics as fiercely as trade on international exchanges. (194) Even women like Swati look like a small fly before their resources—Swati who has had "some kind of power over" her friends and others; "All you have to do is snap your fingers and the rest of us will jump." (181) Her capacity to "manipulate" has been variously recognized. (183) Even Aparna, who has for her a "mixture of revulsion and fascination," "reluctantly acknowledged the power Swati still exerted over her and to a lesser degree over the rest of them." (209) The basic theme of Shobha De's novels can thus be described in terms of the cat-and-mouse syndrome of power play.

Shobha De has brought in pertinently economic aspects of power struggle. "Eventually," she says, "everything boils down to money—that great leveller. There can be no talk of independence for women, without economic self-sufficiency. An independent mind or free spirit, is meaningless so long as the body and soul are being kept together by somebody else."[16] Aparna in *Snapshots*, is a "corporate woman, an *Indian* corporate woman. A businesswoman" who can fend for herself at the time of need, (180) and it is an account of economic considerations that Rashmi and Swati lead 'liberated' life. Having exhausted her passion on Raju and in the wake of the resultant frustration, Reema turns into "an unfeeling, mechanical woman with her eyes fixed on the next big guy—piece of jewellery, a prized acre of farmland, [and] gold in its most basic form. It was greed that kept her going. A greed that no longer excited her." (93) The 'new" Indian women who have attained economic independence are "a breed apart" from others. They enjoy economic independence and their attitude is characterized by a rare seriousness:

> They were no-nonsense women who had 'take me seriously' written all over them. They even wore business suits to work and carried burgandy-coloured briefcases. . . . They took their jobs with an earnestness that was almost terrifying in its intensity. . . . Workaholism for women had become very fashionable.[17]

Shobha De, however, while advocating economic independence of women, would not approve of mania for money. She makes Aasha Rani of *Starry Nights* burst out on her overpowering mother: "Money, money, money. That's all you think of. Well, I'm fed up of being your money machine. I've done enough for everybody . . . now I want to live for myself and enjoy my life."[18] Money is important, she seems to suggest, but living one's own life is even more important.

IV

The institution of marriage is of unrivalled significance in the life of your people in India. In the life of a woman it marks a point of maturing: it signifies the flowering of life. According to Dharmasastras, marriage is a sacrament. The ideal, however, has now got diffused with time and it is being dominated by ulterior considerations. "Marriage," says Simone de Beauvoir, "is the destiny traditionally offered by society."[19] It has been pointed out that "History proves that marriage is essential to the well-being of human society, and that celibacy brings ruin upon states."[20] The institution of marriage has provided for the society's needs for love, security and children. On account of various factors such as sexual promiscuity, women's growing economic independence, increased rate of divorce and, more particularly, "the restless, exacting, often hysterical spirit . . . which tends towards discontent, indiscretion and divorce,"[21] the institution however is now on the verge of breaking up. Marriages are no longer supposed to be made in heaven.

Educated and attractive, confident and assertive socialite women in Shobha De's novels define marriage afresh, in which mutual fidelity till death (*nāticarāmi*) is replaced generally by sexual freedom. Marriage to them is hardly more than a convenient contract to lead a comfortable and promiscuous life, which can be terminated at any time depending upon the whims of the partners. The change in attitude towards marriage represents, according to De, "a big step forward":

> The terms underlying marriage have . . . been redefined in recent times. With some amount of economic freedom, women have changed the basic rules somewhat. If a self-sufficient woman with a roof over her chooses to marry, it is becuase she wants to share her life with someone in the fullest sense, not because she is looking for a lifelong meal-ticket. Divorce, too, has got to be viewed in this light. A woman of independent means is not compelled to perpetuate a bad marriage because she has nowhere else to go.[22]

In *Snapshots*, women have diverse marital status. Reema and Surekha are married housewives, who have had arranged marriages and were able to get "a prize catch" each in "the highly competitive marriage market." (104) Rashmi is an unwed mother saddled with the responsibility of a bastard son. Swati and Aparna are divorcees. Swati led a life of her own with her former husband in London. They led "Separate but friendly lives. . . . We loved each other dearly but we led strictly individual lives." (189) And now she lives the life of a liberated woman. As for Aparna, she is not prepared to repeat the "mistake" of marrying again, (149) and even the term 'husband' is an "Awful word" for her. (24) Noor is still a maid and is doomed to die unmarried at the end of the novel.

Marriage is not regarded as essential in the fictional world of Shobha De. In *Sultry Days*, Deb says: "Who knows about marriage-sharriage. . . . I am happy as I am." (27) When he does agree to marry Nisha, it is out of practical considerations of his "daal-roti, a warm bed, twice-a-week *maalish* and a daily screw." (159-60) That he never marries Nisha even after having a prolonged affair with her, eloquently testifies to his belief in the irrelevance of the institution of marriage. There is also a reference in the novel to "Typical Bombay marriage" in which "She goes her way and he goes his." (183-84) Such marriages do not last long. The incompatibility of the partners may be the chief reason of their dissolution. As one of them confides, "we tried it. But he wanted to walk counter clockwise. And I prefer clockwise. . . . We both wanted to go in different direction." (185) Constancy and faithfulness in married life are just unthinkable in the case of such persons. Reema, in *Snapshots*, represents the majority view when she remarks: "Imagine not knowing any other body, any other feeling, any other sensation. Forever. Sounds terrible. Like eating dal-chaval day in and day out." (152) Fidelity in such persons' conduct and relationships is too much to expect. Their sexual behaviour turns out to be amoral and in many cases even abnormal. To Anjali of *Socialite Evenings*, for example, an illicit love affair is a dream come true. "this is the most beautiful thing to have happened to me," she declares, "This is the experience I've been waiting for."[23] This kind of expedient relationship, devoid of caring and sharing, emotional warmth and mutual fidelity, very often breaks down, resulting ultimately in suicide, divorce or dissipation.

V

According to Shobha De, all people need sex. It is something special, something beautiful, something shared. The woman would get sex on her terms now. "The very fact," she adds, "that sex is no longer the most dreaded and despised three-letter word in India, is enough cause to celebrate."[24] But there is nothing derogatory or clandestine in sex. In fact, sex is "the bedrock of all relationships."[25] The novelist, not unlike D.H. Lawrence, is never in favour of making a 'dirty little secret' of sex. She voices her concerns through her characters in all her novels. Her women are not unaware of their sex potential; only some priggish, tradition-ridden persons speak ill of it. For example, Aasha Rani in *Starry Nights* is "the dream girl of the millions." (14) She says to Kishanbhai: "All of you are just the same, but wait I will screw you. I will do to men what they try to do to me. I will screw you all, beat you at your own game." (8) Anjali's affairs, in *Socialite Evenings*, with the Income tax official, who finds her "exotic and unreachable," is a brief interlude, but she continues to go "mate stalking." Karuna, in the same novel, also concludes that "men like dogs could be conditioned through reward and punishment," (87) and her rewards and punishments would obviously be in terms of offerings and withdrawals of sexual favours. Any sexual experience is a grist to their libidinous mill. Like Anjali, they would declare about illicit affairs:

"This is the most beautiful thing to have happened to me," and "This is the experience I've been waiting for."

Shobha De tears to pieces all notion of respectability associated with marriage. Her women discuss and practise sex with unusual candour. All sexual taboos are broken by them with gusto. The novelist makes them put forth candidly what they always feel but are afraid and inhibited to show. The verbal encounter between conservative Malini and Rita, a frustrated wife and a busybody, respectively, is illustrative of the attitude of the novelist to marriage and sex. Malini cannot tolerate the very idea of free sex and bursts on Aasha Rani:

> SEX! That is all you have—SEX! That is what women like you use. Cheap bitches—part your legs and let any man in. Sex, sex, sex, dirty, filthy sex! Perverts! You must be a pervert. What do you do to him [Akshay]—hah? Suck his cock? Or suffocate him with your breasts? . . . Eventually, a man needs his wife and children. (49)

Rita is pragmatic in her approach. She tells Malini that if she greets her husband with hatred in her eyes when he comes to her every night, he will turn to Aasha Ranis for relaxation and sexual gratification. To Rita, romance in marriage is a figment of imagination, for it "finishes the morning after the wedding night"; men are avid of "variety" and what follows thereafter is a protected life of "boredom." (50) The following words of Rita sum up the novelist's indictment of hollowness and hypocrisy inherent in Indian marriages:

> Most women hate their husbands—it's a fact. They hate marriage. That's also a fact. But what else they can do? What is the choice? The only way to make a marriage work is through sex—and most women hate that too. But the day a man feels that his woman has lost interest in sex, and therefore in him, the relationship is finished and he starts looking elsewhere. Aasha Rani and her kind are always waiting. (50)

Rita pleads for compromise in the maritai relationship. She is not averse to even pretension if it makes the marriage work—"to shut your eyes and part your legs, whether you feel like it or not. Because if you don't some other woman will." "A wife is acting all the time," she adds, "this is the world's best-kept secret. . . . Everything is decided by the bed. On the bed. . . . No woman should be foolish enough to be honest with her husband where sex is concerned." (50) Shobha De's views on marriage and sex would drive the last nail in the coffin of the age-old institution of marriage and patriarchy.

By the time Shobha De wrote *Snapshots* her views on sex crystallized further. Sex to Rashmi is a matter of "mutual need, mutual dependency." According to her, it is mediocre women who use "sex as a bait"; the shrewd ones "hold their men, [and] keep them enslaved." (49) Swati, who acts as the novelist's spokesperson, regards sex as "a hobby": "For some it can be an all-consuming one. For others, a passing fancy." (116) She does not fight shy of her affairs, for "There's nothing to be ashamed of." (164) Women like her rejoice in their sexuality. "We rejoice in our sexuality," says she. "We don't suppress it. We don't dismiss it. We don't find it dirty. Sex doesn't threaten us. I am not afraid to fuck. I feel sorry for all you women hanging on so desperately to outdated ideas of purity, morality, chastity. It's pathetic." (165) She calls herself "a cock-worshipper" and elucidates her stance further:

> Sex isn't filthy, . . . our minds make it so. Look at Khajuraho, Konark . . . have any of you studied the *Kama Sutra*? Fascinating. It's a pity we got brainwashed by some frustrated, repressed idiots. I think sex is a celebration—the highest form of religion. (164)

In a country which nurtured the genius of liberal thinkers on sex like Kalidas, Jayadeva, Vidyapati and, more recently, Rajnish and continues to take pride in erotic art of Khajuraho and Konark, sex would be something prurient only to those who possess a repressed sensibility and a prurient mind. There is Aparna, in *Snapshots*, who, on account of her background and conditioning by her mother's teachings, always has problem with her sexuality. (207) This "reserved, aloof, a bit of a dragon lady" who was left "high and dry" by her husband, can "discover her sexual potential" with a person like Prem. (7) Repression breeds guilt, which is in-built in her:

> Aparna had grown up with shame. Shame about her body. Shame about her adolescent looks. Shame about her background. Shame about practically every aspect of her life. It was the environment she was raised in. Guilt was its defining feature. She couldn't recall a time when she wasn't made to feel acutely conscious of every small pleasure—emotional or physical. (6)

Noor is the product of even a more repressive ethos. She has been presented in the novel as a "prematurely old and exceedingly shabby" person, (61) who looks like a shrivelled up "dehydrated pea pod," (142) and so on, who possesses a "whiny voice," "Thin and reedy like a badly scratched record." (216) The novelist would not be surprised if such a person comes to acquire a "peculiar sexual equation" with her own brother. (121)

Shobha De recommends a mature attitude to sex. It is not like baby food. Rashmi is addicted to sex like a narcotic substance. She says: "I love sex like I love food. It's the same sort of hunger." (134) She also says that 'nympho' should be regarded as her 'middle name.' The novelist is all the more critical of mechanical, loveless, routine sex. The chemistry of bodies has its own relevance in De's novels. Sex should have no other axe to grind. Rashmi and many others like her would care for sex without strings attached to it. (134) The plight of the neglected wife is a favourite theme with De. In all her novels we come across "Neglected wives of men too busy making money to bother with making love to the beautiful women with cold bodies they'd abandoned back at home." (57) Reema's husband, Ravi, for example, "was indifferent to his wife's disappointments and longings most of the time. It was when they impinged on his life and made him miserable that he felt drawn into her world." (65) On account of his strenuous routine, we are told, he is so tired at night that he would finish his dinner in ten minutes and go to bed. (166) There is utter lack of warmth and excitement in his "mechanical, predictable love making," (105) which would leave Reema "completely cold, physically and emotionally." (106) The married life of Surekha is not much different from Reema's. Her husband does demand his conjugal rights periodically, but "Surekha hated having sex with him—detested every coupling." She continues to sleep with him only to keep the marriage going. She would often say: "What is there? It doesn't cost me anything. I open my legs mechanically and stare at the clock on the wall across the bed. It's all over in about six to eight minutes." (158) In her desperation she continues her lesbian relation with Dolly: "Their lives had become inextricably intertwined. Dolly and Surekha were like a well-adjusted happily married couple. There was no passion to deal with any longer. Just enough physical familiarity to provide regular comfort." (159) The lot of Noor' mother is also a "cold, unfriendly bed." (57) While the Nawab is busy elsewhere trying to snare beautiful women, this "distant, cold woman, entirely shut off from her family and, perhaps, the world" continues to live in her "private sealed-off" world. (51) She would ostracize one if her edicts are disobeyed, (57) and the children would see her only when she is ready to meet them. (52) But she would have no hesitation in "weeping prettily in the arms of a man" Noor had never seen. (53)

This "sexless existence" (108) or "unfulfilling relationship" (109) is bound to leave a scar on the psyche of a sensitive woman. One of the results is a widespread "restless feeling," (214) a deep-rooted frustration and disenchantment, which culminates in identity crisis—the crisis of "growing up" and deciding "as to what one is and is going to be." Identity crisis, as Betty Friedan points out, has often been thought to be man's problem only and his exclusive prerogative to search for his identity, women having been told that "truly feminine women do not want careers, higher education, political rights, the independence and the opportunities."[26] What is expected of woman, told a friend to Shobha De, is to be "a passive, obliging receptacle for their semen as and when they feel the urge to discharge in her body."[27] Under such circumstances, the marital bed is hardly different from "a cold battlefield with two unhappy people lying stiffly side by side, year after, dreaming different dreams and yearning for a closeness, comfort and satisfaction that eludes them completely."[28] It is significant to note that in *Snapshots* Shobha De has used the imagery of battlefield and conquest pertinently. Talking about her marital experience, Reema, for example, tells her friends about her husband's "clumsy coupling without arousal":

> Passion wasn't even considered. . . . They'd slipped into duty-fucking without having fucked in the first place! . . . Nights . . . had an in-built pattern and rhythm without the slightest ex-

> citement or variation. Ravi discharged his husbandly obligation—literally. Sex was never discussed—only perpetrated on the other. Like a minor war. (108-9)

After making love to Reema, Raju "raised himself over her body like a conqueror" and the expression in his eyes continues to haunt her:

> Every man behaved similarly, Reema had concluded. Her husband was no better. And these days their love-making had to be squeezed in between her watching *The Bold and the Beautiful* and his business calls. During the cricket season, she recalled at least three sexual encounters accomplished to the drone of Test Match commentary with her husband pausing mid-thrust to applaud a stylish sixer. (93)

Her experience with Randhir has also not been much different. He took her in the lift: "A few swift thrusts and he'd been through. He'd stepped back from her with a triumphant smile." (117) Aparna's husband, Rohit, who appears to belong to a different kind, is not much different from others in this respect. "Boasting like a bloody schoolboy," he tries to impress the gorgeous, pathetic and sexy Swati, with "his conquests—'body counts' as he calls them." (207) Even Swati, who has been described in a different context as "a wild, out-of control cat," (197) finds herself subjugated by Juan, with whom she is "like a captive animal—part of his zoo" and despite her reckless mood, begins "to feel like a snow leopard or something." (201) Placed in such a situation a woman is bound to behave irrationally and resort to abnormal relations such as lesbianism, masochism, air-borne and water-borne sex and so on.

VI

The archetypal Indian male in Shobha De's novels has been painted in the murkiest colours.[29] Her interviews revealed that "Indian men make the world's lousiest lovers," and that "They are high on ego. Low on performance,"[30] their behaviour shows their real nature, and they are not different from animals. Malini, in *Starry Nights*, opines that "Men are all the animals, and we women such fools." (50) Men in *Snapshots* are no exceptions. Rashmi is convinced from her own experiences that most men lead "petty, self-obsessed lives." As for their worth, she asks: "But was any man [worth a woman's love]? She hadn't met one she genuinely felt like sharing her life with. . . . They preferred flirts and flatterers. Even manipulators." (49) When Pip leaves her suddenly, she takes it in her stride. This is replicated in the case of Younes also. She tells her son: "All men leave, baby. That's the way they are." (46) These simple words unfold an endless saga of male callousness. Men, she feels, are "Intrinsically, instinctively, intuitively dishonest." (49) So she asks: "So bloody what? Was being manless such a shame?" (50) Men may come and men may go, "Float in and out of her life like wipsy cotton balls on a summer day," (50) but she can go on for ever with her independence and way of life.

It would be instructive to have a look at the males populating the world of Shobha De's *Snapshots*. There is, for example, the "basic" Prem with "no bullshit," (7) who is "uninhibited" and "brash, arrogant and nauseatingly sure of himself" (7); Rohit, "Selfish and vain" endowed with ruthlessness and a terrifying "self-absorption," (21) and despite his sensitiveness to women, is "A selfish swine" and "A two-ting bastard" (185); the "wirey, nervous" Nawab (51) who can smell women and able-bodied young men in an instant; "Shifty-eyed, fleet-footed, sly and calculating" Nawaz, (52) who takes to pimping for his father, while giving the impression of being a man of fine taste and rare sensibilities so that "Women were attracted to him like bees to honey" (55); "Flambuoyantly dressed" Randhir, "Not good-looking, but rakish," who would not spare even his elder brother's wife; Balbir, "a natural achiever" who is so "full of confidence and bravura" (169) and a perfect womanizer; and swaggering Raju who is "swarthily sexy with foxy eyes, a flashy hungry mouth and a don't-care-a-damn Romeo demeanour." (96) It is not surprising that these men are insensitive to women's individuality, sensitivity and feelings. They can only aggravate women's problems in their own ways. Marriages with their ilk are bound to be doomed. Karuna, in *Socialite Evenings*, comes to realize that she had "married the wrong man for the wrong reasons at the wrong time" and that her husband was just an average Indian husband, "unexciting, uninspiring, untutored" and "not made for introspection." Karuna sums up the average Indian woman's marital life as "an exhausted generation of wives with no dreams left," marriage to whom is "like a skin allergy, an irritant all right." (65) The story in all of De's novels is the same.

VII

Shobha De has created the characters that she has created and treated the themes that she has treated in her novels to call attention to the kind of treatment meted out to women in India. She does not present them for any idealistic purpose or aesthetic effect. Like Deb of her *Sultry Days*, she herself might declare: "I am what I am—take it or leave it." (4) She might find herself in Oscar Wilde's company when he says that ethical matters in a piece of art are "an unpardonable mannerism." We are pertinently told in *Snapshots* that in Bombay, the locale of the novel, "Nobody respected ethics." (71) The novelist has touched upon different facets of an urban woman's life and her plight, but no issue has received the same kind of full-throated expression as the question of matrimony and sex. Attention has been drawn by others also to women's exploitation, discrimination and commodification, but De's voice is the most vociferous and striking. She lashes at hypocrisy with all her might whether she is taking up the issue of arranged marriage[31] or interference from the relatives.[32] She seems to be emphasizing the value of what is most conspicuously missing in the Indian context, namely, 'communication,' full-blooded interpersonal normal relations. Shobha De makes Rita remark sarcastically: "we demand communication, attention. . . . Arrey baba, forget it. We should be happy if they [husbands] don't beat us, burn us, torture us, insult us, discard us. That is all."[33] Modern feminists may learn a lesson or two from Shobha De or her women characters. Frailty's name is no longer woman; given chance she can easily become woe-man.

NOTES

1. Virginia Woolf, *A Room of One's Own* (New York: Harcourt, Brace & World, 1929), p. 105.
2. Wendy Martin, "The Feminine Mystique in American Fiction," *Female Studies*, 2, p. 33.

3. C.P. Surendran, "Just Another De," *The Illustrated Weekly of India*, 6 November 1992.
4. Alice Jardine, *Gynesics: Configurations of Women and Modernity* (Ithaca: Cornell University Press, 1986), p. 25.
5. "Raj Reversal," *Sunday*, 8-13 December 1990, p. 32.
6. Sunanda Swarup, Feature in *Femina*, 8 May 1993, p. 9.
7. Madhu Jain, "Cat on a Cold Tin Roof," *India Today*, 15 October 1989, p. 195.
8. Sunil Sethi, "De in, De out," *Seminar*, 384, August 1991, p. 41.
9. Madhu Jain, *India Today*, 15 October 1989, p. 195.
10. Sethi, *Seminar*, 384, August 1991, p. 40.
11. Sarita Vellani, Interview with David Davidar, *Seminar*, 384, August 1991, p. 43.
12. *The Hindustan Times Magazine*, 12 February 1995, p. 3.
13. Shobha De, *Snapshots* (New Delhi: Penguin Books India, 1995), p. 70.
14. Shobha De, *Shooting from the Hip: Selected Writings* (New Delhi: UBS, 1994), pp. 111-13.
15. Shobha De, "Sex in the Time of Stress," in Khushwant Singh & Shobha De, ed., *Uncertain Liaisons: Sex, Strife and Togetherness in Urban India* (New Delhi: Viking/Penguin India, 1993), p. 6.
16. *Shooting from the Hip*, p. 110.
17. Shobha De, *Sultry Days* (New Delhi: Penguin India, 1994), p. 119.
18. Shobha De, *Starry Nights* (New Delhi: Penguin India, 1991), p. 106.
19. Simone de Beauvoir, *The Second Sex*, trans. H.M. Parshley (Penguin, 1983), p. 445. Simone de Beauvoir again remarks: "There is a unanimous agreement that getting a husband—or in some cases a 'protector'—is for her [woman] the most important of undertakings. . . . She will free herself from the parental home, from her mother's hold, she will open up her future not by active conquest but by delivering herself up, passive and docile, into the hands of a new master." (p. 352)
20. Alexander Walker, *Woman: Physiologically Considerred as to Mind, Morals, Marriage, Matrimonial Slavery, Infidelity and Divorce* (Delhi: Mittal, 1987), p. 80.
21. Charles Cooley, *Social Consciousness*, p. 368.
22. *Shooting from the Hip*, p. 112.
23. Shobha De, *Socialite Evenings* (New Delhi: Penguin India, 1989), pp. 96, 78.
24. *Uncertain Liaisons*, pp. xxi, 208.
25. *The Illustrated Weekly of India*, 6 November 1992.
26. Betty Friedan, *The Feminine Mystique* (Penguin, 1965), pp. 68, 13.
27. *Uncertain Liaisons*, p. 4.
28. *Ibid.*, p. 3.

29. For an analysis of male characters portrayed in *Sultry Days*, see R.S. Pathak, "Shobha De: From 'Starry Nights' to 'Sultry Days,'" in R.K. Dhawan (ed.), *Indian Women Novelists* (New Delhi: Prestige Books, 1995), Set III, Vol. 1, pp. 150-56.
30. *Uncertain Liaisons*, pp. 4, xxv.
31. In *Snapshots*, for example, Reema says: "I was too young and inexperienced when I married Ravi. If I'd known how it would be with him. I'd have said no. But in our community these things don't happen. We marry the person we are told to marry." Swati, reacting to Reema's statement, says: "No, . . . my circumstances weren't all that different from yours. I *made* my choices. And was willing to pay the price—that's what separates the women from the girls." (p. 109)
32. Uncalled for interference from relatives, according to Shobha De, may only compound individuals' problems. In *Starry Nights*, Aasha ruefully states: "What do they care about the people. . . . [like her] Nothing. But they only want to control their lives all right. They want to tell them [women] who to marry, who to sleep with, who to act with, who to be nice to, who to ignore, [and] who to snub." (p. 16)
33. *Starry Nights*, p. 117.

Two Aspects of Feminism: The Expressive and the Explosive in Shobha De

SANJAY KUMAR

It was the French dramatist Alexander Dumas who first coined the term feminism in 1872. Since then 'feminism' has been used and interpreted in numerous shades and shapes of its meaning. The core idea, however, has always been more or less the same; it has always meant a belief that women should have the same rights, power and opportunity that men have. A feminist recognizes the partiality in the phallocentric principles, ideologies and social structure of life and raises a voice of protest against it. For the woman of the third world, feminism means a rebellion wherein she struggles to achieve a racial, social, economic and spiritual equality with man. The cause of such a protest Sarah Grimke traces in a perennial sin the male has ever committed against the female:

> Man has subjugated woman to his will, used her as a means to promote his selfish qualification, to minister to his sensual pleasure, to be instrumental in promoting his comfort; but never has he desired to elevate her to that rank she was created to fill. He has done all he could do to debase and enslave her mind.[1]

In India this struggle for woman's equality with man has been voiced all the more prominently in the last couple of decades. Especially the second generation of Indian women novelists like Nayantara Sahgal, Anita Desai, Bharati Mukherjee and Shashi Deshpande have challenged the male culture that prevails in our country. But the early soft voices of protest gradually turned into an explicit annoyance and finally took the shape of an open rebellion. Shobha De is a modern woman novelist who recognizes the displacement and marginalisation of women and attempts to turn this pattern upside down through her works. The present paper is an endeavour to trace this pattern of challenge and protest in her novels *Sisters* and *Strange Obsession*.

Sisters is the story of two girls Mikki and Alisha who remain isolated from each other as their father, by virtue of his promiscuity, chooses to get them from different women. Mikki is the daughter of a woman whom Seth Hiralal properly weds while Alisha is the offshoot of his unbridled passion with a whore. Mikki grows up in luxury and comfort; she possesses whatever a girl can hope for. Alisha, on the other hand, lives a life of deprivation and scarcity in the suburbs of Bombay despite being the daughter, though an illegitimate one, of the business tycoon Seth Hiralal. As a result she appears to be hostile and bitter to the entire world, especially to her dead father and his legitimate daughter, Mikki. She appears upset as her father's death means no possibility of her going to America. She hardly seems aggrieved at having lost her creator. She reacts sharply at having been ignored by the newspaper reporting her father's death. She sneers at herself and her mother existing as an 'open secret' in her father's life. She slams the door of her bedroom and curses everyone including her dead father. But like a determined and tough girl, she makes up her mind to make up for the loss. She sets out to make sure that the 'open secret' was made 'official' now as she prepares to go to "Shanti Kutir as Seth Hiralal's other daughter the one he fathered but never acknowledged."[2] It is interesting to note that Alisha does not intend to go to the Shanti Kutir to mourn her dead father but to grab forcefully what she does not get lawfully. She seems upset and furious and prepares to take on her adversities. Thus, in the beginning of her novel, the author helps us see how one of the protagonists is going to take on her male counterparts including her father.

Her other main character, Mikki, too hardly appears to nurture any sentimentalism at the death of both her parents. In the beginning itself, she seems to prefer her wish and taste to the social convention. Her hatred for any show of sentimentalism is apparent to us as she refuses to wear white coloured clothes at her parents' mourning and immediately appears to have the faith of the author who seems to be on her side: "Mikki hated white. God, she hated it." (409) She snubs Gangubai for wailing loudly and sounds matter of fact when she says: "Gangubai please stop that, what has happened, has happened." (410) When

Gangubai tries to stir emotions in her by sympathizing in the words "Baby . . . God has dealt you a severe blow: You are orphaned . . . what worse fate can a child suffer?" (410) she appears rather stern and orders her: "Go and get me a coffee." (410) Mikki hardly seems to have been shocked by the tragic death of her parents in a plane crash. She looks focussed and controlled; she refuses to believe that she is a child and orphaned in the real sense of the word, given her maturity and self-reliance. She sounds rather nonchalant as she concludes "Her father has been quite a man . . . quite a bastard too." (410)

In the beginning itself, therefore, Shobha De makes her intentions clear. Her women are not going to be emotional, subdued and weak ladies of manners. On the contrary, they are to be assertive, pragmatic and strong. As the action of the novel unfolds, both these girls continue to indulge in their single-minded pursuit which is to lead a life of luxury, wealth, comfort and pleasure, a perception quite alien to those women who seek a heavenly bliss in the domestic duties and prefer to revel in a spiritual illusion rather than chasing a material reality. Shobha De's women "symbolize the overpowering materialism and the lack of spirituality, that characterized modern age."[3] In *Sisters* too, the moment we look at Mikki and Alisha, we know that these girls won't lead an existence the circumference of which the others, especially males, decide. Both Alisha and Mikki refuse to sulk and appear subdued in order to look sober and domesticated.

The death of their father, in Mikki's case both the parents, does not seem to matter much to them as they want to get down to their business sooner than the society expects them to do. Mikki seems desperate to get back to America to resume her interrupted semester while Alisha appears determined to grab the huge fortune that her father has so unexpectedly left to her. Both these girls appear too much self-centred and preoccupied to waste their time mourning their father's death. Shobha De invests them with the usual male feelings of ambition and purpose and sets on to open her novel in a frank manner. At the very outset we know that the author is going to write from the point of view of these girls.

The focus of the action does not deviate much from these two girls as Shobha De pursues their explorations through the vicissitudes of life. The author first concentrates on Mikki who seems to be a poised, level-headed, strong and mature girl. She takes over the intricacies of the business from her dead father and begins to plough her way through the business world difficulties. When she takes charge of her business, she intends to run it on her own terms and is against unnecessary patronizing. When Ramankaka, a confidant of her father's business complexities, suggests that he be consulted in all her decisions, Mikki shrugs him aside and makes an emphatically decisive pronouncement:

> Thank you for your advice, Ramankaka, I appreciate and value your words. But I'd like you to hear a few of mine now. I can't change my sex, unfortunately . . . But I can change just about everything else . . . and I intend to. . . . This is going to be my show and I intend running it on my terms. If these old solicitors, aren't prepared to talk turkey with me, I'll sack them. That goes for the accountants and anybody else who wishes to treat me like a simple-minded, spoilt little girl out to play being a business woman. My genes are the same as my father's even if my gender isn't. (430)

This is quite a meaningful speech by Mikki as she challenges the usual orthodox vision of a society that treats a girl as mere shadow of the male. Mikki attempts to undo this image of woman and looks almost threatening to treat severely if received with the usual complacency and an air of superiority by her male officials. Surrounded mostly by males in her business empire, Mikki stands tall though aloof and not dependent and yet successful. She hardly regrets her sex and firmly believes in herself, her capability to select the desired and discard the undesirable. In a patriarchal male-dominated society, it is usually the male who decides, guides and directs the female but Shobha De's women are of a different sort. They have the power to resist, oppose and even hit back those who attempt to subdue them. Mikki is projected to be a girl possessing her own intellect, will and intention. She has her own ideas and firmly believes in action. She seems keen to assert her feminine, yet a strong individualistic identity in a habitually male-dominated society. Through the intentions of a tough-minded and level-headed Mikki, we see the design of the author who wants her females to be not just the subordinated counterfoils of their male companions. She intends them to be free and completely self-reliant ladies having an open and free existence. However, if Mikki expresses a notion that clearly is an aspect of her feministic views that are assertive, the ideas of Alisha are somewhat stunningly blatant and violent.

Alisha's initial annoyance with her father soon turns into decisive rebellion as she sets out to level the score with her opponents. In her fury, she moves with a strong feeling of hatred in her heart for her dead father and his legitimate daughter, who got without a stir all that Alisha could not muster with toil. Alisha's animosity continues to prod her. She thinks and behaves widely; mixes with her lover for a free sexual relationship and torments Mikki each time the latter tries to strike a chord of harmony between them. She hates Mikki, her father and the society. She is ferocious at the double standards of the society which discriminates the legitimate from the illegitimate all the more selfishly. She is cross at the injustice and social hypocrisy. To avenge her humiliation, she chooses a subtle way. She beds with a former fiance of Mikki and believes to have tortured her by having sex with him. She is shown to be doing this so earnestly because "her attraction was on a different level altogether. She wanted him only because Mikki had had him." (495)

Though Alisha seems to do it to avenge Mikki, she voices the author's own desire of liberation for women in sexual matters. Alisha is shown to having sex with different men. She shrugs aside the sexual conventionality and runs after the desire of body without any social or moral inhibitions. There are extensive scenes of her sexual encounters with Naveen. Though apparently she seems to always think whether Mikki did the same things with Naveen as she copulates with him. Shobha De also seems to direct us to this part of her silent, subtle revenge as she seems to support our feelings for her, Alisha does this "to obliterate any memory Naveen might have retained of his love making with the women she hated." (497) However, these free sexual encounters, where Alisha seems to initiate, participate and enjoy the sexual acrobatics with Naveen, look like a scornful laughter of the author herself who wants to shock the orthodox reader with the meticulous, graphic details of these physical unions of Alisha and Naveen. One recalls her admission of having a hidden agenda she explained in the "Hard Talk" on BBC on 19 January 1999 as she said, "I don't know why there is so much of noise when a woman chooses to talk about sex" and that by projecting sex in such graphic details she "wanted to jolt the society in a way."

Alisha's feelings of sexual gratification continue to sway her from Naveen to Dr. Kurien. It becomes almost ridiculous the way Dr. Kurien pleads with her to let him free of a physical relation with her. He blurts out his feelings of disapproval for her incessant sexual approach. "For women like you—men are playthings. Today you want to break up my marriage. Tomorrow you'll get bored and move onto some other man. Where will that leave me?" (526) Though Dr. Kurien succeeds in putting off the idea of her marriage with him but has to compromise to the long, uninterrupted love making in the afternoons. And whenever he gets late in turning up from his clinic, Alisha feels furious and shouts at him as Dr. Kurien thus "wasted more than forty-five minutes of their precious time together." (540) She is extremely possessive of him and is pained to see him pick up his wrist watch, a sign of his departure after their love making. It seems she can never be satisfied of having had enough of sex. In an arousing scene that follows, Dr. Kurien expresses a similar idea as he blurts while having sex with her: "All the rich women are the same—you want more all the time. Nothing satisfies you. Here, take it all . . . it's free." (541) Dr. Kurien's frantically brutal sexual assault on Alisha sums up his frustration with her as she seems to have an insatiable sexual instinct.

This frank outlook for sex in Alisha continues till the end of the novel and she continues to pursue males for their physical gratification. Even the last scene of the novel ends on a meaningfully humorous warning by her to the bachelors who pay no attention to her and Mikki: "One of you guys had better watch out. Your bachelor days are numbered. It's all over for you now. Alluring Alisha is on the prowl." (567) The word 'prowl' signifies her position of a tigress that is out to victimize another of her preys. This is how Alisha, one of the two most important characters of *Sisters,* is determined to smash the traditional image of woman and is hostile towards a patriarchal male culture. She approaches her business dauntlessly and indulges in free sex fearlessly using man as a plaything or an instrument whenever required.

It is not only Alisha, but her sister Mikki too, who establishes herself as an assertive, domineering, focussed and sexually frank lady during the course of the novel *Sisters*. She quickly begins to enter her father's business shoes almost successfully. Simultaneously, she begins to accept the demands of her flesh and recognizes a feminine sensibility in herself. She successfully flirts with Shanay who in cherishing her only "was dreaming a hopeless dream," but still fails to get "her out of his system." (438) She proves out to be a tough woman and when Naveen, her fiance, fails to respond to her wishes as he fails to bolster the sagging Hiralal Industries, she breaks off her engagement with him. In fact, she is also troubled by his mother who tries to use Mikki as a pawn. The most hurting moment comes when Naveen's mother begins to show her feelings of sympathy saying, "Bachchi hai. She is young and new to all this. We must encourage her, now that she has joined the business community." (467) This single statement by Sukhaben seals Naveen's fate. This is almost decided that anyone who plays parents to Mikki is going to be snubbed and rejected by this strong-headed lady.

Having already discarded an ineffectual Naveen, Mikki gradually accepts Binny Malhotra's entry into her life and begins to enjoy uninhibited sex with him. She breaks all the taboos and feels "liberated, uninhibited and aroused to the point of primitive abandon." (486) It is clear that like Alisha, Mikki too revels in her sexual union with Binny. Her copulation with Binny has been graphically depicted by the author and it appears as though she does not intend to separate her from Alisha as both of them express an undiminishing, insatiable physical appetite without having any compunction or regret about it. Having thus projected both her central characters, Shobha De sensationally underlines the modern woman's insistence to obtain social acceptance for a free expression of her libido. Sex for Shobha De's women is a palpable, pulsating and compelling reality. They do not hesitate to accept it as an important part of life and do not remain subdued to let man take all the initiative. On the contrary, they think and talk about it openly; participate in it actively, turning upside-down the traditional image of woman for whom sex is a shameful, hidden sin of her existence. In fact, Shobha De seems to herald the arrival of new women who do not lament the existing subordination and passivity of woman and "project their own passions onto others as a female power play in order to deconstruct the male ego."[4]

Thus Shobha De's women seem to be on a demolishing spree as they rip through the male complacency and articulate their erotic sexual fantasies unhesitantly and unmistakably. It is noteworthy that Shobha De achieves a unity in her vision as she shows Taarini, a middle-class woman, too indulging in her extra-marital pursuits. She shocks Mikki with her straightforward approach towards life: "Don't look at me like that. Does it shock you so much? Why? Because you can't imagine a middle-class working mother betraying her husband and children?" (513) By showing a middle-class woman as the one who betrays her family without any traditional pangs of guilt, Shobha De attempts to challenge the conventional male conception. Her attack on the taboo of sex for woman is aggressive and blatant. Mikki is the woman who responds aggressively to a phallocentric patriarchal society and Alisha is the girl who is overtly hostile and violent. While Mikki's is a calculated assault on the malist culture, that of Alisha is a blind slog. In Mikki's aggression it is the feeling of an expression of self which is dominant whereas in case of Alisha it is a vehement charge on the arbitrary male dominion on social views, principles and ideologies.

Shobha De's *Strange Obsession* too depicts a similar pattern which develops in the course of its action. In the beginning of the novel, we see Amrita, an affluent model of Delhi, who aspires to become a top-ranked model in Bombay and leaves her family in order to realize her dream.

Amrita, like any other modern girl of Shobha De, is ambitious, conscious and aware of her strength. She does not hesitate to capitalize on her blessings and believes in downing the world if possible. In an alien city, Bombay, she handles her affairs well, clinching some stunningly lucrative modelling assignments, and unsettling the already established models with her winning performance. Bombay however proves a bit clumsy. She runs into Meenakshi Iyenger (Minx) right in the beginning of her stay in Bombay and starts facing a fearsome turmoil in her hitherto balanced life. Minx, the lesbian sex-monger, chases her and causes her deep anxieties.

Shobha De, however, depicts Amrita to be level-headed and self-reliant. It is interesting to note how she gets into a physical relationship with Rover. It all starts with a forced kiss that he implants on her but in that he wins her completely and despite the fact the people warn her about Rover who is a 'narcissistic bore,' she knows that she has to make relation with him. Such is the spell of his physical charm that she can't resist him. In other words, Amrita's sexual urge for Rover is so much that she decides to forget about its consequences and freely mates with him. It is quite obvious that knowing Rover's nature, there is no dream in Amrita about a permanent relation with him based on love. She has not even once been shown to experience anything tender like love for Rover. All she feels is an irresistible passion which overwhelms her and drifts whenever she gets caught in a physical urge for him. She chooses to neglect an established social convention in order to bed with her lover who she knows "treats his woman like dirt."[5] She has already been told that "he'll use you and discard you." (593) Yet she goes for Rover; goes for having sex without any proper promise for stability in their relationship. This quite easily demonstrates to us the self-willed, liberal girl in Amrita. She treats disdainfully the orthodox conventionality going by which she would certainly have reached for a stable if not permanent relation with Rover. But knowing fully well that her affair with Rover is just a transitory phase in her life, she actively participates in her sexual escapades with him. This attitude of Amrita reminds us of a typical scorn which all Shobha De's heroines manifest. They seem prepared to dump the usual fascination for woman viz. dignity, morality and chastity. Shobha De's women usually take up a revolutionary role and are keen to cherish their passion rather than observing the familial or social decorum usually expected of a woman. Needless to mention that Alisha's move bears the support of the author who advocates her free play of passions. To show the negative and unacceptable side of female sexuality, she portrays Minx, the crazy lesbian. Minx chases Amrita everywhere in Bombay, acts as her protector, promoter and lover, destroys Amrita's business rivals and finally drags her into a lesbian relation with her. She is a wild woman of irrepressible emotions; she is deceptive and dodgy and is prepared to play all the trips up her sleeve to have Amrita in love with her. She disdains males and to justify her hatred for men she narrates the story how she was raped by her own father at the age of thirteen.

Though Minx's father terms her as an extremely clever and manipulative liar and declines to have raped her, the reader is made to harbour the impression that her claims might be true. In fact throughout the novel, the reader vaguely sympathizes with Minx despite her weird obsession to possess Amrita and her bizarre fantasy to own her overwhelmingly.

Though the character of Minx has apparently been created to highlight a negative side of feminism as she seems to have run to extremes to destroy the patriarchal malist culture and its age-old taboos, she too has her moments of glory. Minx, the psychic and obsessed lesbian of Shobha De, attempts to destabilize the continuing complacency in our views about sex and morality as she makes a speech that sounds rationalistic and probing as she blurts out a sarcastic enquiry:

> Why? Why does it make you sick? Why should it? Because I belong to the same sex? Is that my only sin? You find it sickening to accept my love. . . . But what about that animal Rover's love? That's O.K. You enjoy that. How come? And it's normal. Bullshit! there is nothing abnormal about my feelings for you. It is your problem that you have hang-ups. (596)

Considering this speech by Minx, it appears that the entire character portrayal of Minx is a humbug as Shobha De seems to advocate clandestinely her lesbianism and goes out to prove it normal and perfectly acceptable. But she fails to summon up enough courage to put across her ideas boldly. That is why she paints Minx in darker colours as a girl who is just crazy and psychic. The sympathy and advocacy of the author are unmistakable in Minx's actions, behaviour and speech. She appears to be one of her wandering women who would "prefer to identify themselves as radical lesbian feminist separatists."[6]

Thus Shobha De's women refuse to align themselves with the prevailing, partial male ideology. They essentially are the assertive women who, like Amrita and Minx, often take up revolutionary roles and want to destroy the existing malist social structure. In order to prove a point, these women resort to radical lesbianism or an uninhibited sexual play with different males. The author corroborates the feelings of these women by depicting their sexual union with males in detail in her works. As S.P. Swain says, "pornography in Shobha De's novels becomes a symptom and symbol of the female's defiance of a male-regulated female sexuality." (137) In fact, the author is so overtly defiant that she does not hesitate in describing the copulation of even those women who are moderate feminists in her novels. The sexual escapades of Amrita and Mikki in *Strange Obsession* and *Sisters* respectively substantiate such assumption.

Given an open defiance of women, the men in Shobha De's works are usually submissive and timid. Their positions are usually marginalised and it is hardly any male who dominates the proceedings for a long time. It is true that Rover in *Strange Obsession* and Binny Malhotra in *Sisters* fascinate and overpower Amrita and Mikki respectively for a while but it is never too late before the assertive women of Shobha De bounce back triumphantly. Moreover, the author herself deprives the males from playing a significant part in her novels. Consequently, we see the men whose authority has been defied and deflated by the women in Shobha De's works. The males in her novels are either lovable but ineffectual like Rakesh whom Amrita loves and marries but goes out to save him from the clutches of Minx rather than his saving her, or the disgustingly hollow and hypocritical like Binny Malhotra, Rover and Ramankaka. There however are certain level-headed males like Shanay in *Sisters* and Karan in *Strange Obsession* who are virtuous but fail to control reality at any stage of the novels.

It is thus a world essentially carved and shaped by women in Shobha De's novels. They debunk and defy the male hypocrisy and their supposed authority. Casting aside their submissiveness, they run to the extremes of being violently radical, defiantly uncompromising, overly promiscuous and even openly malicious. They revel in an uninhibited universe where the male is pushed into a corner and forced to live a secluded and subdued existence.

NOTES

1. Sarah Grimke, *Letters on the Equality of the Sexes and the Conditions of Woman* (New York: Burt Franklin, 1970), p. 10.
2. Shobha De, *Sisters*, in *The Shobha De Omnibus* (New Delhi: Viking Penguin, 1995), p. 412.
3. S.P. Swain, "Shobha De's *Socialite Evenings*—A Feminist Study," *Feminist English Literature*, ed. Manmohan K. Bhatnagar (New Delhi: Atlantic, 1999), p. 133.
4. *Ibid.*, p. 135.
5. Shobha De, *Strange Obsession*, in *The Shobha De Omnibus*, p. 593.
6. Rosemarie Tong, *Feminist Thought* (London: Routledge, 1993), p. 102.

A Protest against the Patriarchal in Shobha De's Works

PUSHP LATA

Shobha De is one of the famous feminist writers of today. Her writings gained popularity for their inclination towards fair sex and the graphic depiction of their pursuits and attitudes. These raise a protest against the male dominated Indian society where women are denied the freedom to act according to their will and continue to cherish their own dreams in futility. Women are treated as subaltern and mere 'man's shadow-self.' They are considered the otherness of man and not one with men or individuals. However, the role of women in society has been changing with each decade of a century, always with a good deal of social conflict and ideological struggle. These have left a great influence on sexual mores and social codes of the prevalent society which in turn is well embodied by Shobha De in her characters. She voices against the malist culture and strongly detects the marginalisation of women. She does not believe in describing her women characters as love-slaves or bitches or mere helpmates at home. In her novels she presumably mirrors her own feminist and sexist mind set. A broader evaluation of her works reveals her protest against the good old image of woman as 'an appendage' or 'an auxiliary.' Shobha De strives to undo this tilted and distorted image of woman who cries for freedom and equality which still goes unheard in the patriarchal world. From this perspective, the women in her works are more powerful than men. Women are essentially represented sexually liberated and free thinking and have become known as the "New Women" in later twentieth-century fiction. But even more remarkable is the strength of her characters in the very culture that has judged her. Her female characters, especially only after they have gone through their own experiences, come to their real self. Her women may or may not be flappers yet they are much more physical and athletic than their mothers have been. In 1927 an article entitled "Feminist—New Style" in Harper's *Magazine* declared the newly-evolved modern be a composite figure, a boyish girl who combines the flapper's physical freedom, sexuality, and stamina with feminist self-assertiveness and traditional domestic femininity, a woman who can happily combine pleasure, career and marriage. To the advanced young man of the time, this new woman seems the perfect companion—fearless, bright and eager to participate in work, in play, in marital sex.[1] We know this image might be admired but easily accepted by the Indian males. Shobha De, however, shapes her women in the above frame.

In her works like *Socialite Evenings*, *Strange Obsession*, *Sisters*, *Sultry Days*, "Susheela's Secret," Shobha De attempts to portray the above-discussed feminine characteristics. Her female protagonists are just remarkable when measured against men. Men-women relation is almost hollow, ineffectual and compromising. The men-women's complementary image has been completely shattered. In her novels, the world is out of sexual order. She has tried to highlight the discord in marital relationship. It is usually painful and destructive for them to be together. Undoubtedly, the female characters need the companionship of a man in order to satisfy their natural urge. Shobha De's women are daring and establish extra-marital affairs in order to get rid of their marital ennui. These women are not hesitant in using sex as calculated strategy to gain social and financial benefits; marriage for them is merely an insurance against social aloofness. Throughout her novel *Socialite Evenings*, the protagonist Karuna is a woman who declines to dog the traditional path of etiquette and manners. Her marriage is a failure since it is without love, joy and mutual faith. Her husband is just an average Indian husband as he is "unexciting, uninspiring, untutored. He was not made for introspection."[2] We find Karuna saying, "marriage is nothing to get excited or worried about. It is just something to get used to." (68) Though she becomes a well-trained wife but there seems to be no meaningful communication between the couple. Karuna voices her protest about her futile and meaningless marital relationship: "I think our marriage was over the day our honeymoon started. We've got nothing going. I don't love you—never have. As for you—I really don't know to this day why you chose to marry me. I don't think you even know who you married." (185)

There is a complete emotional void; only silence, compromise and adjustment seem to prevail between the two. This marital boredom leads her to establish an affair with Girish, which she considers beyond sin. She is happy to express without any hesitation her sexual urge for a man other than her husband, even to her husband. She makes an ingenious declaration about her inner thirst in the following words: "I love this friend of yours, and I will feel thoroughly disillusioned after that. Maybe he will have some truly foul personal habits that will disenchant me. In which case it will really be *A Death in Venice*." (186) Here it appears that Karuna has just a formal relationship with her husband. Intimacy between the two seems missing altogether. Similarly Shobha De's women who are unmarried also appear expressing their need for sexual liberation. In the novel *Sisters*, Alisha first goes to Naveen for sexual gratification and later it continues to sway her to Dr. Kurien. In an arousing scene while Dr. Kurien was having sex with Alisha, he happens to say: "All the rich women are the same—you want more all the time Nothing satisfies you. Here, take it all . . . it's free."[3] It is not only Alisha but her sister Mikki too accepts the demands of flesh. She successfully flirts with Shanay. Susheela, the protagonist of her maiden story "Susheela's Secret," also confesses her hidden desire to have sex with men other than her husband. She says: "I would think now it could be with someone else—maybe an actor, a film star, Amitabh Bachchan or Jackie Shroff, even Nana Patekar. I'd started to imagine Mr. Deshpande by my side."[4]

Here she attempts to break loose from the traditional sexual conventions. Finally she has it with her boss, Mr. Deshpande. Karuna in *Socialite Evenings*, Mikki and Alisha in *Sisters* and Susheela in "Susheela's Secret" appear to be rebellious modern Indian women who challenge the orthodoxy of sexual and social taboos. They are certainly different from the sexually ignorant Indian woman as described by Khushwant Singh and other Indian writers. Khushwant Singh represents an old age view about Indian women: "This is all most Indian women know of sex—an unpleasant subjection to men's desire—necessary in order to have sons, bearable because of its brevity."[5] But Shobha De antagonizes this view very forcefully in her works. Her female protagonists challenge the traditional set up of the society. In the course of breaking social traditions and conventions, they establish sexual relations with other men without any feeling of guilt.

Shobha De's women are far more assertive, domineering and bold in comparison to their male counterparts. They are not submissive. They are not guilty about their affairs and attitudes. In *Sultry Days*, the female character Sujata once or twice a year invites everyone to her spacious flat to listen to visiting poets from far flung places. "Sujata would play Mother hen and gather all her chicks to her bosom—literally." (727) She feels her duties are over as her children are self-dependent. Regarding her affairs, she boldly claims: "Yes . . . they accept 'Why shouldn't they? I've been a good wife and mother. I'm still here, living in the same house. They are grateful. I could easily have left and gone away. So many men longed to make me theirs. I receive marriage proposals all the time . . . even now."[6]

Sujata is quite gross and repulsive in her mid-forties. She writes pronographic poems. She is comfortable with whatever she does. She goes by her mind. She does not lead a life which is defined by her husband. She follows her natural instincts and makes her own rules. She is not at all a cowardly person. She hardly cares for the institution called 'society.' Similarly in *Sisters*, Mikki, after her father's death takes over his business. Ramankaka, one of her father's inmates and a confidant of her father's business's complexities, suggests to her that he be consulted in all her decisions about business transactions. But it is Mikki who holds the key to decisions and gets an obvious victory as she emphatically declares:

> Thank you for your advice, Ramankaka, I appreciate and value your words. But I'd like you to hear a few of mine now. I can't change my sex, unfortunately. . . . But can change just about everything else . . . and I intend to. . . . This is going to be my show and I intend running it on my terms. (430)

Mikki is not emotional, subdued or weak, like traditional Indian women. On the contrary, she is assertive, pragmatic and strong. Here Mikki challenges the usual orthodox vision of a society. She is a tough woman who easily and without any sense of guilt breaks off her engagement with Naveen, when he fails to respond to her wish. When the actress Aasha Rani in *Starry Nights* finally decides to quit films and live with Akshay, her Amma tries to dissuade her from doing so. Aasha Rani boldly pronounces: "Money, money, money. That's all you think of.

Well, I'm fed up of being your money machine. I've done enough for everybody—you, Sudha and others—now, I want to live for myself and enjoy life."[7] She finally decides not to be a plaything at the hands of her Amma and others. In fact, it is Akshay who is hesitant about the whole affair. He tells her that he cannot consult his solicitor as he might disclose the whole affair to Malini, his wife. But she triumphantly reacts: "I'll handle everything. I'll talk to someone. We will find a solution. You wait and see." (309) This exhibits her confidence and optimistic outlook. Further she suggests that they should convert to Muslims. At this Akshay gets infuriated and expresses his unwillingness. She finally blasts at him: "I thought it could work because I wanted it to. But you, couldn't care it less. You've just taken me up again because your career is in doldrums, and you're scared shitless of your wife." (310) Here Aasha Rani seems to be more powerful and bold than Akshay. She, like other heroines of Shobha De, designs a code of conduct for herself which is free of the prescribed gender roles and sexual restraints of traditional society.

Thus Shobha De's women are more mature than their mates. Yet in their own world, her men have an implied code of stoic manliness by which to define themselves in their relationship to women that code does not assure success. Men seem very passive in response to women: they are either indifferent or insensitive, unwilling or unable to take action or to accept responsibility for the way things turn out. Though in the Indian male-dominated society, women are marginalized by their husbands but Shobha De's women are certainly different. They have the ability to detest the indifferent and callous attitude of the husbands who often keep themselves busy in drab monotonous activities like reading business pages of the newspapers. Karuna in *Socialite Evenings* can realize how Indian women have been assigned a subordinate and relative position, as she says: "We were reduced to being marginal people. Everything that mattered to us was trivialized. The message was 'our priorities.' It was taken for granted that our needs were secondary to theirs." (69)

Karuna is able to recognize how Indian women are made to listen and tolerate and are denied to live as autonomous beings. Though her husband is not cruel but certainly he tries to impose his superiority which we can sense from Karuna's statement: "He brainwashes me constantly. I'm made to feel obliged and in debt. It's awful but even my insistence on working and contributing to the running expenses of the house has become a battleground." (69) This certifies that men in Shobha De's works are traditional and stereotyped. They are not the ideal husbands as they are incomplete and inadequate. So they are not able to dominate their wives. Shobha De has presented men resorting to several defence mechanisms against their self-confident and self-reliant wives but most of the time they do not succeed. They are terribly threatened by their females. In *Strange Obsession* Meenakshi Iyengar (Minx), the lesbian sex-monger, chases Amrita and causes her deep anxiety. After the fire incident, when Amrita inquires from Mr. Iyenger whether Minx's moves and attitudes did not bother him as father, he answers thoughtfully: "I was always afraid of her . . . scared of her rage, unsure of what she might do if I reacted. . . . But my men, the few I trust kept an eye on her most of the time. But Meenakshi outwitted them also."[8] Here we observe Minx's father terming her as an extremely clever and manipulative girl. He is terribly threatened by her ways so he seems unable to control her action. In *Socialite Evenings* we find Karuna's husband accepting Winnie's power and fear from her in the following statement: "She is a very strange and powerful woman. I feel ashamed to admit this but I'm scared of her. I can't do anything because I know she will destroy me. She has that power." (264)

To sum up, we can say that Shobha De writes from a definite feminine perspective. Her female characters are endowed with a vision which penetrates human psyche. They easily outplay their male counterparts with a better control and placidity in their attitude, desire and expression. Mostly the males are subdued and threatened by the self-assured and self-reliant females. Her women revolt against the traditional image of Indian women in words and deeds, be it business or sexual spheres. In a sense, she is the forerunner of the emerging Indian women with her liberated womanhood.

This statement by Karuna's husband exposes subdued position in the event of her superiority. Karuna has successfully achieved the novelist's vision which clearly aspires to belittle the male prominence. In this short speech, the dream of a lifetime for women seems to have been realized. The husband feels powerless and threatened by his wife's strange and domineering position. In fact, Shobha De's women clearly stand their superiority over their male counterparts. For this they may have to resort to any kind of feminine and at times even masculine ploys. But ultimately it is the woman in Shobha De's works who holds all the trump cards up her sleeve. She can easily checkmate and outplay all her male counterparts with a strategy which looks beyond the male comprehension as it is too subtle and manipulative a trick. This way Shobha De's woman is a mouthpiece of the New Indian Woman who shares the vision of many women like herself and that of her creator.

NOTES

1. Dorothy Schneider, and Carl J. Schneider, *American Women in the Progressive Era*, 1900-1920 (New York: Facts on file, 1923), p. 148.
2. Shobha De, *Socialite Evenings* (New Delhi: Penguin, 1990), p. 65.
3. Shobha De, *Sisters*, in *The Shobha De Omnibus* (New Delhi: Viking Penguin, 1995), p. 541.
4. Shobha De, "Susheela's Secret" in *Shooting from the Hip* (New Delhi: UBS, 1995), p. 314.
5. Khushwant Singh, *I Shall Not Hear the Nightingale* (London: John Calder, 1959), pp. 42-43.
6. Shobha De, *Sultry Days*, in *The Shobha De Omnibus*, p. 727.
7. Shobha De, *Starry Nights*, in *The Shobha De Omnibus*, p. 308.
8. Shobha De, *Strange Obsession*, in *The Shobha De Omnibus*, p. 593.

Shobha De:
From 'Starry Nights' to 'Sultry Days'

R.S. PATHAK

In an interview, Anita Desai said that writing "is an effort to discover, and then to underline, and finally to convey the true significance of things."[1] She also confided to the same interviewer that her novels "deal with what Ortega Y. Gasset called the terror of facing, single-handed, the ferocious assault of existence." What Desai said about her own novels applies more pertinently to the works of Shobha De, who has been variously designated as "the Pasha of the pulp"[2] and so on. Her works represent the ferociously militant phase of feminism in Indian English writing.

Shobha De has had a string of best-sellers to her credit. She burst upon the literary scene with *Socialite Evenings* in 1988 and published *Starry Nights* in 1990, *Sisters* and *Strange Obsession* in 1992, and *Sultry Days* in 1994. If we go just by the quantity, this is definitely an impressive score. Most of her novels have been found to be 'un-putdownable' on account of their theme and virtuosity arising out of an elemental passion. The fact that her novel has been prescribed in courses designed by the universities of London and Bombay has made Shobha De even more popular. So has the publication of her anthology on love and sex, which she has co-edited with Khushwant Singh.

Shobha De claims to be writing "popular fiction," saying that she is "a pioneer" in this field. She also claims to be "among the first to explore the world of the urban woman in India."[3] Shobha De is undoubtedly a talented writer and one comes across some original insights and brilliant strokes in her works. Through her novels and essays, she has tried to shatter the patriarchal hegemony in the Indian society fed on well-known injunctions of the *Manusmriti*:

Pita rakshati kaumarye, bharta rakshati yauvane
Rakshanti sthavire putrah, na stri svatantryam arhati

(The father protects her during her adolescene, and the husband in her youth, and when she becomes old she is protected by her sons. A woman does not deserve freedom.) What has made matters worse is the dichotomy between the idealized image of woman in literature (cf. *yatra naryastu pujyante ramante tatra devatah*) and the bitter reality of her position in society. Obscuring the actual predicament of women, the system, instead of working for their liberation, induced them to seek consolation in myths. An Virginia Woolf would put it, "Imaginatively she is of the highest importance. Practically she is completely insignificant. . . . Some of the most inspired words, some of the most profound thoughts in literature fall from her lips; in real life she could hardly read, could hardly spell and was the property of her husband."[4]

Owing to sincere efforts of writers like Shobha De, however, some significant changes have become visible amongst educated members of the Indian society. The change in respect of perspective can be succinctly summed up in Alice Jardine's words as follows: "The putting into discourse of 'woman' as that *process* diagnosed . . . as intrinsic to modernity; indeed, the valorization of the feminine, woman, and her obligatory, that is historical, connotations, as somehow intrinsic to new and necessary modes of thinking, writing, speaking."[5] In any sensible analysis of a piece of literature from feminist point of view, an awareness of this factor is essential. Women's difference underlies and most of their problems arise from her sexuality that has been repressed by patriarchal culture, especially in traditional societies like ours.

Shobha De's latest novel, *Sultry Days*, is about Nisha, an impressionable teenager who meets God (the hero of the novel) on a sultry rainy day in Bombay, whose real name is Deb. Deb has been presented by the novelist as a *beedee*-smoking, smelly guy with his typical "nine-day stubble" and "matted locks" which are "full of lice-nests and other creepy crawlies."[6] One of his hands is invariably engaged in scratching: "I'd never seen a man who itched so much [remembers Nisha]. Scratch, scratch, scratch . . . his hand tore inside his filthy shirt and scratched up a bloody pool. It travelled down to his groin, up to his armpits, right round to his back. Sometimes he'd pause mid-scratch to make some point and then start all over again." (1-2)

De's shabby hero has another uncanny habit. In between his stories and discussions "he'd lift up his thigh and let go without any embarrassment whatsoever." Although Nisha is gassed to death, in the beginning, out of politeness, she would "just sit there unable to move" or block her nose and try to breathe through her open mouth. (4) Deb does not have any charm or social graces that would make him an ideal husband-material. But Nisha falls in love with him as soon as she sees him in the college canteen and is admitted into his 'court'; and their long and passionate romance begins.

God's inordinate ambition leads him into the unreal world of pseudo poetry, art for hire and compromised journalism while Nisha takes up for the time being a job in an advertising agency. Sycophants, court jesters, whores, dirty old men, fixers, pretty boys and party girls drift in and out of their lives and, interrupting their romance, create complications of various sorts. Their careers take off with dizzying speed like that of a meteor. But after some time everything, abruptly and harrowingly, goes wrong. The son of an indigent trade union leader, Deb scoffs at everyone including Marxists, bureaucrats, businessmen, politicians, artists, writers and so on. But as the years go by, he is corrupted by the good things of life that money can buy and becomes the chief confidante of a corrupt businessman-politician called Yashwantbhai Dawani, who is "known for his ruthless wheeling and dealing" and who "controlled the purse-strings of his party and arm-twisted huge 'donations' out of industrialists and businessmen." (99) Commenting on this "very disturbing and difficult to understand" selling-out of Deb, Nisha writes: "God was behaving like a mortal, like all the other journalists in the town, a bum who shamelessly sold his pieces for a few pegs of Scotch and a five-star evening. He'd started dressing differently—flashy horrible clothes that looked absurd on him. He carried Dunhill packs around which . . . he hadn't paid for. He dropped names constantly, particularly one name—and that scared me." (99)

Deb and Yashwantbhai fall out and the former is shot simply because he knows too much about the latter and his activities. Deb, who is regarded as "Yashwantbhai's *chamcha* and pimp" and "a spineless lackey," (226-27) meets with a tragic death, which evokes sympathy in us: "God had probably picked the time to die with care—defiant and alone. I [Nisha] found a packet of beedies smuggled in by an indifferent night-nurse under his pillow. And a half-smoked one on the floor. God had gone off in a puff of foul-smelling smoke without saying goodbye to anyone. Died like a dog. Or like a god . . . if you prefer to reverse the letters." (228) This impressive end lowers the curtain on Deb's hectic and dissipated life. It reminds one of the end of Arun Joshi's *The Strange Case of Billy Biswas*, for the 'cases' of both Billy and Deb are "disposed of in the only manner that a humdrum society knows of disposing its rebels, its seers, its true lovers."[7]

Thus there is not much of a story line in *Sultry Days*. As in her earlier novels, Shobha De deals with neurotic people, amoral and shamelessly engrossed in their blatant enjoyment of life's pleasures in their crazy glitter world, and the novel bristles with bizarre descriptions of all sorts. The novel is dedicated to her children—"finally a book by me that they can read." Her books, says De, haven't changed; only her children have grown up.[8] There is, however, the same sprinkling of four-letter words, though in the first half of the book there are no explicit portrayals of the sex act. But then we do get juicy extracts, despite the novelist's promise to her children, and the itch to confirm the earlier image takes the better of her. Sex, to Shobha De, is "the bedrock of all relationships."[9] We in India, who have had an excellent tradition of erotic poetry right from Kalidasa to Jaideva to Vidyapati, would not fight shy of candid treatments of love and sex in literature. An excess of *mirchmasala,* however, will only make a work repulsive. Unfortunately, Shobha De tends to forget in all her novels the well known fact that art lies in concealing the art.

Although the novel *Sultry Days* is autobiographical to some extent and the entire story is told by the heroine-narrator Nisha, what emerges is a multiplicity of points of view. The novelist has faithfully portrayed the diversity of characters, both male and female, and their individual approaches to life and its challenges. E.M. Forster would have approved of Shobha De's shifting of the point of view. He said: "A novelist can shift his point of view if it comes off . . . indeed this power to expand and contract perception, this right to intermittent knowledge, I find it one of the greatest advantages of the novel form and it has a parallel in our own perception of life."[10] The narrator in Shobha De's novel not only delineates the plights of all other important characters, whom she closely knows and most of whom confide in her, but also voices occasionally the views and philosophy of the novelist herself. It may be for this reason that *Sultry Days* fails to unfold a cogent, unified picture of life.

The image of man that emerges from Shobha De's novels is generally negative. A male character is almost invariably portrayed as seducer, exploiter, wife-beater, rapist, torturer or a cruel and callous husband. Nisha's father, who appears rather "artificial and a little ridiculous," (57) does not desist from having affairs with younger women including his Sindhi Secretary. With his 'vacant eyes' and 'empty smiles,' (63) he is given to 'bullying and hypocrisy,' (147) as his wife herself protests. He degenerates in due course into "a crumpled-up ball of paper, his shoulders sagging, his eyes haunted, his gait a listless shuffle." (217) Basu is an ineffectual artist who is "without much of a personality" and is "driven to inarticulate fury." (45, 44) The head of the ad agency, Roy D'Lima, is also shown as 'a strange man' (69); "His theatricality was so much a part of his personality that it was difficult to know when he wasn't rehearsing for a role." (70) Some other male characters are equally egocentric, mean, selfish and good-for-nothing persons. There is one D.D. Nobody, we are told, "ever asked him what D.D. stood for and nobody knows." He is "a brooding, bearded, silent-as-death, bear of a man . . . so hairy and so quiet." (177) The black man Stash, with his 'dramatic scar,' is 'charming, and a stud to boot.' (168) The novelist has not given a complete portrait of these characters, but the hints and guesses thrown by her are significant.

Shobha De's world is populated by persons like Amar, Lucio, Pebbles, Iqbal and the like. Amar is endowed with the "gift of the gab" and his style of functioning is "bull-doggish and belligerent." To project an impressive image, he keeps a *harem* of girls and lends a futuristic value to his conversation by speaking "always for posterity, his conversation laced with pompous pronouncements and grandiose statements." (202) He has a complex about his looks, and always wears a *toupee* to cover his bald patch and has false front teeth. But, in reality, he is impotent, although he "strutted around as a stud just to keep his secret from getting out." (203) Then, there is Lucio, who is "interested in everything" including "lipstick, pimples, saries." Nisha remembers:

> 'He wanted to know everything. Little things. . . . Lucio was involved and attentive. He noticed when my hair was shampooed

> or if, occasionally, lipstick strayed to my teeth. He wasn't a physical person—not with me. And if he had to point out a pen mark on my cheek, he'd indicate it by making sure his fingers remained a micro millimetre from my face. Lucio noticed my cloths, my make-up, even my pre-menstrual pimples. (67)

As Deb tells Nisha, Lucio, though gifted with a musicality and in great demand to do female voices, is a 'Bloody fairy' and no man. Pebble, on the contrary, is a 'thickset and bull-like' and a 'rags-to-riches type' person. He exudes 'a raw, rough-edged sexuality that most models in the city found impossible to resist' and has had a wild reputation: "It was said that he chewed up half-a-dozen models a day and still had the energy to sample some more." He is brilliant but impossible and is described as "a rough-talking hunk with wolf-like eyes," who reportedly "changed girlfriends as often as he changed bed sheets." (95) Interestingly enough, he is accompanied by one William, who "spent his young life dreaming of Australia and trying his best to pass off as an Irishwoman who'd been accidentally born in the wrong country with the wrong sex." (95) Their company illustrates once again the truth of the saying that like meets like.

As for Iqbal, he is 'a shrewd man' who knows 'how to market himself.' (42) He is 'exceedingly handsome' and is the cause of 'most incredible stories' about his exploits. "The man's hunger for beautiful girls matched his thirst for tea. He loved both equally, though often the tea scored." (42-43) He has a terrible weakness for fresh-faced college girls. His paintings are said to be surrealistic and, to some, 'unbelievable erotic' in their celebration of the male body. He has 'lupine looks' and suffers from a 'ferocious appetite for publicity.' (44) The image that he builds for himself, though 'hollow and phoney,' works beautifully and profitably, for despite 'the patchy quality' of his work, he manages to get 'crazy prices' for them. (44) As a painter, he claims to be "a classicist who appreciates Rubenesque beauty. Pendulous breasts, a big arse—that sort of thing." (60) He is an adept in 'making . . . obligatory passes' and in setting up 'a lesbian orgy with . . . his whores.' (214) He has his own ideas about human relationships. "What's wrong," he would ask, "with immortalizing man-man love?" (43) He makes serious efforts to hide his real identity, as is evident from a one-line comment from the narrator towards the end of the novel:

"Iqbal had tripped into his familiar world and as usual, everything else had melted away leaving him to masterbate with his own ego for inspiration." (214) His 'familiar world' has not been explicitly portrayed, but it is surely not the day-to-day world of common knowledge and experience. Yashwantbhai, to mention one more case, represents yet another aspect of the Bombay world. An ordinary clerk in the fisheries department, he rose to a powerful position on account of his nexus with brokers and ruthless and unprincipled politicians. His early advice to Deb was: "Corrupt them at the top first and then work your way right down to the peon and chaprasi level . . . that way you keep everybody happy." (206) His affairs reveal still another aspect of his personality. He is, in this respect at least, not much different from the producer Suresh Gupta, who has been described as "a real bastard. Filthy, illiterate, uncouth fellow." (142)

Even Anil, who is said to provide 'such a contrast to God,' (76) is not much different from these persons in his general behaviour. He is 'clean . . . and so motivated' and 'all slick and sexy.' (76-77) Although he comes to his office only three times a week, his presence is noted by all. "He smelt of Aramis or Drakkar and used Studio Line gel in his hair. Behind the Warren Beatty glasses were eyes the colour of melting chocolate." (77) He is a yuppie who works on his own with his gadgets and proclaims his philosophy of life as follows:

> It's all relative. Why attach a moral to everything? It's a running shoes hang-up for me and maybe it's a fancy silk sari hang-up for you. Don't tell me you don't feel snobbish about certain things? I have seen it so often. Why do you criticize people who put plastic covers on their car seats and have a showcase full of imported souvenirs in their houses? Why do you look down on Vimal saris and fake silver jewellery made to look antique? (79)

Anil claims to be 'an experimental cook,' loves both jazz and Indian classical music and has a particular liking for Jean- Michel Jarre's 'futuristic and wild' music. Surprisingly enough, he is open to Nisha about his 'beauty routine' —his fortnightly facials and face packs: "No chemicals. Cucumber or yoghurt works well for me. I occasionally do a papaya pack myself when I'm having it for breakfast. Or I pulp a peach and slap it on." (82) Unlike normal males, he takes so much pleasure in "wiping his precious long-stemmed wine glasses and setting the table." (82) His fondness for pink napkins and pink shades is also uncommon. If we believe in Deb's assessment, "The guy looks like a bawarchi. . . . Pansy! Sissy *hai saala*. Hijda!" (83) And again: "Two-way traffic . . . the *chaalu* fucker." (104) In Shobha De's world there is no dearth of homosexuals, heterosexuals and lesbians. But the contemporary society, despite all its degeneration, does not lack normal preople. Unfortunately, they do not seem to interest the novelist. Their conspicuous absence from her novels only falsifies the basic facts about human society.

Occasionally, however, the novelist evinces rare insight into human nature. Iqbal's angularities, for example, are rightly attributed to his childhood deprivations. Through his camouflage, the narrator is able to have a glimpse of 'yet another persona': "This one was almost likeable, almost human. The whole thing worked. It was innocent, revealing and touching. Behind the fancy facade, the great Iqbal was not special at all. He was one of us." (214)

That humans are composed of both good and bad qualities has also been shown through the example of Deb. Superficially, he would appear to be an odious character. He is, in all vital respects an 'anti-hero' but is not without redeeming virtues. This *beedie*-smoking, *pudina chai*-drinking, ever scratching, smelly hobo, who scrounges on others for his meals and drinks and farts in public, is rightly confronted with a natural question from Nisha: "Don't you feel awful? Like a Cheap Charlie, eating and drinking at other people's expense, all the time?" (103) Deb is presented as a "thoroughly detestable," "Coarse, unkempt, ill-mannered," which he knows and revels in. (21) He has no sense of reverence for anyone and is "contemptuous about almost everything." (17) This down-to-earth person is brutally candid. He would not spare anyone. His mother, he says, resembles "a washerwoman or a brothelkeeper, depending on her mood," and his communist father "looks like a handcart puller from Lohar Chawl." (18) He can describe with a clinical objectivity even intimate acts of his parents. His cynicism is a byproduct of his environment, and sometimes he can "get terribly vicious and cross all limits." (17) He does not feel deterred by any idea of obscenity, for "It's all in the mind." (17) He has no patience for 'socially-correct' relationships. (179)

Deb possesses nevertheless certain rare qualities which we would normally not expect in such a person. Notwithstanding his "thick accent and the frequent mispronunciation of the commonest words," (78) he had read Chaucer and Marx at ten, got a scholarship for study at Columbia, and was fluent in German, could understand French and read Spanish. He had shown character at times by teaching lessons to persons like Rakesh, a sugar baron's son, who was given to 'indulging in a few sneaky tricks with the girls.' (9) Deb is not 'boring like the other boys who wore Wrangler jeans and chewed gum.' (8) He likes beauty and cares for good things like a saddle-stitched, all-leather satchel and a fine pair of shoes. One could come across in him certain other unexpected things such as his surprisingly clean and neat hands and fingernails. As for his other talents, we are told that he

> could quote from the Upanisads. He had read *Don Quixote* in the original Spanish. He knew how to pronounce and eat escargots. He could tell you all sorts of interesting things about insects. Or rain forests. He knew all the Beatle songs by heart. And was on first name terms with several painters and poets. He could cook and sew. And he knew how to fix the world's best fluffy omletts. Dogs, cats and other animals were instinctively drawn to him. . . . He was fantastic with electronic gadgets. He enjoyed the opera as much as Bade Ghulam Ali. And he had seen *Citizen Kane* fourteen times. He'd read Ayn Rand when he was twelve years old and could quote extensively from Allen Ginsberg. He had a scrapbook full of Mcluhan's verses which he had illustrated himself using psychedelic ink. . . . While walking down a dirty road, he'd spot a gulmohur tree in the distance and stop to admire it. (14-15)

At times, certain traits in Deb's character seem to be contradictory. But human nature is not wholly free from ambivalences and contradictions. Deb's character is, psychologically, plausible and convincing. In today's highly artificial set up, not many people will have courage to declare: "I am what I am—take it or leave it." (4) The portrayal of Deb's character bears witness to the novelist's capability of creating interesting characters. It is a pity that no other character in the novel has been delineated so convincingly and in such a detailed way.

These 'profiles,' the narrator claims, owe their inception to her interest in details and voyeurism:

> But I was enjoying them. And discovering myself in the process. Discovering a cold-blooded, ruthless voyeur who had no qualms about digging out all the small details that most celebrities take such pains to bury. I found I had a knack with people. I could disarm them and get their tongues rolling. It was surprisingly easy to get the most intimate revelations. I also found .that my eyes and ears missed nothing—the small gestures, the tiny tics, the nervous laughs, the unguarded comments. (214-15)

The novelist seems to be happier when presenting female characters. It is their plight that she is chiefly concerned with. She does not achieve much success with male characters, but her skill in delineating female characters is superb. For obvious reasons, she does not have enough scope for each character, but the few flashes revealed are highly illuminating. Equally interesting is the novelist's treatment of the position of women and their attitude to matrimony.

The novelist has presented a group of modern women, who make interesting case studies. There is, for example, Karen, Roy's wife, who is hardly less than "an overbearing, imperious bitch." (70) She takes pride in being a woman of "exotic good looks" and in tracing her descent to ethnic groups. "I'm one-eighth Turkish—my great-grandmother was a very naughty girl—one-fourth Khasi, one-sixth Goan and one-third Himachali," she would explain. (71) She uses her house like a showroom, and is always ready to sell off her antiques and furniture to her guests who happen to praise them. Roy's lover, Maitreyee, represents "the 'available' Bombay woman—brazen, bold, brassy," whose "energy-levels . . . [are] astonishing." She has hair streaked with gold and purple, but wears a swirling ghagra with a backless choli. Known for her 'enormous vitality' and irresistible 'flirtatiousness,' she would frankly ask: "Is there some special virtue in consistency?" (72) Her dressing style would change dramatically and, loaded with gold and diamonds, she would feel 'warm.' She declares: "I feel like a geisha," (114) and she behaves exactly like one.

The fate of other female characters is not different from that of the ones mentioned in the earlier paragraph. Lotika, for example, believes that she was an *apsara* in her earlier life and that she disturbed a *rishi's* meditation by her ravishing beauty. Now she is destined to have only 'one night stands' and then would commit suicide. (212)

Lotika, the narrator tells us, "was a sought-after woman on the social circuit," her biggest asset being her single status; and "it was her colourful past that sent out signals" although she was "attractive in her own way." To an interviewer, she confided that she became the victim of child abuse at eight, was raped by a raunchy cousin at fourteen, was married off at the age of nineteen and was divorced at twenty-four. Her attitude to all these experiences is reflected in her brief, but meaningful, comment: *"Chalta hai."* (212-13) Aarti, an account executive, is another emancipated woman in the novel. She wears "cut-away sleeved choli blouses without shaving her armpits" and smokes Charms cigarettes holding them "awkwardly between her fingers and blowing smoke out of nostrils." She is not very careful about her person, her kaajal being "invariably smudged," and wears thick handloom saris. (77) She keeps on raising her arms constantly, which to Deb means that "It's the animal in her." (78) Her hands being "busy as usual tugging at her underarm hair," (175) she would giggle and giggle "jangling the two hundred silver bangles . . . on both arms from wrist to elbow." (78)

Some other female characters may also be referred to briefly. Chandni, the D.O.M.'s 'pet,' (186) in her wildly colourful ghagra and tunic, looks "like a horny *banjaran* or a sexy sweepress." (156) To her 'the most beautiful thing' was her lover's masterbating 'right there' in front of her. (92) Shona, the model from London, knows how to 'look so different—from Cleopatra to Sridevi' and wears a 'skilfully cut wig' to hide her 'major beauty flaw,' i.e. her forehead that is 'as large as a *papad*.' (106) The most sought-after playback singer, Tanya the Temptress has 'bedroom eyes,' which look 'like luminous dishes the size of a full moon.' (134-35) Feroze, who wants to be the first woman Parsee director of Hindi films, has "lived, breathed and dreamed movies." (148) In reality, however, she is a weird lesbian and a sex-maniac. She follows the actress Kiki "like a puppy, Sending her flowers and poems, Fetching her food, Carrying her clothes [and] Generally behaving like a lovelorn maiden." (151) Kiki is like a dynamite on the set, and elsewhere 'instinctive and phenomenal.' Deb is particularly struck by 'something primal' and a 'Basic attraction' in her. (151) "That female is like *bijli*," he says. (150) Kiki's chief rival, Zainab takes pride in being "the film industry's first unwed mother," the father of the child being "a mysterious stranger"—a foreigner not connected with showbiz at all. (152) As the narrator reminds us, "In these filmi affairs, anything goes." (151) Cheetah, the Goan girl, looks "like a hooker from Hamburg and behaves like one." (169) None of these women can be called normal human beings.

It is through these characters' actions, assertions and behaviour that Shobha De has shed significant light on the important issues pertaining to matrimony and gender bias. Traditionally, the institution of marriage has been believed to be a religious sacrament in Indian society. The institution has provided for the society's needs for love, security and children—the things which one needs most in life and for which we have no real substitute. "History proves," writes Alexander Walker, "that marriage is essential to the well-being of human society, and that celibacy brings ruin upon states."[11] The institution of marriage, however, is now on the verge of breaking up. Amongst chief causes of the disintegration of family are: sexual promiscuity, women's economic independence which makes marriage less necessary, increased rate of divorce, and "the restless, exacting, often hysterical spirit . . . which tends towards discontent, indiscretion and divorce."[12] Marriages are no longer supposed to be made in heaven.

The age-old institutions of marriage and family are under tremendous strain in Shobha De's novels. The neo-rich Indians in her novels, particularly educated, beautiful and attractive and competent, confident and assertive socialite women, seem to define marriage afresh, in which fidelity in married life is replaced by sexual freedom. Marriage to them is hardly more than a convenient contract to lead a comfortable and promiscuous life, which can be put to an end depending upon the whims of the partners. Mutual fidelity till death (*naticarami*), the highest ideal for both the husband and the wife,[13] has no sense for them. Their sexual behaviour is amoral and in many cases abnormal. Like Anjali of *Socialite Evenings*, most of them would declare about their illicit affair: "This is the most beautiful thing to have happened to me," and "This is the experience I've been waiting for."[14] This is not surprising that this kind of expedient relationship, devoid of emotional warmth and mutual fidelity, often breaks down, resulting ultimately in suicide, divorce or disruption of family bonds—'little nameless unremembered acts of kindness and love' which make life worth living.

Marriage is not regarded as essential in *Sultry Days*. Deb remarks: "Who knows about marriage-sharriage. . . . I am happy as I am." (27)

When he does condescend to marry Nisha, it is out of practical considerations: "If you want, I don't mind a shaadi-waadi—I know that will make you feel better. *Theek hai*—we can be bourgeois and go through with that marriage rubbish. . . . Give me my daal-roti, a warm bed, twice-a-week *maalish* and a daily screw. That's all I expect." (159-60)

The fact that Deb never marries Nisha, although he has a prolonged affair with her, speaks voluminously about his belief in the irrelevance of the institution of marriage. The views of the novelist get reflected better through women characters. Pramila, a non-conformist lady from Nagpur, suffers from 'a big-city hang-up.' Married to a mechanical engineer, she has "everything a woman could ask for—a husband with a 'solid' job, security, lovely children, a moped of her own and all the time in the world to pursue her interests." (160) But she runs to Bombay, leaving behind her family, to save herself from suffocating 'boredom and frustration.' (161) In Bombay, she tries to get around in 'the right circles' and to make 'the right moves,' her chief aim being to be regarded as a 'Woman of Substance.' (163) Ultimately, Yashwantbhai and his people see to it that she is accepted in society as nothing better than a 'divorced woman of bad character' or even 'a borderline whore.' (226)

The Khannas and Baroohas also typify dissipated marriages. Ruki Khanna is "a vibrant, bright person who attracted all sorts," loves to receive "post-coital gifts" from her lover, is regarded as "outrageous, witty, sharp and sexy" and flirts in a seductive way. (166-67) Commenting on their marital status, the narrator confides:

> They'd been married five years now. Five stormy, tempestuous years. It was the second time round for both of them. His first wife had left him for his best friend, while Ruki had driven her husband to suicide. . . . She was looking for a home. Not just any home. Preferably, a penthouse. He wanted a glamorous woman to prove to the world he wasn't impotent. He actually was. (166)

Their 'best friends' the Baroohas have been married for twenty years and have yet 'survived.' Mrs Barooha has one thing in common with her husband—booze. She is terrified with her children, who call her anything from 'nympho' to 'bitch.' Although Bubli is 'an incredibly ugly woman with a cave-like mouth, painted mud brown,' she is 'anything but bubbly.' She is married to a 'male whore.' "Theirs was certainly a strange marriage," we are told. "What in their circle was referred to as a 'Typical Bombay marriage. . . . She goes his way and he goes his.'" (183-84) Bubli herself underscores their incompatibility for each other when she says: "We tried it. But he wanted to walk counter clockwise. And I prefer clockwise. It was then that I realized how that simple preference symbolized our marriage—we both wanted to go in different directions." (185) It is but natural for such marriages to end pathetically.

Although Shobha De says that her female characters do "not fall into the 'New Woman' category," for they missed this label by a generation, yet they are "a breed apart." (119) They enjoy their economic independence and their attitude is characterized by a marked seriousness:

> They carried the awesome weight of an MBA degree . . . on their padded shoulders. These were no-nonsense women who had 'take me seriously' written all over them. They even wore business suits to work and carried burgandy-coloured briefcases. . . . They took their jobs with an earnestness that was almost terrifying in its intensity. Even the married ones insisted on being addressed as 'Ms' or stuck to their maiden names. Their male colleagues were not permitted to crack jokes or flirt lightly. . . . Workaholism for women had become very fashionable. (119)

If married, they would nevertheless permit the husband to expect "his high-powered wife to make him his evening cup of tea and even sing an occasional ghazal in the kitchen while stirring a dekchi full of mutton-do-piazza." (119) Many of them also have to deal with their old-fashioned mother-in-law who expects the daughter-in-law "to sit for an hour-long morning puja with her" and take care of "all the other botherations." (119) There is yet another group of modern women taking great care to dress in "vampish" clothes. (194) Kiki's *Kamasutra* shenanigans are nothing but 'porn disguised as arty erotica.' Her hostess, Tarantula, regards her simply as 'the tarty little bitch,' though she herself is one. These women dress very carefully and refuse to grow after a particular age. As for Tarantula, "The socialite queen was dressed not just to kill but commit a gruesome murder. . . . Very Forties and very vampish. Someone had told her recently that she resembled Rita Hayworth. The queen had promptly changed back the colour of her treated red hair to its original black, making sure one eye was permanently covered with a tantalizing lock placed over it." (194) Some of these women may even sleep their "way to the top" of their profession, "using every man along the way." (204) They may also have abnormal, lesbian or pervert relations with people and even with animals.

Women in all cases are victims of male chauvinism. A typical male attitude to them is enshrined in Deb's assertions that "once a bitch, always a bitch" and "One bitch is as good as another." (154) Pratimaben, who meets her Ahmedabad-based businessman husband, only once a week, calls him her 'weekend husband' and passes her time arranging 'matkas and chatais with mirrors everywhere,' associating herself with social work, and going on pilgrimages. (145) She also has plans for a boutique or an art gallery to make money by selling imitation dresses. "Everybody copies everybody else," she would declare. "I can also copy from film stars—you know, what Madhuri or Juhi wears." (146) Nisha's mother was originally 'far more subdued and silent.' (20) But even she cannot be expected to go on tolerating nonsense on the part of her husband. His affair with his Secretary provoked her to assert:

> I have had enough of your bullying and hypocrisy. I have kept quiet for far too long. Go to hell with your corporate nonsense. Who cares what your boss thinks? Or those bloody women think? Where were they when my world was collapsing and you were with that Sindhi whore? . . . And you want me to bother about them? Why should I? Why should I bother about you either? You can also go to hell with your pompous talk and empty boasts. I am sick, do you hear, sick of living this false life. Varnishing my nails, setting my hair, wearing these silly saris and smiling through your office parties pretending nothing is wrong with my life. . . . you don't deserve me. . . . Whether you like it or not, henceforth I will make the decisions about my life. (147-48)

So strong are the bonds of tradition in Indian society that she still makes compromise and continues to live with her husband under the same roof. G.K. Chesterton is right in a way when he says that in married life one has to make perpetual compromises. That Indian feminist model is not a replica of the Western one is also evident from another fact. Most 'old wives'—spinsters, divorcees, widows and other singles—keep on hoping against hope that some day somehow "a group of gorgeous guys will walk in and marry" them all. They live only with one hope that they would be 'saved' by some man. Their bitter realization comes to them rather late: "No men, no future. . . . Being single wasn't such a hot alternative"; their married friends had at least "husbands to call their own" and "They were Mrs. So-and-So." (211) This weakness for 'husband material' is so typical of the Indian situation.

Writers like Shobha De have concentrated on examining the position of women in the urban and modernized sector of our society, but the percentage of the privileged educated and liberated women in it is conspicuously small. The real problems of uneducated rural women are entirely different. Another limitation of a work like De's is that (to put it in Paulina Palmer's words), "it gives simplistic and inexact impression of women's relations with men as invariably antagonistic, it treats their oppression in a transhistorical light, ignoring those occasions . . . when the sexes have worked together as allies. . . . it fails to take account of the social and economic differences dividing them."[15]

Despite limitations, Shobha De's treatment of women's problems is not without interest. The focus of the novelist in *Sultry Days* is rather diffuse and not so precise as in *Socialite Evenings* or *Starry Nights*. In *Sultry Days*, far too many women characters emerge on the scene for very little time. The novelist has nevertheless been able to present her viewpoint in her own inimitable manner.

Over the years, Shobha De, the *bete noire* of the contemporary Indian literary circuit, has become synonymous with an enviable appeal and an undeniable charm. The time-tested populist ingredient of sex and a tempestuous style go to make her one of the most popular writers today. Her *melange* of themes, variety of characters, startlingly captivating thoughts, all forcefully and colourfully expressed, lend a fascination for her readers. Also there is a lot that is amusing, outrageous, thought-provoking, even shocking. She has developed for her use a curious brand of English, which may be called Shobha De's 'Hinglish,' which helps her immensely in presenting her narrative with an unsparing transparency. Her use of language evinces a greater mastery over the medium and less of earlier self-consciousness.

Notwithstanding all the achievements, Shobha De remains a 'popular' writer who banks too heavily on a proliferation of four-letter words and uninhabited employment of salacious details. We must make a distinction between a popular writer and a good writer and a great writer. A popular writer is a nine-day wonder and his appeal is hardly more than seasonal. Even if we restrict ourselves to Shobha De's own works, there seems to have come a decline in her art as a novelist. She seems to have written herself out. Hers is a case of a novelist at the crossroads, and the old tricks may not help for long. The time has come when she has to embark upon fresh fields and new pastures. After reading her early novels, a perusal of her latest novel is like passing from 'Starry Nights' to 'Sultry Days.'

NOTES

1. Interview with Yashodhara Dalmia, *The Times of India*, 29 April 1979.
2. C.P. Surendran, "Just Another De," *The Illustrated Weekly of India*, 6 November 1992.
3. *Ibid.*
4. Virginia Woolf, *A Room of One's Own* (New York: Harcourt, Brace and World, 1929), pp. 45-46.
5. Alice Jardine, *Gynesis: Configurations of Women and Modernity* (Ithaca: Cornell University Press, 1986), p. 25.
6. Shobha De, *Sultry Days* (Delhi: Penguin India, 1994), p. 1.
7. Arun Joshi, *The Strange Case of Billy Biswas* (Delhi: Orient Paperbacks, 1971), p. 240.
8. Nandini Banerjee, Review of *Sultry Days, The Hindustan Times,* 9 April 1994, p. 4.
9. *The Illustrated Weekly of India, 6 November 1992.*
10. E.M. Forster, *Aspects of the Novel* (London: Edward Arnold, 1960), p. 78.
11. *Woman: Physiologically Considered as to Mind, Morals, Marriage, Matrimonial Slavery, Infidelity and Divorce* (Delhi: Mittal, 1987), p. 80.
12. Charles Cooley, *Social Consciousness*, p. 368.
13. See Pandharinath H. Prabhu, *Hindu Social Organization: A Study in Socio-psychological and Ideological Foundations* (Bombay: Popular, 1958), p. 209.
14. Shobha De, *Socialite Evenings* (Delhi: Penguin India, 1989), pp. 96, 78.
15. *Contemporary Women Fiction* (London: Harvester Wheatsheaf, 1989), p. 69.

The Image of Man in Gloria Naylor's *The Women of Brewster Place* and Shobha De's *Socialite Evenings*

SUBHASH CHANDRA

With the rise of feminism in the sixties, the feminist literary critics came to believe that women had to create a literature of their own, in which the feminine sensibility could consider and confront the peculiarly feminine issues and experiences. It was essential to do so, because a large part of the feminine experience is out of the reach of the male psyche and, therefore, an authentic and sensitive portrayal of the conflicts and traumas, in all their nuances, ambiguities and contradictions, could be achieved only by women writers. Such women writers as Virginia Woolf who held forth the concept of "androgyny," were castigated. Elaine Showalter's criticism of Woolf was that her "androgyny" was "myth that helped her evade confrontation with her own painful femaleness and enabled her to choke and repress her anger and ambition."[1] Showalter saw "Woolf's insistence on the androgynous nature of the great writer as a flight away from a 'troubled feminism.'"[2] Woolf's writing has a certain elusiveness which is interpreted by Showalter as a "denial of authentic feminist states of mind, namely the 'angry and alienated ones.'"[3] The seventies and the eighties saw a spurt in feminist writing which condenses in its pages the livid rage of the exploited female against the "male dominion" that characterizes both the Western and Eastern patriarchal cultures. Such works presented women as oppressed, exploited, tortured, cheated, angry, alienated and rebellious (rebellion taking different forms—mostly sexual promiscuity and lesbianism). But this towering rage against the patriarchal categories and male domination resulted in biased and distorted (at times even calculatedly vicious) presentation of man in these books. It is not mere coincidence that Gloria Naylor's (an American Black American Woman writer) *The Women of Brewster Place* and Shobha De's (an Indo-English woman novelist) *Socialite Evenings* written in the eighties, conform to this type of feminist rhetoric, creating male characters who serve the postulates of the writer's ideology more than the artistic needs of the plot and structure of the novels.

II

The image of man that emerges in *The Women of Brewster Place* is that of seducer, exploiter, wife-beater, cruel and callous husband, rapist and torturer. Mattie Michael, in the story of the same title, is seduced by Buch, who has followed her relentlessly. Even though he has often been rebuffed by Mattie, he eventually succeeds in cajoling her into the act. Having been impregnated by him, she is subjected to brutal beatings by her father, Sam, who nearly kills her in a fit of rage. She is thrashed so mercilessly that she is reduced to a "pile of torn clothes and bruised flesh on the floor."[5] But her misery does not end here. She continues to get exploited and hurt by yet another male—none else but her own son, Basil—for whom she has toiled, suffered and gone through all kinds of trying situations. It appears, Buch has not left chasing and harassing her, because Basil, right from his childhood, looked exactly like his father and turned out to be a bounder. Struggling incessantly and braving the world, Mattie brings up the child with all the maternal care and love. She has not cared for and has not been broken by the queries, "Where's your husband?" But Basil grows into an egocentric, mean and selfish son, a good-for-nothing individual, who sponges on his mother till finally, she exhausts her last penny and loses her house in an attempt to bail him out of the manslaughter charge he has been arraigned with. He expectedly jumps bail and drives the last nail in the coffin of her misery. Mattie loses everything, including her sanity (though temporarily). Here Basil conforms to the image of an absolutely spoilt son (Mattie had excessively indulged him as a child and young boy) and Mattie is the typically doting mother, gone blind in love of the son. However, in the case of Mattie, the doting mother part has been overdone, as she goes on getting beguiled by the cock-and-bull stories that Basil reels out to her. She has known her son to be a scoundrel, which is why he has landed up in jail, but even then she insists on standing the bail for him, much against the advice of the lawyer engaged by her to defend Basil. The lawyer's suggestion, "It's only a matter o two weeks. . . . Some defendants spend months waiting for trial. Perhaps you should reconsider," (50) is only met with an angry retort from her, "If it was your daughter locked up in a place like that . . . could you stand there and say the same thing?" (50)

The Women of Brewster Place abounds in women who have been betrayed and exploited by men. Etta Mae Johnson, in the story titled after her name, has nurtured dreams of marriage and settling down to a quiet life. She does meet Moreland Woods at the Church, who gets fascinated by her: "Her firm brown flesh and bright eyes carried the essence of nectar from some untamed exotic flower, and the fragrance was causing a pleasant disturbance at the pit of his stomach." (71) Etta, in his company, felt herself in another world, "weaving his tailoréd suit and the smell of his expensive cologne into a custom-made future for herself." (72) But Moreland's plans were different, and somewhere in her consciousness Etta knew about them: "It took his last floundering thrusts into her body to bring her back to reality. She arrived in enough time to feel him beating against her like a dying walrus, until he shuddered and was still." (72) Moreland dropped her off near Brewster Place. As he was driving away, he "glanced into his review mirror and saw that Etta was still standing in the corner, looking straight ahead into Brewster. There was something about the "slumped profile of her body silhouetted against the dim street light, that caused him to press down on the accelerator." (73) Ciel's husband, Eugene, in "Lucielia Louise Turner," can give her nothing but babies and pain and anguish. And ironically, he hates the babies he foists on her (the one that is already there and the one that is on the way). He shouts: "With two kids and you on my back, I an't never gonna have nothing." (95) Eugene had deserted her the first time when the baby, Serena, was one month old, and Ciel was alone and sick. Her humiliation got reflected in the meaningful blue eyes of the caseworker's blue eyes which conveyed the unanswerable observation, "you can find him to have it [the baby] but can't find him to take care of it." (91) Her disorientation on account of the abortion of the second baby elicits no sympathy but only an abuse: "Moody bitch." Eugene leaves her a second time, even though she has gone in for an abortion, and cut off a part of her flesh for his sake. And his departure indirectly becomes the cause of Serena's death, because she had put the baby to play while she pleaded with Eugene to take them along and the baby got herself electrocuted. Eugene becomes responsible for throwing Ciel into a long, dark night of pain and despair, and becomes a stereotype of the torturing, betraying husband who is selfish, mean, hard-hearted and unloving. "Cora Lee" makes a strident statement about the unlimited lust of man who treats woman as a mere instrument of satisfying his sexual appetite. Cora Lee grows in body, but not in mind. Even as she enters puberty, she continues to want to play with dolls and feels miserable when she does not get a doll on Christmas. And how does this male-dominated society treat her? Men give her real babies instead of baby-dolls. Each man satiates his lust and leaves her with a baby in her lap. Out of the whole lot of babies she has begotten, only two—Sammy and Maybelline—have the same father. The rest are individual gifts to her by several men, who are not even mentioned in the story to suggest the universality of man's exploitation of vulnerable women. The imperatives of the story requires innocent, vulnerable woman and the writer has succeeded in portraying Cora Lee as such, but then working under the twin demands of feminism and the Black's struggle, Gloria Naylor puts a statement in Cora Lee's mouth, which is too profound and subtle for a simplistic character who is totally ignorant of the shrew and complex ways of the world. She goes to the park, along with her brood of children, to watch a Shakespeare play. At the end of the performance, Sammy, her son, asks: "Mama . . . Shakespeare's black," and her response condenses in it the suffering, deprivation and the struggle of the Blacks for an identity, when she says: "Not yet." (127) Caught between a dual commitment, the novelist creates a character, ridden with a contradiction.

The one story in which the artist in Gloria Naylor takes over is "The Two"—a story about the two lesbians who come to live at Brewster Place. This story becomes a touching, moving account of Ben's (the caretaker of Brewster Place) attempts to form a tender parent-daughter relationship with Lorraine, one of the two lesbians. A lonely, heart-broken man, he finds Lorraine like his long-lost daughter whom he could not protect from the ill-treatment and cruelty of her mother who forced her into prostitution. Lorraine responds to his tender overtures and feels good. But the most cruel irony fate contrives in Ben's death at the hands of Lorraine, who bashes his head to pulp, with a stone, when he is in a drunken state, because she mistakes him in the early morning fog, to be one of her rapists (she has been gangraped by the Brewster Place hoodlums, CC, and his gang).

III

In *Socialite Evenings* the picture of man as husband is determined by the dictates of the feminist ideology. An important form of feminist rebellion against the patriarchal structure is the attack on family which gets manifested in sexual freedom, that is, extra-marital relationships. While the women in the novel go round indulging in promiscuous sex, the husbands are made to tolerate or ignore it. Even when a promiscuous wife divorces her husband, the rich husband settles a handsome alimony on her, thus enabling her to carry on her sexual amours uninterrupted, or he takes the deviant wife back, after she has had her fill of sex with the man of her choice, without his asking any questions or suffering the jealousy pangs. In the case of the husband of the central character, Karuna, the husband (his name is not mentioned throughout the novel—probably an attempt to obliterate his identity) is made to grovel at his wife's (divorced) feet to come back to him, in spite of her violent extra-marital relationship with his friend, Krish. He had pleaded with her to desist in her affair with Krish, but it is he who is made to beg her to be his wife again, after the divorce. Of course, he is unceremoniously rejected and even humiliated, because he had been mean in his dealings with her. He had cheated her of the money he had promised her while getting the divorce papers signed by her. The writer's prejudice against the "husband" seems intense and bitter, coloured as it is with the feminist bias. In the husband-wife relationship, in which the wife has blatantly betrayed the trust of the husband, the wife fights her way up, professionally establishes herself in the highly competitive world of advertising, and becomes emotionally and financially independent while the husband is made totally helpless. Yet another instance of a husband's unconvincing generosity (of course, required for the purpose of fulfilling the ideological stance) is Ritu's husband's action. Ritu, a flirt par excellence, first has an affair with a young ex-huckster-gigolo of Anjali and then lands herself in the hands of a shady, but extremely rich N.R.I., Gul—a builder—and lives as one of his concubines. She gets into heavy drinking, even drugs, puts on a huge weight, and everything seems to be over for her. But then like a fairy-tale resolution to her problems, her husband takes her back and everything becomes hunky-dory for her again. Such improbable situations militate against the credibility of the plot and make characters rather simplistic, one-dimensional mariönettes. Anjali, a woman perpetually on heat, has a husband who is leading a promiscuous life and is not one bit bothered about her amorous activities. Ironically, it is she who divorces him, because he is taken up with other women openly and blatantly. The husband, Abe, is generous with the alimony.

In both the novels discussed here, there is a negative portrayal of man. Ideological bias triumphs over the artistic (novelistic) requirements. The ideological predilection impinges on the aesthetic worth of the works on the one hand, and undercuts the element of verisimilitude on the other, making it difficult for the novelist to bring about what Coleridge called the "willing suspension of disbelief."

NOTES

1. Toril Moi, *Sexual / Textual Politics: Feminist Literary Theory* (London: Methuen, 1985), p. 2.
2. *Loc. cit.*
3. *Ibid.*, p. 3.
4. Gloria Naylor, *The Women of Brewster Place* (London: Sphere Books, 1984), p. 24.

From Purdah to Popular Culture: Anees Jung's *Unveiling India* and Shobha De's *Socialite Evenings*

BHARGAVI P. RAO

Pita Rakshati Koumare
Bharata Rakshati Yauvane
Rakshanti Sthavire Putra
Na Stree Svatantra Marhati

Said Manu, centuries back while laying down the social codes. But those were the days when male domination had not grown to monstrous proportions. Women were happy under their protective veil and enjoyed their due respect. But the structure of the society has changed due to different political and social ideologies. Women had to come out of their "Purdah" and help their counterpart in fulfilling the social obligations. She took up the burden willingly besides the traditional role which was imposed on her. But this was not appreciated. She was scorned, insulted and humiliated in the process. There came a time when she had to assert herself and this assertion was labelled as "feminism." Many decried that "feminism" is an off-shoot of western "women liberation movement" and looked down on it as a sacrilege of tradition.

Feminism has no apt definition. Feminism in the west is treated as an off-shoot of Marxism which existed in the capitalist countries as a "defensive body of orthodoxy surrounded by protective walls, encrusted with fear, stiff with terror, brittle with bitterness, acting with disillusionment. The oppression and the vacant feeling of women lay buried, unspoken for many years has now given expression to a new consciousness."[1] The intention here is not to discuss the feminist movement in the west and its influence on Indian thought. The object is to say that India too needs feminism as a social and literary movement. It is essential for women's emancipation. When we claim progress, a country cannot progress leaving behind its women. At one end, women are opting for careers in space research and "manning" many important scientific and technical projects and at the other end they are the targets of sexual exploitation and getting "burnt" for the sake of dowry. It is time for women to unite and strive towards a set goal where men and women enjoy equal status.

The women's problem in our country is totally different from that of west. The lower middle class, rural based women who contribute their labour for agriculture and industrial production, are illiterate and bound by superstition. They are not even aware of the extra burden which is put on them and they suffer willingly. The middle-class whose number has swelled enormously in the recent years, face a different kind of problem. They are educated and some of them are gainfully employed. This has not given them much relief. These women have to cope with the burden of domestic responsibilities as well as the demands of their career. The upper class, a few of them are aristocrat and the rest are the neo-rich and the first generation educated. They have leisure and money, more than they can digest. The Indian "feminism" spans all these categories.

Women creative writers have contributed their might to Indian writing in English. Kamala Das, Anita Desai, Shashi Deshpande, Kamala Markandaya and a few others have written novels projecting fine feminine sensibility. Bharati Mukherjee, Gita Mehta, Shobbha De and Anees Jung and a few more writers have entered the fray and are making their presence felt. I have chosen Anees Jung's *Unveiling India* and Shobha De's *Socialite Evenings* for this study to discuss how women writers are weaving feminism in their works. Anees Jung has explored the problem in her brilliant study *Unveiling India*. It unveils a story of population, a survey, a subjective personal experience. She travelled to every nook and corner of the country to "know" women. They are not mere statistics to her. As she travelled, "each face becomes a person, numbers cease being an abstraction."[2] Anees Jung belongs to a city founded by Quli Qutubshah to commemorate his love for a village girl who became his queen and lent the city her name. She comes from a family where her mother was not allowed to be photographed even for a family portrait. As a young girl she drove in darkly draped Plymouth car to go to school. Later she studied at Osmania University and went abroad for higher studies. But she confesses that she is a Muslim woman from Hyderabad, "a city whose name conjures up images of fragile women languishing behind veils." (18) She has met women of Bihar, Rajasthan, Kerala, Maharashtra and Mysore and they are not just women—they are Gomati, Amita, Shagufta, and Bolamma. She has recorded their opinion about marriage and widowhood, sexual servitude, bearing and rearing children, sexual discrimination and other forms of exploitation. The women in her book reveal their fierce brilliance and make themselves felt.

The journey "into those energy filled spaces of silence" begins at Bihar. Barkapur is a hamlet. Pottery is the village industry. Nothing has changed there. Pots are their bread, part of their family and part of their life. Pots carved with fish, parrot and mango leaf augurs prosperity and fertility. Hospitality is their strength and Anees Jung is touched to see a family who share "pride, love and hunger." Amita of Kerala, ebony coloured, strong boned, twenty years old is earning and saving for her marriage. Rukkammavva is another soul, married, but abandoned by her husband. She works for a cloth mill.

Religion is more meaningful to women and gives them solace—be it Islam, Christianity or Hinduism. The author begins with Islam in which she is born. She meets the Muslim women at Bidar of Karnataka and tells them that "Purdah" is only a state of mind. She quotes from Koran to say that modesty is the same for both, men and women. "A brazen stare by a man at a woman is a breach of refinement. Where sex is concerned modesty is not only good form, it is not for the good of the weaker sex but also to guard the spiritual good of the stronger sex." (33)

The journey goes on and Anees Jung meets Balachandra Sastri of Dharwar. Women are barred from his school, the Sanskrit Pathasala. According to him, "A woman does not have the necessary detachment to commit herself to a goal, a discipline or a journey. She is blessed to bear life, to nurture and sustain it whatever its form or shape; be it good, evil or indifferent." The author has also met Jain Sadhvis, the women with the shaven heads who move on and beg and eat their food and withdraw into the dark precincts of the ashram during the night. Faith, whether it travels or stays rooted, pervades the life of India. It is not only the illiterate peasants, even the educated—doctors, scientists—seek faith in mystic religion. She quotes a doctor who believes in a hill woman whom he calls mother, with divine power. He says that the flower touched by the Mother gets miraculous power. "A petal a day keeps the ulcer away, makes a lame one walk, a barren woman fertile." (18) Rituals are meaningful part of religion and all go through them religiously—be it a Collector or a Doctor or a commoner.

The author travels on, meets several men and women in her sojourn and gathers their opinion on marriage, love, family, children and various other things connected with women. The ideals have not transformed much. After surveying the villages, Anees Jung arrives in the city. City for her is the city of Hyderabad, to which she has a sense of belonging. Modernism has not affected the society life. Even in cities, being a single woman is still a curse. Women get married to get out of the stigma and bear children to prove their fertility. Young women are driven to suicide or killed by dousing them with kerosene and setting them ablaze. The law is proving inadequate and inefficient in preventing such crimes. Anees Jung has included ten true life incidents from newspapers to emphasize the atrocities committed on women. But the picture is not bleak. The women are waking up to a reality: "And the women in the forest are awake. Each one now has a name. Also an identity, realized and shared. Despite isolation and dire poverty these women have acquired a collective power that stems from a felt need. The voices have soared above the hills, finding echoes in distant corners of the country." (108) This is what is feminism in the Indian context.

II

Shobha De's *Socialite Evenings* begins where Anees Jung has left. This first novel by the journalist author has evoked mixed responses. For some reviewers it is shocking, for others it is "un-put-downable." Karuna, the heroine, is a prominent Bombay socialite, the book is in the form of her memoirs. As the story unfolds, we see the girl from middle-class metamorphose into a star and there are friends—neurotic, manhungry. Anjali, gorgeous, vivacious, Ritu, who has developed flirting into a fine art and deserts her second husband and prefers to live with a smuggler. Pitched against them are men—Si, Abe, Varun, a high profile editor, Krish, the pretentious adman, whose wife actively helps him in his extramarital affairs, and Girish, the art-film maker. The story revolves round these characters in a predictable way exposing sexual perversities and fake Sadhus.

Karuna is born in a dusty clinic in Satara, a remote village in Maharashtra and does not remember much of her childhood except the strict vigilance of her father. Her mother who was preoccupied with domestic chores does not devote much time to "know" her daughter. Karuna's life starts only when they migrate to Bombay because of her father's official transfer. She meets Anjali, a prominent socialite and the wife of a wealthy playboy. Her whole world changes and Karuna starts dreaming of a career in films and holidays abroad. When she enters college and gets married to Bunty, a rich businessman, the family accepts him because of his social status. But he is not the right "husband material," discovers Karuna. "He was just an average Indian husband—unexciting, uninspiring, untutored. . . . He wasn't looking for any stimulation either intellectually or emotionally."[3] She gets bored with her husband who does not share her interests, tries to down her blues in reading books and crossword puzzles. Anjali suggests that she should try an affair as an antidote. Krish comes her way. Ritu her friend who had practised flirting as an art educates her about the rules laid down for adultery—"no calls on Sundays, no calls at home, letters to be destroyed immediately after reading . . . no presents." (171) She meets Si, another friend who ridicules her for not having a car. She tells Karuna, "you mean after so many years of slavery you haven't earned a car yet?" (130) All the women in the novel are attractive, self-assured, conscious of their plus points and clever enough to hide their drawbacks. They are happy with wealth, happy with the pleasures which they could buy with money and the new-found freedom. Anjali leaves behind her teenage daughter under her husband's care, allows her to take any man to bed, as long as she did it discreetly. The pretty, young wife was only another status symbol for him. Karuna did not want to have a baby, and seeks abortion when she gets pregnant, and later learns that she cannot conceive any more. In the process of establishing her identity, she divorces her husband and takes up journalism as her career. Ranbir, her colleague, is interesting enough to have fun but not to live with. Finally he ends up a loner who finds her evenings lonely in spite of her active participation in "socialite evenings."

The book has been reviewed as "the lingering intimations of a paradox" and as "the liberated woman's celebration of a new dawn of total freedom." No one can deny the existence of such character. Human interest and crime stories from the daily newspapers will give us ample evidence. The "pulp" novel is not cinematic and neurotic but is a realistic representation of the present-day popular culture. Incidentally, Bombay is the backdrop. It could be New York, London or Calcutta or Bangalore. One cannot overlook the popular television programmes and the suggestive advertisements, which project the image of the modern liberated women.

Karuna is the hollow woman of our modern wasteland. Her kind are sick as they are unable to face the shocking realities after discarding the veil, the protective purdah. Religion does not give them solace as in the case of her rural counterpart. She feels "oppressed" in spite of her freedom. The right kind of feminism can give them solution as well as solace. The women creative writers should take up to explore the area of oppression—be it urban or rural. "The act of oppression not only disfigures the oppressor, it also maims the oppressed."[4]

NOTES

1. Sheila Rowbotham, *Woman's Consciousness, Man's World* (England: Penguin, 1986), p. x.
2. Anees Jung, *Unveiling India* (New Delhi: Penguin, 1988), p. 12.
3. Shobha De, *Socialite Evenings* (New Delhi: Penguin, 1989), p. 130.
4. Sheila Rowbotham, p. xvi.

Shobha De's *Sultry Days* and Gita Mehta's *A River Sutra*: A Study in Orientalism

INDIRA BHATT

Shobha De's *Sultry Days* and Gita Mehta's *A River Sutra* have the narrator-protagonists who are detached observers of the world around them. Both the novelists attempt to present the view of life in their chosen aspects of Indian society. Shobha De chooses to depict the modern life-style of the nouveau rich people with their physicality given full swing whereas Gita Mehta selects aspects of traditional spiritual heritage of Indian society. These are the aspects which the western critics and readers consider to be the essential image of India, what they term as orientalism.

Shobha De's *Sultry Days* opens with the filmy-style girl-meets-boy in a college-canteen episode. The boy named Deb who is known as God—a literal translation of his name as also an indication of his domineering personality in college, is attractive in a repulsive manner. Nisha the narrator-protagonist is attracted towards him: "A sort of infatuation towards him that simultaneously attracted and repelled,"[1] her. She gives a detailed description of this God who calls her his *Nasha*:

> . . . his hair. I hated that too. Matted locks—which I was sure were full of lice-nests and other creepy crawlies. One hand of his was invariably engaged in scratching. The hand didn't stop at the head. I'd never seen a man who itched so much. Scratch, scratch, scratch . . . his hand tore inside his filthy shirt and scratched up a bloody pool. It travelled down to his groin, upto his armpits, right round his back. Sometimes he'd pause mid-scratch to make some point and then start again. He really was most revolting . . . what he really needed desperately was a bath. (2-3)

like a filthy dog. What is so attractive about this figure who claims to be God to Nisha? Nisha who comes from a respectable family of a company-officer is gratified that this filthy young man claiming to be a communist accepts her as his companion. Besides God is a parasite living on other people for all his needs. He is a sponger and does not hesitate to borrow money from any one, nor does he feel embarrassed for this habit of his. So begins their relationship—he obliges her by borrowing from her and taking her in his fold and she is happy to be of use to him in whatever way she can.

Their relationship continues even after their graduation. Nisha takes up a job in a mediocre ad agency and God takes up journalism. The type of jobs they select gives them ample opportunity to come in contact with varied types of public figures, the business people and the models, the painters, photographers and politicians, the whores, homos and lesbians. What with the Bombay fast and fashionable life of the nouveau rich, the artists and social workers, the film stars and political brokers—one and all of the upper class of society come within their purview. The reader gets the overview of the surface life of these people who move in and out of the novel without creating any positive impression. It is a world of the film-magazines, fashion-periodicals and gossip columns of newspapers which present the strange and weird life of these people catering to the sensation-loving common man who is bored with the harsh realities of his routine life.

Nisha is an omniscient yet evasively neutral observer and can tell us what these men and women are, how they dress and address, a little of their past and nothing of their personal private life. They belong to the offices, restaurants, studios, art-galleries and night-clubs. This world is conveyed as an impression: "a moving collage without any depth. It is a flickering, quickly rendered world of characters who are shadows without substance." (1)

Though Nisha claims to be a detached observer of these whimsical people, she describes her own experiences of these people in full details: "Iqbal the painter was known to be arrogant, temperamental, unpredictable and disgustingly attractive. . . . The man's hunger for beautiful girls matched his thirst for tea. He loved both equally." (42)

Iqbal is a weirdo who thinks of using a model's body as a canvas for his painting. Nisha describes her encounter with Iqbal at his home:

> Iqbal who was now down on his knees, in front of me, pulling up my sari. . . . I knew it was time to scream . . . but I couldn't do it. I was too scared of this mad man whose eyes had dilated, whose nostrils were flared. . . . A voice within me kept repeating, irritatingly, "you asked for it. Don't blame him. . . ." I waited expecting something else to happen. It didn't. Iqbal, the great womanizer was limp. He looked pathetic at that moment with his jaw open and eyes shut in pseudo-orgasmic bliss. (158)

The man who is always surrounded by models and whores and poses as an aggressive lover in public is really a pitiable impotent man in his private life. Nisha too is bared in her willingness to accompany him to his home and is disillusioned.

God's experience is not very different. It is at Mrs. Bhalla's Theme party, what she calls a Rich-Bitch party with fantasy dresses that God is presented in a ridiculous situation. God appears in a crushed foil tube outfit stapled into place on him and in a ridiculously high-heeled pair of sandals which is torn off by Ron and God looks: "so puny, miserable and ridiculous, standing there starker on his high heels, his beard full of bread crumbs, a half-smoked cigarette in one hand, a glass of tequila in the other . . . and his exposed genitals." (182)

If Nisha finds herself in an absurd situation with Iqbal, God too must be so exposed in public and must be depicted as a weird character. Nisha considers herself superior to God and would permit him to score a point over her. She must show that she always remains in control of the situation.

It is Pramila the Ghatan and her relationship with the politician-broker Yashwantbhai which bring about the full degradation of God though Nisha keeps on warning him. God attaches himself to Yashwantbhai's various operations and presents him in periodicals and newspapers as a noble and generous man. Yashwantbhai needs a reputed journalist to look after his publicity and to present a perfect public image, God needs a sort of God-father to provide him his needs and comforts. So he becomes Yashwantbhai's "Chief minder and henchman." (165) In return, he receives all the comforts of life and shifts from the communists' chawl to the comfortable bungalow with a brand new Maruti car.

When Nisha turns down God's casual proposal of marriage he turns to Pramila, a divorcee with a young daughter, and they live together. Though it is clear that Yashwantbhai has a greater claim on Pramila; she is a woman of substance with dignity but all the same she had accepted Yashwantbhai as her mentor when he states:

> "We need women like you," Yashwantbhai leered at their first meeting, scratching his groin thoughtfully. (163)

She understands the implication and accepts to work "full time" for him and his party! It is when she finds herself pregnant with his child that the trouble starts both for her and for God. With the women organization taking up her issue and taking out morcha, Yashwantbhai gets bad publicity. Besides, Nisha's write-up on Yashwantbhai in full details is published at the same time. She is threatened by Yashwantbhai and his goons. God is frightened and worried for her safety. Nisha and God's relationship follows the familiar hot and cold pattern, and his attitude changes gradually towards her, he cares for her much. They become real friends overcoming their sexual life. Though she feels hurt by his attitude at times. She asserts: "I felt at ease with God perhaps for the first time in our relationship." (120) They both could enjoy the spectacle of the people around them heartily: "God and I laughed over these stories telling ourselves they didn't touch us. We weren't like them. We were different. We had depth. A sense of purpose. We were real people." (120)

The novelist is conscious of the characters she has created that they belong to some fantastical unreal world who have no roots in realities of life. Time and again Nisha comments on the unrealistic people she has observed and described in great detail.

When Yashwantbhai finds God of no use and feels betrayed by him he arranges God's murder—God is worried about Nisha but it is God who receives his punishment. God's is a journey from rice to riches and in drifting to riches he leaves off any values that he had. The novelist attempts to present God as a disintegrating figure in this grotesque world of chaos and confusion, of disorder and lawlessness where the only order is the self-centred craving for material gains and sexual fulfilment.

Though Nisha claims again and again to be an indifferent observer on the side-line of this procession of weird people, she too seems to belong to this same world with her physical relationship with various persons. Ultimately she realizes that she really loves God when she attends to him and cares for him at his death bed.

God and Nisha jointly observe life as outsiders, trying not to get involved in the people around them. Since she is intelligent and comes from a well-to-do family she could remain aloof and indifferent whereas God is a needy person and wishes to acquire all the comfortable things in life through a short-cut without thinking of the consequences of antagonizing Yashwantbhai. They provide a constant link to the episodes in the novel. Though innumerable characters from the Punjab to Kerala and Bengal to Gujarat, from poets and painters to pauper princesses and whores are protrayed, the reader only gets a dim glimpse into their real life.

The novelist tries to raise such questions as "what I am" and "from where to where I am headed to" in Nisha's mind, these queries do not sound true and appear mere posers adorning the pages of the novel. But God is depicted as a typical drifter who never takes stock of his deeds and his surroundings, who is never bothered by the basic questions of life. He is over-confident and is satisfied that he has moved from sponge-like existence to the worldly possessions and a name in journalism. Both God's father and Nisha's parents remain shadowy figures serving merely as a back-drop to God and Nisha. God can find no resolution, no redemption in his life and dies a dog's death. Nisha is left with her lost love for God but is likely to pick up the threads of life and begin a new life.

Though De attempts to show the society as a whole with her vast range of characters, what she succeeds in doing is to create a picture of a fragmentary world. The comic mode fails to give life to these characters. They are mere paper-thin journalistic caricatures without any deep roots in the realities of life. They remain a bubble on the surface of the river of life, here to-day, gone tomorrow people in this grotesque world of disorder. They have almost a brainless existence presented with their mannerism, wit and gossip. Nisha and God with some sort of family background move through this jungle of inhuman animal-like beings and record their public appearances, their brief history given like the bio-data on the flap of a book. Their private life is neither seen nor felt by the narrator-protagonist. They do not interact, nor do they build up the story but remain static characters having no dimensions.

The personal, private, inner life evades the novelist. It is a world full of chaos and disorder, a world without any values, a world which boasts of sexual affairs and parades in flimsy fashionable apparels, a world which has no habitation and no locale.

Gita Mehta in *A River Sutra* encompasses the total Indian ethos, the Hindu, the Muslim, the Jain, the Adivasi and the anglicized as does Shobha De. Set on the bank of the river Narmada which is in news all over the world with the environmentalist's enthusiasm, the next best to the holy river Ganga with all its cultural and spiritual implications, *A River Sutra* easily finds the simple pattern of the pilgrims' voyage in search of Moksha. The narrator is a semi-retired bureaucrat whose wife is dead and has no children. Having no family and no job, so to say, he in a simple traditional characteristic way thinks of Vanprastha, the retirement from active life as the new way of life seeking redemption on the Narmada bank. Mehta has chosen the river bank for the protagonist to stay put which facilitates him to come across a vast section of people with their varied predicaments and problems, seeking spiritual peace. The novelist has presented different aspects of life and its problems through the life-stories of various characters. It is not the protagonist's first hand experience of life, his active participation in the happenings that the novelist presents. She has portrayed the finished-stories or events that have happened in the near past. Though the narrator has searching questions to understand the philosophy of life, he does not ask them to any of the people he encounters on his way. It is left to Tariq Mia to explain the true way of living.

The story of the Jain Monk is picked up by the novelist from the recent newspaper reportage of the millionaire's son opting for Diksha. It is the Jain monk himself who tells the story of his life and how he gave up all the luxuries and beautiful wife to seek his Nirvana. All the details of wealth and the procession flouting the riches in a vulgar show are given with arrogance. He could have talked about his doubts and provided some answers to life's questions. Instead he describes with great relish his final procession that outdoes the great Mahavir's renunciation of royal life. Then there is the story of the Bengali music teacher Master Mohan who takes up a blind but gifted Muslim boy with a beautiful voice as his pupil.

But before he could make a name for himself, this young boy's neck is slit by a Saheb out of jealousy. This tale reminds one of the practice of the kings to cut off the hands which built or sculptured their buildings. This story is narrated by Tariq Mia to explain the place of love and passion in life which the rules and regulations-minded bureaucrat hardly understands.

The Executive's story is the case study of Nitin Bose who feels that he is haunted by the tribal woman Rima's soul and thinks that he would be cured by the Narmada waters. He decides to undergo certain tribal rituals to free himself of this spirit. It is Chagla who explains to the narrator: "It is not a woman who has taken possession of Mr. Bose's soul" and further that: "It is Mr. Bose who is making no sense, pretending desire is some kind of magic performed with black arts. But desire is the origin of life."[2]

Nitin Bose does not understand his tensions of desire and reason pulling him in two directions. But he feels redeemed by the rituals performed by the tribals on the bank of the Narmada. Once free from his obsessions, he writes some interesting essays on the tribal practices. Through this story, the novelist introduces the mythical stories of serpents which the filmy world has made quite popular. Perhaps that is where Mehta found it and picked it up.

The story of "The Courtesan's Daughter" too belongs to this category of filmy remake. As Hasan Saroor points out, it is based on "the real-life story of Umrao Jaan. . . . who has been the subject of some Hindi films on courtesans."[3] The novelist refers to the old practice of initiating the princes and the noble men in the art of love-making. Here too the details are given at great length. First the courtesan mother tells the story of her daughter's kidnapping by the bandits. Then the daughter appears out of nowhere and tells the narrator about the bandit Rahul Singh and his love for her and their marriage. But Chagla tells the narrator that the daughter had drowned in the river. The novelist gives no explanations for the appearance and disappearance of the daughter. It only adds to the mystification of life.

The Musician's story tells of an ugly female musician who learns to perfect her singing. She tells the narrator about her broken engagement and unrequited love. This depresses the narrator. Again it is Tariq Mia who comments: "I still say you should envy your musician, not pity her" (229) and that it is the narrator's misfortune that he has no knowledge of the world, "only hearsay, not experience," "To hear of love without ever having melted in its embrace." (229) The man who has not loved is a man who has learned nothing from life.

The final story, The Minstrel's story of the Naga Baba, is narrated by Tariq Mia to prove that life's experiences are to be deeply felt before one thinks of renouncing the worldly life. The Naga Baba who had meditated in the caves of the Narmada reenters the world and becomes a scholarly archaelogist and comes back to the Narmada and the guest house where he meets the narrator. It is the active life, the life of Karma and not a passive renunciation that brings not only knowledge but also enlightenment. As the Naga Baba turned Professor Shankar explains: "Don't you know the soul must travel through eighty-four thousand births in order to become a man?" (281) This story helps the novelist to introduce the mystical story of Lord Shiva and his meditations.

The novelist has brought together characters from different fields representing all those not-so-common class of people. She has used the device of the grandmother's style of telling stories to unfold life's experiences which pass by the narrator. The semi-retired narrator remains a bewildered person who has neither seen life nor felt it deeply. Such persons can never attain any enlightenment, nor can they think of Moksha even if they stay on the bank of the Narmada. The narrator's attempt at alienating himself from the outer world, renouncing the outer-world, a mere ritual of the ancient tradition only because he has reached a certain age appears somewhat unrealistic since he is a government officer who has come across cross-sections of people. Uprooted from his job, he tries to implant himself on the bank of the Narmada seeking spiritual freedom, yet he remains an alien here too.

A River Sutra presents the interestingly narrated stories which the protagonist learns second hand. The novel which is about the narrator and his enlightenment does not carve out a full-dimensional character. Both the narrator and Tariq Mia remain cardboard figures. The novel is episodic and misses that extra dimension which turns a simple story into an artistic novel. Mehta presents the different fragments of the Indian society through many eyes "committing herself to extended episodes, allowing herself to make acerbic moral points and judgements. The novel portrays a theatre of unrelatedness and indifference and gives the reader a dim picture of life to be felt and lived and experienced in the real societal world of participation.

It is indeed "a designer effort for the west and confirms the stereotyped image of India that the West admire so much. The Western critics and readers admire the spiritualism, exoticism and the myths of Gods and Goddesses on one hand and on the other wonder about the sex-starved Indians. Mehta caters to the western critic's image—the spiritual India with all her mysticism, tribal rituals, courtesans, bandits, gods and goddesses, whereas Shobha De caters to the western critic's image of the land of Vatsyayan. Both these novels mirror the surface, super life of characters who move in and out of the pages of the novels as and when so required by the novelists without making any impact on the readers. Both Mehta and De portray "the observed life" as opposed to "lived life." They are less interested in presenting their protagonists with their inner experiences. Nisha in *Sultry Days* and the narrator in *A River Sutra* remain almost untouched by any real yearning for meaningfulness in life. Though the novelists have chosen quite opposite aspects of Indian life, their superficial treatment of the themes and the protagonist-observers are quite comparable in their manner of presentation.

The opening upto the west for the purpose of self-definition is orientalism or Indology. It is this Indology that flouted the myth of spirituality as the essence of Indian culture and Vatsyayanism as the essence of Indian materialistic life. Shobha De portrays the world of sexually-infatuated people and Gita Mehta the spiritually hungry characters. Both cater to the western idea of India and hence are hailed high in their eyes. But if we see through these novels the picture that emerges is the picture of the king in the Emperor's clothes.

Here in India such books assume significance only because the Western press has considered them; we still remain the colonized readers to accept their judgement. Had the novels been written in any regional Indian language, neither the reader nor the press, and certainly not the critic, would have taken any note of these.

NOTES

1. Shobha De, *Sultry Days* (Penguin Books, India, 1994), p. 1.
2. Gita Mehta, *A River Sutra* (Viking, Penguin Books, India 1993), p. 143.
3. Hasan Saroor, review in the *Hindu*, Sunday, July 4, 1993.

Socialite Evenings: Toward a Feminist Romance?

PRAMOD K. NAYAR

But in order to make you understand, to give you my life, I must tell you a story. Virginia Woolf, *The Waves*

Categorisation is always a risky and uncertain project. With the current penchant for labelling, it becomes almost a procedural feature, to call a work this "-ist" or that one. "Isms" float around unbounded and frequently get attached, sometimes violently, to texts. Such a categorisation precludes other, variant readings ("kategorein" originally meant to accuse publicly. Hence a label could be accusatory too). To avoid this trap I have tried to read Shobha De's *Socialite Evenings* (1989)[1] as a combination of the romance novel and a feminist work. The paper necessarily locates within De's novel elements of both kinds of writing. The essay is divided into sections. Section I discusses *Socialite Evenings* as a romantic tale. Section II seeks to pin down the feminist features of the novel.

I

The feeling that *Socialite Evenings* first induces in us is of incompleteness. De's novel is populated with more stereotypes than characters. I shall be arguing later in the essay that this very stereo-typification is a feminist narrative strategy in De. First, however, the characters.

The stereotypes are mainly of women. The heroines (since I believe the novel has more than one) all subscribe to a role-model tailored by the patriarchal set-up. The character Anjali, described very early as "memsaaby," (9) is a good example. In Anjali, we are given the portrait of an apparently independent lady: rich, confident and beautiful.

De however etches a subtle mark onto this near-flawless picture. We are told that "like most women in her circle, she [Anjali] had started dabbling in fashion designing and advertising." (10) This suggests that she is one more of a type. We are also informed that she "filed her nails straight across," though they had been "truly spectacular" when she weds a second time. (10) This event is meant to puzzle us till much later. Anjali informs Karuna that she cut her nails because her husband does not like her long nails. (24) Thus she had conformed to the husband's wishes. Therefore the early comments about Anjali are meant to put us on our guard in viewing her as truly independent, and anticipates her character development later on. Eventually Anjali takes to inhabiting a traditional woman—space: religion.

In what is obviously another stereotype, the women characters are shown as gold-diggers. Anjali marries Kumar only after thoroughly researching his financial status. She declares that men like "dependent dolls." (69) She is candid about her materialist outlook: "The only thing I didn't ask him was the number of his Swiss bank account. And that too, only because I forgot." (116) Monetary dependence of the woman is constantly harped about. Ritu, another heroine, is married to an underworld don. She is so dependent on Gul's mercy that she agrees to procure other women for him. (220) Gul's subsequent ill-treatment of Ritu stems from this dependence. In another case, even a qualified lady surgeon is shown as dependent. (69)

A more effective mode of male control is reflected in De's portrayal of the woman's sexual dependence. The heroines start off as sexual libertines. And yet, they all fall prey to the "I-cannot-live-without-a-male" syndrome. Anjali gives up her career, independence and a husband for the homosexual Kumar. Ritu's villainous Gul goes so far as to humiliate her in public. (220-21) She then returns to her first husband, who "accepted her without any questions asked." (228) The heroines are attracted to the masculinity of the male in *Socialite Evenings*. Anne Cranny-Francis in her essay on feminist romance believes that there is a fetishisation of the hero in gender terms.[2] There is a "dangerous masculinity," as Cranny-Francis calls it, of the hero. Anjali's affair is inevitably begin with her fervent admiration of the male (47, 74, 76, 96). Ritu even claims that her husband looks more masculine when he beats her, provided "he doesn't touch . . . [her] . . . face." She claims: "I think the beatings have brought us closer. I respect him more. He looks so macho in those moments." (130) Karuna is herself attracted to a different kind of masculinity: the intellectual snobbery of Girish and Ranbir. Thus, as is typical of romances, the heroines in De ascribe to their men a definite higher status—sexually and intellectually. The men therefore automatically become protector-provider for the women, again a truly romantic "knight-in shining-armour" feature.

The "dangerous masculinity" of the male is kept under "control" through marriage. For Cranny-Francis (195) this is an attempt to keep the threat of rape away. The fear of rape is neutralized by marrying the source of the threat, or affiliating oneself with another *male* protector. The threat (real or perceived) of intimate relations is legalised, permanently, through marriage. Ritu's return to her husband is a crucial illustration of this argument. She seeks to escape from her oppressive life with Gul by escaping to another male.

The dependency and vulnerability of the heroine is tied to the theme of chastity/purity. Northrop Frye in *The Secular Scripture* argues that heroines in romances are generally "modest" and "pure."[3] In *Socialite Evenings* women fail in their relationships until they turn monogamous (monogamy for women being a male-prescribed requirement). Extramarital affairs do not fetch happiness for the women. Hence Ritu's return, like a repentent sinner, to her first husband's "familiar kind of boringness," (229) as the "original Earth Mother . . . finally com[ing] home to roost." (231) Anjali turns to religion in order to salvage some wifely pride. In religion, she aims for a transcendental purity to help ignore her material (bodily?) needs. I suggest, after Frye, that the established model of the "pure" heroine of the romance is brought in by the back door. This is achieved by painting the non-conformist lives of Anjali and Ritu as mistakes. By returning to more conventional "female" spaces—religion, housewifery. Anjali and Ritu are kept "quiet" in continual marital dependence upon their husbands.

The stories of Anjali and Ritu end in marriage. This type of conclusion, the "happy ending," is an important and usually inevitable, feature of romances.[4]

If the characters in De are traditional romance stereotypes, we need also to look at their insertion into the "Symbolic Order" (to borrow a serviceable term from Jacques Lacan) of patriarchal society.

Heroines in De's novel institute their identities in line with male pre-determined ideals. Karuna is initiated into the life of a model by her mentor Anjali. (10-12) Karuna had always "yearned to be a part of the smart and beautiful set." (10) Modelling helps her create an identity for herself. The glamour is retained upto a point and then quickly tarnished. We are told of Anjali's own tragedy with her husband Abe. Karuna wants Anjali "to remain her queenly self." (29) Ironically it is Karuna who provides information of Anjali's tragedy. She compares Anjali with a seedier character Si: "it took me . . . forever to tumble to the realities of Anjali's world, a world where Si and Anjali were only two sides of the same expensive, if badly tarnished, coin." (31)

De is revealing here, I suspect unwittingly, the helplessness of a woman who attempts to fashion her own identity. Anjali's identity is one she creates based on her husband's *sanctioning* of it. Her dependence (and humiliation) is an offshoot of this.

One can then say that the women do not accumulate any capital—economic, academic or cultural—through this self-fashioning. Pierre Bourdieu in *Language and Symbolic Power* argues that all credentials and identities have to be approved of by society and its institutions. The value of the bearer's credentials increases with the institutional belief in this value.[5] Anjali and Ritu cannot capitalise on their identities as independent women because the male-dominated society in which they exist disallows this identity. Anjali's conversion into a devout Hindu wife is this institutional re-fashioning of her identity. The men control the institutions through financial power, (Abe, Gul) intellect (Girish, Ranbir) or sheer sexual dominance (Karan, Pierre the Frenchman). The only identities allowed to women are: mothers, models, (or "dumb beauties") housewife, or bed-mates. These roles make the woman dependent.

It is also significant that most males in *Socialite Evenings* offer marriage to the women. This offer stems from the notion that marriage is the end-all, escape and sole means of survival for the women. This notion remains persistent even when women like Anjali are "quite prepared to settle for an affair." (116) Karuna rejects Girish's son Kunal's offer to come and live with them. Kunal retorts: "He [Girish] doesn't expect you to shack up with us. He wants to get married." (269) On both these occasions the male is demarcating the woman's sphere—as a housebound wife—*for her* within the institution of marriage. It is conveniently ignored here that for males a relative degree of automony is retained even within the identity of "husband" and the institution of "marriage." This is adequately illustrated by Abe and Gul in the novel. Simultaneously the woman's space is shrunk. Thus, to adapt Bourdieu's argument, marriage in De is an institution which seems to embody all male-favouring equations of power.

If an institution ascribes an identity to an individual, it also places him/her under an obligation to fulfil certain requirements of this identity. (Bourdieu 121) In this case the women must suit their notions to the word "wife" pronounced by the institution. Anjali demonstrates this "fulfilment." She forgives Kumar's denial of conjugal rights on account of his homosexuality to her. Her new-found religious ardour is a public acceptance of the role thrust upon her—a traditional Hindu wife. Similarly, Ritu's unquestioning tolerance of humiliation at Gul's hands or Karuna's acceptance of her husband's "kindnesses" (especially after her affair with Krish) are symbols of this submission to expectations of behaviour. The women thus accept their oppression within marriage, in a kind of Gramscian "consent."

It does not suffice that the woman obtains (seldom creates) an identity. There must be, according to Bourdieu, a public acknowledgement of this identity. (121-22) As in romances, the heroine's purity, heritage and virtues must be acceptable to society. In *Socialite Evenings*, the woman is constantly reminded of her identity until she assimilates this identity as her self. In De's novel, this assimilatory process is helped by the role of media and the flow of information. Unlike in early romances, the heroine's virtues are not narrated in epideictic speeches to people but embodied as images. Karuna's identity as a model is first created when a series of her photographs appear in the newspaper. (24) This public recognition of her self occurs, we must notice, at the very beginning of the narrative. Hereafter she lives this role into which she is cast as a result of this spread of information. To adapt Jean Baudrillard's arguments,[6] Karuna has no defence against this flow of information *about* her. A few examples may be noted in favour of this argument.

Karuna's father reacts violently to her modelling career describing it as "cheap" and "not something girls from respectable families do." (24) Karuna's career begins on this note. She has, at least for her father (and probably for other males), assumed the identity of a "cheap" woman who lacks respectability. I believe that Karuna herself internalises this view of her. Through the rest of the novel she strives to maintain "respectability." She marries because everyone (especially her parents) find the man "acceptable," (58) of "good family . . . prominent people." (63)

As a result the affair with Krish makes her feel despicable. She believes that she is "a harlot self-consciously sneaking up to solicit customers." (175) The first real expression of her sexuality makes her feel unworthy of respect because she has imbibed the phallocentric notions of sexuality (favouring males and within marriage). She naturalizes the concept of a "loose" woman, incorporating and inculcating it. This is the result of the institutional power over female sexuality and behaviour.

It is also relevant to note here that Karuna fits not only the male engendered identity of a "characterless" woman, but also of the woman-as-romantic. The woman, traditionally associated with emotion, sentiment and romance is portrayed as hypersexual. Karuna believes this of herself. Her husband accuses her of seeking a movie-style romance. (187) She herself needs "a Grand Romance with violins and roses." (301) Karuna has then inserted herself into the role of a vulnerable romance heroine who seeks and is swayed by gestures of affection or flattery.

Romances are populated by "fair" and "dark" heroines generally placed antithetically. The community of women is generally divided on these lines. For recent feminist theory this concept of women's community or "sisterhood" has assumed great significance.[7] Paulina Palmer in her *Contemporary Women's Fiction: Narrative Practice and Feminist Theory* argues that feminist fiction of the 1970s and 80s affirm the ideal of sisterhood and women's collectivity. Later fiction however focuses more on themes of women's betrayal.[8] In *Socialite Evenings* the sisterhood motif is seldom portrayed favourably. Envy, class differences and hatred inform relations among women. For example, Karuna's vicious comments greet any narration by Anjali or Ritu. Members of the family with whom Karuna lodges are all snoopy and interesting. Characters like Si are uninhibitedly creede.

Only one favourable sketch of sisterhood occurs in De. Anjali's care of Karuna after the latter's abortion is also, however, tinged with a lofty condescension on Anjali's part. (223-28) Karuna's mother is non-supportive as are her sisters.[9]

Hence a collective resistance by women is not suggested in the novel. David Tetzlaff in his essay "Popular Culture and Social Control in Late Capitalism" has discussed this aspect of resistance-culture. Tetzlaff argues that individualistic rebellion is constantly validated but rarely do these rebellions merge into a totalising movement.[10] Likewise, in *Socialite Evenings* any token resistance (Anjali's, Ritu or Karuna's) remains solitary and unsupported. Anjali does not understand Karuna's continued rebellion. Ritu settles for a boring but secure life rather than go along with Karuna.

The antipathy displayed by De's women towards their fellow-women derives from the same foundations of socially constituted differences. In this case it is wealth and class which assumes greater import than gender. Women's solidarity does not occur as long as they remain conscious of their class affiliations.

Practically every page of the novel bristles with overt or covert references to class. Karuna does not wish to write of her middle-class origins. (9) Anjali likewise works at forgetting her poor origins. Wealth and its accompanying social status is therefore constantly sought, displayed and reinforced by the heroines. Talk of French perfumes, foreign holidays, jet setting lifestyles, designer clothes form the "atmosphere" in *Socialite Evenings*. In portraying a rags-to-riches romance in the stories of Karuna and Anjali, De glorifies material success, class mobility and glamour. The heroines "make it big" in spite of their lower origins which, Cranny Francis has pointed out, is an indispensable feature of the romance. (194) Simultaneously, however, De deconstructs this glamour by showing how pain and suffering inhabit this world too. Ritu's torture, Anjali's humiliation and eventual near-asceticism reveal the pathos of the "high life." Affections of people percolate, if at all, through notions of class and status. We note for example, how Anjali behaves distantly when Karuna attains a better social grade. (66-67) De, I believe, places a large interrogative over the world of "glitz" (a term usually found describing the "high life") and romance. At this point we may begin to re-read the novel's status as a romance.

II

De's novel offers a few pointers for us to view it as a feminist work. We have, early in the essay, noted that the novel relies upon stereotypes, I suggest that the reduction of women characters into stereotypes is an overall narrative strategy on De's part. Karuna, Anjali and Ritu are flat and stereotyped because they are made so in a male dominated social context. De is suggesting that such a discourse about/of women (as seductress, tramp, mother or wife) reduces them and assigns them to these types. It denies individuality to the women, and forces them to adopt attitudes, faces or ideals envisioned for them by the males (we have already noted Ritu's complete dependence upon her "forgiving" husband or Anjali's retreat into the traditional woman's sphere of religion). Other ideals of independence or individuality are scuttled for good.

One of the ideals so demolished is of financial (and career) independence. The heroines of *Socialite Evenings* seek financial security. Anjali, Ritu and Karuna become vicitms to men precisely because of their economic dependence. However, it must be stressed that in De, the economic interest is seldom sundered from the erotic one. For example, Anjali's fascination for men is inevitably two-pronged: physical beauty and wealth. In a similar fashion, Gul practically "buys" Ritu. This dual motif characterizes all feminist romance.[11] I would like to argue that in De, women are victimized on account of this dual "interest." They become, ironically, economically subservient and sexually dependent, unless sexuality is "sublimated" into religious fervour as in Anjali.

Karuna marks a deviation from this norm. She refuses a "good life" (offered by Girish or Ranbir) if it entails a loss of individuality. She attempts to see, and keep, the erotic and economic as separate realms. This is so particularly after she realises that sexually appealing "playboys" like Krish actually live off their doting women-patrons. (192)

Karuna's resistance to the idea of marriage (or rather, her second one) is also significant. She talks tough to prospective husbands, especially Ranbir. (301-2) She prefers a "friendship" (304) to permanent subjugation. She refuses the institutionalising of her personality, and thus her stereo-typification, within marriage. She also refuses to allow others to fashion an identity for her. This is seen in her rejection of Ranbir's proposal to make a documentary about her. In a Baudrillardian sense, she refuses to be a mere screen "reflecting passively the image of other surfaces." (116) This refusal to allow the "imaging" of her life by others is the creation of space where she possesses the freedom to write her own self. This is strongly suggested in her remarks to Ranbir: "If anyone is going to cash in on this, baby, it isn't going to be you. . . . I'll try and write you in somewhere." (306) Karuna is here reversing the standard pattern. She is writing the identity of the men in her lives while projecting her point of view. Karuna is disallowing male "versions" of herself. De has thus found a way for the heroine to re-write, literally, the gender equations in a manner she chooses.

Karuna has been mauled by the patriarchal society. It is difficult for her to accept or reject this indelible feature of her life. The only way she can come to terms with it is to write about her life, the way she wants, "packaging" it her way (as she terms it in the epilogue). The writing is thus the assertion of a self-hood created by oneself.

Anne Rosalind Jones suggests that feminist novels seldom have a positive ending while romances do. Jones believes that in feminist fiction "doors open tentatively into uncertain future." (215) Paulina Palmer on the other hand argues that novels which end on (re)affirmation of values of a woman defined sexuality and acts of marriage-resistance are truly positive endings. (160-61) I believe that there is no uncertainty at the conclusion of *Socialite Evenings*. The decision to write actually opens the doors to a new identity. Karuna's acceptance of single-woman status is an affirmation of her self.

Is De then suggesting an alternative culture? I believe she is at least providing glimpses of a "resistance culture." The lone-rebel motif (Karuna) is the validation of individualistic rebellion against the system. We may term this an oppositional stance. David Tetzlaff defines an oppositional culture as one which resists a primary form of power in effect *at the site where it occurs* (61-62, emphasis mine). This argument illustrates Karuna's behaviour at the conclusion of *Socialite Evenings*. Karuna resents, resists and rejects (in that alliterative order!) male dominance where it is at its most effective: marriage and (mis)representation. Karuna refuses marriage and prefers to create her own representation.

It could be argued that Karuna is being self-centred in her rebellion. It may be perceived as her individual act of courage where other proto-feminists like Anjali and Ritu have succumbed. To borrow Jean-Francois Lyotard's formulations,[12] the aura that surrounds Karuna's human, female experience is being dissolved into the calculation of profitability, the satisfaction of needs, self-affirmation through success. Indeed, it is this very self-affirmation through success that creates a self, personality and identity for Karuna. And since it occurs in traditional sites of male dominance (marriage or representation of women), it becomes a feminist stance.

Thus I believe *Socialite Evenings* to be suggesting a feminist romance. The text swings between these two strains of thought, attempting a compromise (marriage?, to borrow a traditional trope) between the two. To identify De's novel as a specifically feminist work would be to ignore the conventional romance elements in it. At the most we may term it a "cultural feminist" work since it focusses on an alternative woman-created culture. However, this attempted paradigm shift into cultural feminism carries the dangers of a lapse into topics, ideas, representations traditionally associated with women: modelling, marriage, religion or such (ineffectual?) arts. Karuna's act of writing her life is an attempt to write and represent it on her own terms, emphasising and narrativising her experiences. This, I believe, is the inauguration of her individual rebellion against patriarchy.

NOTES

1. Shobha De, *Socialite Evenings* (New Delhi: Penguin, 1989).
2. Anne Cranny-Francis, "Feminist Romance," *The Polity Reader in Cultural Theory* (Cambridge: Polity, 1994).
3. Northrop Frye, *The Secular Scripture. A Study of the Structure of Romance* (Massachusetts: Harvard University Press, 1976), pp. 73, 78-89.
4. Anne Rosalind Jones, "Mills and Boon Meets Feminism," *The Progress of Romance: The Politics of Popular Fiction*, ed. Jean Radford (London: Routledge and Kegan Paul, 1986), pp. 215-16. Jones's work discusses the slow seepage of feminist thought into popular romances such as the Harlequin.
5. Pierre Bourdieu, *Language and Symbolic Power* (Cambridge: Polity Press, 1994), pp. 119-20. See specifically the essays "Rites of Institution" and "Did You Say 'Popular'?" For an excellent summation of Bourdieu's work, see John B. Thompson's Introduction to the above volume. For a more critical perspective, see John Lechte's section on

Bourdieu in *Fifty Key Contemporary Thinkers*: *From Structuralism to Postmodernity* (London and New York: Routledge, 1994).

6. Jean Baudrillard, "The Masses: The Implosion of the Social in the Media," *The Polity Reader in Cultural Theory*, pp. 116-18.
7. The concept has been elaborated from different perspectives in works like Nina Auerbach's *Communities of Women*: *An Idea in Fiction* (Massachusetts: Harvard University Press, 1978,) Janet Todd's *Women's Friendship in Literature* (New York: Columbia University Press, 1980) and Janice G. Raymond's *A Passion for Friends*: *Towards a Philosophy of Female Affection* (London: Women's, 1986).
8. Paulina Palmer, *Contemporary Women's Fiction*: *Narrative Practice and Feminist Theory*. New York: Harvester Wheatsheaf, 1989), pp. 127-28.
9. A more positive picture of female sisterhood is to be found in De's second novel *Starry Nights* (New Delhi: Penguin, 1991). There is a lesbian relationship between Aasha Rani and Linda. The conclusion of this novel shows the two siblings Aasha and Sudha Rani coming together.
10. David Tetzlaff, "Popular Culture and Social Control in Late Capitalism," *Culture and Power*: *A Media, Culture and Society Reader*, ed. Paddy Scannell, Philip Schlesinger, Colin Sparks (London: Sage, 1992), p. 67.
11. Cranny-Francis, pp. 191-95.
12. Jean-Francois Lyotard, *The Inhuman*: *Reflections on Time*, trans. Geoffrey Bennington and Rachel Bowlby (Cambridge: Polity, 1991). An elaboration of Lyotard's views on representation and such can be found in Geoffrey Bennington's *Lyotard*: *Writing the Event* (Manchester: Manchester University Press, 1988).

From Victim to Non-Victim: *Socialite Evenings* as a Version of Künstlerroman

URBASHI BARAT

Perhaps the most ubiquitous and enduring theme in the novel is the search for identity and selfhood. As Rosalind Miles points out, "the novel has been and is a prime area for acts of definition and self-definition, both personal and social"[1]; it is the form, therefore, that the woman writer most often chooses, for it is through fiction that women have most often and most successfully managed to "construct themselves as women within new social structures."[2] If the Bildungsroman most clearly embodies the individual quest for personhood and authenticity, it as clearly underlines the ambiguity of the quest for the woman, who has through the centuries been confined to submission to patriarchal norms, exemplified by marriage and by Manusmriti, which envisage femininity and personhood as being inherently contradictory. Marginalization and victimization have been fundamental to the woman's situation: if patriarchal society is to survive, woman as a person cannot.

Consequently, in the early woman's Bildungsroman the female protagonist grew "down" rather than "up,"[3] learning to accept and to conform and to deny the self, whether or not the novel itself endorsed the desirability of such a position. It is only with the rise of feminist consciousness that the woman began to be seen as survivor, a person in her own right rather than only a role of a function, growing successfully from exploitation, subjugation and victimization to become what Margaret Atwood terms "a creative non-victim."[4] Such a Bildungsroman has more often than not been a Künstlerroman, dealing with the growth and development of not just an individual protagonist but of an artist; artists are after all almost by definition anti-normative, whose rebellion can be presented more easily as successful and whose unconventionality is acceptable even in a conformist society.

It is not surprising, then, that the first Indian Bildungsroman in English by a woman should be a Künstlerroman: Shobha De's *Socialite Evenings*. All Dé's protagonists, from *Socialite Evenings* to *Snapshots*, engage, in a search for identity, but it is only in her first novel that the woman succeeds, and finds fulfilment and self in a creative occupation. Thus *Socialite Evenings* becomes a Künstlerroman, whereas the later *Starry Nights*, which traces the growth and decline of a film star's career, remains a Bildungsroman. This is not because film-acting is less creative than film-making, but because Aasha Rani in *Starry Nights* becomes a film star not of her own volition or any desire for self-fulfilment but by virtue of the efforts of an impecunious, unscrupulous and ambitious mother. In the end Aasha Rani finds a vicarious selfhood in her dreams for her daughter—but nothing more.[5]

In *Snapshots*,[6] De's latest novel, Aparna, Rashmi and Swati are all engaged in what could have been creative vocations and which could have enabled them to reach beyond victimization. All three of them are very successful professionally, but in their personal relationships they do not make use of the qualities that enabled them to forge ahead in their public lives, and so remain mired by their patriarchal conditioning in their Basic Victim Positions One and Two, as Atwood defines them: denial of victimization, and acceptance of victimization as inevitable. In spite of the fact, then, that the novel affords the reader glimpses of their childhood and upbringing and the several stages in their journey towards adulthood, it is no Künstlerroman, nor indeed even a Bildungsroman. The structure of the novel itself indicates this. Building on the implications of its title, the novel rejects the conventional linear mode of narration characteristic of the Bildungsroman/Künstlerroman: its story begins with childhood and ends in maturity and independence, as Karuna looks back to the past in order to assess where she has reached. The novel ends with the sentence that had begun Karuna's tale—'I was born in a dusty clinic in Satara, a remote village on the outskirts of Maharashtra'—to point out that now she can go forward, that selfhood lies in acknowledging and accepting the past and learning to go beyond it. The protagonist is the third and youngest daughter in a middle-class Maharashtrian family living in a succession of small towns until she reaches adolescence and her father is transferred to Bombay: it is a move that transforms her and her way of life, and engenders within her the sense of alienation from society and family that is such a mark of modern Bildungsroman/ Künstlerroman. Karuna reminisces, "The move to the big city came just at the right time—for me but not for the rest of the family . . . we were country bumpkins transplanted for the first time into the impersonality of big city life." (13) This change of residence, then, corresponds in many ways to the Bildungsroman protagonist's journey from province to metropolis.

There are differences, however. For one, unlike as in the traditional Bildungsroman, this is not a journey that she undertakes alone, or voluntarily; this is after all a woman's Bildungsroman. Nevertheless, the young Karuna feels at home immediately in this "dirty, overcrowded, impersonal and entirely wonderful" city, (13) though her family finds it difficult to adjust to the new environment. Her own ease here is thus the first stage in the development of her own identity. In their new English-medium school while her sisters struggle with the unfamiliar language and "prefer to concentrate on their percentages, [Karuna] prefer[s] to discover Bombay and Bombayites." (14) Consequently, her sisters find their way to societal approval—or so it seems at the time—marked by paternal grunts of satisfaction at their academic performance; but Karuna becomes defiant, both at home and at school, showing her anger and resentment at her victimization in whatever way she can, assuming the role of "A sassy kid, small for her age, oppressed at home and hungering for things she didn't have." (15)

Karuna thus begins her quest for selfhood from Atwood's 'Basic Victim Position Three,' in which the protagonist "acknowledge[s] the fact that [she is] a victim but . . . refuse[s] to accept the assumption that the role is inevitable. . . . *The basic game* of Position Three is repudiating the Victim role."[8] She is thus very different from the traditional Bildungsroman hero, who moves from innocence to experience: certainly she has much to learn, but she does not begin from the innocence that lies in ignorance. She is clear-eyed about the implications of her social status and the patriarchal regimentation of her middle-class life; she recognizes the hypocrisy of "this business of being part of the Indian middle class," (37) with its clichés about the necessity of discipline and austerity and the evils of money and privilege, its fetish about following religious ritual and its ability to ignore the flouting of these rituals by individuals, its belief in the value of sexual segregation for adolescents. Indeed, as she observes later, "I doubt I'd have done the things I felt compelled to do if we hadn't been so middle class." As a result she rebels, especially against the domination of an overbearing father who decides everything for his family—even laughter—because he believes in parental control over the lives of children, (34) and invariably blames his uncomplaining wife if anything goes against his preconceived ideas. (13) There is thus no communication between Karuna and her father, and because her mother and sisters accept their victimization, there is soon a chasm between her and them as well. This sense of alienation is of course an inevitable part of growing up, but it is the special mark of the Künstlerroman protagonist (see, for instance, Joyce's *Portrait of the Artist as a Young Man* or Plath's *Bell Jar*).

With this kind of realization behind her, Karuna can only go forward, becoming a creative non-victim once her anger and resentment are channelled. Her story becomes, accordingly, a variant of a "recurrent narrative archetype, [in women's fiction] that of the rebirth journey," in which the protagonist experiences "a transformation of the personality, a centering upon personal, rather than patriarchal, space. . . . The radical otherness of women's experience is borne out in the eccentricity, a patriarchal outcome, and arcane symbolism that characterize fiction dealing with women heroes who complete the ultimate quest for human adulthood."[9] The first phase of this journey, therefore, is an acute consciousness of the importance of the self and a rejection of familiar/ familial toes: a journey that Karuna has already begun, and on which she is soon propelled further by the friends she makes. First there is the unconventional, undesirable and tarty Charlie, who makes her aware of her sexual identity and needs—although, of course, she herself remains middle-class enough to shrink from following Charlie's example, because "good girls didn't" (26)—and who introduces her to the world of modelling (a profession that had not yet acquired its present respectability) that will soon help her to spread her wings. Her father reacts violently to her modelling, but when he sees that it has no effect, "a strange truce" is effected between them as they engage in the "elaborate charade" of "what-I-don't-see-I-don't-know," (24) the hypocrisy of the situation serving to strengthen her resolve to reject her present.

Through her modelling stints she gets to meet Anjali, who in the beginning is her guide to a new world—"she offered me the opportunity to be everything I ever wanted to be" (15)—and whose story later becomes an ironic parallel to her own, as indeed do all the stories of the women whose lives soon entwine themselves with hers, making *Socialite Evenings* De's comment on the institution of marriage and in Pratt's terms the archetypal woman's novel of marriage. (41-58) There are of course several points of resemblance between the Bildungsroman and the novel of marriage:

> In the woman's bildungsroman tension between the hero's desires and society's dictates results in archetypal narrative patterns of pursuit and submission, accompanied by images of suffocation, dwarfing, and mental illness. In novels of marriage similar archetypes occur, the authors depicting matrimony as one of the primary tools for dulling a hero's initiative and restraining her maturation.[10]

That is, in both cases and at all times, the woman is invariably the victim.

Nevertheless, Charlie and Anjali become Dé's ironic counterparts to Pratt's "green-world guide." (139) Anjali's role in this matter is made clear when she provides Karuna an opportunity to travel on her own to Delhi to model, a journey that resembles the primary Bildungsroman/Kunstlerroman one, except, of course, that it is from metropolis to metropolis and not from provincial town to city, and is, moreover, swiftly dismissed in half a sentence. This is because it is by itself unremarkable; what is important is that she is able to go there at all, bearing in mind her parents' opposition and her own realization that "modelling was not quite my thing." (32)

It is a watershed in her life for another reason, too; it enables her to see the reality behind the show of glamour in Anjali's life. Earlier, Anjali had seemed to her to be "invulnerable" because she "didn't have to be anything or anyone. She just had to be." (9) But the intimacy of the Delhi journey brings Karuna closer to her. Anjali begins to call on Karuna's house, and the young girl is at first embarrassed and ashamed at her own dowdy, unfashionable middle-class surroundings, which are such a contrast to Anjali's "terribly stylish," "perfect" home, "the height of good living." (37) But she soon learns that her ideal's background had been very much like hers, and the gulf between them closes considerably, so that their relationship becomes a more equal one. Abe, Anjali's husband, may be rich, but he is a boor, and unfaithful to boot and Anjali's tramp/vamp ways are, Karuna realizes, the product of her unhappiness. Karuna cannot however, despise her: "I can only give her the most fulsome praise for achieving what ninety per cent of India's middle class spend two-thirds of their lives trying to achieve—the step up to the glories of the rich and famous." (36-37) Both, that is, belong to Basic Victim Position Three. Karuna, however, is able to move on, because she can think beyond men and marriage for her salvation.

The friendship between them takes a new turn when Anjali discovers that an ad-film-maker she herself is interested in is actually attracted to her protegee, while Karuna is disgusted that her erstwhile mentor should encourage her to respond to her husband's advances. The young girl seizes the opportunity to break with Anjali when she goes to New York on holiday "the original yokel, well, perhaps with a superficial polish—in a state of suspended excitement prepared for anything—everything. For the very first time, I felt ready. On my own, free of family influences and pressures, free of Anjali, prepared to discover the world on my own terms." (50) This is of course the real Bildungsroman/ Kunstlerroman journey of self-discovery. For though the ad-film-maker renews his acquaintance with her and offers her his protection, the decisions she makes from now on are completely her own.

When she returns home, her estrangement from her family seems total. Her sisters now appear "provincial and pesky" and "superficial," and, feeling "assertive," she declares she needs her own "space," to "find" herself. (55) These terms might seem meaningless to those around her, but that does not stop her from breaking off her four-year-old engagement to someone she is merely fond of or from cleverly evading Anjali's inquisitive questions. And she suddenly agrees to marry an old college friend with whom she had lost touch, because his "head-on, dead on approach" is so different from the hypocrisy she sees around her; she is simply "Pushed into it [marriage] by an 'acceptable' male who wouldn't take no for an answer." (58)

Her parents are happy at last about their daughter, for she is for the first time conforming to the middle-class dream of a financially secure marriage for a daughter. Within a year, though, Karuna's hopes about marriage are destroyed. Not that her husband is a villain: he is "just the average Indian husband—unexciting, uninspiring, untutored." (65) This is the reality of marriage: "All the husbands of my friends more or less fell into this pattern. They were not evil men, but what they did to our lives went beyond evil. We were reduced to being marginal people. Everything that mattered to us was trivialized." (69) Boredom is the essence of the married woman's condition that "self-induced anomie or claustrophobia" that characterizes the modern woman in the modern Bildungsroman.[11]

All around her Karuna sees marriages and relationships with men collapsing, even within her own family, with the woman inevitably at the losing end, at the mercy of a society which demands of a woman eternal conformity and submission and perennial youth and good looks and of time that destroys face and figure and human hopes. Anjali herself, divorced by Abe, goes from man to man, getting more and more hurt in the process, until she meets someone who offers her all the emotional and financial security she craves for. She marries Kumar Bhandari in what seems to be a fairy-tale wedding, but the marriage itself turns out to be no fairy-tale (the wedding festivities themselves are a pointer to this) for Kumar is a homosexual who uses marriage to provide him respectability. Anjali turns to religion and to interior decoration for consolation, to be faced with betrayal here too; being Anjali and not Karuna, she tries to make the best of what she has instead of walking out. She remains, that is, a victim.

It is only Karuna, of all the women in the novel, who learns from life. As the archetypal Kunstlerroman protagonist, whose sensitivity forces her to rebel against a philistine society and its bourgeois straitjacketing, she must suffer before she discovers how to bridge the gulf between the claims of selfhood and of society and to defeat time by standing outside it. Before she achieves this, she has to make another wrong decision, to enter another blind lane, before she is able to find the true path. This happens when she falls in love for the first time with an old acquaintance of her husband. Her friends warn her about him, and she herself realizes that he is exploiting her, (173-75) but it is as though she were mesmerized. It is not until she goes to London in order to snatch a stolen holiday with him in Venice that the truth of the matter bursts upon her (the journeys in this novel all occur at significant moments, as is characteristic of the Bildungsroman/ Künstlerroman).

For while she is away Karuna's husband and mother-in-law discover Krish's letters to her, and the former flies to London to "deal" with her. (183) Helped, undoubtedly, by her sister's support—this is in fact one of her major discoveries in her journey, that the sisterhood of women exists, and offers much more support than anything that a man can give—Karuna holds her own against a man who allows her a farewell holiday in Venice with her lover before she leaves him forever. To her surprise Karuna enjoys her brief interlude in Venice with her husband more than her days with Krish; evidently there is in the last analysis no real difference between the two men. If her husband is hollow and superficial, so is Krish. She had always suspected that the latter was a "phoney," (187) and the way in which he goes along with her husband's plans, and dismisses her dreams of a grand passion as "so much *dramabaazi*," makes her see him "for what he really [is]—a shallow, exploitative, utterly ordinary, no he was even less than that, human being." (191) Krish is, then, an ironic representation of the archetypal "green-world lover," "an ideal, nonpatriarchal lover" who does not dominate the woman but constitutes, rather, a phase through which she must pass before she attains selfhood, and who either helps her towards "social development" or leads her "away from society and towards her own unconscious depths."[12] Though he is certainly no ideal, nonpatriarchal man—no man in Dé's fictional world ever is—unconsciously and unintentionally he is the precipitating factor behind her realization that the woman has no-one to turn to but herself.

Karuna's brief fling with Krish undoubtedly seems to make her marriage more tolerable once she returns to her husband. Then she discovers she is pregnant. So far they had decided to remain childless (a symbol of their barren relationship!) and she still feels she does not want the baby. But when she informs her husband about it, he immediately takes the opportunity of telling her he wants a divorce. His attitude is highly moralistic, but it is soon evident that he has been planning this for a long time, for, as Krish will soon tell her, he wants to marry someone else. His show of reconciliation was just that: a show, and betrayal is endemic in all man-woman relationship; indeed, as she learns later, Krish's wife had actively encouraged their affair.

It is a woman who comes to Karuna's help again: her old friend Anjali. With her abortion and her hysterectomy, Karuna is freed of the most potent symbol of femaleness, and is ready to progress towards androgyny and creativity; creative women, as Rosalind Miles points out, are more often than not childless. (23-34) She starts out life afresh on her own, staying in PG accommodation and beginning to earn her own living and to search for fulfilment in the theatre. She is tempted several times to return to the past, by Krish and later by a repentant husband, but she has gone beyond them.

The last of the tests Karuna has to face comes in the form of a famous art-film-maker, Girish Sridhar, who with his son Kunal takes to her immediately and with whom she herself feels an instinctive affinity. Girish offers a role in his adaptation of *Shakuntala* (note the appropriateness of his choice) and makes her feel so comfortable with him that he becomes much more the "ideal, nonpatriarchal lover" than Krish. Karuna is now secure enough to return to her parents and to come to terms with her past—an important phase in the progress towards identity. This sparks off her creative spirit, and she begins writing scripts for ad-films almost as though inspired. There is no Künstlerroman-like epiphanic moment, perhaps, but the easy relationship she shares with everyone around her has charged her emotionally and intellectually. So when the gossip magazines are full of spiteful stories about her and Girish, and he offers to come to her rescue, she is able to refuse him, even though her parents urge her to marry him and even though she cares for him as a friend. She is now close to achieving androgyny; she believes, instead, in her responsibilities towards her elderly parents (much as a son would do) and she is able to tackle Varun, the powerful editor of the scandal-sheet that has attacked her, with equanimity and poise.

The friendship between Karuna and Girish and his son tapers off—no man can, after all, face rejection—and she enters into a new relationship with an Indian reporter from America (the country that had first nurtured her ambition to find herself and her own space). Ranbir Roy is a married man, and what he gives her is something that goes beyond sex or romance: the ability to believe in her own creativity. As he tells her, "Put yourself on the line. Find out what you're all about. I think you've got the stuff in you." (300) Most significantly, he suggests that she creates a work of fiction out of her own life. The result is this book that Karuna has written. She has to look back to her past and work it out of her to create not just a film script or a novel but her present and future: she has discovered herself through her fiction. It is this simultaneous realization of identity and creativity that makes *Socialite Evenings* a Künstlerroman. As such, it is a landmark in the history of Indian fiction in English and of the Indian women's movement. Its value as literature? Well, that's another story.

NOTES

1. *The Female Form: Women Writers and the Conquest of the Novel* (London: Routledge and Kegan Paul, 1990), p. 61.
2. Juliet Mitchell, "Femininity, Narrative and Psychoanalysis," *Modern Criticism and Theory: A Reader*, ed. David Lodge (London: Longman, 1988), p. 426.
3. Annis Pratt, *Archetypal Patterns in Woman's Fiction* (Bloomington: Indiana Univ. Press, 1981), p. 14.
4. Margaret Atwood, *Survival: A Thematic Guide to Canadian Literature* (Toronto: Anansi, 1872), pp. 36-39.
5. *Starry Nights* (Delhi: Penguin India, 1994), p. 234.
6. *Snapshots* (New Delhi: Penguin, 1995).
7. *Socialite Evenings* (New Delhi: Penguin, 1988).
8. Atwood, pp. 37-38.
9. *Pratt*, pp. 135-38.
10. *Ibid.*, p. 41.
11. *Ibid.*, p. 31.
12. *Ibid.*, p. 140.

Socialite Evenings: A Feminist Study

S.P. SWAIN

Kate in Jane Wagner's *The Search for Signs* says:

> I am sick of being the victim
> of trends I reflect
> but don't even understand.[1]

Thus she becomes painfully aware of her position in the system whose trends incarcerate her. But Karuna in *Socialite Evenings* is a different woman. She is all agog to break-out of such thralldom which "compel her to assume the status of the other."[2] A problem child both at home and at school, she declines to dog the traditional path of etiquette and manners. At home, she refused to cower before elders and at school she wore her sash hipster style. As she grows in age there develops in her the emotional urge to identify with the outside world, the modern crowd, the bewitching and fascinating world of affluent girls who had everything. Her slap-dash entry into all that is modern lands her in the lewd and clandestine world of modelling with her secret assignment as the Terkosa Girl.[3] Throughout the novel Karuna figures as a woman who asserts her feminine psyche through protest and defiance. She figures as a woman, not victim. Shobha De deals with the sullenly skewed power equation between the genders and its transformation into the stuff of art. We do not have here the stereotypes associated with male artistic representations of women. Karuna's initiation into the fashionable world of modern life begins at Anjali's fancy place in Malabar Hill. But Anjali accuses Karuna of bitchiness and lechery, her insatiable appetite for sex. This is borne out when Karuna dates with the New Delhi ad film-maker in London. Further her stay in the US gives her a feeling of superiority and makes her assertive. Karuna, with all her attempts at ego-assertion, refuses subscription to stereotypes, to succumb to the hegemony of the malist culture. Simone de Beauvoir finds man-woman nexus quite unsymmetrlcal and uncomplementary for "man represents both the positive and the neutral, as is indicated by the common use of man to designate human beings in general; whereas woman represents only the negative defined by limiting criteria, without reciprocity."[4]

A woman is never regarded as an autonomous being since she has always been assigned a subordinate and relative position: "Man can think of himself without woman. She cannot think of herself without man. And she is simply what man decrees . . . she appears essentially to the male as a sexual being. For him she is sex—absolute sex, no less. She is defined and differentiated with reference to man and not he with reference to her; she is the incidental, the inessential as opposed to the essential."[5]

Socialite Evenings gives us the picture of the marginalization of Indian women at the hands of their husbands. Shobha De's is the picture of women not only as protagonists but also as motivating factors in society, initiating and regulating their own lives as well as the lives of others in the voluptuously fascinating world of Bombayites, its enticing glitter and glamour enamouring many a Karunas to its ensnaring and captivating gossamer. Karuna's marriage is a failure since it is loveless, joyless and bridgeless. There is no understanding between the husband and wife. She feels that she has married "the wrong man for the wrong reasons at the wrong time." Her husband is just the average Indian husband, "Unexciting, uninspiring, untutored. He was not made for introspection." (65) The average Indian woman's conjugal life is to her "an exhausted generation of wives with no dreams left" and "marriage" is "like a skin allergy, an irritant." But she is not afraid to face this irritant, this allergy. She boldly and defiantly encounters it, for she realizes "marriage is nothing to get excited or worried about. It is just something to get used to" (68) and she gets used to this stereotyped social institution in the course of time. She detests the standoffish and callous attitude of the husbands who often kept themselves busy in drab monotonous activities like reading the business pages of *The Times of India*. But despite these laxities, a husband was above all, a sheltering tree, a rock to the wife. They were not wholly bad or evil and the wife as a woman was only a peripheral being. Karuna says:

> We were reduced to being marginal people. Everything that mattered to us was trivialized. The message was "you don't really count, except in the context of my priorities." It was taken for granted that our needs were secondary to theirs. And that in some way we ought to be grateful for having a roof over our head and four square meals a day. (69)

In a patriarchal male-dominated society, it is the male who shouts, hurls abuses, bullies, reproaches, criticises and it is the woman who listens, tolerates and remains passive. But Shobha's women are different. Like Karuna they are not mere binding vine, "yes-persons" to bow down in meek subordination. They are like the new woman who fights back, resists and shouts back.

Subaltern attitude of women finds expression in the deletion from their mind of all thoughts of feminine liberty and equality. This is exemplified in the life of a qualified surgeon who was deliberately humiliated by her husband due to his repeated nagging that she married him for money. And what of the wife? She was "feeling humiliated and demoralized enough to actually half-believe what he was saying." (69) Look at the pitiable plight of such a woman as a housewife: "He brainwashes me constantly. I'm made to feel obliged and in debt. It's awful, but even my insistence on working and contributing to the running expenses of the house has become a battleground. I don't know what to do—either way I'm stuck." (69)

The subordination of women as housewives stems from a castration-panic on the part of the husband. The Indian male is presented by Shobha De as a person "terribly threatened by self-sufficient women." (69) He is inadequate and incomplete as a husband since he lacks the traits of an ideal husband. Fear of the loss of domination and control over the self-affirming wife makes him resort to several defence mechanisms. One of this strategies is his male chauvinism and power-assertion ventilating in bullying and committing atrocities upon his wife. But his stupid self-conceit and ego restricts a free exchange of views among sexes. Karuna inquisitively wonders: "how could we communicate anything at all to men who perpetually sat reading pages of *The Times of India* while concentratedly picking their noses?" (68)

Karuna learns from Ritu, whom she chances upon at a finance director's party that "men like dogs could be conditioned through reward and punishment." (87) But could she condition her husband in the like manner? She was fed up with her husband's compulsive socializing, his horrible safari suits and the gum he constantly chewed. She could not turn to anything in such a boring milieu save her books and her fantasies. Crosswords and newspaper chess were other alternatives to utter boredom. She realizes that despite her little acts of protest, she is "a well-trained, Indian wife" (51) but she shares the same rational human nature as men do. Karuna is not "the toy of man, his rattle," which "must jingle in his ears whenever, dismissing reason, he chooses to be amused."[6]

Rabindranath Tagore said in one of his early songs:

> O Woman, you are one-half woman
> and one-half dream.

So too with Karuna who combines in her both fact and fantasy. Her imaginary craving for the fulfilment of her physical desire finds reflection in her fantasies. Anjali's fancy place in Malabar Hill, the regular haunt of Karuna is symbolically the projection of her fancy, her dream which in reality is but a myth. A woman lives in a world of fancies, insignificant but profoundly imaginative. Talking of women, Virginia Woolf says: "Imaginatively she is of the highest importance. Practically she is completely insignificant. . . . Some of the most inspired words, some of the most profound thoughts in literature fall from her lips; in real life she could hardly read, could hardly spell and was the property of her husband."[7] In this context it would be worthwhile to examine Karuna's views about the meaningless marriage in which she is trapped:

> I think our marriage was over the day our awful honey-moon started. We've got nothing going. I don't love you—never have. As for you—I really don't know to this day why you chose to marry me. I don't think you even know who you married. You don't have a clue what sort of woman I am. I'm tired of your

> smugness, your irritating mannerisms, the way you take me for granted and expect me to fall into your overall scheme of things—I was another one for your well-calculated deals. (185)

Locked up in a fragile and futile marital knot, Karuna was leading a life of emotional frigidity. There was no meaningful communication between the partners. No smiles and laughter, no free exchange of thoughts and ideas, no queries and questions but silence. Only silence. Karuna admits: "It wasn't that I never tried, but there was no question that my husband and I inhabited different planets." (68) Despite these emotional voids in her conjugal life, Karuna toed the track of an ideal housewife conforming to the demands of tradition. She did not protest but dutifully obeyed her husband. The house was kept in order, everything was well-trimmed, clean and tidy. Her husband is a compromising and forgiving type of person who is not a cruel and merciless individual to throw her away for her affair with Girish:

> I've thought over the whole thing carefully. I would've thrown you right now—but I'm prepared to give you one more chance. I'm not a mean man. You've been a good wife—I'm prepared to cancel this one black mark on your performance record and start with a clean slate. But you have to swear you'll never see or keep in touch with that man again . . . you have sinned but I must be generous and forgive you. (184)

I would rather call this act of forgiveness on the part of her husband as an act of his male ego, his assertion of superiority. What right has he to say that "I am not a mean man" when he himself has denied his wife the conjugal bliss of a marital life by often keeping himself at a distance from her? In what way is he "fair" which he in the course of his tirade admits to be? He is unable to look deep into the biological need of Karuna's female self. If Karuna had any affair with Girish, it was only a means to fulfil her psychological and emotional need. It was her attempt to attend wholeness of personality for without a man, a woman is a fragment, a partial self. Such an involvement on the part of Karuna may also be a strategic escape from the claustrophobic and cloistered milieu of her marital life where they lived as two separate islands. Karuna says: "You never cared to understand me as a woman." (185) Basically Karuna is pure, for she is spiritually untainted and unsullied. The modern New Woman, independent in all respects, Karuna is a respectable, conservative Hindu housewife, wrapped in yards and yards of sari. The role of a wife restricts a woman's self-development. It circumscribes it. Rosemarie Tong maintains: "Sometimes women play their roles not so much because they want to, as because they have to in order to survive psychologically. Virtually all women engage in the feminine role playing."[8]

Karuna in *Socialite Evenings* plays different roles at different times to quench her emotional and psychic thirst. She is a model, a housewife, a society lady and an actor-writer and a paramour. Marriage subjugates and enslaves women. It leads her to "aimless days indefinitely repeated, life that slips away gently toward death without questioning its purpose."[9] But not so with the new women like Karuna. Unlike other married women who have practically no choice left to them save what their husband wills and desires, Karuna has independent thoughts. She has her own say and is free to choose her ways and means. The husband interferes but it is only by way of guidance and advice. There is no superimposition on her thoughts. Karuna's is a life of instincts and urges. Unlike other married women slavishly tagged to tradition, she has her own say. She unveils and unfurls herself to activate the creative urge stifled within her self and this act of unburdening herself is a compromise with her self. Like Shashi Deshpande, Shobha De does not overdo women's suffering. She transforms it into a creative principle of art and beauty.

The subordination of women in a malist culture is symptomatic of hierarchization of socio-moral values between the sexes. It symbolises the polarity between activity and passivity, between meek obedience and defiance. Helene Cixous observes: "A male privilege can be seen in the opposition between activity and passivity. Traditionally, the question of sexual difference is coupled with the same opposition: activity/passivity."[10] Women are often the symbols of passivity. Cixous further maintains: "Either the woman is passive; or she doesn't exist. What is left is unthinkable, unthought of. She does not enter into the opposition, she is not coupled with the father who is coupled with the son." (288)

Woman is thus reduced to matter, a mere object. This reduction of woman to matter or a commodity is in the main a phallocentric pattern. Karuna's husband treats her as matter, a mere object subjected to his own will. Karuna's humorously sarcastic approach to her problems in the patriarchal male culture apparently deconstructs the traditional gender hostility used to elaborate the polarities of connubial ties. Karuna undermines male superiority. She loathes her husband's dwelling in "post-mortems." (186) She makes an ingenuous declaration about her inner urge to express herself through love:

> I love this friend of yours, and I want to be with him in Venice. There is a good chance that I will feel thoroughly disillusioned after that. Maybe he will have some truly foul personal habits that will disenchant me. In which case it will really be *A Death in Venice*. You know by now that I'm not the flighty sort. I don't flirt at random like my other friends. I'm steady and grounded. It's the Taurean in me that's surfacing these days. Treat this as a short-term mania that will wear itself out. (186)

It appears that Karuna has just a formal relationship with her husband. Intimacy between the husband and wife is lacking for Karuna who never calls her husband by his name but derogatorily as 'Black Label.' Shobha De resorts to the technique of manipulating language in order to deconstruct the male ego: "the fact that his wife had taken a lover excited him. It seemed immoral that we should make love under the circumstances, but there was no point in resisting—it would have only consumed more time." (188)

She views woman not only as meekly/passively defiant but also as the embodiment of power. In Karuna this power (Shakti) syndrome assumes a positive figure but in Winnie it is a negative force, the destructive image, the image of Kali. Let us have a look at what Karuna's husband says about the bewitching Winnie: "She is a very strange and powerful woman. I feel ashamed to admit this, but I'm scared of her. I can't do anything becuase I know she will destroy me. She has that power." (264)

Women in De's novels symbolise the overpowering materialism and the lack of spirituality, that characterises modern age. With the crumbling of moral and ethical values there is an inner conflict which drives the modern Indian women to seek shelter in different identities for momentary solace. One of the most notable features of these women is they lack an identity. But we should not lay the whole blame on women only because in De's novels we do have the type of men who use and abuse women and then discard them. In *Socialite Evenings* we do encounter a liberal Indian husband who allows his Indian wife to go abroad and get herself screwed once for all as the last gesture of goodwill! From the individual, let us come to the family. It is the family which is the centre of deviance. Subhash Chandra regards family's disintegration the instrument of degeneration in *Socialite Evenings*.[11] The first tentative assay at the vamp ideology, Shobha De's *Socialite Evenings* is a lust-laced work of sexploitation.

Anjali throws off the traditional conventions of moral values and seductively rises to the social status of the upper classes. She enacts a marriage of choice with Abe, "an experienced rake with a wild reputation" (12) and rejoices in orgastic acrobatics. Having a passion for illimitable sex, she has frequent sex encounters. Be he the die-hard rake Abe or the innocent Karan, she is after the desire of the body, the itchings of the sensations. Karuna too discards the dogmatic rules of a hackneyed and worn-out tradition for sustaining and cherishing her extra-marital relationship with Krish. Even she does not hesitate to restrain her husband from a week-long sexual orgy with Krish in Rome. Anjali, Karuna and Ritu are the proverbial succubi who reign supreme in their world of licentious and unrestricted libido. In *Socialite Evenings*, Shobha De articulates her own inclination towards vamp art and displays the troika of female characters who symbolise absolute freedom of womankind from all forms of patriarchal inhibitions. A housewife, Karuna encapsulates the plight of the Indian woman: "I felt like an indifferent boarder in the house, going through the motions of housekeeping and playing wife but the resentment and rebellion remained just under the surface, ready to break out at the smallest provocation." (69)

Thus De's novel shows the struggle of woman against the predatory male-dominated society. But her vamp ideology of feminism provides no redemption for the deviant and fallen women who in their frantic struggle to escape male-domination and attain individuality, meet with failure and are victimised in one way or the other. In enacting the drama of seduction and betrayal in her foray against patriarchal structures, the glamorous vamp in De's novels "may end up being as seductively treacherous to women as to men."[12] In dealing with the problems of women in the androcentric society, she fails to provide viable solutions to the plight of the ailing woman. A woman in Indian society marries not just the man but also his family and subsequently loses her identity in marriage, relinquishes her freedom and sets about pleasing everybody. But the new generation of women with their new-found release from matrimonial bondage adopt different perspectives, and revolt against the old order. De's women are such liberated individuals in search of a niche in their lives through escapades and sexcapades.

Karuna detests her husband's flattering nature, his duplicity and deviousness. He who had earlier rebuked and reproached her for having an illegal child is now satisfying her female ego by sly and base flattery, by saying that it was their legitimate child. But this is wrongly timed and too late for Karuna, for she has already undergone the protracted pangs of an abortion. Hence her demolition of the male ego: "you are even more of a worm than I thought. You deserve Winnie. I hope she's got a wax doll of yours. I'll send her some extra pins to stick into it." (264) Karuna is a different Bombay socialite. Unlike them, she defies the preconceptions and presumptions of a phallocentric patriarchal society, a world poles apart from her own rationale of life. Other women hardly defy the norms of the androcentric world. Anjali for instance has her own hangover following her separation from Abe. She is in search of a suitable life-partner. Hence her amorous drift into the life of Kumar whom she chooses as her husband. As a woman she "projects her own sexual breakthroughs, energy, desire, onto a man, (or sometimes another woman) as if such power has nothing to do with her."[13] De's women like Anjali and Karuna project their passions onto others as a female power play in order to deconstruct the male ego. They like to be "eroticized as objects" and to view "themselves as erotic objects, not subjects."[14] But eroticism for these pervert women may either be a means to regain their sexuality or may be an expression of the confusion of their emotional and carnal urge. It may also be "a measure between the beginning of our sense of self, and the chaos of our strongest feelings . . . an internal sense of satisfaction to which we can aspire."[15]

Ritu exploits her sexual breakthrough, her female potentiality to keep her husband within her reach, within her control. Look, what she tells Karuna about her strategy: "make them feel you have done them a favour by marrying them . . . make them feel insecure. Let them think you'll walk out on them if they don't toe the line. That's what keeps them in their place." (86) Like Ritu, one has got to play the game, by flattering their male ego to suck anything out of them. Such an ideology of sexual power politics where the female is assigned a superior position and the male "a conditioned dog" has not been fully exploited and elucidated by De's vamp feministic ideology culminating in cheap sexual encounters between the male and the female, almost a vile pornographic picture of man-woman relationship. But such a perspective does not promise one a safe life. Hence Karuna's mother prefers the traditional way of life:

> A woman cannot live alone. It is not safe. We are here today—but who knows about tomorrow? A woman needs a man's protection. Society can be very cruel . . . a woman's real place is in her husband's house—not in her parents'—Take your time but marry. And marry the right one—that is important. . . . Before we die, we want to see you secure and at peace. (275-76)

But the mother's view is fraught with a lot of improbabilities and fallacies for is it possible for a girl to "marry the right one" and is it possible to attain 'security' and 'peace' in the modern society, especially in the urban milieu which forms the backdrop of De's novels? No longer in the Indian society, the institution of marriage carries with it the traditional sense of security. As Karuna questions:

> But, mother why does security rest with a man? I feel confident now that I can look after myself. I am earning as much money as any man, I have a roof over my head. I don't really have any responsibilities. I am at peace with myself. I'm not answerable to anyone. . . . I can't make any "sacrifices"—not now. (276)

Karuna rejects the hierarchization of male values where the female factor is reduced to a negative, and almost nullified. Her statements express her desire for the affirmation of her feminine self. It is in fact a search on her part for the genuine female self in a male-centred phallocentric world. But hers is not a traditional one. It is an esoteric quest, something weird and grotesque on the part of an Indian woman. But Karuna never bothers about the social repercussions her esoteric quest might entail. She is isolated from the traditional Indian heritage and its social implications. Taking up a non-conformist stance, she adopts a radical feminist point of view all agog to "destroy the sex/gender system—the real source of women's oppression—and to create a new society in which men and women are equals at every level of existence."[16] In order to avoid sexual exploitation or eroticisation of women as mere sex objects, Millett advocates a society having a single standard of "sex freedom" for boys and girls without which the equality between men and women will remain ephemeral. Shobha De has fully exposed the feminine world of the characters since for her, humanness should be identified with "femininity" because as Marilyn French observes: "A masculine world is less fully human than a feminine one."[17] With dissident women like Karuna and Anjali oppressive gender roles will be deconstructed and women will take up a revolutionary role, flouting androgyny. A new generation of "wild," "lusty," and "wandering" women like those of De's female protagonists will be created who would "prefer to identify themselves as radical lesbian feminist separatists."[18] Pornography in De's novels becomes a symptom and symbol of the female's defiance of a male-regulated female sexuality. De's women suffer in an androgynous world for they do not cherish genuine passions but only plastic passions which make them passive without a sense of purpose living in a frustrating world of anxiety, guilt, hostility, bitterness, boredom and resentment. These women cast off the conventional sense of morality, the old, tired and repressive sexual moves and revel in the erotic celebration of the body. Could we call Shobha De, a pornographic and vulgar novelist since she depicts the naked sexual description in her novels? Then how should we justify the rationale of the people who patronise XXX porn films? The probable answer may be they do it to release or relieve their sexual tensions. And Shobha De may be aiming to do the same thing when she describes the lusty sexual scenes. She may be aiming to provide the readers "with the mechanism that will, if all goes well, carry off the effluvia of socially banned sexual expressions into the realm of fantasy."[19] It seems that Shobha De views women as nothing but sex, a means to satisfy masculine lust.

The plight of women's present psychological situation is thus only one aspect of the problems involved in the growth of individual freedom. Viola Klein observes: "Being in the position of outsiders, intruding into a finished system, and restricted by a century-old history of submission, which had bred in them a sense of inferiority women's chief claim in their struggle was, as a natural result, to prove that in all respects they were just as good as men."[20]

These new women were like Shobha De's Karuna "disgustingly self-assured and revoltingly self-sufficient." (305) Shobha De presents women with a lot of "pot passions." She exhibits the traits of neither the liberal feminists nor the radical feminists. At the most her novels are pulp-fiction, which sell well and read well but they fail to meet the aesthetics of feminism. Shobha De's novels may simply be called as vamp feministic ideals of an experimenter in feminism. She has a long way to go in order to carve out a niche for herself as a genuine feminist novelist, for what she most exhibits in her novels is gross pornography. She has yet to "prove her first commitment to feminism and shed off the popular stigma of being a mere peddler of pornographic fiction."[21] A.G. Khan rightly regards "her entire acrobatics as an attempt to reduce 'fiction' to 'fucktion.'"[22] Her novels portray her feelings of alienation from the traditional fictional craft of other women writers especially her predecessors. They are pieces of self-dramatization. They symbolise a woman writer's struggle for artistic self-definition, an attempt at self- differentiation from her male counterparts as well as an urgent sense of her need for a female audience coupled with her dread for the orthodox and traditional male readers. Shobha De's *Socialite Evenings* fails to offer a viable strategy to the readers for socialization though it may to some degree offer some panacea to the sex-starved unsociables.

NOTES

1. Jane Wagner, *The Search for Signs of Intelligent Life in the Universe* (New York: Harper and Row, 1978), p. 53.
2. Simone de Beauvoir, *The Second Sex*, trans. and ed. H.M. Parshley (London: Penguin, 1974), p. 85.
3. Shobha De, *Socialite Evenings* (New Delhi: Penguin, 1990), p. 24.
4. R. Selden, ed., *The Theory of Criticism: From Plato to the Present: A Reader* (London: Longman, 1988), p. 534.

5. *Loc. cit.*
6. Mary Wollstonecraft, *A Vindication of the Rights of Woman*, ed. Carol H. Poston (New York: W.W. Norton, 1975), p. 34.
7. Virginia Woolf, *A Room of One's Own* (New York: Harcourt, Brace and World, 1992), pp. 45-46.
8. Rosemarie Tong, *Feminist Thought* (London: Routledge, 1993), p. 200.
9. Beauvoir, p. 500.
10. Lodge, *Modern Criticism and Theory: A Reader* (London: Longman, 1989), p. 288.
11. Subhash Chandra, "Family and Marriage in Shobha De's *Socialite Evenings,*" see the next article in this book.
12. Sandra M. Gilbert and Susan Gubar, "The Mirror and the Vamp: Reflections on Feminist Criticism," *The Future of Literary Theory*, ed. Ralph Cohen (New York: Routledge), p. 145.
13. R. Morgan, *The Anatomy of Freedom: Feminism, Physics and Global Politics* (Oxford: Martin Robertson, 1983), p. 143.
14. *Loc. cit.*
15. *Loc. cit.*
16. Kate Millett, *Sexual Politics* (Garden City, N.Y.: Doubleday, 1970), p. 62.
17. Marilyn French, *Beyond Power: On Women, Men and Morals* (New York: Summit, 1985), p. 72.
18. Tong, p. 102.
19. English Deirdre, "The Politics of Porn: Can Feminists Walk the Line?" *Mother Jones* (April 1980), p. 44.
20. Viola Klein, *The Feminine Character* (London: Routledge, 1989), p. 34.
21. Sudhir Kumar, "Artist as Vamp: A Feminist Approach to Shobha De's *Starry Nights,*" reprinted in this book.
22. A.G. Khan, "Shobha De 'Vatsyayani'," *Indian Women Novelists*, ed. R.K. Dhawan (New Delhi: Prestige, 1995), Set III, Vol. I, p. 78.

Family and Marriage in *Socialite Evenings*

SUBHASH CHANDRA

Males like fox, martin, wild cat, and mole, the eagle, sparrow-hawk, pigeon, stork, black-bird, swallow etc. whose young are difficult to provide for, select one from among several females at the first period of oestrum. They remain attached to each other even when the time of propagation has passed. They journey together, remain side by side in flocks, "provide for themselves, and at each succeeding period of oestrum, again yield to love," and do not "seek a new mate till the former is dead."[1] Homo sapiens belong to this category, and therefore, promiscuity in sex is as unnatural to them as it is to such animals and birds. The behaviour of anthropoid apes, man's nearest kins, further confirms the instinct for family and absence of promiscuity. They "always live in pairs and are not promiscuous,"[2] and do not part company until separated by death. Among men, even the savage races of the world are known to "live under a well-regulated marriage system."[3] Havelock Ellis says, "Marriage in the biological sense is a sexual relationship entered into with the intention of making it permanent, even apart from whether or not it has received sanction of law or the Church."[4]

Family, the smallest sociological unit, implied marriage, implicit or explicit, which in turn lent this unit stability, togetherness, and mutual care. Commenting upon the benefits resulting from family, Alexander Walker observes:

> The advantages resulting from the states of marriage are that the two sexes may reciprocally satisfy the natural desires which are felt equally by each . . . that they equally submit the exercise of the reproductive organs to a healthful regularity; that they may equally perpetuate their common species; that they may equally

> by respective duties, provide for the children proceeding from their mutual union; that they may equally assist each other throughout life by reciprocal affection and cares; that they may in old age receive the cares of their common progeny; and that they may, in health and well being, reach that age which all these circumstances generally enable married pairs to attain.[5]

Walker goes on to assert, "History proves that marriage is essential to the well-being of human society, and that celibacy brings ruin upon states."[6]

II

But these hoary institutions of family and marriage have come under tremendous strain in the modern times, primarily in the Western culture, and also in the rich stratum of the Indian society. Commenting upon the breaking up of the family, David McReynolds observes: "Nor can a person find his identity in the family—for that institution is breaking up."[7] One of the major causes of the disintegration of family is the rampant promiscuity in sexual relations. Another factor is the lack of a set routine of work and excessive leisure among women of the richer classes which becomes "a chief cause of the restless, exacting, often hysterical spirit harassing to the owner and everyone else, which tends towards discontent, indiscretion and divorce."[8] Yet another cause is that by winning the right to enter the labour market, women have found a degree of economic freedom that makes a marriage less necessary and has increased the divorce rate. *Socialite Evenings* presents a picture of the institutions of family and marriage obtaining in the wealthy classes of the Indian society. The portrayal is authentic, being an inside story, because the narrator (the writer) belongs to the rich set, which is the focus of attention in the novel. In the fictional cosmos of the book, the family is crumbling and marriage comes to be re-defined. The new definition of marriage postulates complete sexual freedom, with no notion of marital fidelity. Economic security for wife seems to be the cornerstone of this marriage arrangement which appears more like a contract than a vibrant, living, emotional relationship. Devoid of emotional warmth and entered into for expediency, such marriages often break down, leading to divorce and sundering of the family ties.

III

Anjali, the narrator's friend (and one time mentor) typifies the concept of marriage prevailing in the rich classes. The dubious factors instrumental in her marriage set the tone of her marriage and that of other marriages in the novel. Anjali, not interested in studies, had keenly wanted to get out of her middle-class background. She was a pretty, young girl, interested in seeing places and meeting people. So, like other beautiful and smart young girls of her time, she had joined Air India as a hostess. Abe (Abba Tyabjee) had been an "experienced rake with a wild reputation. Something about Anjali's almost frigid demeanour had attracted him. Initially, he had imagined she would be just another quick pick-up. But, by the time they landed in London, Anjali had managed to hook Abe. Or he her."[9] Trickery becomes the basis of marriage. "Marriage and family are the means used by society to control promiscuous sex and dissipation of man's energy which could be directed and used in many other usual channels, without at the same time, suppressing sex."[10]

But marriage, in no way, puts any restraint on Anjali's and Abe's respective sexual orgies. Arjun, Anjali's brother, works for Abe in some "vague capacity," which actually means being Abe's boozing partner and pimp. He "rounded up the pretty Hindu virgins whom Abe was partial to whenever he threw one of his wild parties." (11) Abe has some regulars with whom he sleeps, apart from the occasional pick-ups. No jealousy pangs are aroused in Anjali who is quite preoccupied with her own sexual encounters. The Belgian photographer, who had been taken along to Bhavnagar residence of Anjali's rich Gujarati friend, Jinx, for some modelling photographs of the narrator, Karuna, was won over by Anjali for her bed, though she and Jinx had competed hard to have sex with him. Feeling bored, with nothing meaningful to do, Anjali starts taking French lessons and lands herself in the bed of the young French teacher, even though she had declared to him (perhaps to make herself more insistently desired) that "she was a married woman, much older and really not one of those sleep-around types." (77) Nothing could be farther from truth, because later she comes to Karuna: "This is the experience I've been waiting for." (78) She hops to France with the French lover for a fortnight orgy of sex with him. To an unhappy Karuna, her sagacious advice is: "You are bored with your husband, you need an affair." (95) Even as she is giving her this suggestion, Anjali announces her next affair. In the narrator's words, "she was in love again, but this time she managed to stun me," (95) because this time she has picked up a boy, fit to be her son, as he is approximately her daughter Mimi's age. There is consistent repetitiveness in her description of the affair: "This is the most beautiful thing to have happened to me. . . . What Karan and I share is a very tender and beautiful relationship." (96)

After her divorce from Abe, Anjali is so desperately on the look-out for a catch to marry that her situation becomes simultaneously amusing and pathetic. She tells Karuna that she would grab a rich person, who was "available," and Karuna promises to be on the prowl for one. Eventually, Anjali does get her rich and "available" man. Kumar (K. to her) is exceedingly rich. He promptly divorces his second wife to get married to Anjali. But it is most ironical that Anjali—a woman perpetually on heat—gets saddled with a husband who is a "gay" and has his work-outs on the young boy, Murty. But, then from now on, rather abruptly and unconvincingly she turns to spiritualism, and maintains a beatific relationship with God Krishna, leaving K. to carry on his homosexual amours with Murty and other young boys. With all her penchant for variety and frequency in extra-marital relations and with her slogan, "Give me sex any day," she is transformed into a sexless relgion-minded devotee. In return for her leaving K. alone with his quirk, she gets all the financial security and the luxuries she cannot do without. But her stormy sexual affairs (before her marriage with K.) have taken their toll on her daughter, Mimi, who grows up to be a hurt, withdrawn girl, finding her security and solace in drugs.

The fate of other marriages (except for one, which becomes a point of contrast and to which I shall revert later) is not much different from that of Anjali's. The narrator's sister gets divorced from her Engineer husband in England and lives alone, practising as a doctor in London. The narrator herself, restrained by her middle-class background and morality for some time, breaks loose of the marital bond and starts a "torrid" affair with the husband's friend Krish, who is a married man, but a confirmed rake. Significantly, neither the narrator nor her husband's friend Krish, who is a married man, but a confirmed rake. Significantly, neither the narrator nor her husband refers to the other by name; each calls the other only "husband" and "wife," which denotes the impersonality of one of the most informal and intimate relationships. Karuna is conscious of the fact that she is committing adultery (the Biblical word "adulteress" sounds old-fashioned to her and she wishes for a new name for the act), but she continues to plunge deeper into it with feelings of spite against the husband, as it were. "I'd feel like a harlot self-consciously sneaking up to solicit customers," (175) when she goes to Krish's hotel for her rendezvous. In response to her friend Ritu's query, whether he wants to marry her, Karuna pours forth her passion: "I don't know. I don't care. I want him. I'll go crazy." (173) Ritu's advice in the matter is to give him up, for he cannot and will not marry her. Interestingly, each advises the other against some "affair" or the other, but the reason for dissuading is not morality: it is mainly that the lover is not "husband material" (husband becomes commodity) or is not rich enough to provide a life of luxury. Karuna cannot be dissuaded, like Anjali or Ritu could not, and plans a holiday (a sexual orgy in fact), with Krish in Rome. They (Krish and she) fix up a meeting in London, from where they would go to Rome and have uninterrupted, unrestrained and uninhibited sex. So, Karuna leaves for London on the pretext of spending some time with her sister there. But then her affair is exposed and her husband suddenly lands in London to thrash things out with her. She not only does not feel ashamed of the betrayal against her husband, but adopts a belligerent stance about her intended trip to Rome. No amount of reasoning by the husband succeeds in making her see reason. He is prepared to forget about everything, if she desists from her intended holiday in Rome with Krish. But she holds her ground, declaring, "I love this friend of yours and I want to be with him in Venice." (186) Anjali's (the paragon of sexual licence) comment on Karuna's affair later speaks volumes of the attitude of the upper class towards sexual morality: "Your little infidelity whatever it was and with whosoever is so trivial." (224) So, there is nothing to feel guilty about.

Orgasm seems to be the only thing that matters in marriage. So, Ritu loves the thrashings she receives from her husband, because they lead to "terrific orgasms." But her marriage, too, goes haywire, because she, too, is bitten by the love (promiscuity) bug. She falls for Gul—a shady character in Bombay who is rolling in wealth. She speaks the same language which the promiscuous women use in the novel: "Gul is the best thing that could've happened to me." (206) But this supposedly love relationship turns her into a whore and a pimp, who literally procures virgins for Gul and his friends. She begins to booze, consumes drugs, puts on a lot of weight and looks eminently suitable for the part that Gul makes her play—that of the procuress. But having suffered mental and physical torture at the hands of her "lover" she returns to her husband, who readily takes back a sexually violated, physically and mentally wrecked wife. Everything is forgiven and forgotten which makes it appear like a fairy-tale.

As against these families and marriages, we have Karuna's parents—a middle-class family which suffers the paints and hurts life is vulnerable to. But they stick together, through thick and thin, lending each other the much needed moral support, providing to each other the feeling of togetherness, and maintaining an affectional relationship. Marriage for them is the bedrock of faithfulness, fidelity and mutual support. They exemplify the traditional Hindu view of marriage according to which "Mutual fidelity till death" is the "highest law for the husband and wife to follow."[11] All of their three daughters are facing problems. Alka has lost her mental balance and is admitted in the nursing home. The other two daughters have become divorced. But they weather these back-breaking and nerve-racking crises (of course these have taken their toll in terms of their withdrawal from the hectic social life) primarily because they have continued to stand by each other.

The feminine sensibility and the spirit of feminism determine the direction the novel takes towards the end. The betrayed "husband" finds himself saddled with a woman who is a veritable shrew and, therefore, comes a-begging Karuna to come back and remarry him. But since he has been shown to be a mean individual (he deprives Karuna of financial assistance after divorce, even though he had promised to help) and since the militant feminism will not permit any woman to buckle under, the narrator vehemently refuses to be his wife again. Even though she is not precisely gifted or trained for any profession, she is made to fight her way up, getting recognition in advertising and television productions. She becomes financially self-dependent, carves out her own niche in the professionally competitive world of advertising and acquires all the resources to flirt *ad infinitum*, which she is shown doing with a married journalist, Ranbir Roy. The novel closes on the same tenor on which it had opened—unlimited freedom to flirt. When young, Anjali was the narrator's ideal. She wanted to emulate her, be like her.

Towards the end of the book, the narrator is another Anjali in the making. The value of the family and marriage is undermined and the traditional concept of marriage with fidelity as its cardinal principle stands discarded. There are marriages of convenience in the novel, with no obligation to emotional faithfulness and sexual fidelity.

NOTES

1. Alexander Walker, *Woman: Physiologically Considered as to Mind, Morals, Marriage, Matrimonial Slavery, Infidelity and Divorce* (Delhi: Mittal, 1987), p. 75.
2. A.K. Sur, *Sex and Marriage in India: An Ethno-Historical Survey* (Bombay: Allied, 1973), p. 3.
3. *Ibid.*, p. 3.
4. *Ibid.*, p. 2.
5. Alexander Walker, p. 78.
6. *Ibid.*, p. 80.
7. David McReynolds, "Hipsters Unleashed," in Seymour Krim, ed., *The Beats* (Greenwich: Fawcett, 1960), p. 203.
8. Charles Cooley, *Social Consciousness*, p. 368, qtd. in Pandharinath H. Prabhu, *Hindu Social Organization: A Study in Socio-Psychological and Ideological Foundations* (Bombay: Popular, 1958), p. 238.
9. Shobha De. *Socialite Evenings* (New Delhi: Penguin, 1989), p. 12.
10. Pandharinath H. Prabhu, p. 209.
11. *Ibid.*, p. 236.

Socialite Evenings: An Initiation Tale from Innocence to Experience

INNA WALTER

Shobha De's first novel *Socialite Evenings* is the initiation of Karuna, a young college girl, in the mega city of Bombay. Karuna was born in a 'dusty clinic' in Satara, a remote village in Maharashtra. From Satara to Bombay is a big leap and Karuna's mentor is Anjali, a middle-aged sophisticate who was the portal to the big world of fashion-designing and advertising. Anjali with her satiny polished nails, French perfume and the silver grey Impala were enough to make a stunning impact on the gauche mind of the native Karuna; but coming from a middle-class family as she did, Anjali somehow seemed to symbolize everything that was wrong and evil, and therefore irresistible. Anjali, from a conservative Jain family, had married Abbas Tyabji whom she had met as a young air hostess in Air India, her reason for the alliance being to escape from middle-class boredom to the exciting world of money and sophistication was, in turn, attracted to Anjali's 'frigid demeanor.' Karuna's parents disapproved of her contacts with Anjali. Her mother had a 'psychic' awareness of the unsuitability of their friendship. Anjali's introduction of Karuna into the modelling business only served to further exasperate Karuna's mother.

Karuna was a problem child both at home and at school. At home she refused to cower before elders and at school she wore her sash hipster style. Her hunger to be 'in' with the mod crowd increased as she grew up and she desperately longed to be in 'that charmed circle of rich girls who had everything.' The systematically snobbish way in which she was kept out by the smart set, diverted Karuna's impotent rage into a discovery of books encouraged by her father. (16) While Shaw and Shakespeare interested Karuna, her adolescent interest 'Playboy' and 'Photoplay' were equally great. Her college friend 'Charlie,' was a disreputable character who 'scored so many firsts of the non-academic kind' and was the first to discover boys and soul-kissing. Karuna's first modelling for a newspaper and her father's rage on discovering the secret assignment as the Terkosa Girl (24) was enough to earn her a tight slap.

Anjali's fancy place in Malabar Hill was soon the regular haunt of Karuna—the gaudy and cheap imitation of a third-rate Hollywood film set that impressed the young girl as the height of fashionable living; the mirrors, the bar with the naughty stickers along with a portrait of Anjali's daughter Mimi (Mumtaz) looking down with all the loneliness of a traumatic home life. Abe (Abbas) was Mimi's rakish father who played around with all the fashion models including the one who won the Miss India contest. (29) Karuna's meeting with Si, a regular at Abe's orgies, a sluttish woman with false eyelashes and a Mary Quant wig, who smoked incessantly and vulgarly suggested that Karuna be introduced to Abe—'he'd love her he has this thing about Hindu virgins!' shocked her profoundly. Karuna realized that 'Si and Anjali were, only two sides of the same expensive, if badly tarnished coin.' (31) The Delhi trip to model Maganbhai's jewellery and the models dressed in simple Grecian style sarees in pastel shades proved to be an ego-boosting experience to Karuna.

Anjali's unannounced visit to Karuna's house was another eye-opener when she discovered that Anjali was just as middle-class as she was. Anjali's father, a Gujarati doctor, who had practised in suburban Bombay had sent his daughter to the New Era School where Anjali had learnt her brand of English with its grammatical lapses. (36) In Karuna's middle-class home education with a capital was one of the gods while austerity, discipline and denial were the highest prized virtues. Anjali was just an unsure Gujarati, basically insecure, trying hard to fit into a world where she was always an alien and an intruder. In Anjali's circle everyone was thrice married and divorce a commonplace. This explained Anjali's marital relationship with her husband Abbas Tyabji, which reminded Karuna of Aristotle Onassis, "With the same crude arrogance that money breeds." (41) Anjali was treated like a baby and she enjoyed the feelings of indulgence; but the vital area of difference between Anjali, the half-Jain, half-Hindu girl and Abe was the "mussulman part." Anjali continued to wear a bindi when she wore saris, and celebrated Diwali at home. Religion was of no consequence to Tyabji. Another such jaunt on fashion shooting was in the house of a Gujarati heiress, with the odd nickname of Jinx, at Bhavnagar, with her penchant for speaking French and insatiable appetite for sex and 'dressing up.'

Karuna's experience at the beach-party on the occasion of Holi with its *bhang* and free and easy capers among the assembled guests, movie-stars, businessmen, models and diplomats, and Anjali egging Karuna on to "enjoy herself" with the ad-film-maker, a middle-aged man with a quiet and scholarly manner and his "professionalism," was enough to cause the first rift between Anjali and Karuna. Anjali accused Karuna of bitchiness and it was obvious that Karuna posed a threat to her.

Karuna has a trip abroad—a round-the-trip-ticket took her to New York and London. In London the New Delhi ad film-maker called and her date with him inevitably led to Karuna's comparing him with her fiance, Bunty, a management trainee in a multinational firm; for weeks the ad-man impelled Karuna to break off her engagement. Karuna's stay in the US was enough to give her a feeling of superiority and made her assertive. She returned home to find her sisters "provincial and pesky." She had discovered "privacy" and "space," commodities that were lacking at home. Her final break with Bunty, a loving and caring companion of four years, came when she discovered his 'ordinariness.' Anjali's jealousy of Karuna is further aggravated when she finds the latter flaunting an expensive Lanvin watch and exotic purple and white orchids on her shabby bedroom table. Karuna's sudden marriage took place to a comparative stranger who walked into the Sea Lounge one evening as she sat with Anjali advising her "to fix" her husband Abe with her new-found American militancy, and imperiousness. Her husband Shetti was the heir to a hundred-year-old export-import firm. He had innovative ideas and soon dismantled the cabin system and had to open work-stations in the American style. The old munimji and the peon were retired and xerox machine took their place. Karuna found that the working style of the firm reflected her husband exactly, flashy but lacking in depth. His mother was the business partner from whose business conversations she was scrupulously excluded. Karuna soon realized that she was caught up in meaningless marriage. As a liberated woman who gloried in reading the feminist writing of Germaine Greer, Karuna advised Anjali to forget her husband Abe but only to hear Anjali was unwilling to really divorce her husband. Karuna's own assessment of her tottering marriage was that she had "married the wrong man for the wrong reasons at the wrong time." Her husband was just the average Indian husband, "unexciting, uninspiring, untutored. He was not made for introspection." (65) Karuna summed up the average Indian woman's marital life as "an exhausted generation of wives with no dreams left." Marriage was "like a skin allergy, an irritant all right."

The men were always busy reading the business pages of the *Times of India* while picking their noses in abstraction. A second time that made Anjali jealous of Karuna was when her husband rose in the Bombay business community's "pecking order" and Anjali could no longer patronize Karuna. But Anjali always managed to be superior by regularly criticizing Karuna's hairstyle, the cut of her blouse and her husband—on the rebound, Karuna met a man with "a pair of gentle gray-green eyes behind large spectacle frames" at a cocktail party. He offered all the mental stimulus she had longed for and soon caught up on poetry, books and films, discussed Turgenev and Camus. Unfortunately the new-found friend and Karuna had to part and soon after she heard he had died—perhaps, thought Karuna, of boredom.

Anjali's affair with the income-tax official who got excited by her painted nails—who thought she was "exotic and unreachable" was a brief one but she continued to go "mate stalking." Anjali's next affair of the heart was with Pierre, the young French instructor at the Alliance and discovered life French style.

Karuna learnt from Ritu, whom she had met at a finance director's party that "men like dogs could be conditioned through reward and punishment." (87) Attracted to all sorts of men, from little servant boys she mothered, to silver haired industrialists, (107) Ritu suffered from a shoe fetish and wondered why the world made fuss over Imelda Morcos's collection. (109-10) Anyway Karuna's marriage was definitely on the rocks. She was utterly bored by the husband's compulsive socializing, his horrible safari suits and the gum he constantly chewed. She had nothing to turn to except her books and her fantasies. Crosswords and newspaper chess were other alternatives to utter boredom. All her mother-in-law's thrifty house-keeping methods were distasteful to Karuna as she preferred crosswords to conversation and scrabble to cocktail parties. She realized sadly that in spite of all her little "rebellions," she was "a well-trained, Indian wife." Anjali's affair with Karan, a Punjabi masseur young enough to be her son diverted Karuna for some time. Karan had a cocky "John Travolta swing" and looked like one of those typical Punjabi teddy boys from Delhi's Karol Bagh. (98-99) The death of Anjali's father made her realize what an embarrassment she was to her family as her mother was not too pleased to see her divorced and debauched daughter. Anjali soon turned to Nisha, a starlet and an inveterate gossip. Karuna soon met Nisha, the Indian Marilyn Monroe in flesh and blood. Karuna's eldest sister's divorce from her engineer husband, in England, who had soon after taken an English mistress, made Karuna realize again what "a witless little charade" (107) she herself was still playing. Anjali's next affair was with Kumar Bhandari, a businessman with a factory exporting machine tools, with two wives—one each at Madras and at Juhu. Anjali became his third wife and it was her first marriage with the Gujarati *sari*, *mehendi* and *haldi*.

Kumar Bhandari's Punjabi high spirits could be seen all over the place with the *shehnai* players greeting the guests on the one hand and Michael Jackson entertaining the gathering with "Beat It" on the other. A mixed cuisine of Chinese, Mughlai, Gujarati, Polynesian and Continental was lavishly spread on the long tables, the out-of-town guests included 'a clutch of Pakistani cricketers.' Quite a sensation was created when Zafar the Pakistani Vice-Captain lay bleeding on the floor, Feroz, Bombay's macho-est film star having pulled a gun on him after the two men had fought over a flashy starlet. A month after the wedding, Anjali confessed to Karuna that Kumar was a gay and a homo with Murthy, an orphan he'd picked up somewhere. Bhandari's three wives were to give him "a respectable front." But he made up to Anjali by letting her do her boudoirs with shocking pink bows, frills and canopies—the sort that would have given Barbara Cartland nightmares, (132) and order shower curtains from Harrods.

A new aspect of Anjali's nature was revealed when Si, Anjali's trampy friend and Karuna were invited to go over Anjali's house with its expensive decor and artefacts collected from world capitals. Anjali invited her friends to her Puja room, instructing them to please remove their shoes before entering. She went in first and bowed her head to the floor and rose with "a beatific expression on her face." She confessed, "I have found him, I am at peace at last." She pointed to the exquisite deity of Krishna installed in an inner shrine. Si twitted Anjali about having joined "the Hare Krishna guys" who operated from Juhu. Anjali even had a *mandir* built out of Makrana marble with its lovely milky tone. She then revealed that listening to bhajans was far better than all that "tuck-shuck." Anjali now claimed that though she had not joined an ashram, or given up luxuries, nice saris and jewellery, she could feel her *Kundalini* rising and lifting her up out of the spiritual and mental morass she had been in. Karuna was obliged to add that "Hindu revivalism is going to be the big trend of the 80's." Anjali was, in fact ahead of her times. (140) Si's aversion to religion and her mockery of Anjali whom she nicknamed 'Mirabai,' are all of a piece where such an arty-tarty woman is concerned. Anjali sums up Si's reaction in her remark, "I can feel her bad vibrations everywhere. She spreads *paap* wherever she goes. She is so morally corrupt." Anjali's life with Kumar now oscillated between pujas and parties. Murthy, Anjali explains to Karuna, is cute like Sabu the Elephant Boy and is great for Kumar's ego. Kumar even gave jewellery, cuff-links and rings to Murthy and bought him National Savings Certificates for future security. Anjali's business enterprise to start an interior decoration partnership with an ex-movie star Mrs. Kripalani, nicknamed Kuku, on *Janmastami* day kept her pleasantly busy. Karuna's invitation to her husband to accompany her to the launching of the interior business at Anjali's only aroused his ire and he accused Karuna of being unrealistic and compares her to Scarlet in *Gone with the Wind*; she had "no gratitude, no loyalty, nothing." (151) Such women expected all men to be Clark Gable, life is not a movie or a book, he sneered. Karuna, a childless wife now, was accused of being idle and pampered with the servants doing everything. Karuna's thoughts flew at such times to her New York flame and there rose in her mind's eye the image of the two of them walking hand in hand down 5th Avenue.

Karuna's visit along with Ritu for the *Janmastami* party at Anjali's was an eye-opener to Karuna when she saw the chief character on the scene was Babaji a "Sexy Sanyasi." Anjali explained to her friends that Babaji was a "Sufi Saint" and "the incarnation of Gautama Buddha and the final *avatar* of Krishna." And there was Mataji who led the *bhajans* and made everyone's *Kundalini* rise and told people about their past lives and past sins. (154) Both Babaji and Mataji were highly evolved people. But Ritu insisted on calling Babaji and his vast entourage "free loaders." Hot vibrations or sweating in the palms or the feet of the Babaji or Mataji meant that there were evil presences in the crowd around and so one of the disciples was applying sandalwood paste to cool them down. Ritu's interest in the Babaji went to the extent of "turning her on" and very soon Mataji approached her and told her *Kundalini* was getting stuck at one of the *chakras* and suggested that she go to the Baba for relief. Karuna and Ritu pay a visit to the Baba and what they saw there was a revelation to both. The Baba was being massaged with almond oil by a masseur who resembled "Hercules unchained," to the musical accompaniment of romantic ghazals instead of *bhajans;* an aristocratic Gujarati woman supplied the Baba with goat's milk and fruit as any other drink upset the Baba's *chakras*. The woman a widow had stripped her home of all the priceless antiques her husband had collected, to buy the Baba a bungalow. She had "offered" her two young daughters to the Baba, so gossip went the rounds but Anjali refused to believe these stories, for Babaji's heart was pure, asserted Anjali, and he really did need Mataji for she represented the Earth Mother, she was Shakti. (151) Anjali's confession that her husband Kumar had now become a believer and had even taken up *Yoga* calls up some cynical remarks from Ritu, who accusses Anjali and Kumar of "marketing Babaji." Photographs of Babaji were taken of him dressed in robes stitched at Maharajas, a Juhu boutiqe, complete with sequins and bead work. Anjali justified the Baba's rich attire as he was now a *rajyogi*, a prince on earth. He wore the clothes that his devotees gave him as he did not wish to hurt their feelings. Babaji was being increasingly quoted by the press and he started holding press conferences in five star venues giving his frank views from virginity to *sati*.

Karuna's frequent bickerings with her husband who accused her of being "a no-hoper" led to her becoming involved with theatre, and Krish, a hot-blooded Bengali rebel from the late '60s. He was known to be a Naxalite sympathizer though he himself came from an affluent background with a barrister father and law school in America. Krish Mukherjee turned his back on law and took up a job in an ad agency, but theatre was his great love. He even attempted to stage Shakespeare in Bengali.

Krish and Karuna soon launched into a torrid affair which lasted three years but broke off when she was told over the phone by Krish's servant that the Saab had taken the memsaab out for an ice-cream. Karuna's husband, after threatening to divorce her, took her on a trip to Venice pre-empting Krish's plan to take her there himself and Karuna found the trip with her husband to be "great fun."

Karuna's two sisters had each her own traumatic experience. Swati who was on the seminar circuit in a big way at London was now passing through a rough time in her marital life. Her second sister Alak always a moody and emotional person had to be given psychiatric treatment. Ritu was under a spell of boredom. Karuna's advice to her was to join the Sisters of Charity, or organize an anti-sati cell in her locality that was the "in" thing these days to involve oneself in women's issues. But Ritu soon found excitement with Gul the builder, a don and a smuggler, whom she had met at the party the Patels gave; they had made their money in cement. Ritu was going through a 'trial marriage' with Gul.

Meanwhile Anjali's house was raided, by the income-tax people who found much evidence and incriminating documents from the puja room. Gold coins and jewellery were found in Babaji's Puja room and blue films in Murthy's room. The Babaji himself was at California as his foreign disciples were organizing a major celebration. Anjali's husband Kumar was now a heart case and Murthy was blackmailing Kumar. The newspapers soon carried the news that the Babaji was arrested for trying to smuggle gold and drugs into this country. Gul could help as he was well acquainted with all the underworld.

Karuna's expected child creates a crisis in the household as her husband suspects the paternity of the child and sues for divorce. As always during trouble, Anjali helped out with advice and accommodation. Karuna's strait-laced father had no sympathy for her and told her that as she had made a mistake, she must also pay the price. Ritu herself had problems with her latest lover Gul for whom she had to procure virgins. At Anjali's anniversary party Ritu lunged at one of Gul's new interests, the starlet Sonia and got knocked up herself. Ritu attempted suicide the next day but was pulled through by Gul and his associates. Karuna's fear was that her present predicament was the consequence of 'divine justice' (224) and plans to live on her own in lodgings hired out by a Parsee woman Mrs. Jeroo Mehta. Her daughter Shireen and their maid Savitri and the dog Brutus made up the household. Between the three of them, they lived a life of 'heightened sexuality' (233) and Karuna referred to them as 'the three witches.'

Karuna's efforts to land a job and become independent landed her in theatre and she had a small role in the Hindi version of "Desire under the Elms" directed by a hysterical Delhi woman Swapna trying to make good in the Bombay film world. She had arranged for applause at the end of the show though the opening night was a complete disaster—the only encouraging thing was the presence of the great art film-maker, Girish Sridhar in the theatre. Girish told Karuna that her role was badly directed but she had acted well in spite of it. Girish was on the look out for someone to play the lead role in his magnum opus "Shakuntala," a contemporary version of the Kalidasa classic with no deer or birdies and seemed to think that Karuna would make the perfect Shakuntala. Girish was a widower with a young son Kunal, with whom he had a loving relationship. He was a loner and was known to be one of the 'angry' film-makers who made powerful statements through his films. His forte was women's subjects. Swapna's 'hostile vibes' over Karuna's obvious friendship with Girish were clearly unwarranted. Karuna and Girish, however, 'shared a lot of cultural affinities' and Girish took it as a good omen that Karuna's mother was named Shakuntala. And soon Girish offered the keyrole in his forthcoming major production "Shakuntala" to Karuna but Karuna wasn't too enthusiastic about intellectual cinema life. She preferred modelling for suitings and dresses. Karuna confesses that she was soon "sucked into a ruthless world without scruples," and then she read in the gossip columns 'Hits and Flops,' a filmy trade paper run by the powerful hotshot editor Varun, that Karuna was now busy having an affair with both father Girish and his young son Kunal and just when Karuna felt like drowning herself, Kunal walked in with a marriage proposal from his father. Karuna felt she was now obliged to care for her aged parents as they were quite alone and refused to give her 'version' of the gossip columns or be in the scandal. Varun was notorious for 'inventing stories' and ruining the reputations of those who thwarted him. He was rich enough to send his editors abroad for holidays. An older film critic however let out the lowdown on Varun, he was a homo who preferred 'Young chikna boys.' Karuna won the Ad Club award for the Best Ad of the year and was advised by friends to 'set up her own shop' but she still preferred to be a freelance Ad writer prizing her freedom more than the money that now flowed in.

Varun had announced an anniversary party, his 'annual jambooree,' to celebrate 'Outlook.' He was known to be lobbying for a Rajya Sabha seat and he was shamelessly indulging in *chamchagiri*, supporting the most absurd policies of the PM. He would probably be rewarded with a future ambassadorship. There was no doubt that Varun was going to be a politician. He had the machinery to buy the votes and definitely win in the elections. He might even join the PM's Secretariat and become his press advisor. Varun's 'Outlook' party in the concrete shiplike building was complete with lots of booze, food and action: the film star guests rigged up in the most fantastic garbs imaginable, and pot-bellied, dhoti-clad ministers, video boys and disco lights with the London-based news writer who specialized in pornographic accounts of social events completed the whole backdrop for the violently whirling dances and Anjali's discomfiture at the hands of the foreign news man and Kumar's running away from the embarrassing scene of his wife's humiliation because he was too weak to handle the situation.

Karuna soon graduated from writing to making ad films and she struck up a relationship with Ranbir Roy, the reporter from the 'Washington Times' a second generation American. He appeared to be a serious man who hid behind a buffoon's mask. He was a married man with two kids completely Americanized but nevertheless invited Karuna to go with him to Washington as an assistant. Ranbir's ambition was to reach the top as editor but he found it difficult 'to lick the system.' Karuna was after all, as Ranbir found, the respectable and conservative Hindu woman, wrapped in yards and yards of Sari. Ranbir's efforts to involve Karuna in a project involving the 'status of the urban Indian woman' giving it 'an Indira Gandhi angle,' failed to draw her out into any intimate relationship. Ranbir's suggestion to use her own life story for a possibly stirring documentary on the Indian woman, did indeed, give Karuna the idea of writing out her life story herself and so she sat typing before her personal computer.

Karuna is the modern New Woman, independent in every way. Her defiant attitudes in dress and manners and her ability to keep herself at a safe distance from wolfish males, and the leering expressions of men who had maintained a formal distance through the day but thought it was OK to drop the mask in the evening and take a chance. (304) Her breaking out of the bonds of matrimony and finding her feet into a profession of her choice were all of a piece with her character. As

Ranbir Roy summed her up she was 'disgustingly self-assured and revoltingly self-sufficient.' (305) She is presented by the author with as much unromantic realism as Bernard Shaw portrayed his women characters in a Raina or an Ann Whitefield. Karuna's defiance of her elders and wearing her sash hipster style at school is reminiscent of Maggie Tulliver's refusal to do a patch-work quilt and cutting off her hair and then again refusing to be a prey to male predatory manoeuvres. Shobha De's heroine is very different from the heroines of other Indo-English women writers. Whereas Anita Desai makes psychological forays into the minds of her women characters, and Kamala Markandaya depicts rural or urban women as victims of their circumstances. Shobha De depicts Karuna a young Indian from a middle-class family as a capable woman able to circumvent her lot in life and launch into the kind of life-style of modelling and independent journalistic essays that is still not acceptable in conventional Indian society. Bharati Mukherjee's heroine Jasmine, the Punjabi widow is an independent and psychological character, but as Mukherjee herself asserts, her American immigrant characters are too belligerent and assertive in their survival tactics to be compared with their less agressive Indian counterparts owing to the difference in locale, circumstances and patterns of lifestyles, all of which Mukherjee points out makes even herself a non-Indo-English writer. She claims a fully Indo-American identity for herself.

The Quest that Led to Take Decisions: *Socialite Evenings*

G. SHEELA SWARUPA RAVI

Socialite Evenings[1] the first novel of Shobha De is about the journey of a prominent Bombay socialite Karuna, from a gauche middle class girl to a self-sufficient woman. Knowing about oneself enables a person to set his goals and directions properly according to his own interests which give him satisfaction. In Karuna's life too finding out about herself gives her the capacity to take decisions which she thinks would make her happy.

Karuna's quest to find out about herself springs from her discontentment with her own life which doesn't come upto her expectations. With all her discontentment that engenders mental struggle and rebellious nature, she walks the unreasonable ways in the eyes of society and remains a different person throughout. Karuna's sister says,

> You were always the strange one, right from childhood, I wouldn't ever figure you out. I used to think you were slow or vain or both. But there was always something secretive going on inside your mind that none of us knew about. You weren't like the others. (180)

The people who don't have any expectations of life and who complacently be content with the life that fate has ordained them can never understand the people who have certain expectations of life. Karuna remains an enigma to that contented sect. To use the words of Meera, a character in Shashi Deshpande's *Binding Vine*:

> To you who are satiated, content
> how do I speak of my wants?[2]

If Karuna's life is divided into three phases: life before marriage, married life, life after the separation from husband—one can see how Karuna has been a different girl, a different wife and a different woman with her expectations of life, and how the quest to know about herself, which started towards the end of the first phase, is stopped abruptly with her marriage and is under control in the second phase only to spring up in the third phase more powerfully making her "disgustingly self-assured and revoltingly self-sufficient."

The first phase is marked by her discontentment with her middle class origins. The hatred of middle class pedantic life and inadequate facilities runs throughout her life. Her fear to be one among this pedantic class which leads to her major decisions like marriage and taking up a job after her separation from husband. "I was terribly self-conscious and awkward and resented with all my being my middle class origins." (10)

Like her sisters and her classmates, she cannot placidly accept her middle class origins. She wishes to be one among the sophisticated people: "I didn't care that probably half the class consisted of other girls just like me. It was the luckier other half I wanted to belong to." (15)

This unfed hunger to be part of the smart and beautiful set, her helplessness to achieve this, her humiliations at the hands of these sophisticated dolls, her realization that none can understand her feelings make her behave differently. With the turbulent feelings hidden in her breast, she becomes the most indisciplined girl both at school and home. Unable to understand her feelings, her sisters and parents feel puzzled about her.

Her continuation in the modelling profession and her friendship with Bunty (her boy friend) are acts of rebellion. She is aware of this, still she continues in a vague sort of way, unconsciously trying to find the proper direction. At one of her shows she feels convinced that modeling is not fit for her: "After the show I was more than ever convinced that modelling was not quite my thing. I wasn't an exhibitionist." (32)

At that stage, she is mature enough to think that modelling is not her field, but not mature enough to know which field would suit her. She feels vague about her decision to marry her boy friend. Unable to take any decision, she feels restless. Humiliation at the hands of Anjali who introduced her to modelling and the sophisticated world makes her come to a conclusion that it is high time to take decisions on her own, free of all influences. With her hard earned money, she buys a "cheapie round-trip-ticket" to go to the USA. The journey is supposed to be an expedition to find herself. She says, "This was going to be my Brave New World trip. I was going to find out about myself. America was supposed to be my experiment with adulthood. I wanted to take charge, assume responsibility, find direction. All in a vague sort of way, of course." (51)

Unfortunately, she hardly gets any time to do so. The ad-film maker whom she had met at a party in India intrudes with a proposal. He helps her to come to a decision about breaking the engagement with her boy friend because marrying him is going back to inadequate middle class life which she hates. She knows she cannot marry the ad-film maker also as she would 'not spend her life swooning over flowers and gorging chocolates.' She comes back to India with no decisions taken about her career and marriage. To take such decisions she needs to find about herself. It requires privacy; her Indian home hardly affords that. When her boy friend comes to her to know her decision, like a caged animal she cries out: "You know—SPACE—I need my own space. I feel claustrophobic—I need to find myself." (55)

In such a situation, she is pushed into marriage by her boy friend at College "an 'acceptable' male who wouldn't take no for an answer." Marriage with all its bondages puts a temporary stop to her quest.

She remains discontent. She has taken a wrong decision without finding out about herself completely. It becomes clearer when her marriage becomes "increasingly meaningless" and their love making "a listless affair," "a vague habit" and a "passionless mechanical encounter." She realizes she has "married a wrong man, for a wrong reason at a wrong time."

Her discontentment springs mainly from a world of difference between her concept of marriage. As per the conventional standards, the marriage becomes "OK" and "a pretty terrific one" if the husband is rich, prominent, generous, good, tea-totaller and not a wife-beater. The question of common interests, intellectual and emotional compatibility do not figure in the picture. But to her, marriage is, "A marriage full of laughter and conversations. One in which the two of us were perfectly in tune. Speaking the same language, thinking the same thought, enjoying the same thing." (68)

This is possible only when compatability in all realms between the spouses exists. To her disappointment she realizes her "flashy lacking in depth" and "average Indian husband" can never come up to her expectations to make marriage lively and interesting.

> My husband was not a villain. He was just an average Indian husband—unexciting, uninspiring, untutored. . . . He wasn't one for introspection. . . . Unless things went radically wrong he preferred to let things be. . . . I didn't have to prove myself. . . . He wasn't looking for any stimulation, either intellectually or emotionally. (65)

She can't be an average Indian wife who though minimized to a marginal person fashions herself as per the likes and dislikes of her husband. She cannot stoop to conquer—pretending something which she is not. It is not for her to gain control over her husband by pretending a "dependent doll" as per Anjali's suggestion, or use body and pretend love as per Ritu's suggestion.

She is not "cut out for domesticity with all its happenings" and is not a "wife material" to adjust herself to this kind of marriage which doesn't come upto her expectations. She cannot expect anything better from her average Indian husband—they belong to two different worlds. Karuna's sister throws light on this incompatibility as a probable reason for Karuna not being happy with her husband:

> In all departments, he was all right, I suppose. In fact, better than most. Yet, I always felt he was the wrong man for you—maybe because I never saw you talking to him—Not idle chatter—you know—but the sort of conversation husbands and wives have . . . your worlds were different and you didn't want to belong to his.
>
> Mother used to say, "It's all right if a woman marries above her, but a man never should." Though your husband was a rich man, with you he didn't feel confident. (180)

Impossibility of leading a happy life makes her disappointed and rebellious. But she cannot shake off her marriage as she has shaken her modelling profession. She doesn't have that freedom now. She senses a "well trained Indian wife" behind this: "And most of all I wondered why I didn't get the hell out of the marriage? . . . I don't know, perhaps it was because, for all my little rebellions, I was a well-trained Indian wife!" (94)

In her helplessness—not able to adjust, not able to get out—she even fears to think about her problems, because thinking means taking decisions—that she wants to avoid: "I felt passive and powerless and tried not to think about my problems. For if I thought about them I'd have to take some decisions, the last thing I wanted to do." (95)

To suppress her anger and rebellion, she takes refuge in books and in her "private worlds" of fantasy—reliving her college days and enjoying a liberated woman fantasy.

A step she takes innocently to come out of boredom turns out to be an extra-marital relationship. It results in her broken marriage which leads her to the 'SPACE' which she cried for before her marriage.

Separated from her husband, she is endowed with privacy to find about herself. But she cannot think anything of that sort in the beginning as she is terribly upset with her state. Termination of pregnancy, undergoing of hysterectomy, agony over her husband taking another woman, make her feel depressed and dejected. She goes through all these physical and mental turmoils with no one except the caring Anjali beside her.

For the first time she feels the need of a room and money of her own. She takes up odd jobs but realizes that the meagre amount coming from these can afford her only a middle class way of living. With Anjali's help, she takes up a lucrative job which transports her to a luxurious life.

Once money starts flowing in she starts to analyse herself. She finds out that the freedom to do what she likes gives her absolute joy. With this realization she starts encashing joy through the acts she likes, however insignificant they may be. Sticking on to the part-time job and staying with parents looking after their needs like a responsible daughter are little acts of independence which bring her great joy. When people ask her to quit her part-time job for a lucrative business, she muses: "I suppose my real concerns were different. It wasn't money or success I was looking forward to in my life at that point; it was the freedom to do what I wanted. My part-time job gave me that." (273-74)

She looks after her parents and enjoys their company, care, love and concern. She has privacy and freedom in her parents's house. She feels content and happy. She cannot sacrifice this independence and happiness.

That's why she rejects downright her husband's proposal to come back to him. At the same time she cannot sacrifice this state of happiness to some thing which she is not sure about. When Girish, the art-film maker, comes to her with a proposal, she doesn't like to take a hasty decision: "I feel all closed-up and insulated. I need little time. I'm discovering stuff about myself. I enjoyed this little patch of independence. I'm reconnecting with my parents—they need me. I'm enjoying their presence. . . . Don't rush me please." (255-56)

She realizes that she cannot be happy with Girish in spite of their common interests, in that sense she cannot be happy with any man which deprives her of her present state of independence. So when her mother with her motherly anxiety asks her to settle soon in her life saying, "A woman cannot live alone. It is not safe. We are here today—but who knows about tomorrow? A woman needs a man's protection." (275)

Karuna feels she is not ready 'now' to sacrifice this independent, peaceful single life to marriage which requires lot of sacrifices. A constant search of herself must have allowed her to give a statement like this.

> But Mother, why does security rest with a man? I feel confident now that I can look after myself. I am earning as much as any man. I have a roof over my head. I don't really have any responsibilities. I am at peace with myself. I'm not answerable to any one. I don't feel like complicating my life by getting into a second marriage. I like and respect Girish. We share a lot of common interests. But I am not sure I'll make a good wife to him. Or he a good husband to me. Perhaps we are both far too selfish for marriage. I can't make any "sacrifices"—not now. (276)

Being single in the society means inviting problems. Her mother has brought before her all the problems a single woman has to encounter. She knows how Anjali has been terrified by the thought to remain single. She has experienced men trying to take advantage of her because she is not escorted by a man. She knows it is difficult to live without a man in this society. But at the same time, she can't make her life miserable for the sake of society. Sharing her hard earned room with a wrong person will spoil the beauty of the room totally. She can't be another Anjali who in her fear to be single marries a person who turns out to be a homo.

Towards the end, Karuna confidently comes out with the statement—"single is good for me." She is so sure of her decision that Ranbir the journalist comments: "You are now disgustingly self-assured and revoltingly self-sufficient." (305)

NOTES

1. Shobha De, *Socialite Evenings* (India: Penguin, 1990).
2. Shashi Deshpande, *The Binding Vine* (India: Penguin, 1992), p. 146.

A Woman More Sinned than Sinning: A Study of *Starry Nights*

SANDHYARANI DASH

By choosing a nymphomaniac as the central character of her novel *Starry Nights* (1991) the sexo-feminist writer Shobha De has set a stir to the feminist literature in India. Followed by *Strange Obsession* (1992), a novel about lesbians which has further labelled her as a lesbian feminist, thus challenging the phallocentric myth of writing as an "erectile and ejaculatory activity."[1] Her first novel *Socialite Evenings* published in 1988 dealt with the unhappy marriage and divorce of Karuna and her consequential sordid affairs. In *Starry Nights,* De moved far away from depicting characters in the tradition of Indian womanhood. She stepped out of the threshold of family and tradition to portray the harsh realities that await a woman outside the four walls of her house. *Starry Nights*, her most sensational and controversial novel, is the story of the struggle and survival of a woman in a sex-starved society.

The purpose of this paper is to focus on the character of Aasha Rani—the central character of the novel taking into account the factors that lead to her explorations vis-a-vis her sexploitations in a male-dominated society.

Aasha Rani, the unrivalled, ravishing beauty of Bombay stardom, is a woman with an insatiable libido, thus susceptible to indiscriminate sex with film people—producers, directors, heroes, cameramen, high society celebrities, sheaths and other non-filmi people also—everywhere used, soiled and exploited.

Aasha Rani's first lesson in exploitation begins with her scheming mother who, for the sake of money, uses her fifteen-year-old daughter, forcing her to be the bed-mate of producers and distributors. She also thrusts Aasha Rani into the orgy of blue films. For the hungry people of the film world, it is the forty inch bust of this fifteen-year-old girl which becomes the centre of attraction.

Aasha Rani's irresistible sexual desire is not inherent but the manifestation of a suppressed sense of vengeance of the male world which has its roots in the ill-treatment of her Amma by her Appa, or it is because of her own exploitation by the male world since her childhood:

> Perhaps it had something to do with appa and the way he'd mistreated her mother. Or maybe she felt soiled, used, exploited by them—she often told him bitterly: All of you are just the same, but wait, I will show you. I will do to men what they try to do to me. I will screw you all—beat you at your own game. (8)

This hatred has even a deeper root. Aasha Rani recollects the nightmarish experience of her childhood when she was sexually assaulted by her uncle:

> She remembered queing up outside the enormous tent with this man holding her hand. Soon her hand had been slyly slipped into his mundu. And his hand had been replaced by what fell like a firm hard stick. Aasha Rani wanted to scream. But she was terrified. . . . Finally, he had turned limp and she had felt her small hand go damp with something sticky and smelly. (196)

An incomplete childhood with a single parent, poverty, starvation, her mother's cruel dream to make her a film star, the devilish attitude of the people of the stardom to bruise and batter her feminity, the jealousy and unkindness of her sister Sudha, the collapse of her marital life and separation from her own child—she stoically endures a series of shocks one after another.

Viji was given the new name Aasha Rani and was given the first break by Kishen bhai. It was he who taught her for the first time how to "part her legs." During the first sexual intercourse she looked at Kishen bhai with the innocent eyes of a child sleeping on the impersonal bed in the hotel:

> "Are n't you afraid?" he'd asked. . . .
> "No, not at all. Why? should I be?"

> Those eyes had regarded him coolly and he'd wondered briefly if she was as innocent as she looked. (5)

Thus the long agonizing story of Aasha Rani begins. Her physical exploitation starts with Kishen bhai but her mental agony has a regresive link with her past—the innocent days of her childhood. When her amma was facing a lot of hardship to rear up her children, as her appa never turned to look at them, the days that passed in utter deprivation. When Kishen bhai wonders to see her fetish for toys she reveals a part of the sad story:

> "You don't know about my childhood," she'd tell him hugging a doll. "I never had anything to play with—no toys nothing." He'd heard the story before. The father who had deserted them. The mother who had been left with three children to raise. The poverty, deprivation. The struggle. (4)

Throughout the novel, Aasha Rani remains a passive character. She is always acted upon. While reading an article concerning her acting in blue films, she thinks: "nobody had asked her whether or not she wanted to do those sickening films and nobody had listened when she'd cried herself hoarse and protested." (53) On the other hand, her mother had said: "Don't be stupid. These films will not be shown in the theatres. Nobody will know you have done them. There's lot of money involved. I've committed on your behalf." (53) When she gets scared of taking off her clothes in front of strangers, her mother tries her best to convince her: "Think of it like going to the doctor's. Don't you allow him to examine your body? These people are the same. They see bodies all the time. It does not make any difference." (53) Amma further tries to emotionally blackmail her: "It is all acting. You just pretend and follow the doctor's orders. Close your eyes and think of other things. Think of your poor sister and your amma struggling to make you a big star. Do you know Sudha hasn't paid her fees?" (53)

In her struggle for survival, Aasha Rani also comes in contact with Seth Amirchand, a member of the parliament who keeps his "Godfather image" and calls himself a protector of the weak. Seth Amirchand takes special interest in Aasha Rani when he discovers that she is not body only but has a mind also. Under his patronage, Aasha Rani's career swings to the top.

Akshay Arora, who is known to the entire film industry to be a "mean spiteful bastard" who had symbolically fucked his way to the top, casts a deep impression on Aasha Rani. He takes interest in her because at the time of his first flop Aasha Rani was the "pricy hit" and he thought "this was only surefire way for him to hold on to his niche at the top and it involved Aasha Rani." (39) But she looked at him with the "besotted eyes of a woman" without realizing the mystery of his magic which had charmed every woman: "Every woman in the audience believed he was doing it to her and her alone. While everyman thought he was Akshay—screwing the women of the world." (39)

Aasha Rani has to suffer a lot due to this relationship. She is humiliated, insulted and rebuked by Akshay's wife Malini who curses her for trying to break her marriage. She is even beaten by Akshay later on. Her next meeting with him ends in disaster. She proposes Akshay to marry her but he does not agree to change his religion, become a muslim and marry her. Frustrated, betrayed and humiliated, she tries to commit suicide but fortunately escapes death. Aasha Rani's journalist friend Linda who knew all her secrets betrays her by revealing the secrets which comes as a terrible blow to her.

Abhijit's interest in her in spite of his beautiful fiancee Nikita whom he marries later on fills Aasha Rani with further remorse. After going through Nikita's interview in the magazine about her husband, Aasha Rani feels like the courtesan Chandramukhi in the great epic *Devdas*. She feels tortured by Abhijit who comes to her only for sex, and has no love for her. Her relationship with Abhijit makes her feel like no body but a sexy Madrasi girl a "celebrity fuck." She tells Abhijit, "you are not making love to me! You are screwing my own image—my screen image. Get out of here, Abhijit. Go back to your wife and make a man of yourself." (97)

At the peak of her career Aasha Rani takes the decision to marry a foreigner—Jamie (Jey) Phillips whom she had met in Wellington. She is blessed with a daughter and also promises to her husband—"You are a good man Jay. And I promise you I'll be a good mother to Sasha." (129)

But Aasha Rani's homecoming after five years marks a drastic change in her fortune. By that time her sister Sudha had emerged as a big star and people had not forgotten Aasha Rani. Watching the enthusiasm of the people and Aasha Rani's popularity, Jay suggests a comeback. He realizes that Aasha Rani cannot stay in New Zealand for ever leaving behind her own country. Besides there is amma's persuasion that she has become old, suffering from joint pains, hypertension etc. She also tempts Aasha Rani by saying that her price in the film market would soar up if she takes up her career once again.

Sudha's interview to the magazine disturbs her "bechari akka, I can understand how she must be feeling, now that I am the star and she is a poor nobody." She fails to understand the mystery of Sudha's indifference, her hostility. At a criss cross of her life when her ailing father needs her support but her daughter Sasha does not want to stay in India for whose sake Jay decides to leave for his country.

After Jay's departure, Aasha Rani tries for roles in films but to her disappointment, she is offered role of a mother in which she is not interested. She comes in contact with Jojo and the unhappy incidents that take place one after another breaking her down completely. The most shocking of it all is Akshay's death. Sasha tells her crying over the telephone that she misses her mother as her father spends most of his time with Nanny. Aasha Rani decides to go to New Zealand. Her trip to New Zealand lands her in further remorse. The birthday party of Sasha where she wears a saree which her daughter does not like and screams and clings to Nanny: "Don't touch me, I'm not your daughter. I don't want to be your daughter." (207) Then Jay returns and tells Aasha Rani about his affair with Alice:

> I love the girl. She loves me. And she loves Sasha. Things just worked out that way. I hadn't planned it. I love you too, but differently. We've grown apart. We've been drifting off for quite a while now. I guess it was Sasha who was the common factor. Now that she's older and has a mind of her own, we should allow her to choose the sort of life she wants herself. (202)

After this incident Aasha Rani comes to London to hide herself. It becomes impossible on her part to go to Madras with the problems of amma and appa. She feels utterly lonely and completely broken down. She decides to live the life of an exile in London. But here also she falls a victim to many people. Sonali, who gives her a new job, her second encounter with Gopal Krishnan, his threat to keep Bhaskaran in her room, the murder of Bhaskaran, Sonali's arrangement of her return to India—all these events take place in quick succession.

Coming back to India, Aasha Rani decides to meet Sudha who after an accident is in a horrible condition. When Sudha sees her she is full of repentance and counts her misfortune to be the punishment for her sin. Aasha Rani consoles her that they will stay together, they will reopen appa's studio, they will work together to make their banner the greatest banner of the South. She is confident enough about their success, "We are going to succeed and never look back."

Later that night, in a twilight state between dream and waking, Aasha Rani has a vision of her daughter's future. She dreams to fulfil her dreams through her daughter by making her a superstar. Sasha will live her own life on her own terms. Aasha Rani thinks of bringing up her daughter in a different way than her amma. With her daughter she would conquer the world without any heart break, any disappointment and compromise. A series of misfortunes, circumstantial compulsions and the failure of her marriage do not let her down. She emerges as a phoenix from the debris of the past with a beautiful dream for the future which she wants to share with her daughter. Thus the novel ends on an optimistic note.

Shobha De has been subjected to serious critical appraisals since the release of the book *Starry Nights.* A.G. Khan calls her the 'Vatsyayani' who is "educating the ignorant Indians about the sublime world of cunt and cock."[3] Sunil Sethi considers her work as "bodice ripper"[4] and Madhu Jain calls it "high society potpourri, bland and banal bristling with orgy laced parties and voyeuristic servings of souped-up four wheel-drive—sex in all directions."[5]

Despite the blatant criticism it has to be admitted that De's novel reveals the realistic pictures of hypocrisy, degenerated values, double standards both of the filmi people and also the celebrities who come from a higher social strata and are successful to hide their real personalities with money and power. Her writing seems abominable and bizarre to us as she is a woman and we are not habituated to listen to a woman talking so much about sex so freely and so frankly. But the novel is not simply a treatise on sex, it depicts the modern woman's search for identity in a male-dominated society. Shobha De's bold and transparent language with which she portrays the intensity of grief of a tormented, discarded and anguished soul saves her writing from being a mere pornography and establishes it as a further extension of feminism and a protest against the established patriarchal order of the society.

NOTES

1. K.K. Ruthven, *Feminist Literary Studies: An Introduction* (1984).
2. *Starry Nights* (Penguin, 1991).
3. A.G. Khan, "Shobha De Vatsyayani," *Indian Women Novelists*, ed. R.K. Dhawan (New Delhi: Prestige, 1995), Set III, Vol. 1.
4. Sunil Sethi, "De in De out," *Seminar*, No. 384, 1991.
5. Madhu Jain, "Cat on a Cold Tin Roof," *India Today*, Oct. 15, 1989.

Rise and Fall of a Star: A Study of *Starry Nights*

GEETA BARUA

Starry Nights is primarily the story of a film star, Aasha Rani, who comes from a small town background to the tinsel world of Bombay and after struggling for sometime she ultimately becomes a star, 'sweet-heart of millions.' This paper aims at studying the career of Aasha Rani, how she is able to become super heroine reigning as the queen of, the film world, her many affairs, her glory and tribulations, her loneliness and yearning for a family. She comes from a broken home. Even though she has married, yet she is not able to enjoy marital bliss and family warmth because of her deep rooted attachment to the film world and her desire to continue to be associated with the film world, although not in the capacity of a heroine. The novel is also a faithful portrayal of the film world with all its perfidies, glamour, crimes, lies and deceits and sexual exploitation. Since Shobha De the novelist has been long associated with the Bombay film world as a journalist, she knows it first hand and has been able to portray it well.

Aasha Rani, before becoming a film star was Viji, bastard child of a film producer. After the father deserts Viji's family, she has to suffer deprivation and poverty and in order to survive, her mother pushes her into the under-world of blue films. Like any other girl, she is scared of seedy people who are making the film. She breaks into tears but has to submit to her mother's command:

> And that porno session? Dammit! She was just a child at that time. It wasn't her idea . . . 'Amma please don't, I'm so scared. . . . How can I take off my clothes in front of all these strangers? 'Amma . . . said patiently, 'Think of it like going to the doctor's.

> . . . Haven't so many doctors seen your body? Examined it? . . . They see bodies all the time. . . . Besides that man won't *really* do any thing. I mean, it is all *acting*.' . . . Aasha Rani had unbuttoned her blouse. . . . She [Amma] had gesticulated with her hand indicating how the bra was to be unhooked. Aasha Rani had shut her eyes and reached for the clasp. . . . After that, she hadn't really registered anything . . . along with her eyes, she'd also shut her mind.[1]

That was her first exposure to the camera. In order to earn money, her mother takes her to Bombay and as she has a voluptuous figure, with the help of a small-time producer Kishen Bhai, she is able to get a film contract. But no body in film world would survive without the blessing and patronage of a rich politician with shady dealings; in this case it is Sheth Amirchand who is not only a womanizer but also a sodomite. Any heroine would feel privileged to be called over to Amirchand's place which had elaborate arrangements for preparing the women to be presented to Amirchand. And the person in charge for this is Mastaan. She is served an intoxicating drink, not alcohol, and she feels 'transported . . . into a hallucinatary world. She was weightless and floating. Her head was full of colours and sounds. Her senses had been heightened to an extent that she experienced no pain even when the Shethji entered her savagely from behind and whipped her with a small leather thong. She was far away in some distant world, listening to bird calls and looking at a dozen rainbows.' (61)

When she reaches at the top in her profession, she falls headlong in love with another top hero Akshay Arora who is a married man. Knowing fully well that the love would always remain unfulfilled because the lover is a married man, she continues her affair, for she so desperately loves him that she can't help. There are a couple of ugly scenes with Akshay's wife Malini. Things become so bad that when she goes uninvited to a *mahurat* of Akshay Kumar's film, she is not only humiliated but also beaten by him. Still she cannot turn away from him and suggests religious conversion, for Islam permits polygamy. But the very idea is repugnant to Akshay: 'You are so stubborn and so stupid. . . . Just forget it. Besides I don't want to become a Muslim. I believe in my religion. I don't want to give up my faith. I was born a Hindu. I want to die a Hindu. I want to be cremated, not buried.

I don't want to change my name to Aslam Khan or something. How could you think such an absurd plan would work?' (108)

After doing many hit films, earning popularity, fame and wealth in formula films, Aasha Rani does an art film with low budget and totally different work culture. While shooting the film somewhere in Rajasthan, she sleeps with the director, a bohemian devoting his evening to rum and glass. One night when he comes to his room she pounces on him and wants to excite and prepare him for the act but the man has no erection and after various futile attempts he leaves the room. The film is successful and receives critical acclaim. In all the opulence, fame and luxury, Aasha Rani misses one thing, one big thing, genuine love. She has had numerous bed partners, but no partner in real sense who could share her feelings and reciprocate. The one man whom she really loved, and who also loved her, was unable to marry her because of his family, his image and other constraints. Frustrated in her love, dejected because of her loneliness, she goes on sleeping with various men, even with some who in spite of her glamour are not subjugated to her, like Jojo, the director of her last film which could not be completed because his wife sent three toughs who threatened Aasha and put her house on fire. Unfortunately most of her affairs are with married men.

In the novel and also in Aasha Rani's career, Linda, a journalist of a film magazine, plays an important role, more during her declining phase after her return from New Zealand. Linda does everything to spoil her image by quoting Sudha Rani and also by making public many secrets of her life which she knew since during the peak of Aasha Rani's career she was her intimate friend. Linda is very fast and knows well the tricks of the trade and because of her frank manners and strong personality, she almost intimidates Aasha Rani. It is she who initiates her in the mysteries and pleasures of lesbianism. The novel describes almost every kind of sexual behaviour; lesbianism is one of them and it is suggested that in many ways it is superior to hetero-sexual contact. Even though it is Aasha Rani's first lesbian experience, yet she likes it when Linda pulls her down on the bed and kisses her on the lips:

> It was a pleasant feeling, Aasha Rani thought. No rough bristles scraping her face, just smooth cheeks and soft lips over her own. . . . Her hands move from Aasha Rani's neck to her breast. .

> . . Reaching under Aasha Rani's shirt she unhooked her bra. . . . Her head moved down till her mouth found Aasha Rani's breast. . . . Linda's warm thigh wedged itself between hers and her hand moved between Aasha Rani's legs. . . . Her mouth still between Aasha Rani's legs, 'But let me ride you first. Let me show you that I can take you like a man too.' Linda . . . moving over her, rubbing herself against her, till both of them came together shuddering and shaking, not wanting it to end. . . . Then Linda began . . . 'THIS is love, understand. This is love making, not what those bastards do to our bodies.' (79-80)

After this, they meet again and indulge in lesbian pleasures. But in spite of such physical intimacy, Linda does not hesitate to use her pen against Aasha Rani when she comes back from New Zealand. Through Linda's character, we come to realize the power of a journalist in making or marring a film star's career. Like other characters in the novel she is guided by selfishness, professional gain and other considerations rather than human relationship. It is this hollowness of the film world that makes the life of film stars miserable and empty, driving them to alcoholism and suicide. Aasha Rani in one of her desolate moments does attempt suicide and although with all possible secrecy maintained, the news leaks out to the press. If one looks at Aasha Rani sympathetically, one would find that in spite of her bitchery, she craves for genuine love which she never gets except from Jamie and in a limited sense from Akshay.

Aasha's affair with Abhijit is also futile because he is also a married person and his wife is in the family way. But since both she and Abhijit want to get away from Bombay, they decide to go to an obscure country, neither Europe nor America but to a country where no one would recognize them. And they decide to go to New Zealand. But ill-luck always dogs Aasha. Abhijit's father who is a big man in the film world somehow is able to find out their destination and when they reach New Zealand with a journey break in Singapore, they find Abhijit's father at the airport. Like a truant boy caught by the teacher, Abhijit docilely follows his father back to India. Aasha is given ample money by Abhijit's father and once again she is lonely and this time in a strange country where no one knows her. Once while sitting in a disco, she is accosted by a young man who recognizes her. She is surprised that she has been recognized even in this obscure country.

The young man, Jamie Phillips, while in London, had an affair with an Air India hostess who was Aasha Rani's fan and along with her, he had seen each and every film of her's many a time on video. Jamie is attracted by Aasha Rani not only because she is sexy but also because of her being an Indian, for his grandfather was posted in India during the British rule. He proposes marriage to her and she accepts it. She also gives birth to a beautiful girl Sasha who because of mixed blood has an unique beauty. For five years she lives in New Zealand perfectly happy with her husband and child even though her in-laws had not accepted her. She is fortunate to have an understanding husband. After five years they decide to come to India via London. In London, she is welcomed by the NRIs. After five years of anonymous life, once again she tastes the blood of filmstar popularity. Back in India, once again, in spite of her unwillingness, she is drawn to the film world. Jamie sympathetically leaves her to decide her own way of life and to be near her ailing father who now at the fag end of his life wants to own up the family he had deserted. Meanwhile her younger sister Sudha has become the queen of Bombay films and ironically she is living without marriage with a one-time friend of Aasha Rani, Amar who is a bi-sexual.

Aasha Rani's last film venture is with director Jojo who is also a married man. Since his wife comes to know of her affair with her husband, she spoils the plan and the film would not even begin. This is the last phase of her film life. In the film world, she is known as destroyer of families. She is despised by all, loved by none. By now Akshay has died of cancer and in spite of her long-drawn affair with him, no film journalist offers her words of sympathy or condolence for the departed man. Her family is away in New Zealand and in India she is all alone, friendless. The biggest irony is that her daughter who is born and brought up in New Zealand has no attachment to her mother's country. She makes it very clear that she hates India and does not want to be called a bloody Indian, a darkie.

The novel ends on no definite note. Aasha Rani imagines and visualizes Sasha's return to India to become a popular heroine 'gracing movie hoardings and gossip magazines.' (234) Her father asks her to run his studio. What is strange is that in spite of having seen the film world from inside and knowing its hollowness, intrigue, lies, deceptions, exploitations, crimi- nalizations, she still continues to be associated with it. She dreams of her daughter, who has by now bloomed into a young girl, to become a film heroine in India. We do not know whether she comes back but Aasha thinks she would. It is suggested that because of severe burns of Sudha Rani, a vacuum has been created in the film world and Sahsa is to fill that vacuum under the banner of Aasha Rani productions. Money which is always at the centre of the novel, remains most important thing till the end. The novel ends with a reference to Goddess Laxmi who is the presiding deity of Diwali, the festival of lights. 'It was Diwali festival of lights. She would need to tell Laxmi to prepare the *diyas.*' (234)

Summing up, we can say that *Starry Nights* is the story of the rise and fall of Aasha Rani, a popular film star, who actually never leaves the film world, even though she ceases to be a heroine and is not too happy with it. The film world is an addiction to her and she continues to be associated with it, if not as heroine, as a producer at least. She imagines that Sasha would become what she had been earlier, the sweet-heart of millions. 'She would rule the film world through her daughter who had the makings of a star. An unforgettable star. The Golden Girl of the silver screen! Oh yes, Sasha would be tomorrow's Lover Girl!' (234) And thus, as the saying goes, the show must go on.

NOTE

1. Shobha De, *Starry Nights* (Delhi: Penguin, 1991), pp. 53-54.

Search for Identity in *Starry Nights*

NISHA TRIVEDI

Indian fiction in English after establishing its foothold in Commonwealth literature, is now producing third generation novelists. We are in the last decade of the twentieth century, progressing on to the twenty-first century. We witness the rapid changes in the social, cultural and moral norms of the society. The writers of the post-independence fiction have focused on contemporary problems. They have explored the vital areas of individual consciousness and have projected the fascinating images of cultural change, rather transformation.

Shobha De who started her career as a journalist in 1970, has emerged on the literary scene of Indian fiction dealing with the vital aspects of existence and survival in high class society of India. Her works have no existential and psychological bearing. Closely acquainted with the Bombay cinema and the world of modelling, she has beautifully mirrored the shattering human values of this glittering society. Her novels occupy themselves with the themes of over-powering materialism, lack of spirituality and the resulting inner conflict, the lack of identity of women, and the crumbling moral values. Her women characters represent a true picture of the modern Indian women.

The modern Indian woman who is at the centre of fiction of Shobha De, is no longer a model of Vedic, or pre-Vedic dignified woman, nor is she modelled on the post-Aryan woman who is passive in nature and accepts the dominance of men in society. Born in the era of woman's lib, they are to a certain extent an extension of the woman based on mythic models from the *Ramayana* and the *Puranas*. Modelled on Sita, Savitri and Gandhari, "she becomes shy, gentle as a person, pure and faithful as wife, and selfless, loving and thoughtful as a mother."[1]

The modern Indian woman born in post-war generation in an atmosphere of bewilderment and confusion has become bold and capable of surviving in degrading moral values of life. These characters suffer a humiliation as far as their social, economic and cultural life is concerned but they also find themselves capable of struggling, compromising and realizing their existence in the end.

The search for identity has been a popular theme in fiction. Many writers have portrayed the problem of the place of woman in society, her true belonging and her place in marital relationship. But often the novels end where these problems begin; writers, no doubt, raise the problems without offering any solutions. Sometimes there is an escape from the misery of the world, sometimes they yield to sorrows of the world. Shobha De has very realistically presented the models before us. Her women, rather strong in character, take bold decisions to survive in society.

Aasha Rani, a ravishingly beautiful film star, 'the dreamgirl of the millions' is the central character of *Starry Nights*.[2] In her childhood she suffers the agony of unsuccessful relationship of her parents. Her father, a renowned film producer in Madras, leaves his wife and two daughters for a younger star girl. The girls with their unaffectionate, ununderstanding mother find themselves deprived of emotional security in childhood. In Aasha's early teens her scheming mother pushes her in the never-ending gluttony of blue film and then through sex in the crass-world of Bombay cinema.

Aasha's downfall begins as she rises in her career. Beautiful with a perfect and appealing figure, she finds herself in the hands of Kishanbhai, a small film distributor. He first exploits her physically, but later on finds himself in love with her. Meanwhile her mother, acting as her first-pimp, compels her to 'please' big personalities of cinema in order to get good roles. "As the social psychologists believe the central elements of her personality are acquired in the bosom of the family and men continue to need the warmth, security and intimacy they experience, as children."[3] Due to the lack of these feelings and interactions of childhood Aasha grows with a disguised feeling of hatred for men. She often tells Kishanbhai: "All of you are just the same, but wait I will show you. I will do to men what they try to do to me. I will screw you all, beat you at your own game." (8)

Soon Kishanbhai finds her words true. Rejecting his love she falls in love with the top star of cinema Akshay Arora. Later in her life she realizes that it all began as an infatuation towards him. It was his top position in the industry, his aristocratic manners, high standard of living that swept her off her feet. She admits: "I feel like a villager in his presence." (130) Being a middle-class woman her one strong desire is to become modern by emulating his life. Though soon they found that there was 'something' between them.

This step is to prove fatal to her career. But deprived of true love and sympathy, she seeks shelter in his bosom. Her yearning for freedom from the world of bondage seems obvious when she compares her mother to Akshay's brother. She thinks all the relatives are just the same. "What do they care about the people who slave in the studios to make money for them. Nothing. But they only want to control their lives all right. They want to tell them who to marry, who to sleep with, who to act with, who to be nice to, who to ignore, who to snub." (16) It just shows a typical woman's fantasy to roam into the imaginary world of love but filmi persons too have to follow the social norms. There are taboos which have still not made men free.

Akshay, a typical representative of the society, has no courage to take a bold step. He keeps enjoying both worlds. His wife Malini, who has already given up her career as a ghazal singer for her marriage, and who is repulsive of sex tries to get Aasha out of their life with the help of her friend Rita. A meeting is arranged in Rita's bungalow to humiliate Aasha. There Akshay's wife rebukes her and curses her to die as a spinster. Aasha, confident of her love, makes her realize that she herself is responsible to break the bond between her and Akshay for she does not greet him properly when he comes back home and does not give proper celebration in the bed. Malini thinks, "Men are all the same animals, and we women such fools." (50)

Akshay begins to feel Aasha's presence in his life possessive and embarrassing. So, he decides to get rid of her. He becomes afraid of her true love and manipulates against it.

Her love for Akshay is from the depth of her heart. So, when he rebukes her and slaps her in an orgy, she remains silent and if she speaks it is only an apology. Crossing the limits of earthly love her ego remains untouched. But the incident gives a great shock and she falls ill.

The feelings of compromise become prominent when, desperate and sad, she is shown sympathy by Seth Amirchand. She plays her part very cunningly to please him, and he receives a good impression of her. Though deeply connected with the underworld activities, Sethji is a member of the Legislative Assembly. He not only provides her money but also helps her in getting into films.

The Indian woman, in spite of her economic independence, does not feel secure without the protection of men. In her childhood, she receives protection from the parents, in her married life man protects her and later she is protected by the son. Passionate Aasha too, deprived of Akshay's love, craves for protection which she has expected from him. Unable to find this protection she recollects her childhood and longs to relive a seven-year-old child in the lap of Amma who rubbed coconut oil into her scalp. She wants to cry as a child. Physically and emotionally drained she feels tired.

Aasha, still longing for Akshay's love, manages to attend the mahurat party, in which he is to come. But her friend Linda advises her to lay off, "keep some dignity yaar, don't go after him like a bitch on heat." (87) Lost in the pleasant memories of Akshay, Aasha thinks she cannot forget Akshay and the lovely days spent with him. In the party, instead of Akshay she meets Abhijit Mehra, the only son of a top industrialist Amrish Mehra.

Boredom and loneliness in life do not inspire Aasha to work hard in three shifts. Her heart craves for a normal life. Normal persons, to her, are those who live outside the film world. Her heart craves for marriage and parenthood. That is why she rejects the offer of Abhijit who is attracted by her appealing personality. She asks him to find love in his family, his wife: "you are not making love to me. You are screwing my image—my screen image. Get out of here, Abhijit. Go back to your wife and make a man of yourself. I have my own life to lead." (97)

But what is her life? Obsessed with the thoughts of Akshay she catches him suddenly one day, begs an hour of him and even after his humiliation she gets the matter on once again between them. The feeling of victory of love makes her so crazy that she decides to leave her career to become his wife, the mother of his children. She makes funny plans for marriage when Sethji calls her and makes her see reality.

Ignoring his advice Aasha still thinks of carrying the plan when she is caught by her mother who calls for an explanation. For the first time rebelling against the over-powering mother she bursts out: "Money, money, money. That's all you think of. Well, I'm fed up of being your money machine. I've done enough for everybody—you, Sudha and others—now, I want to live for myself and enjoy my life." (106)

Since none of her plans work, the frustrated Aasha tries to commit suicide. As usual Akshay refuses all interviews. He remains silent in every matter related to them. Betrayed by Akshay, Aasha reluctantly tries to find peace in her relationship with Abhijit who offers him a holiday in a distant land where nobody can distrurb them.

They leave for New Zealand but his father surprises them by catching them at New Zealand airport. He offers a big sum of amount to Aasha for leaving his son. Aasha at once agrees because she was never in love with anyone except Akshay Arora.

Partially banished from India, Aasha goes to Wellington. There, an admirer proposes marriage. Bored, troubled and confused, she accepts the offer and becomes Mrs. Jammy (Jay) Phillips. Far from the world of cinema she leads a family life with a farmer. Her life fills with love; satisfied with her present state of life she tries to forget the past. She does not want to even think of India. When in one and a half year, she becomes the mother of a beautiful girl child, she finds her life filled with every happiness of the world. To enjoy this important event of life, she decides that she will share the mutual trust and understanding—the most beautiful aspects of a mother-daughter relationship with Sasha, her daughter.

When Jay, her husband, proposes that she visit India with the child, the thought of her mother shatters her. "Nothing doing, no way. I never want to go back. And please don't give Amma the news. I want to protect Sasha from her. I want to bring her up with all the love in the world. I never want her to meet her grandmother, never." (130) On reaching India she finds herself in totally strange circumstances and feels a kind of responsibility towards her Appa (father) who is back home and is suffering from illness. Amma has lost her dictator's image and totally depends upon the mercy of Sudha, her younger daughter, who has skilfully taken Aasha's place in Bombay cinema. During her stay in Madras Aasha receives an invitation as chief guest for the Mahurat of a film from her old acquaintance Rita. She accepts the invitation and as she steps into a blaze of flash bulbs inside the studio, she feels as if she had never been away. Everything comes back to her. The peculiar atmosphere of the studio, people crowding around, trying to touch stars, get near them, smell them. She thinks she missed it all. It is only after such incidents that it strikes her how much of an alien she was in New Zealand. She had tried to adapt, adjust, accept. And she thought, she had succeeded. Now back in familiar territory she realizes how deluded she was. No. She didn't belong there. This was home. And home was Holi and Diwali and other rituals in the same manner year after year, down several centuries.

She prefers to stay in India, specially in film society. Jay cooperates and leaves for Wellington along with Sasha. He gives Aasha a chance to fulfil her wishes, her responsibilities and above all to have a feeling of working and doing something in her life—a feeling of achievement. But soon, Aasha realizes that five years have changed everything in the world including Bombay cinema. She gets offers for the roles of mother or mother-in-law. The shock is unbearable to her and once again she is ready to have an adulterous relationship with the young producer Jojo for getting main role. Meanwhile she receives a call from Wellington from her daughter that Jay is having an affair with her nanny. Confused and desperate, she feels shattered. "Whichever way one looked at," she thinks, "there was always a man in the picture. A man using, abusing and finally discarding a woman." (157)

Afraid of failure and rejection she decides to find out the truth with Jay. On reaching Wellington she comes to know that her marriage is over. Once again she confronts the problem of existence and belongingness, what is her real place in the world? Where does she really belong? Who are her relatives? For whom does she live and who needs her? These problems haunt her during her return journey. Her unpromising state of mind makes her land in London and find a job. She comes in contact with Shonali, a high class call girl of London's political and upper class society. There she finds herself trapped in the web of Tamilian terrorists.

Having escaped from and horrified by the cruel realities of life, she comes back to Madras. where she is welcomed by every member of her family. Her younger sister's inability to make name as a star disturbs her. Appa's faith in her gives her strength and courage to restart their old family film studio in Madras. Now she has existence, belongingness, and opportunity to do something creative in her life. She, then, manages to bring beautiful Sasha to India to live with her so that she can give her daughter what she could not receive from her mother.

Instead of escaping from life's responsibilities, or yielding to the problems, Aasha chooses the right way of struggling and surviving through it. She realizes that her roots are very deep in the soil of India, specially in Madras where she can and will grow.

The glittering world of cinema is in reality so ruthless, so miserable that it can shatter the moral values and innocence of any human being. But Aasha survives and achieves success.

NOTES

1. Alladi Uma, *Woman and Her Family* (New Delhi: Sterling, 1989), p. 2.
2. Shobha De, *Starry Nights* (New Delhi: Penguin, 1991).
3. Cited in Mrinalini Solanki, *Anita Desai's Fiction: Patterns of Survival Strategies* (Delhi: Kanishka, 1992), p. 45.

Artist as Vamp: A Feminist Approach to *Starry Nights*

SUDHIR KUMAR

> I'm not waving a flag to Indian women saying you have nothing to lose but your hymen. . . . Oh, what the heck, I may as well sit back and enjoy it. You'll see, I'll have the last laugh.[1]

That's how Shobha De, "the softporn star" and the writer of the latest "bodice-ripper,"[2] *Starry Nights* delights even in her affirmative denials. De. proverbially speaking, sowed the wind by launching her lust-laced *Socialite Evenings* and reaped a whirlwind, in turn, with the phenomenal release of her *Starry Nights,* her orgiastic marvel, that virtually caused to the puritans of art much heartburning, wrathful introspection and bitter pangs of sour-grapeism. Shobha De appears to be a sweet timer as she jumped into the fray of professional fiction-writing when feminism was fast making deep forays into the citadels of male-hegemony in India. She is in the jocund company of Anita Desai, Shashi Deshpande, Bharati Mukherjee, Rama Mehta, Geeta Mehta and a host of others like Nina Sibal and Namita Gokhale, raring to join the select band of feminists in India.

Shobha De frenziedly forages for the erotica in her novels and bestows on her femmes fatales a bestial lust that mockingly upsets the apple-cart of all the patriarchal institutions and conventions. With her startling imagination that often appears fertile to the youth and fetid to the old, her female protagonists like Karuna and Anjali, in *Socialite Evenings* and Aasha Rani in *Starry Nights* unabashedly unleash a blitzkrieg on the seemingly topless towers of male-chauvinism. The sexual taboos tumble haplessly like a pack of cards as and when her women walk. With a disconcerting penchant for the pornographic details in her fiction, Shobha De futuristically foreshadows the form (and fate??)

of feminism in the India of twenty-first century. Her novels have often evoked hostile reviews in spite of their grand sales. *Socialite Evenings* was labelled as a "high society potpourri, bland and banal," bristling with orgy-laced parties and "voyeuristic servings of souped-up, four-wheel-drive-sex-in-all directions."[3] Another review flays its reeking sensuality as the novel is "choked with listless lust and witless dialogue."[4] *Starry Nights* with its brazen portrayal of sex and 'sexploitation' in the Bombay film-world clearly steals a march over its predecessor, which was dubbed as "confession of a man-eater."[5] Both the novels indicate the arrival of Indian woman in society with a rebellious defiance against the well-entreched moral orthodoxy of the patriarchal social-system.

This paper attempts to analyze Shobha De's *Starry Nights* in the light of the contemporary feminist critical theories put forth by Sandra M. Gilbert and Susan Gubar. Taking a cue from M.H. Abrams' much-celebrated *The Mirror and the Lamp,* they use the symbols of 'mirror' and 'lamp' to illustrate and illuminate "the intellectual assumptions and strategies of most contemporary feminist theorists." The mirror, for the feminist critics "becomes a space in which to capture the shifting historical images of gendered reality."[6] Often, holding on to the belief that literature "is a reflection of objects and events,"[7] they employ texts to explore social and psychological contexts and issues. What Gilbert and Gubar postulate about the feminist critic is largely true of the feminist author/artist also. The feminist author belonging to the 'mirror' category tries to rebuild the past, often questioning the misinterpreted and distorted cultural history. But he does not challenge the concepts of reality which underlie the very activities of periodization and evaluation under the partriarchal umbrella. To name a few feminist novelists that may be said to fall in this mirror category in the Indian English fiction, one can easily recall the likes of Anita Desai, Kamala Markandaya, Nayantara Sahgal and even Bharati Mukherjee, who have fearlessly probed into the question of the subordination and liberation of woman in the Indian milieu. Their female characters, generally speaking, display a remarkably new sensibility and sensitivity that enable them to protest against the timeworn shibboleths of a pharisaical patriarchal order. They, no doubt, ask for a re-interpretation of Indian social and cultural history. But, even making allowance for thier bold initiatives in feminism in Indian English fiction, they do not turf out the ground-realities that hem in an Indian woman in their vicelike grip. Shobha De, as we will see later on in this paper, is not content with only protest and petition formula. Hence, her separation from this 'mirror' category.

The second category in which Gilbert and Gubar place the more vocal and violent feminist critics (substituted by artists in this paper) is that of vamp. The lamp that stands for the artist's subjectivity and inspiration in M.H. Abrams' work, undergoes a mutational metamorphosis in their critical framework and becomes a vamp serving as a paradigm for the artist's expressive autonomy as well as "for rebelliously antirational and anti-hierarchical impulses that have been repressed but not erased by patriarchal culture."[8] The 'vamp' artists, like other feminists, also demand total liberation from the male-domination, a re-writing of female discourse and deconstruction of the binary opposites of culture/nature, man/woman, mind/body, day/night, reason/imagination etc., in their works. They hate, nay dislike, the phallocentric standards of art, culture and history. The singularity of the 'vamp' artist lies in his "defiantly inspired and demonically sensual attack on, indeed, a seduction and betrayal of patriarchal system of thought."[9] Silhouetted against the camp of 'vamp' artists the authors in the "mirror" category appear distinctly rational and classical. The "mirror" authors are definitely full of decorum and rationalism and do not believe in breaking down the aesthetic taboos in pell-mell fashion. To the contrary, "like a dark double, the vamp acts out the desire for the apocalyptic revolution against law and order that lurks on the other side of the mirror."[10]

It is important to remember that the 'mirror' critics believe in the entity called author while the 'vamp' critics deny the existence of the creator of the text—thanks to the new critical theories of deconstruction and 'intentional fallacy.' Here I beg to differ from the 'vamp' critics. The identity of an author, in my opinion, shapes to a great extent, the texts of history, culture and literature. That is why I have deliberately used the epithet of 'vamp' for the "author" of the feminist text. Truly speaking, Shobha De flaunts a frightening flippancy in flagrantly flouting the conventional canons of maorality and decency prevalent in the patriarchal social order. My attempt in this paper is, therefore, to show Shobha De's striking affinity with the "vamp" group of feminist authors with special reference to *Starry Nights.*

It is worthwhile to start our analysis with a brief discussion of De's first novel *Socialite Evenings*, which was her first experimental attempt at the vamp ideology. Anjali is the first sketch of Aasha Rani of *Starry Nights*. Highly attractive and charming, Anjali throws off the conventional moral values by wayside as the seductively rises from her middle-class background to the upper-most rung of society. She enacts a marriage of convenience with Abe, "an experienced rake with a wild reputation."[11] Both of them revel in the orgiastic rituals. Her passion for sex is illimitable indeed as the novel bristles with her frequent sexual encounters. The range of her sexual exploits is bewildering from a die-hard rake Abe to an innocent, baby-faced Karan. All is grist that comes to her libidinous mill. Even Karuna discards the traditional role of a wife and fondly relishes the extra-marital relationship with Krish. Taking a lesson from her mentor Anjali, Karuna brazenly adopts a militant attitude towards her husband when he tries to prevent her from enjoying a week-long sexual orgy with Krish in Rome. Anjali, Karuna and Ritu are the proverbial succubi who reign supreme in their world of limitless libido. Shobha De displays the first signs of being a vamp artist in *Socialite Evenings* in which the troika of female characters symbolizes the absolute freedom of womankind from all types of patriarchal restraints. As a wife Karuna epitomizes the misery of a woman in India: "I felt like an indifferent boarder in the house, going through the motions of house-keeping and playing wife but the resentment and rebellion remained just under the surface, ready to break out at the smallest provocation." (69) What De experimented with in *Socialite Evenings* crystallized into a terra firma of her convictions in her latest "bodice- ripper"[12] *Starry Nights*. Aasha Rani, the highly seductive star of the tinsel world of bollywood and the heroine of the novel displays disarming nonchalance in her torrid sexual affairs—with men of all hues and variety. Once trapped in the mire of lust and vaulting ambition, she knows no turning back, till the end of the novel.

It is important to remember that Shobha De makes Aasha Rani's peculiar circumstances responsible for her being launched into a world of abominable lust and greed. Her father led a dissipated life abandoning her mother and marrying a dancer. Her mother had to prostitute in order to support her family and lived with her daughters in the slums. It is only by selling her flesh that her mother could pay for Aasha's dancing-lessons. It is, now, Aasha's turn to repay the debt. Upto this point, Shobha De appears to be in line with the feminists of the 'mirror' category. *Starry Nights* is a blend of the mirror and the vamp approaches to feminism. Both approaches launch a frontal assault on society and its various male-dominated institutions. The vamp approach to feminism is at full play in the novel after Aasha Rani's first surrender to Kishanbhai. Thereafter, Shobha De makes Aasha Rani embark upon a dazzling round of sexual encounters with her rather persistent references to the erotic zones and the private parts, and characteristics of the female body. With her satanic seductiveness and boundless libidinal energy Aasha Rani breaks all sexual taboos with a gusto. Her elan vital is sex. Once the repressed in her is aroused, it becomes a colossus mauling up the flotsam and jetsam of the patriarchal order. She and the likes of her enthrall and enslave the males and become 'successful' as it is evident in Shonali's (Aasha's friend in London) exhortive speech:

> These men who seek out company are powerful, rich and influential. They control the world. They find us relaxing, charming and desirable. We are doing them a favour—they spend their days under stress and tension. Their lives are complicated, their wives are bitches, their children hate them and their English girlfriends use them. We are safe. We give them whay they want. That's why we are successful.[13]

Starry Nights furthers the theme of a liberated woman; it is but an extension of the frontiers of feminism. This is how its shocking pornographic details that jar the sensibility of an untrained reader should be viewed and appreciated. Aasha Rani may appear to a hypocritical Kishanbhai who first took her, "all fucked up and fucked out," (5) but she continues to soar up in the realms of dizzying prosperity and popularity. Once launched in the tinsel town of Bombay, she, with an unfeminine vehemence, becomes a liberated woman who lives for her own pleasures and knows no value-system. Sexual encounters and compromises are a routine affair in her life. In her infatuation for Akshay, the reigning star of the film-world, she feels no qualms of conscience in performing oral-sex with him. Immersed in the ecstasy of tremendous excitement, she only remembers how "all the hirsute, sweaty men she'd been forced to lick—all over—whose body hairs would get into her mouth and make her feel nauseous." (17) Why should there be any compunctions about having sex with the desired man when she was, even as a child, sexually assaulted by her uncle. Shobha De vividly portrays her nightmarish experience with her uncle that exposes the hypocrisy of the male-centred and male-dominated value-system of our society:

> She remembered queuing up outside the enormous tent with this man holding her hand. Soon her hand had been slyly slipped into his mundu. And his hand had been replaced by what felt like a firm hard stick. Aasha Rani wanted to scream. But she was terrified. . . . Finally, he had turned limp and she had felt her small hand go damp with something sticky and smelly. (196)

Shobha De as a vamp author makes no bones about the sexual exploits of a 'bitchy' Aasha Rani. She candidly and boldly puts forth in her novel what a woman always feels but is ever afraid to express. This is evident again when Shobha De records the reaction of the audience to the enthralling charms of Akshay Kumar in the words of Ajay, his elder brother. Ajay holds that every young "woman in the audience believed he was doing it to her and her alone. While every man thought he was Akshay—screwing the women of the world." (39) Shobha De shows Malini in *Starry Nights* as a traditional wife existing on one extreme of femininity who wants to possess her husband for ever. She is all devotion and dedication to her star-husband, Akshay Kumar—who consistently shares his bed with Aasha Rani. De wants to convey the message that marriages are a means of the perpetuation of the patriarchal order. A woman's being is annihilated on the altar of marriage. De seems to believe that a marriage is but an infructuous exercise undertaken by two partners to realize each other fully. Malini, Akshay's wife, could never enjoy the consummation of sex with her legitimate husband. She is more of a woman tied up in the shackles of a lopsided moral order than an individual, a free bird like Aasha Rani. She is ignorant of the simple logic that "being a wife and being a whore were not all that different. It needed Aasha Rani to educate her." (43) She fails to possess her husband because she cannot do an Aasha Rani to her husband—who wants novelty and freshness in sexual intercourse every time.

Be it Malini or Rita, each partner in marriage is denied full individuality. Praful Bidwai, a columnist of repute, writes, "Marriage involves a terrible seductionism. It can encompass and envelop the complexity of most relationships only by simplifying them grotesquely."[14] On meeting Aasha Rani at the residence of a busybody Rita, another frustrated wife, Malini gives a free vent to her violent vituperations showing her wifely jealousy and possession:

> Malini screamed, 'SEX! That is all you have—SEX! That is what women like you use. Cheap bitches—part your legs and let any man in. Sex, sex, sex, dirty, filthy sex! Perverts! You must be a pervert. What do you do to him—hah? Suck his cock? Or suffocate him with your breasts? . . . Eventually, a maan needs his wife and children. (49)

Aasha Rani coolly takes all this in her stride and in a revealing manner answers all her misgivings: "Let me show you your face, Malini. Just look at the hatred in your eyes. Is this how you greet your husband when he comes every night? And you wonder why he comes to me?" (49) Obviously she insinuates that a sense of crucifixion in bed is repulsive to her husband. Denied this pleasure, he turns to the Aasha Ranis of our society. Malini continues to negate and repress her sexuality and becomes a frigid body in bed. Akshay has to turn to Aasha Rani for sexual gratification. Shobha De, through the character of Rita, tries to find a way out for waylaid and betrayed wives like Malini. Rita is a pragmatic wife who pleads for a compromise in the marital relationship. To her, romance in marriage is a figment of imagination as it "finishes the morning after the wedding night." (50) After that follows a painfully protracted period of "boredom" (50) for women because husbands or men like "variety." (50) Rita understands Malini's predicament but sees nothing unusual in it. Shobha De in the following words of Rita seems to sum up her indictment of marriage from the vamp point of view:

> Most women hate their husbands—it's a fact. They hate marriage. That's also a fact. But what else they can do? What is the choice? The only way to make a marriage work is through sex—and most women hate that too. But the day a man feels that his woman

> has lost interest in sex, and therefore in him, the relationship is finished and he starts looking elsewhere. Aasha Rani and her kind are always waiting. (50)

Rita reiterates the feminist fears that a wife has to pretend in this pharisaical, conservative patriarchal order. In her desperate yet revelatory advice to Malini "to shut your eyes and part your legs, whether you feel like it or not. Because if you don't some other woman will" (50) lies the biggest discriminatory dilemma faced by women in India. Shobha De's "vamp" brand of feminism proves to be the last nail in the coffin of the institution of marriage as it is obvious in her observation: "A wife is acting all the time—this is the world's best-kept secret. . . . Everything is decided by the bed. On the bed. . . . No woman should be foolish enough to be honest with her husband where sex is concerned." (50) This is the feminist coupde grace on the hollowness and hypocrisy inherent in marriage.

The wheel comes full circle when even the much-dreaded man-eater called Aasha Rani experiences the throes of infatuation and marriage. Her passionate yet abortive attempt to marry Akshay and later on her actual marriage with the Kiwi Jay, are proven failures as Aasha Rani and her kind are not meant for marriage. Yet, for once, Shobha De describes her intense longing to be a wife and mother. She is even ready to renege her religion and come to the fold of Islam to legitimize Akshay's second marriage with her. Her marriage formula is rather simplistic: "we can both become Muslims! It's easy. . . . I'll be your legally wedded second wife. Muslims can have four, but you'd better stop with me." (108) To Seth Amir Chand she confesses: "You don't understand Sethji. I love this man. I really do. I want to marry him. Bear his child." (105) So deep and strong is her resolve to marry Akshay that she is ready to sacrifice everything—her career, her fame, "Sub Kuch." (105) She has been foiled in her attempt to realize her dream through strong-arm tactics used by Malini. A desolate Aasha Rani tries to commit suicide in sheer desperation. Ironically, while she can have sex with Akshay at will, she can't have marriage with him. But after a period of convalescence, she rises like a phoenix to be an emancipated woman again.

With Linda, Aasha Rani experiences what lesbianism has to teach her. New horizons are opened to her though Linda, the lesbian who made her feel wild with excitement. In Dubai where she goes to recover from the trauma of the Akshay-affair, she is offered lavish hospitality by Badshah, the Gold King. In his harem, she enjoys the sandwich message administered by two Thai girls. Shobha De gives highly sensual description of her experience:

> It was an experience so sensuous, so arousing, so complete, that it was weeks before she could forget the feel of two, smooth, soft, oiled, practically breastless bodies on either side of her, touching, licking, stroking every naked inch, making her skin tingle and come alive in a way she couldn't have imagined possible. (66)

Aasha Rani has just too much of oomph to be controlled in a wedlock. Traditionally speaking, marriage is the be-all and end-all of a young woman in India. Aasha Rani is also disillusioned in her attempt to be a wife and mother. Her marriage with Jay in New Zealand also ends up in a fiasco, underlining the futility of marriage at large. What Rita tells about the plight of married woman in India is also a matter of deep concern for the feminists of today: "we demand communication, attention, pampering. Arrey baba, forget it. We should be happy if they don't beat us, burn us, torture us, insult us, discard us. That is all." (117) To an emotionally shattered Aasha Rani Jay proves to be a doting and caring husband. She bears him a baby girl as well. But their marriage was, at best, a compromise, not a wholesome identification with each other. Jay's family members continue to ignore Aasha Rani because of her colour. Shobha De exposes her lecherous father-in-law who tries to tease Aasha sexually. A woman as a wife suffers if she fails to compromise with what remains her fait accompli. That's why, Aasha Rani is lured back into her original fold—the film-world where she continues to reign as a liberated queen. On her way back, she has airborne sex with Gopala-krishnan in the toilet of the plane, the details of which are rendered and nauseum. As a 'vamp' writer Shobha De describes such wild experiences with a deliberate violence: "They began a swinging motion that was so perfectly co-ordinated, Aasha Rani felt they'd done away with gravity. . . . Both of them came together, with such force that the tiny toilet shuddered with the impact." (198) For the likes of Aasha Rani the days have to be sunny and nights starry since they are free from the shackles of androcentric moral order.

Shobha De also reinforces her plea for liberation through the examples of Sudha and Sasha, Aasha Rani's sister and daughter respectively. Towards the end of her reign as a starheroine, enters Sudha, her own sister, whom her mother throws up in the film-world. Sudha takes the entire society by storm. Shobha De depicts her to be even more calculating and designing than her elder sister and mother put together. She lives with Ajay, a hero, without marriage in the same bungalow. Cohabitation, and not marriage, is the watch-word for her. She becomes a rage till she falls a victim to the wicked designs of her enemies. Towards the end of the novel, we see her as a badly burnt-up figure asking for death. She really pays a very heavy price for her material achievements. She confesses that she has been rightly punished: "God has punished me. It is nothing else but that. I deserve it. I have been evil. I have sinned." (232)

Shobha De conforms to the vamp ideology of feminism in the sense that she shows how self-destructive the attempts to achieve liberation have been for Aasha Rani and Sudha and will be for others as well. It is precisely because of the inherent lopsidedness and orthodoxy of the patriarchal system that perpetuates male-hegemony. But the ending of the novel does not sound a note of despair; it is symbolic of a new beginning once again. This time it is Sasha, Aasha's daughter, who has to continue the show, the struggle and the survival of a woman against the predatory male-dominated society. Aasha Rani aptly thinks that together "they would conquer the world. . . . Sasha would live life on her own terms. And she would bring her up as amma never had." (234) Aasha fantasizes that Sasha would be the "Golden Girl of the Silver screen! Oh yes, Sasha would be tomorrow's Lover Girl!" (234)

Shobha De's vamp brand of feminism admits of no redemptive formula for the 'fallen women' and no millennium, for the liberated women. Her women characters who endeavour to liberate themselves often meet with disaster. Before this happens, they send a whole host of taboos devised by patriarchal order cartwheeling. This is how we should appreciate the crusaders of a different kind like Anjali and Karuna in *Socialite Evenings* and Aasha Rani in *Starry Nights.* Shobha De sees through the male-operated conspiracy of silence that is the sorry lot of Indian women at large. Her women characters act according to the dictates to their own will and defy the farcical codes and phoney mores of the social system. Anita Desai, the great Indian woman novelist and a pioneer of feminism, brilliantly exposes the grinding suppression of women in India:

> Even if in reality she is nothing but a common drudge, first in her father's house and then her husband's—a beast of burden bearing an endless string of children, putting up with any brutality or disloyalty or failing of her husband—she has no alternative: she must live as Sita did, as Draupadi did; she is Durga incarnate. The myth keeps her bemused, bound hand and foot. To rebel against it—either in speech or action—would mean that she is questioning the myth, attacking the legend, and that cannot be permitted: it is the cornerstone on which the Indian family and therefore Indian society are built.[15]

Shobha De, in her fictional world, seems to suggest that we have not only a deep need to demolish the mythical and iconographic images of woman imposed by patriarchal structures but also a deeper need to conceptualize woman as a composite energy of production, protection and love, both earthly and sexual. Shobha De's heroines protest against this massive oppression and exploitation carried through various patriarchal ideological constructs manifest in history, philosophy, culture and arts. Try as they do to break the shackles, they do not attain total liberation and are victimized in one way or the other. Shobha De here is in line with the vamp school of feminism:

> Delectably sensual and transgressive as some of the writings of the vamp critics has been, it, too, has the faults of its virtues. The vamp is glamorous, an actress in a kind of guerilla theatre, but the drama of seduction and betrayal that she enacts in her foray against patriarchal structures may end up being as seductively treacherous to women as to men.[16]

Thus, Shobha De provides no solutions or alternatives to the problems the Indian woman faces in the androcentric society. The path of liberation chosen by her heroines is also fraught with frustration, mental break-down and disasters. If it flouts the canons of the patriarchal order, it violently disturbs the concept of femininity as well. After a stage, feminism becomes deconstructive. De is also caught up in this dilemma. Whither feminism? is the question that one often encounters even in the writings of the staunch feminists of today. The Indian brand of feminism has still a long way to go. Here I can't help quoting Jaidev: "A feminist novel for India is not a novel which a woman will write just because she is a woman and knows how to write. It will be written by one who has understood a woman both as a woman and as a person pressurized by all kinds of visible and invisible contexts, by one who is not carried away by fetishes but is mature enough."[17] This is a sort of statutory warning to Shobha De as she has to wean herself away from the lure of pulp-fiction that sells well. Ironically in India as anywhere else "vamp" feminism may be bad aesthetics but is certainly good economics. Shobha de has yet to prove her first commitment to feminism and shed off the popular stigma of being a mere peddler of pornographic fiction.

NOTES

1. *India Today*, Feb. 15, 1992, p. 180.
2. Sunil Sethi, "De in, De out," *Seminar*, 384, August 1991, p. 40.
3. Madhu Jain, "Cat on a Cold Tin Roof," *India Today*, October 15, 1989, p. 195.
4. Sunil Sethi, p. 41.
5. Madhu Jain, p. 195.
6. Sandra M. Gilbert and Susan Gubar, "The Mirror and the Vamp: Reflections on Feminist Criticism," in *The Future of Literary Theory*, ed. Ralph Cohen (New York: Routledge), p. 145.
7. M.H. Abrams, *The Mirror and the Lamp: Romantic Theory and the Critical Tradition* (1953; New York: W.W. Norton, 1958), p. 34.
8. Gilbert and Gubar, p. 145.
9. *Ibid.*
10. *Ibid*, p. 157.
11. Shobha De, *Socialite Evenings* (New Delhi: Penguin India, 1989), p. 12.
12. Sunil Sethi, p. 40.
13. Shobha De, *Starry Nights* (New Delhi: Penguin India, 1991), p. 213.

14. Praful Bidwai, "Heaven can Wait," *The Times of India*, 16 February 1992, p. 22, col. 4.
15. Anita Desai, "Secret Connivance," *Times Literary Supplement*, 14 Sept. 1990, p. 972.
16. Gilbert and Gubar, p. 154.
17. Jaidev, "Feminism and the Contemporary Hindu Novel," in *On Literature*, ed. Jaidev (Shimla: Indian Institute of Advanced Study, 1990), p. 63.

Tender, Beautiful and Erotic: Lesbianism in *Starry Nights*

PRABHAT KUMAR PANDEYA

Cheek to cheek and breast to breast
Locked together in one nest.

Christina Rossetti, *Goblin Market*

Lysistrata [inspecting Ismenia]: I should have known—look what a fertile vale she's got there!
Calonice: Yes, and with all the grass beautifully cropped, too.

Aristophanes, *Lysistrata*, I

Some women of the harem
When they are amorous,
Do the acts of the mouth congress
On the *yonis* of one another.[1]

Vatsyayan, *Kamasutra*, XIV

Shobha De in *Starry Nights* has graphically depicted the Bombay film world and how could Bollywood be complete without sex and fleshly pleasures. And not to fall short on this count the novel is heavily laced with sexuality and almost every conceivable variety of sexual behaviour is presented in the novel, to wit, masturbation, sodomy, fellatio, cunnilingus, lesbianism, male homosexuality, and certainly normal heterosexual copulation. That sex sells De knows well and no wonder she is a best seller and who cares if she is called soft-porn queen and her fictional world is described as "Beastly Beatitude."[2] Her writing about sex is nothing new. It has been a perennial favourite with writers. If one were to write about all sex episodes in the novel it would be too long for a paper, hence, I confine myself to lesbianism in the novel. This paper aims at discussing this sexual behaviour, female-female contact and tries to see this phenomenon not merely as one form of sexual behaviour but to study its extra-literary aspects to find out whether it has any relevance to the story and the heroine around whom the novel moves. In the story De does not give much importance to the lesbian episode but its implications cannot be denied. The epigraphs covering different cultures prove that it is a universal phenomenon but of late it has come out of the closet and has been used even as an expression of feminism with political overtones.[3] Before coming to the novel it would be useful to know something about this kind of sexual behaviour. Some may wonder how there can be sexual relationship between two women. It has been ridiculed too, as by the Arabic poet Abu Nuwas:

> What sense is there in tribadism? None—I know that game full well:
> It's fat rubbed up by fat, and nothing more.
> And rub as one may, when down to bare skin, there's nothing to rise in response.
> There's no wicked shaft that is smooth at the tip to drive itself home and sink into place.[4]

Female homosexuality has several names: lesbianism, sapphism, and tribadism. The word lesbianism is derived from the Greek *Lesbios*, a Greek island in the Aegean sea which was the native place of Sappho, the 7th century B.C. lyric poetess who addressed her love poems to women. Sapphism is self-explanatory. Tribadism, according to *Webster's New World Dictionary*, is derived from the French *tribade* meaning a lesbian. But a better explanation is given by the editor of *The Glory of the Perfumed Garden* whose name we know only in initials, H.E.J.: "Tribadism (from the Greek *tribas*, a woman who practises 'pounding,' 'grinding,' 'rubbing' with another woman) is a more accurate translataion of the Arabic *sihaq* . . . than 'Lesbianism.'"[5] Lesbianism has psychological implications about which we would talk later and the physical part of it would become clear when we come to the novel. With this background information we are ready to go to the novel for analysis.

There is one elaborate description of the heroine Aasha Rani's lesbian relationship with her journalist friend Linda when she is away at Manali for shooting. But even before that she has tasted the pleasures of the female flesh. After the fiasco of her affair with Akshay Kumar she goes to Dubai to nurse her lacerated nerves by courtesy of Sheth Amirchand: "A Gulf Air ticket to Dubai. First class. On the back of the ticket . . . written in black ink: 'He's not worth it. *Jao aish karo.*'"[6] Her host in Dubai, a goldsmuggler, is not interested in sleeping with her but she is provided with every comfort. She is attended on by two Thai masseurs from Bangkok and this is her first exposure to lesbian pleasure:

> She got her shopping done, plus she had her body dexterously worked over by the Thai girls, who giggled at the size of Aasha Rani's breasts ('like melons') and took turns rubbing coconut oil over them. Aasha Rani found their ministrations most pleasurable. . . . The Thai girls asked her flirtatiously whether she wanted to try a 'sandwich massage.' Game to try anything once, Aasha Rani agreed readily.
>
> It was an experience so sensuous, so arousing, so complete that it was weeks before she could forget the feel of two smooth, soft, oiled, practically breastless bodies on either side of her, touching, licking, stroking every naked inch, making her skin tingle and come alive in a way she couldn't have imagined possible.
>
> When she returned to Bombay . . . she had . . . experienced some of *the greatest orgasms of her life*. (66, emphasis added)

Aasha has several sexual relationships in the novel but what is important is her description of "the greatest orgasms" derived from the Thai girls.

Her second lesbian experience, described in great details, comes from Linda. This is the central lesbian experience of the heroine and hence is to be quoted *in extenso*:

> "Come here," she said to Aasha Rani, "take a sip [of brandy]. . . . With that she pulled Aasha Rani down on the bed and kissed her on the lips.
>
> It was a pleasant feeling, Aasha Rani thought. No rough bristles scraping her face, just smooth cheeks and soft lips over her own. A memory flashed in her head of the Thai masseuses. Linda's hands were in Aasha Rani's hair, expertly undoing the

clasp. . . . Her fingers began massaging her neck as once again she bent over her to kiss her, saying, "Open your mouth, let me taste your tongue. . . . Your tongue looked so sexy and pink—relax baby, relax. You will love it. Just leave it all to me. Trust me."

Her hands moved from Aasha Rani's neck to her breasts. She kept kissing her gently, probing her mouth with an eager tongue. Reaching under Aasha Rani's shirt she unhooked her bra. Aasha Rani tensed and tried to cover her breasts. . . . "Don't stop me, it will be beautiful. Like nothing you have known before," Linda whispered. Her kissing was more passionate now and her fingers rested on Aasha Rani's taut nipples. "Look, you want me. Your body can't lie." Her head moved down till her mouth found Aasha Rani's breasts.

There was no resistance left any more. Aasha Rani's entire body was floating—her mind was adrift. She let her arms drop . . . as Linda's warm thigh wedged itself between hers and her hand moved between Aasha Rani's legs. "Close your eyes, let me do to you what no man could have done. Let me make you come like you've never come before. Stay loose, stay with me, you will forget men, you will forget everything you've known before. My hands, my mouth, my tongue, my thighs will set your body on fire. Enjoy it. . . ."

Aasha Rani groaned with pleasure. Linda refused to stop. She'd become more aggressive now and her hands pummelled Aasha Rani's body, exploring every inch of it. Unexpectedly she grabbed the bottle of brandy and poured some between Aasha Rani's open legs. "The only way to drink it," Linda said and placed her mouth over the dampness, licking each drop as it trickled. The sensation was unbelievably arousing. Aasha Rani wanted to growl and scream with excitement . . . "Come . . . come . . . not once but a hundred times!" Linda urged, her mouth still between Aasha Rani's legs, "But let me ride you first. Let me show you that I can take you like a man too." And she climbed roughly over Aasha Rani, whose head had fallen back, over the side of the bed.

"Do you like it this way?" Linda demanded gruffly, moving over her, rubbing herself against her, till both of them came together, shuddering and shaking, not wanting it to end. Aasha Rani collapsed with Linda over her. For a while they didn't say anything. . . . Then Linda began caressing Aasha Rani gently and kissing her fingertips. "THIS is love, understand? This is love-making, not what those bastards do to our bodies." Aasha Rani was lulled to sleep by Linda's fingers stroking her. Yes, she thought,

> this is what it should be, tender, beautiful and erotic. In a way it could never be with a man. (79-80)

This the only real lesbian experience that she has but the memory of it never leaves her completely. It lingers pleasantly in her mind. After she has married Jamie Phillips, a considerate understanding man who "concentrated on pleasing her" and was able to, but the memory of the lesbian pleasure never fades from her consciousness. And even though half-jokingly she comes out: "Once Aasha Rani told him, 'Only half-joking, actually, if you must know, I prefer girls. They are so sensitive and soft. This, only another woman can know—how to turn a woman on. Can't you find a sexy girl friend here?'" (120) Now that we have seen Aasha Rani's lesbian experiences we have to work out its implications.

A pertinent question is whether lesbianism is "natural," and why at all such sexual behaviour? If "natural" is taken to mean what applies to animal behaviour, it would be a revelation to many that such behaviour is found among several other species. Alfred C. Kinsey believes that calling homosexuality "perversion" has no scientific validity and elaborating this he writes:

> The impression that infra-human mammals more or less confine themself to heterosexual activities is a distortion of the fact which appears to have originated in a man-made philosophy, rather than in specific observations of mammalian behaviour.
>
> In actuality, sexual contact between the individuals of the same sex are known to occur in practically every species of mammal which has been extensively studied . . .
>
> Homosexual contacts in infra-human species of mammals occur among both females and male. Homosexual contact between the males have been observed in such widelly separated species as rats, mice, hamsters, guinea pigs, rabbits, porcupines, martens, cattle, antilope, goats, horses, pigs, lions, sheep, monkeys and chimpanzees.[7]

Thus we find that lesbianism is a natural phenomenon, scientifically speaking. That many people don't like or it is a socially unaccepted behavicur is a different thing. But the more important question is why lesbian behaviour and this takes us beyond the physicality of it. The answer is to be found more in woman's psyche than in her body, not that the body is any less important. We know that among the humans sexuality is not only confined to the genitalia, it is in the mind, the genitalia is only the medium. That is why it is also called the "tool." The psychological implications of lesbian behaviour are more pertinent to the novel in context of the heroine. In lesbian relationship physicality is not all, rather the physicality is a part of the greater emotional relationship. When Linda says, "let me do to you what no man could have done" she is not exaggerating for the simple reason that man can never be woman either in sexual advances or in his body. Man in order to be macho is always harsh and rough in approach, not that violence has no place in *ars amatoria,* and his body can never be soft like a woman's. And therein lies the difference. Writers have known and written about it. Here is an example from a late nineteenth century French novel *Aphrodite by* Pierre Louys:

> A woman is a perfect instrument. From head to toe she's made solely and wonderfully for love. Only a woman knows how to be loved. Therefore, if a couple is composed of two women, it's perfect; if it has only one woman, it's only half as good; if it has no woman at all, it's completely idiotic.[8]

Similar preference to woman is expressed in the following poem:

> My source of happiness is a soft skinned girl . . .
> The moisture of her mouth is sweet and fresh to those who care to taste it.
> Between her legs a fissure lies as pretty and alluring as the neck of some gazelle.
> And when her beauty was first laid bare to me I said what I felt in my heart:
> "Praise be to Him who has moulded such beauty . . .
> My night was one of sucking at her mouth and throat,
> And if to love a girl in such a way is sinful, to love a man's unlawful.[9]

This preference is also because of a different kind of psychic rapport between two women not to be found in heterosexual relationship in which woman's role is inferior. She is rode over by the male. She is made love to, not made love with. One of the lesbian partners may assume active part, called "butch," as Linda, yet in such relationship there is a mutuality, not duality as observed by Simone de Beauvoir:

> Between women love is contemplative; caresses are intended less to gain possession of the other than gradually to recreate the self through her; separateness is abolished, there is no struggle, no victory, no defeat; in exact reciprocity each is at once subject and object, sovereign and slave; duality becomes mutuality. Says Colette in *Ces plaisirs*: 'The lover takes delight in being sure of caressing the secrets of which she knows, and whose preferences her own body indicates to her.' And Renee Vivien's poem (from *Sortileges*) expresses the same idea: 'Our bodies are made alike. . . . Our destiny the same. . . . In you I love my child, my darling, and my sister.[10]

Tender approach is an important thing in this behaviour. A woman can work up another woman better than a man. The man has to "perform" and after doing it he doesn't care for the partner. In a recent survey[11] a woman gives following reasons for her lesbian preference: it is much easier to give emotionally to a woman, to surrender ego; her skin is soft and smooth; no worry whether my body is "adequate"; no worry about the partner's sexual-moral judgment, where I was going to be placed on the spectrum of female frailties (angel or whore). Here surrendering of ego is important, the implication being it is easier to surrender before one's own sex than to the male who always rules, exploits and dominates the female. And herein comes another facet of lesbian behaviour, independence from the male which is an important principle of feminism or Women's Lib Movement. It also has political implications. Hite[12] writes that lesbianism can be political. Sex with another woman could be better "because of the more equal relationship possible. Sex with woman can be a reaction against man and our second class status with them in society." One of the subjects in the Hite survey says, "Sex with a man is often the beginning of a political education. Sex with a woman means independence from man." There is a kind of reciprocity and similarity between two women and as a psychiatrist has pointed out, "Only another woman knows." Going deeper into the woman's earliest feeling of secured fleshy haven, she writes, "There is something uniquely satisfying in a woman's body that cannot be had with a man. As sexually exciting and elegant as a male body may be, it lacks the obvious physical attributes of our first source of love, mother. It isn't just the breasts: it's the texture of skin, the smell, the whole mysterious aura of that first body we laid against, which fed, warmed, and overwhelmed us with its power."[13] This observation applies to what Linda says to Aasha Rani, "let me do to you what no man could have done. . . . This is love-making, not what those bastards do to our bodies." Thus we notice that in Linda's arms Aasha Rani feels cozy and happy, even though initiative was not hers and after the act she admits superiority of lesbian pleasure to heterosexual: "yes, she thought, this is what it should be, tender, beautiful and erotic. In a way it could never be with a man." (80)

In the context of *Starry Nights* it is an important point. This paper does not aim at studying the novel as a feminist one but Aasha Rani is certainly not very happy with male and his exploitation. Even her mother has exploited her, treating her as a money-making machine. The only man whom she really loves, Akshay Kumar, cannot treat her better than a kept since he is married. Thus her lesbian affair also implies her escape from lesbianism yet the only such affair that she has with Linda leaves such a powerful impact on her mind that she is not able to forget it and as observed above, "It could never be with a man." On a deeper level of her consciousness this experience also implies independence from man.

To conclude, Aasha Rani's lesbian experience in *Starry Nights* is not just a variant sexual behaviour but it has relevance to the heroine's character. It is her short-lived abandon in the arms of another woman, Linda, fleshy warmth giving her emotional security, love and certainly sexual pleasure, as in Dubai with the Thai girls "she had experienced some of the greatest orgasms of her life." In the turbulent life of the heroine and her many sexual escapades and many affairs the lesbian affair is something different, something fulfilling, an emotional oasis. Aasha Rani's lesbian affair may not be central to the novel and she cannot be called a lesbian, for she does not show much preference for it, yet it does have bearing on her character.

NOTES

1. There is one more reference to lesbianism in this classic of Hindu erotica: "Dhātréyikām sakhim dāseem vā purushavadalamkrityākriti sanjuktaih kandamulaphalāvayavaip-dravyairvātmābhiprāyamnivartyeyuh." *Kamasutra*,V. (The sexually starved female inmates of the harem contrived to attain sexual gratification through the daughters of a nurse, a woman friend or a maid servant, who dressed and acted like a male by penetrating a root or a fruit, resembling a male organ fastened to the front part of her waist.) In another Hindu treatise on statecraft and penology, *Manusmriti*, we find mention of punishment for spoiling a young girl through lesbian contact, mutual sexual gratification: "Kanyaiv kanyām yā kuryā tasyā syād dvishatodayah/Shulkam cha dvigunam dadyācchiphashaivapnuyādrish/Yā tu kanyām prakyryātstri sā sadyomoundyamarhati/Angulyoreva vā chedam kharenodvahanam tathā." *Manusmriti*, VIII: 369-70 (If an unmarried girl spoiled another raw girl and taught her the lesson of self-abuse or gratified her with her fingers or other counterfeit male organ or cylindrical substances she was liable to pay fine of two hundred currency coins. Besides the fine she was to subsidise the parents of the deflorated girl with double the amount of the calculated dowry and also was to receive ten lashes. But if a married woman exercised similar guilt she was to be awarded a more merciless punishment. Her head was shaved, her fingers were excised and she was paraded in the public streets on the back of a donkey.)
2. *India Today*, September 30, 1993.
3. See Shere Hite, *The Hite Report: A Nationwide Study of Female Sexuality* (New York: Dell, 1987), pp. 414-16.
4. See Shekh Nafzavi, *The Glory of the Perfumed Garden* (London: Granada, 1978), p. 31.
5. *Ibid.*, p. 21.
6. Shobha De, *Starry Nights* (Delhi: Penguin, 1991), p. 65.
7. Alfred C. Kinsey et al, *Sexual Behaviour in the Human Female* (New York: Pocket Books, 1965), pp. 448-49.
8. Quoted by Nancy Friday, *Innocent Love* (Publisher's name and place not given, 1980), p. 78.
9. *The Glory of the Perfumed Garden*, p. 30.
10. Simone de Beauvoir, *The Second Sex* (London: The New English Library, 1966), p. 155.
11. *The Hite Report*, p. 409.

12. *Ibid.*, p. 414.
13. Nancy Friday, *Women on Top* (New York: Simon and Schuster, 1991), p. 182.

The Dialectics of Self-Assertion: The Liberated Woman in *Sisters*

E. SATYANARAYANA

> . . . a female character . . . can potentially be construed as a marginalized entity based on what we know about women's relative powerlessness in society, regardless of her position as represented in the fiction.
>
> Phillip Brian Harper

A distinct feature of the creative writings by women during the last two and a half decades has been one of increased awareness of the abuses which the women are subjected to. This sensitivity among the writers can undoubtedly be attributed to the influence of the feminist movement, in spite of their denial of any ideological commitment. In fact, the advent of feminism with its varied implications has given a new direction to the creative literatures. Many women writers seem to have realized the need for a separate literature that can speak for the feminine issues and experiences which have been either misunderstood or distorted by their male counterparts. As a result, a major part of creative work by the women writers is preoccupied with the dated traditions of the patriarchal society. A casual reading of the novelists like Kamala Markandaya, Anita Desai, Shashi Deshpande, Bharati Mukherjee and Shobha De reveals a common concern in their experiences as women and writers. They portray the tortured consciousness of the urban middle class woman, who, in quest of her identity undergoes a metamorphosis—from a silent sufferer to a hard-core rebel, breaking with the age-old and restraining ethics of the male-dominated world. At times, the rebellion of the woman takes the extreme forms such as sexual promiscuity/extra-marital relations which serve as a device for her to assert her "self." And it is this theme of self-assertion which is also central to Shobha De's third novel *Sisters* (1992).

Shobha De, though dubbed as the "Pulp Queen" and "Desi Jackie Collins," has established her reputation as a novelist. As Janaki Ramachandran rightly states, "you may love her or hate her, but it is difficult to ignore"[1] her. In fact, she has found a wide readership as her stories, in her own words, are meant for "both men and women from sixteen to ninety."[2] Having been provoked by the pervasive 'hot sex' sequences in her novels, critics have completely ignored Shobha De, a writer with feminist leanings. Her tales are an attempt to create a space for feminine reality. She makes no bones about her obsession with what is called a 'taboo subject' in her works. She confesses: "It is important for women to talk about it. Our mother endured it silently because it was a taboo subject. Nobody was interested in women's view on sex. Whether it was erotic poetry or prose, the perspective was always that of a man. It is only now that women are expressing the way they feel about this most elementary . . . aspect of conjugal life. It is a kind of catharsis."[3]

Besides three works of non-fiction, Shobha De has so far authored half a dozen novels which are characterized by her sense of empathy for the women who, having come out of the bound of domesticity and marriage, assert their identity. The present paper aims to examine how the major characters in Shobha De's *Sisters* go through the ordeal of self-assertion and how they realize their freedom—a freedom to live a life of their choice.

Like her earlier novels, *Socialite Evenings* and *Starry Nights,* Shobha De's explosive novel *Sisters* is unique for its 'pacy narrative quality' and its 'ostensibly intimate view of glitzy side'[4] of Bombay life. But unlike its predecessors, *Sisters* for the first time deals with the psychic conflict in its liberated woman-protagonist who is caught between a 'personal self' and a 'societal self.' The novel thus focuses as much on the seamy side of the business life as on the inner turmoil of the protagonist.

Shobha De's *Sisters*, set in the corrupt world of big business, appears to tell an interesting story of two wealthy and socialite women who, driven by ambition and lust, are involved in an unending rivalry. But it is in Mallika (Mikki) that we encounter a woman who struggles against the constraints of being a woman and finally completes her odyssey towards being herself.

When the narrative opens, Mikki, the protagonist, compelled by the untimely death of her parents in an air-crash, leaves America for Bombay to take charge of her father's industries which are verging on collapse. It is too much burden for a woman like Mikki, whose "twentieth birthday was just three months away."[5] She is in reality, unprepared for any responsibility that can deprive her of her personal freedom. Her initial aversion for the corporate business is mainly due to her fear of losing the colourful life in America where she has had her first taste of life. The narrator tells: "Given the choice, Mikki wanted this nightmare to end now. Her parents were dead. There was nobody she cared for. And nobody who cared for her. . . . Her life in India . . . was over." (9) But left with no alternative, Mikki decides to lead the sprawling industries. Once she gets into her father's shoes, she begins to show her managerial skills. In no time she is beset on all sides by the creditors, takeover tycoons and unreliable associates. Having learnt that she has a sister, Alisha, her father's illegitimate child, Mikki feels obliged to make her a partner in the business.

In reality, Mikki, with the demise of her parents, feels lonely. The existence of Alisha, although strangers to each other, gives her a sense of solace and she is strengthened morally. It is not Alisha's wealth that makes Mikki think of her, but her faith in human values that prompts her to establish relationship with Alisha.

Preoccupied as she is with her own self, Mikki is determined to save the industries from going bankrupt. Advised by Shanay, her cousin, Mikki decides to borrow from her fiance, Navin. But it takes her no time to realize that Navin is a putty in his mother's hands and she is repelled by his lack of self-respect. She calls off her engagement with him. Being aware that "there are enough vultures waiting to pounce upon" her (11) Mikki goes in for a middle-aged Binny. What attracts her to him is his uncanny aggressive manner. It is he who helps Mikki learn about the other side of her personality. Amy, an old hand and friend of Mikki, says: "Maybe he lacks finesse . . . refinement . . . nevertheless Malhotra type men are better. . . . An older man . . . an experienced one. And together you'd make quite a team." (58)

Despite being warned, Mikki marries Binny. It is indeed surprising to note that unlike Shobha De's other women-heroes who generally tend to free themselves from the clutches of married life, Mikki deliberately gets into wedlock. Though she has been enamoured of the life of freedom, she is not averse to being a wife. What she does not like is the inhuman subordination of the woman and confining her to four walls of the kitchen. With her education in America and progressive thinking, Mikki gives in to Binny whom she loves very much. In the beginning, Binny appears to be all attention towards Mikki who "enjoyed his experienced approach and found herself discovering aspects of her own sexuality, she hadn't guessed existed." In his company, she not only gets an insight into her real 'self' but also feels a sense of security. Thus she prides herself on being his wife. The narrator tells:

> She felt liberated, uninhibited and aroused to the point of primitive abandon. If this was what her man wanted, if this was what made him happy, should give it to him. She would give him every bit of herself, her body, her mind, and her soul. She was in love with him. And he was finally hers. (109)

It is this total submission, a characteristic of the traditional woman, which adds to the superiority of man and consequent exploitation of women. However her honeymoon with Binny is to end in a fiasco. Binny, a womanizer, has already got a family and his marriage with Mikki is only to keep up his image in the society. Strongly enough, Mikki, having learnt this, remains silent, for she does not care for his past life. But she cannot tolerate Binny's indifference to her. Except for a few moments when "he poured falcon of joy on her limbs" (108), her life with him becomes a veritable hell. The process of dehumanization of Mikki begins, when all her property is transferred to Binny. Besides, she is denied motherhood, for she has to keep always fit for him. Being a representative of the oppressive system, Binny does not like Mikki's desire to be an active partner both in life and business. He is characteristically outspoken when he tells her that he needs a wife "who stays at home and looks after me . . . our women stay at home and make sure the place is perfectly run. They fulfil their husband's every need and look good when their men get home in the evening. No office going." (109) This is exactly what puts Mikki off but, as she is conscious of her precarious condition, she pleads with him: "I can look after you and look after at least a part of the business. We could work together. . . . I won't have to wait hours to see you." (109)

Mikki's situation in the novel throws light on the harsh realities of the patriarchal society. It also hints at the growing awareness among the women who begin to rise from the eternal slumber and call shots. Mikki's continual protest with Binny results from her innate desire for freedom. Ironically, she never thinks of a life beyond marital bounds. It is her dream to be both an ideal wife and a responsible social being that gives the novel a moral dimension. For Mikki, materialistic pleasures without freedom of the 'self' mean nothing. In fact, Shobha De's women have been liberated from the economic constraints. What they search for is the personal freedom, and when they are denied this, they turn rebellious. They express their anger by resorting to what might be termed as unethical acts, that is breaking the marriage oaths or indulging in extra-marital relations. Shobha De observes: "It is not enough to have mind of your own, if you don't have income to match. . . . With this economic freedom has come assertiveness, confidence and refusal to be treated as doormats."[6]

Mikki is constantly at war with herself as a woman and as a human being. Although she fails to find in Binny a man with whom she could share her life, Mikki is "willing to compromise her own life if it meant he'd notice her, listen to her, acknowledge her existence." (140) Her dream to enjoy the fruit of marital life is shattered when Binny, suspecting her chastity, turns her out of his home. She pleads innocence and tells him: "Binny. . . . I love you. Only you. . . . I can't live without you." (141)

In fact, her disillusionment with Binny is total when he goes in for a divorce. All her efforts to live with him fail. Mikki is determined to retain her industries with which she identifies herself. However, long before she does anything, she again finds herself in the saddle, when Binny along with his illegitimate family meets his death. Mikki is a changed woman now. Her experience with Binny gives her an insight into her 'being' as a woman and an individual. The transformation of Mikki from a mere social butterfly to a mature woman and to a kindly mother-figure is apparent when she turns her attention towards her estranged sister.

Unlike Mikki, "a prim and proper mistress of the manner, all correct conduct and sober talk" (187), Alisha, an insecure and lovable young woman, leads a flirtatious life which, though it seems a breach of the moral code, is a sure pointer to the arrival of a new value system, and a mode of self-assertion. Alisha's hatred for Mikki is based on her sense of being neglected by her father. She is a victim of her own illusions. In fact, she needs her sister more than Mikki does. Mikki's efforts to improve the strained relations between them, become worse when her enemies poison Alisha's ears. Alisha imitates her sister and finds a sense of satisfaction when Mikki is in trouble. She moves closely with the men whom Mikki rejected. She traps Navin and indulges in fornication, not to satisfy her carnal yearning but to show Mikki that she is not inferior to anyone. She misses no opportunity to insult her sister. In fact, Alisha serves as a foil to Mikki. Being unaware that Binny has been already married, Mikki accepts him, while Alisha knowingly leads an amorous life with a married person. Her emotional involvement with this man is so deep that she becomes a drug addict. Although they attempt alike to find fulfilment in their life, both the sisters are different from each other. Mikki's encounter with different men helps her grow into an independent-minded woman, while Alisha, failing to get any hint from her experience, becomes an introvert.

Ironically, Mikki and Alisha are united only after the death of the latter's mother. With her motherly affection, Mikki attempts to soothe the wounded self of her sister. She helps her get over all the emotional hurdles in her life. The novel comes to an end with both the sisters realizing the need to live together.

The structure of the novel is cinematic with its climax, being reminiscent of one of the most make-believe scenes of the modern pop cinema. But *Sisters,* which covers four years in the life of Mikki, is a fine study in the traumatic experiences of a woman caught up in the whirlpool of complex human situations. The narration, simple and direct, adds to the authenticity of the story.

NOTES

1. Janaki Ramachandran, "Survival Tactics," *The Hindu*, Feb. 2, 1997.
2. *Ibid.*
3. *Ibid*
4. Janaki Ramachandran, "Call it a Day, De Did," *Indian Review of Books*, vol. 3, no. 7, p. 26.
5. Shobha De, *Sisters* (New Delhi: Penguin).
6. Ramachandran, "Survival Tactics."

An Analytical Study of *Sisters*

NEENA ARORA

The well-known columnist and a free-lance journalist Shobha De came into limelight as a novelist in 1988 with the publication of her first novel *Socialite Evenings*. *Socialite Evenings* gave her both instant wealth and fame, though she has never ceased to be a cynosure at socialite parties or in newspaper columns and for adopting new surnames as quickly as she brought out new novels. And of late she has made a niche for herself as a script writer of television soaps too.

The success of *Socialite Evenings* was supplemented by her second best-seller *Starry Nights* (1990)—a tale of gossips about dons of Bollywood. And after that there has been no looking back. While her regular contribution to newspapers continued, she was out with her third novel *Sisters* in 1992, followed by her fourth novel *Strange Obsession*, where she plumbed new depths, delving into the dark caverns of lesbianism. *Strange Obsession* succeeded *Snapshots* which captures the patois of Indian yuppie and cruelly caricatures desi celebrities. In her world, all men lust for only two things—money and women—and all women chase after men and money. All relationships centre around sex and all the scenes revolve around sexual encounters.

Some recent works to her credit are: *Sultry Days*, *Second Thoughts* and *Uncertain Liaisons* (with Khushwant Singh). In fact, De is the most prolific Indian woman writer writing in English in present times. Her latest is a non-fictional work: *Surviving Men: The Smart Woman's Guide to Staying on Top* (1997), which has made her a controversial writer. Here she shows her guts in frankly writing about taboo ridden topic of male sexuality especially about Indian male.

This paper makes an attempt to analyse De's *Sisters* (1992) critically. In *Sisters*, she focuses her attention neither on the aristocrats of high social circles nor on the stars or starlets of the Bombay film industry, but on the "richie-rich" intriguing corporate world of business tycoons.

The story unfolds in a Gujarati milieu, with a young girl Mallika Hiralal returning from the U.S.A. to attend the funeral of her rich parents who have died in an aircrash. Very soon, she is exposed to the duplicity of her father as she discovers that she has a half-sister Alisha Mehta born of a mistress four months after her. She feels betrayed. She was not told anything about Alisha by her mother or by anybody else for that matter. Now, when she thinks of her father: "Her father, always distant, now seemed a total stranger. A stranger who's led a sneaky double life."[1]

She wanted to know from her parents the truth about what really happened but now both of them are gone. She, however, decides to claim the only blood-relative she is left with. While the lonely Mikki wants to befriend Alisha and help her out, she finds the latter to be rude, unfriendly, jealous and full of hatred towards her. Things are already in a bad shape at her father's 'Hiralal Industries.' Her father had

> made some hasty decisions during the last two years and borrowed heavily. He also got involved in ventures floated by entrepreneurs of dubious character. He lost a great deal of money on his Malaysian adventure. In other words, H.I. can be described as close to bankruptcy. (48)

Nevertheless, Mallika takes the reins of her father's empire in her hands, and soon realizes that her father's trusted employee Ramanbhai could not be relied upon as he was "keeping things from her," (30) and had been discouraging her to take interest in business. He once remarked to her:

> Had you been a son your father might have taken you into his confidence from a young age and guided you properly from the beginning. But as a daughter, all he wanted for you was a good husband—that is all. . . . My advice is—leave these serious matters to me. I am there to handle them. Trust me. I will guard your interests like a father. But you will make things difficult for yourself if you do things without consulting me. (30)

Soon she finds that it is Alisha who gets the pulp and turns into a rich heiress, while she (Mallika) holds on to her father's crumbling empire.

The central event of the novel is the quest of Mallika to win her sister Alisha and Alisha's to be a rich lady. After many vicissitudes, the novel ends on a happy note with the two sisters finally reconciled to each other:

> The sunlight came pouring into the room through enormous bay windows of Mikki's—and Alisha's—beautiful home, bathing the two sisters in its golden glow. Mikki surrendered to its warm embrace as her fingers played tenderly with the silken tresses of her sister's hair, and she drifted off into a light sleep full of dreams . . . the future shimmered tantalizingly before her half-closed eyes . . . and Mikki reached out her hand to touch it. (217)

Shanay, Navin, Binny Malhotra—the suitors of Mallika are the big sharks ready to swallow her. It is, however, Binny Malhotra who not only gets Mikki but also fabulous assets and Industries of her father.

Amy, Anjanaben, Leelaben—mother of Alisha, Dr. Kurien, Lucio and many other characters in the novel remain in the backdrop and hardly emerge as powerfully drawn characters.

The plot sounds good, rather perfect for a super-hit Hindi formula film with well measured doses of suspense, romance, imported locales, sex, drugs, accidents, rape and love-hate relationship finally ending on a happy note.

De's novels, no doubt, are instant hits and are being printed and reprinted. And almost every year she is coming out with another new one. To be known as a columnist or a popular T.V. soap writer is different. To be recognized as a classic novelist is a separate matter altogether which so far appears not to be her forte. Critics go to the extent of saying that De's books are packed with strange facts and handy tips, useful for only growing teens. However, in her T.V. interviews, she vehemently denies the charge and claims to have exposed the realities of life alone. A serious reader, however, fails to discern subtlety, sobriety or even understanding of complexities of human life in her novels.

N O T E

1. Shobha De, *Sisters* (New Delhi: Penguin, 1992), p. 12.

Lesbian Relationships in *Strange Obsession*

NEELAM TIKKHA

The novel *Strange Obsession*[1] is a masterpiece by Shobha De—her tour de force. It is a rebellious novel highlighting lesbian relationship. A look into lesbian philosophy will give a better comprehension of the novel. This essay attempts to explicate lesbianism and elucidate lesbian relationship in the novel *Strange Obsession*.

As lesbian, a woman's sexuality becomes the focal issue of dissent. Majority of women, both lesbian and heterosexual, are taught that their sexuality must conform to certain modes of behaviour. The society with its existent culture voices shame upon a woman if she goes beyond the criteria of passivity and repression, and doubts her virtue if she refuses. A woman is taught to suppress sexual desires and needs by conceding all pleasure to the male; even talking about participation and satisfaction in sex is taboo. So most women learn to hate their bodies and usually possess little knowledge of their bodies and their reproductive systems or their own physiology. Most just do not look down there.

Not loving the body affects how a woman perceives herself as a sexual being. As lesbians, however, they have no choice but to confront their sexuality before they can confront their lesbianism. Thus the commonly held viewpoint among heterosexuals that lesbians are "defined by their own sexuality" is, in a way, partially true. If lesbians did not bring their sexuality into consciousness, they would not be able to confront themselves and come out.

After confronting and then acknowledging the attraction, a lesbian must, in turn, learn to reclaim that what they are told is bad, wrong, dirty, and taboo—namely their bodies and their freedom to express themselves in them. Too often a woman internalizes the homophobia and sexism of the larger society, as well as that of their own culture, which attempts to keep her from loving herself. A woman must learn to love herself, both as a woman and a sexual being, before she can love another. Loving another woman not only validates one's own sexuality, but also that of the other woman, by the very act of loving. This means that she has to learn to love not only her own vagina, but someone else's too. It is only then that the subsequent experiences of love and commitment, passion and remorse can also become their dilemmas, much like those of everyone else. The effort to consciously reclaim her sexual selves forces a lesbian to either confront her own sexuality, or in refusing, castigate lesbians as blasphemers to God and atrocious to nature.

For many women, the identification is as complete women comes from the belief that they need to be connected to a man. Getting rid of this parasitic identification is not always easy, for a woman grows up defined in a male context: daddy's girl, some guy's girlfriend, wife or mother. Competing for a man's attention, she compromises her own personal and intellectual development. A woman exists in a patriarchal society that undervalues women. A woman is socialized to undervalue herself as well as anything associated with the concept of self. Her voice is considered less significant, her needs and desires secondary. The toleration of unjust behaviour from men, the established order, is considered an attribute. How much pain a woman can bear in the here-and-now that she may be better served in after-life? Martyrdom, the cloth of denial, transposes itself into a gown of cultural beauty.

Yet, an alliance with a man grants a woman heterosexual privileges, many of which are reified by the law, the religion and families. But, the woman has to pay its price at her own cost, since she has to destroy herself, her voice, intellect, and personal development, for a man's need, in these alliances. Moreover, in refusing to the ideal pattern of behaviour, the lesbian shuns the machinery, the main cog of which is respect for patriarchal dictates of ownership, thereby threatening to destabilize the system by usurping male privilege. In order to discourage such behaviour, the lesbian is marginalized, stigmatized and censured. Thus homosexuality is seen as counter-revolutionary.

Time and again, men insult a woman when they are unable to belittle her intellectual capacities. Historically, women have been viewed as property. Though some laws have changed ideologically little else has changed. The behaviours necessary in the act of pursuing a man creates a competition among women leading to betrayal of one another, in a way also sexual suspects to one another. The responsibility is placed entirely on the woman with little thought given to the suspected infidelity of the man.

A lesbian does not fit into this scheme, since she rejects compulsory heterosexuality. She also refuses to partake in the game of competition for man. She confronts her own sexuality and challenges the norms placed upon her by culture or society. The desire of the society is to overthrow her into proper roles and places. The very aspect of her existence does this whether consciously or unconsciously.

II

Shobha De in her revolutionary novel discusses the obsession of a lesbian called Minx. Meenakshi was the only child of her parents. Her father was in a powerful position in police—an I.G. Her mother's sickness and later institutionalization makes her psychologically sick. Moreover, she had got no motherly love and care. All love and care that she gets is from her father. She loves him so much that her love changes to obsession. She gets badly spoilt because of her father's love, affection and pampering. Her whole personality changes. To achieve what she wants she becomes a sly, clever and strong-headed girl.

Her father concedes even to her most unreasonable demands, as he puts it, when as a grown up girl she comes to him requesting him to destroy Partha:

> Mr. Iyengar answered thoughtfully. "I was always afraid of her . . . scared of her rage, unsure of what she might do if I reacted. She was crying. And I remembered the little girl without friends who used to crave her mother's company. I felt sorry and would've done anything she wanted me to." (204)

She longs for physical relationship with her father. Her father was denied sex since her mother was institutionalized. She feels it to be her moral duty to satisfy him. One can read between the lines from what she tells about her father to Amrita, that he was an upright man:

> He wasn't drunk. He doesn't touch the stuff. He was just horny. And frustrated . . . so frustrated I was too scared to do anything . . . say anything. I didn't ask . . . but he told me about my mother . . . that she refused to have sex with him. That she hated him. "I only have you now," he told me. And I felt guilty . . . of course I did. He made me feel it was my duty. You understand? My duty. If your mother doesn't you have to. (45)

Her transformation into a lesbian is due to an Electra complex. Minx is attracted towards her father when she is hardly thirteen years old. She deludes herself to the belief that it is not she who wants physical relationship but her father. Since sex with her father is incest so she imagines that he rapes her and colludes her to have sex. She rather pities her father for his sexless life and believes it to be her duty to fulfil his needs. This creates a psychological rift and leads to a pathetic condition. She is able to get what she wants but here she fails. She thus becomes a sexual competitor of her own mother. She also experiences a kind of patriarchy and also associates it with her childhood beatings, which she had got from her father. This also makes her counter revolutionary to the existent culture and society.

She withdraws from society. In childhood itself she becomes friendless. The isolation makes her psychologically sick. This failure in life makes her associate with bad company. She falls out of school and becomes friendly with local dadas. She develops hatred for her own father and every man. She becomes a lesbian and forcefully falls on an upcoming model—Amrita.

So strong is her obsession and desire for Amrita that she even murders Lola—a model—a competitor of Amrita. "Why what more do I have to do to prove myself? Kill? I'll do that too. Just tell me—who? You want me to kill someone? Anyone? I'll do it. I'll kill for you. I will Amrita . . . maybe then you'll love me . . . Will that make you happy? Will that please you? Then I'll do it—just tell me to, and I'll do it. I'll kill myself. I'll give you my life—what more can I give you?" (62-63)

Minx's obsession is nothing less than a mania. She cruelly and sadistically attacks Lola. "'It wasn't just an acid attack—the poor girl was carved up nicely. Her insides were minced and shoved through her vagina.'" (68)

She is so head-strong to win her love that she even undergoes surgery to remove her breasts. She somehow wants to please Amrita.

> No sweet heart. Nobody hurt me. Maybe I hurt myself. I thought it would make you happy. . . . It's a tits job. . . . Well . . . most women go to this surgeon for cosmetic surgery to enhance their breasts—boy! I could give you a few names—but I actually asked him to reduce mine. You know, slice them off. (93)

The use of the word slice them off shows how much she hates men. She is unable to bear what men like. "Don't ask me why, but I got the feeling you didn't like them—that their huge size put you off. I didn't like them either." (93) It is a kind of a counter-revolution against her father and society. She very potently challenges the society and its existent norms.

> Amrita had stared at the sight of Minx with her shirt off and those uneven red scars on her chest were making her feel sick. But she felt pity too, and perversely, for the first time, a feeling of sympathy for the wretched woman before her. She heard Minx's voice cracking as she carried on, "And then I met you . . . fell in love. A love so intense I felt my body would burst. I thought I saw revulsion in your eyes when you looked at me, especially when I thought I saw you staring at my ugly enormous breasts. Two weeks ago I decided to chop them off." (93)

This is the point when Amrita is initiated into perversion and develops feelings for Minx. Minx works her way to win Amrita's heart by undergoing through pain and torture. So deep is her desire and so strong her obsession that she is ready to do anything for her. She expresses herself thus:

> Believe me, baby, it wasn't easy. I was scared. I could tell no one, consult no one. But each time I was nervous and tense about the step I was going to take, I thought of you and the expression in your eyes. And then I knew I had to do it. And I knew you'd like what I'd done and like me also. (93)

Amrita feels pity and is drawn close to her. This is the point when she starts feeling for her:

> Minx removed her clothes one by one and placed them neatly on a chair close to the bed. Amrita was suddenly conscious, very conscious, of Minx's touch as each nerve ending in her body came alive under her probing fingers and tongue. The crickets outside her window set up a noisy chorus as Amrita struggled not to lose herself entirely to what was happening to her. Minx had taken each one of her toes into her mouth and was massaging them with her tongue, while her hands reached between Amrita's legs and touched her with rhythmic stabs. She felt her legs open *almost voluntarily*, as Minx climbed upon her, straddling her slim hips with her own, covering her breasts with her hands, cupping the nipples and circling them repeatedly till they ached with a sweet pain. Amrita had never known anything like this . . . never. She moaned with pleasure as Minx brought her to peak, again and again, starting where she'd left off each time she felt Amrita's body going slack under her. After what must have been two hours, they fell into a light sleep with Amrita's head cradled in the crook of Minx's arms, their legs entangled. (94)

This is where her future gets inextricably linked with Minx. Amrita in fact starts responding to the crazy love of Minx except the relationship hurts her for the reason that she will never be able to become pregnant. Despite all this after sometime Amrita's life falls into a pattern. As she admits to Minx's father: "I began to enjoy it. To respond I became dependent I thought we'd spend our life together." (204) In fact, it is a mutual response from both. Amrita feels close to Minx since she fulfils most of her needs, so love is from within and not without. She also helps her in developing her career. Amrita has everything, a good house, somebody taking care of her finances. She is taken care of very well. The only thing she lacks is a child. If that need could be fulfilled, she would prefer this relationship to a heterosexist one.

She is divided into two: to accept relationship that goes against the norms of society and the relationship that makes her safe and secure but cannot fill her womb.

She always feels love and pity for Minx. She cries for help when Minx is caught in fire. She shudders when she reads her obituary. Her captivity was self-imposed.

For Minx, lesbianism was a result of hatred and fear of deception from men. It was a revolt against society and norms laid down to under-rate women. By belonging to Amrita, protecting and helping her, she posed a great threat to male dominance and disrupted patriarchal oppression.

NOTE

1. Shobha De, *Strange Obsession* (Delhi: Penguin, 1992).

Strange Obsession: A Critical Study

GAJENDRA KUMAR

Shobha De burst upon the literary scene in 1988, with her tour de force *Socialite Evenings* which was followed by *Starry Nights* in 1990 and *Strange Obsession* in 1992. She shot into fame and popularity on account of her thematic choice, narratology and brilliant use of language. In the theoretical and structural analysis, her novels are considered to be the modern edition of picaresque novels. As a leading exponent of journalism, she founded and edited three covetous magazines—*Stardust*, *Society* and *Celebrity* and worked in the capacity of consulting Editor to *Sunday* and *Megacity*. Because of her profound experience as a journalist, she is capable of exploring and analyzing the content and context of the creativity with courage and conviction. De's creative output seems to be a monument of her intimate understanding of the psyche and self of women.

Shobha De is considered to be an *avant garde* in the realm of popular fiction writing. She also claims to be "among the first to explore the world of the urban woman in India."[1] De's novels and essays are supposed to be a creative endeavour to shatter patriarchal hegemony. Just after the publication of the best seller *Socialite Evenings*, De was branded as a "high society potpourri, bland and banal," bristling with orgy-laced parties and "voyeuristic servings of souped-up, four-wheel-drive-sex-in-all-direction."[2] One of the critics analyzed it "choked with listless lust" and criticized its "witless dialogue."[3] Even *Starry Nights* is described as "confession of a man-eater."[4] De's novels are not simply a series of 'bodice ripper.' According to Penguin's editor David Davidar, they are serious attempts at "discovering India through Indian eyes."[5] De's treatment of the "contemporary Indian woman's challenges, predicament, values and life-style is surely not without significance."[6] She herself would examine the treatment of the woman question as the most significant contribution made by her work. She once said, "I write with a great deal of empathy towards women. Without waving the feminist flag, I feel very strongly about the woman's situation."[7]

Shobha De's explosive novel *Strange Obsession* revolves around the life and lustful relationship of two young women, Amrita and Meenakshi. Fundamentally, it seems to be a psychological documentation of sexual obsession of mysterious woman Meenakshi, also known as Minx, and her calamitous end. Amrita, who comes from a noble and educated family, decides to search her lot in modelling. In order to execute her long cherished desire, she settles down in Bombay. In Bombay, she encounters Minx, a modern high flown lady, free from all taboos and values. Being a daughter of Inspector General, she is always conscious of exploiting the power and position for her gimmicks. She is very much pervert and polluted in her thought and plan. Even in the initial meeting with Amrita, "Meenakshi stared into the most beautiful eyes she had ever seen and forgot what she wanted to say." (5) Amrita finds herself unable to conceive the unusual and crazy feeling of Minx and utters: "But let alone a woman, no man had ever looked at her the way Minx just had. And no previous compliment had affected her in the same manner."[8] Both of them represent the different kinds of typology of modern urban set up. They seem to be hardly better than school girls playing adult games. It is through their behaviour and conversation that Shobha De throws significant light on the predicament of these two young women.

Strange Obsession does not deal with the struggle for power and feminism. Minx is a lesbian, an eccentric who behaves like a male. She is thoroughly deprived of womanliness. On the thematic plane there does not seem to be a question of power. But on the theoretical plane, it is difficult to disagree with the basic questions of power-pleasure as Foucault underlines. In her theoretical perspective, Shobha De argues: "Eventually, every relationship is a power struggle either on an overt or subliminal level. The very concept of the sexes locked in eternal battle is negative and destructive."[9]

In the sociological context, Shobha De's novels have emphasized the values of different socio-economic set up and the value of equivalence of power. Whenever this balance collapses, there is tension in society and double-dealings and hypocrisy predominate. Even in the relationship between Minx and Amrita, there is social and mental imbalance. The problem of social equivalence is due to difference in social set up. Bombay is different from Delhi. Bombay is more self-centred and profession-oriented than Delhi. Karan, a photographer before snapping Amrita says, "but to me, a model is a model—a subject for my camera. Nothing more. You could be a vase of flowers or an ice cube." (11)

Creative writing often has two-fold dimensions. First of all it functions as a safety valve to release the pressure mounting up within the artist and secondly as a sensitive being, an artist wants to project the picture of society. Unlike R.K. Narayan, Mulk Raj Anand and Bhabani Bhattacharya who have devoted themselves mostly to the portrayal of socio-political reality, Shobha De explores the inner and psychic reality. Her creative venture does not focus the one-tenth visible section of the iceberg that one sees above the surface of the ocean but the remaining nine-tenths of it that lie below the surface. She prefers to delve deeper in a character or a scene, rather than going round about it. She prefers the private to the public world.

Psychologically, Minx is a case in study. In psycho-analytical framework, Minx is a fit case to be treated as pervert, obsessed and crazy who manipulates Amrita, a young lady full of love, warmth and innocence. Even in fictive terms, Amrita proves to be a nectar for Minx as her name connotes. Amrita once rebukes Minx by saying "Weird and abnormal.' Minx through her shrewd effort tries to allure her:

> What are you talking about? You think I'm a bloody lesbian, don't you? Well, guess what? You are wrong. And so are all of them who've been telling you that. I'm not a dyke. I'm not kinky. And I'm certainly not crazy . . . but I'm in love with you, I love you. I adore you. It is not sexual. I don't wish to go to bed with you. All I want is to be around you. (22)

Minx knows what she is. She, consciously or subconsciously, identifies herself in negation. She is extremely passionate for Amrita and sometimes becomes violent. Out of her intense sexual feeling, Minx utters: "Sweet, Sweet Amrita, you have become a part of me. You live right here in my body. I can feel your presence inside me all the time." (23)

To the novelist everyone needs to get sexual encounter. It is something special, something beautiful, something shared. The woman would get sex on her terms now. The very fact, De adds, "that sex is no longer the most dreaded and despised three-letter word in India, is enough cause to celebrate."[10] But there is nothing derogatory or clandestine in sex. In fact, sex is the bed-rock of all relationships. De nowhere approves the role model of Minx. A woman cannot be contented with lesbianism, she needs to get a loving support of man. In no way, lesbianism can be a substitute of heterosexuality. In *Starry Nights*, Shobha De shows a conflict between tradition and modernity. It is true that the sexual act could not be considered as something to be avoided in life or in literature. The lower animals are there to make it as public as possible. But in his inborn sense of superiority to animals, no man would accept behaving like them. Thus, through Malini in *Starry Nights*, the novelist focuses on the traditional sanctity of the sexuality though she herself does not believe in such orthodox views. "Sex! That is all you have—Sex! That is what women like you use. Cheap bitches—part your legs and get any man in. Sex, sex, sex, dirty, filthy sex!"[11]

In any given society, the attitude its literature shows towards sex is largely shaped by the attitude of its Religion and Morality. In India sex is accepted as one of the legitimate functions of man and woman. The only restriction is that the description must be in accordance with the rules both of Kamasastra and of Rhetorics. In case of the relationship between Amrita and Minx, the socio-psychological situation is altogether different. This kind of relationship cannot be termed as adultery, incest or illegitimate; rather it is something unnatural, unexpected or a part of abnormal psychology. Amrita has natural inclination for heterosexuality but Minx has almost developed abhorrence for it. She is not ready to allow Amrita to get or select a boy friend for her. Minx, out of her utter possessiveness, says, "I love you. I have to protect you. It's my duty." (36)

Minx does not have any emotional feeling for Amrita. She compels Amrita to search her love and lot in her (Minx). To Minx, same sex does not create any hurdle. Minx says, "Why does it make you sick? Why should it? Because I belong to the same sex? Is that my only sin?" (44) She says that "there is nothing abnormal about my feeling for you." (44) Shobha De recommends a mature attitude to sex. It is not like baby food. She says, "I love sex like I love food. It's same sort of hunger." But nowhere she pleads woman to woman sexuality. Minx enjoyed sexual encounter with Amrita. But just after this experience, Amrita became conscious of her guilt. She is conscious of her sexual identity and so she raises a question to Minx when she argues for the satisfaction of Amrita, "You want a prick to enter you—I'll go out and get one." (110) The woman in Amrita replies, "You may be able to get some quack to stitch on a plastic disk. But will that make me pregnant? Will you be able to fill my womb with a child?" (110)

Lesbianism is a psychological perversion, an obsession and something like eccentricity. It should not be a part of feminism. Feminism as such has to attempt a new definition of woman's role in the wider social frame. In the name of women's lib Minx and Minx-like cannot be justified. Shobha De herself makes her stand clear when Minx's mother says, "My daughter is the severely disturbed child of a disturbed mother. She suffers from delusions, she tells lies, she make s up stories, the number of schools she has been expelled from have their own tales to tell." (203) Amrita is saved by her husband. At last Minx dies and Amrita feels liberated.

According to the feminist theory, sex does not mean sexuality or sexual preference which stands for a person's pattern of erotic attraction. Similarly, gender does not apparently correspond to sexuality. Robyn R. Warhol analyzes this complexity: "a person of the female sex who is erotically attracted primarily to persons of her own sex (who may or may not refer to herself as lesbian, another term whose definition is under debate within feminism,) might be either strongly feminine or strongly masculine in her gendered self-presentation, or most likely—her gender identity would, like most homosexual persons, be made up of a complicated combination of gender 'differences within.'"[12]

NOTES

1. C.P. Surendran, "Just Another De," *The Illustrated Weekly of India*, 6 Nov. 1992.

2. Madhu Jain, "Cat on a Cold Tin Roof," *India Today*, 15 October 1989, p. 195.
3. Sunil Sethi, "De in, De out," *Seminar*, August 1991, p. 41.
4. Madhu Jain, p. 195.
5. Sarita Vellani, "Interview with David Davidar," *Seminar*, 384, August 1, 1991, p. 43.
6. R.S. Pathak, "Feminist Concerns in Shobha De's *Snapshots*" in *Feminism and Literature: New Points of View*, ed. K.K. Sharma (Delhi: K.K. Pub., 1996), p. 61.
7. *The Hindustan Times*, Magazine, 12 February 1995, p. 3.
8. Shobha De, *Strange Obsession* (New Delhi: Penguin India, 1992), p. 6.
9. Shobha De, *Shooting from the Hip, Selected Writings* (New Delhi: UBS, 1994), pp. 111-13.
10. Khushwant Singh and Shobha De, ed., *Uncertain Liaisons: Sex, Strife and Togetherness in Urban India* (New Delhi: Viking/Penguin India, 1993), pp. xxi, 208.
11. Shobha De, *Starry Nights* (New Delhi, Penguin India, 1991), p. 106.
12. "Feminism," *The Oxford Companion to Women's Writing in the United States* (New York: Oxford University Press) 1995, p. 310.

Return of Shobha De to the Mainstream'New Woman': A Study of *Sultry Days*

SHARAD SHRIVASTAVA

At the outset it needs to be clarified that the 'new woman' of this study is not merely an aggregate of certain personality traits to be studied through the methodology of social sciences. She is a being in her own right who is in the process of becoming. She seeks self-fulfilment through self-expression in a milieu where there is mutuality, understanding and tenderness. In this sense the 'new woman' is different from the modern woman whose prime concerns are dominance and self-assertion. The study treats such women as "aberrations." Majority of the women characters of Shobha De's novels belong to this category. These women totally disregard the basic spiritual and moral concerns of the woman. They represent an entirely different value-system.

However, in the process of development of art, one often comes across such 'sallies' but they are always brief; art returns to the mainstream of spiritual and moral values. So, such 'sallies' which might dazzle for a short spell cannot become a different or a parallel stream which branches off from the mainstream and continues its separate course. Hence, we have called the women characters of Shobha De as "aberrations."

Shobha De begins this dazzling 'sally' with her first novel *Socialite Evenings* and continues this through *Starry Nights, Sisters* and *Strange Obsession*. Yet a stage comes when she, too, acknowledges the need that the author must return to the mainstream for after these she comes out with *Sultry Days*, about which she says on the title page itself: "Finally a book by me, that they [my children] can read."

The fifth novel of Shobha De, *Sultry Days* does contain women who are obsessed with men; they, too, indulge in beating men at their own game but here we also come across some glimpses of commitment, thereby giving credence to the fact that not all writings of Shobha De are 'aberrations' and that there is a possibility of even her returning to the mainstream of writing after a few 'sallies.'

Unlike *Socialite Evenings* and *Starry Nights, Sultry Days* has apparently a man as the central character. The narrator or the protagonist, is, however, a woman but it is through the male character Deb that Nisha discovers herself. From the beginning we become aware of Nisha's attraction for Deb who is also referred to as God by most of his college chums. She is attracted to Deb because he is a mixture of opposites. His appearance is shabby, wears days's old stubble, always scratches his 'matted locks which were full of lice-nests,' smokes 'beedies,' is a man of loose morals, 'has had several girls by the time he reached college.' His attitude towards girls is also simple—'use them and leave them.' Despite his shabby appearance, 'God's hands and fingernails were surprisingly, neat and clean.' He knows many languages such as German, French and Spanish. He had already read Chaucer and Karl Marx before leaving school. He is the son of a communist and himself a communist, gets arrested while taking out Morchas.

God's entry into the 'literary circuit' is through proof-checking but he soon discovers that he can do more than just read other people's proofs. With his association with Art Magazine *Plume*, God's career takes an upward turn. It is actually the beginning of the death of the rebel and the visionary in him.

Now, God starts sinking in the estimate of Nisha. To her God had at one time symbolized 'commitment' but gradually he loses all shreds of self-respect. As for Nisha, hers is a very ordinary course of life wherein she tries to make her mark through sheer hard work and application. Although herself a member, yet she always remains at the periphery of affluent and glamorous life. In other words, she is quite unlike the other women of Shobha De who revel in the life of glamour and sex. Here it may be remarked that it is the 'commitments' of God that help Nisha to remain at the periphery of such a life.

As God gets more and more the taste of 'power' and 'money,' his commitments appear to be psuedo-commitments. Although Nisha does not have any pronounced commitments of her own yet her constant companionship with Deb reveals the gulf between herself and Deb's psuedo-commitments. That she does not approve of God's 'new' way of life is made clear several times by her in the course of the narrative. One such reaction would suffice here:

> No I didn't like what was happening to God at all. We were beginning to see less and less of each other now that he didn't need to touch me for cash that often. He was getting ahead professionally, meeting all the VIPs in town, interviewing culture-vultures and generally being wooed by 'all those who mattered' in the high-life of the city. (100)

Even the occasional meeting between Nisha and God turns out to be a confrontation. After one such 'meeting' God calls her 'Jhooti bitch' and Nisha's rejoinder is 'capitalist Kutta.' This is the nadir of their relationship. It is actually the point when Nisha has completely seen through his co-called 'commitments.'

And simply by not becoming a part of God's psuedo-commitments, Nisha begins to discover her own commitments. Her commitment towards the end of the novel emerges as a commitment to a cause. She exposes Yashwantbhai through her write-ups and remains undeterred despite God's warnings 'to keep herself off by having anything to do with Yashwantbhai and his underworld connections.' She is joined in her 'cause' by her mother and her activist friend Pratimaben. Nisha's mother and Pratimaben are out to expose Yashwantbhai on the issue of his 'atrocities' on Pramila with whom Yashwantbhai had an illicit relationship for some time. Thus, we see that by dedicating herself to a 'cause,' the character of Nisha rises. Actually Nisha's rise has to be seen in the context of the degeneration of God's character. It is only when Nisha has some inkling of her 'commitments' that she is able to seek some kind of an identification with the women and menfolk of the middle class also.

In the novel, there is one woman character whose experience sums up in a nutshell the cause charted by women characters whom we have called 'aberrations.' It also shows that the only ray of hope for such women is to return to their roots and join the mainstream. This woman character is Pramila.

Pramila is a Nagpur woman who has everything that a traditional woman can ask for—"a husband with a 'solid' job, security, lovely children, a moped of her own and all the time in the world to pursue her interests," (160) yet she feels bored, suffocated and frustrated in this environment. She has talent. This puts ideas in her head and she sets on the road of becoming an emancipated woman. She starts writing poems and within a year she decides that Nagpur is not the place for her and her talents. Suddenly, without informing anyone she goes to Bombay. There her poems are translated into English and she moves from success to success.

In order to become 'the completely emancipated woman' she divorces her husband and takes her two daughters with her. These, then are the stages in the path of her becoming the emancipated woman: boredom and frustration with her surrounding, disappearing from Nagpur and appearing on the Bombay scene, taking up English writing and discarding Marathi and divorcing her husband. In this world of glamour, a stage comes when she overreaches herself. She miscalculates that Yashwantbhai, an underworld king and mafia don is in her power. This results in a traumatic experience wherein her life is threatened and she is forced to go in hiding.

After the traumatic experience, Nisha is for some time a shattered woman but when her mother and Pratimaben find her out and take up her cause against Yashwantbhai, she discovers a new meaning in life. She fearlessly exposes Yashwantbhai. Though she does not succeed in making any impression upon Yashwantbhai and though she knows that Yashwantbhai's present inaction does not mean that he has accepted defeat and that he is coolly waiting for the time when he can strike back, yet Pramila has found a cause. The cause is to join the movement which seeks to expose persons like Yashwantbhai. This changes her life and she returns to the roots where she belongs. The narrator describes her 'return' in the following way:

> She was back with her old Maharashtrian publishing cronies. Back to the people she had arrogantly rejected before moving on to the glamorous world of English language journalism. Shruti (her daughter) was going to a neighbourhood Marathi medium school and Pramila was busy putting together a collection of Marathi poems in tortured metre. (224)

Snapshots: A Postcolonial Text

MADHUMALATI ADHIKARI

Colonial consciousness/ patriarchal power structure creates, encourages and nurtures typical psycho-physical tendencies that construct different perceptions in the colonizer and the colonized. The characteristics of colonization—suppression, domination, assumed superiority, exploitation—penetrate deep into the culture and literature of the particular society. As a result, various forms of retardation, reaction and inferiorization continue to play their damaging roles. It is reflected in the warped psychology and fragmented personality of the colonized people: a paradoxical attitude that adores and condemns concurrently the imposition of a foreign rule and a way of life. "Colonialism is not only about the exploitation of countries with resources, cheap labour and less technological power. It is also about assuming unquestioningly, the right to change these cultures, economically, and more invidiously, textually, in ways entirely foreign to them."[1]

Colonialism gives rise to open rebellion or secret revolt carried out by defiant groups who despite outward submission continue the slow process of carving out a free space for themselves through inscribed or oral literature. Inscription of this process is accelerated in postcolonial text and yet, one becomes conscious of two paradoxical forces that act and react on each other: first, a nostalgia for things when slavery was a blessing and second, a condemnation of the degrading experience. Thus, valorization and denunciation of colonialism, quite often, is to be found in the postcolonial literature. Along with this blending, one can perceive the absorption of certain cultural and intellectual traits of the ruling powers into the native consciousness. It tends to become embedded firmly and as a result, it becomes difficult to recognize it as an alien attribute; it is accepted as a prevalent reality:

a step towards modernity and progress.

In India, postcolonial literature is marked by an awakening of the 'self.' The male writers have concentrated on the socio-economic changes and conflicts and the female writers, inspired by the Western Feminist Movement have moved inward to record the intimate experiences and demands of the female psyche. On their widened canvas, they have projected and accommodated the needs, ambitions and struggles of the modern woman. The articulation initially subdued, is now clear, confident and vociferous. Female Commonwealth writers like Margaret Atwood (*The Handmaid's Tale*), Jean Rhys (*Wide Sargasso Sea*), Shashi Deshpande (*That Long Silence*), Shobha De (*Starry Nights*), Kamala Markandaya (*Pleasure City*), Bapsi Sidhwa (*An American Brat*) and many others have visualized patriarchy as a colonial system. Feminist literature compares woman's culture to colonial culture wherein she is exploited, abused and silenced by masculine power: the controlling authority is no outsider but an integral member of the community. Colonial inscription historically, mythologically and socially depicts women as archetypes of powerlessness. Bound and tamed with St. Paul like injunctions, 'I permit no woman to teach . . . she is to keep silent,' woman is ruled by the dominant gender. Shobha De in *Snapshots* has rearranged the equation of the power game wherein woman either controls power or is in a position to ignore the prescriptions of male authority. The drama of the novel has the backdrop of Bombay in the last decade of the present century. In this paper, I would like to argue that historically, thematically, psychologically and culturally *Snapshots* portrays the ambience of a postcolonial era.

Judith Fetterly rightly observes, "Literature is political" and it has a "palpable design" on the reader; it claims to enjoy "universality" but it has "a different reality and different vision."[2] The bulk of Indian literature claims to be universal but its spirit is patriarchal. It seldom records a Woman's story in its entirety. Shobha De reconstructs the tradition and explores the experiences of six women—Swati, Aparna, Reema, Noor, Surekha and Rashmi—now living in magnified domestic bliss. These six characters form the core of the novel and the males are shifted to the periphery. This revolution in gender politics could never be envisioned in the age of aggressive imperialism.

In *Snapshots*, the British colonial regime is a long forgotten chapter of history and yet, these six girls while being students of Santa Maria

High School, had absorbed the traits of colonial education. Despite their childhood training, they are very much Indian with a leaning towards western outlook and life-style. This is the result of East-West cultural integration, a post independence phenomenon. De presents a candid picture of metropolitan life-style through a modified or more often, a transformed version of traditional values. Not many writers have dared to bare the postcolonial scenario. Surekha, a middle class housewife, pretends to be very concerned about her mother-in-law but the hard truth behind this praiseworthy act is her homosexual interest in her friend Dolly. (152)[3] This truth of cosmopolitan Bombay reflects the psychological separation of Indian women. Surekha manages to keep her husband happy and yet, insures a space of her own. The scripting of female ownership is a recent development in Indian-English literature. Manu's diktats regarding female behaviour is openly flouted by De. No longer is woman a scrubbing maid and a docile bed-partner. She manipulates to live lavishly like Reema by controlling her husband's sexual urges. Reema claims confidenlty, "My husband is lost without me . . . feed them well. Fuck them regularly and sit tight." (151) She enjoys an illicit relationship with her own brother-in-law Randhir and suffers from no 'guilty' feelings. The "patriarchal enclosure of marriage"[4] had failed to trap her. Interestingly, matrimony has granted greater power to her. She negates the concept of marriage present in Hawthorne's *The Birthmark* that paints the picture of man's power and woman's powerlessness. The colonial rule of the husband is deactivated in *Snapshots*. Reema has only one daughter and she has refused to become a child-producing machine. During her school-going years, she had conceived her boy-friend Raju's child. At that point of time, she was the victim and he the victimizer. But very soon, Raju had lost the battle; his body as was found near a "sewage dump." (101) Postcolonial fiction of Shobha De is not an effort to reclaim lost treasures of tradition but to move ahead with the changed moods of society.

Aparna's metamorphosis in the novel is very transparent. She moves from the colonial to the postcolonial emotional dynamics of woman. "Aparna had grown up with shame. Shame about her body. Shame about her adolescent looks. . . . Shame about practically every aspect of her life. It was the environment she was raised in. Guilt was its defining feature." (6) But she is not fragmented by the psychology of "guilt" and "inferiorization"[5] instilled in her by society. She revolts and uses her "sexual potential" (7) to enjoy life. Very often, she participates in erotic sexual behaviour and initiates the entire exercise. (7) She is aware that it is "lust" and yet, she is ashamed of her feelings. With a vengeance she goes for "demaximization"[6] of the self. Aparna is a divorcee; undeterred, she reaches the top rung of the corporate ladder; nothing can undermine her confidence and wholeness. In her social and professional sphere, her conduct is anti-patriarchal/anti-colonial. To her, "husband" is an "awful" word. (24) "Marriage the destiny traditionally offered by society"[7] to woman, is rejected by Aparna. She refuses to become the "colony" of man. The patented brand of truths associated with the institution of marriage is erased by De. Fidelity, once a test of womanhood, is turned into a concept of limited possibility. Implicitly or explicitly, all the participants of this drama seem to agree with Reema's point of view, "Imagine not knowing any other body, any other feeling, any other sensation. Forever. Sounds terrible. Like eating dal-chaval day in and day out." (152) The emancipated psychology and roles of women have an "imaginative continuum" in postcolonial literature varying from bold to very bold.

The novel erases all impressions of the British Raj though the legacy of servility is reflected in a preference for convent education for the girls. The world of these characters is surely more occidental than oriental but it must be realized that cultural isolation is a concept of the past. The relation with the opposite sex is very much liberalized, for women. Gender prejudice entertained by the patriarchal society is reduced to a great extent. In the literal sense, racial discrimination, the hallmark of the colonial temper, is quite absent from the novel but metaphorically, Swati, now a resident of London, exemplifies the superior psychology of the masters. As a representative of the colonial power, she treats her native friends with condescension; she always had "some kind of power" (181) over them. Her capacity to "manipulate" (183) is recognized universally and yet the novel closes with the impression that despite her power, generated by the "electronic bugs," (218) she is made powerless. The dissolution of cultural imperialism and scientific advantage is denoted by Swati's loss of power. The indigenous way of life, though quite westernized, triumphs in the end.

In colonial literature woman's desire for economic self-sufficiency is either ostracized socially or ignored completely. But De's women, realizing that female empowerment is a product of financial independence, are very often career-minded personalities. Man's insistence on economic control emerges from his knowledge of the best way to keep women/slaves paralyzed. Shashi Deshpande's female protagonist in *That Long Silence* is less independent than her illiterate maid who earns her own livelihood. Shobha De has granted financial freedom to her female creatures in *Snapshots*. They either earn individually or control the finances of their husbands by their cleverness. De has given a new format of conflict that stems from the desire to monitor money-matters.

Each female character in *Snapshots* desires for power, enjoys power and battles to control power. Power-conscious ambitious females are the product of postcolonial culture. The realization that their power is rooted in their sexuality, it has a "potential" (7) and it is not a "danger,"[8] has enabled them to challenge the traditional concept of morality. Champa Bai the prostitute is self-aware to claim, "We are here to satisfy their lust not for sex but for power." (43) Her claim concretizes woman's role in the game of power. The conventional woman is a model of physical exploitation but De's women, in this particular novel, are the masters of their destiny. This makes Balbir, Reema's brother-in-law, ask the girls, "Do you fuck because you enjoy fucking? Or is it power-play." (162) De, along with other feminist writers, challenges the traditional values of womanhood. The institution of marriage and family, work culture related to woman's domestic and non-domestic duties are openly questioned and deconstructed. In De's fictional world, successful working women are no Utopian dreams. They live their lives as they please and take care of their mental health.

Jean Rhys in *Wide Sargasso Sea* creates a colonial background, narrates a colonial story but conveys a non-colonial theme. Shobha De boldly rejects all kinds of subterfuge and communicates the unprintable aspects of woman's story. The general ambience and the style of communication, are postcolonial. For De's women, silence is not golden; they speak distinctly; use forbidden words and have gained the right to use the male sexual vocabulary. Though De often reflects on the plight of neglected wives, yet in *Snapshots* the married women enjoy an autonomy that can be a matter of envy for many. De has transformed the traditional images of women and opposed the move to relegate woman's experience and woman's body language to the second rank. *Snapshots* embodies the spirit of postcolonial literature that concretizes the adventures of powerful, emancipated new woman.

NOTES

1. Elivi Whattakar, "Towards Feminist Ethic and Methodology," *The India-Canada Relationship*, ed. J.S. Grewal and Hugh Johnston (New Delhi: Sage, 1994), p. 346.
2. Judith Fetterley, "On the Politics of Literature," *Feminism: An Anthology of Literary Theory and Criticism*, ed. Robyn R. Warhol and Diana Price Herndle (N. Brunswick, NJ: Rutgers University Press, 1991), p. 492.
3. Shobha De, *Snapshots* (New Delhi: Penguin, 1995).
4. Annis Pratt, *The Archetypal Patterns in Women's Fiction* (Bloomington: Indiana University Press, 1981), p. 45.
5. Sandra M. Gilbert and Susan Gubar, *The Mad Woman in the Attic: The Woman Writer and the Nineteenth Century Literary Imagination* (New Haven, Conn.: Yale University Press, 1979), p. 50.
6. Nancy K. Miller, "Plots and Possibilities in Women's Fiction," *The New Feminist Criticism*, ed. Elaine Showalter (New Pantheon Books, 1985), p. 341.
7. Simone de Beauvoir, *The Second Sex*, trans. H.M. Parshley (Penguin, 1983), p. 445.
8. Patricia Meyer Spacks, *The Female Imagination* (New York: Avon, 1975), p. 200.

"The Medium is the Message": A Study of *Snapshots*

URBASHI BARAT

The title of Shobha Dé's latest novel[1] says it all. If this assessment sounds rather flippant, it is deliberately so, for Dé herself seems to be rather flippant in her novel. Pop fiction at its most readable, *Snapshots* is also pop philosophy and pop sociology, everything, that is, that the word "snapshot" calls up. A snapshot represents a snatched moment in time, a frozen memento, a source of reminiscence, but it is not associated with the sophistication and artistry of a "photograph." Obviously meant to be a bestseller in the Jackie Collins-Sidney Sheldon mould, Dé's *Snapshots* seems to be written in haste: there are several lapses in style and occasional slips in time-sequence, and episodes and characters are sometimes quite gratuitously introduced without being integrally linked to the story and having, therefore, quite frequently the effect of mere titillation: its picture of society is apparently based on popular women's fiction and soap operas of the West rather than on the Indian reality. Not, of course, that the rape, incest, lesbianism, the sexual promiscuity and perversions described in the novel do not exist in India (the agony-aunt columns in our newspapers and magazines are enough proof that far more shocking things go on under the facade of conventional morality); but the overemphatic exclusion of everything else, the occasionally contrived situation, and the crude language the characters speak, are unrealistic, and cheapen the impact of the novel. Dé is, moreover, surprisingly careless about details. For instance, someone called Aruna is suddenly mentioned as late as on page 218 as being present at the party, but she does not appear anywhere else; and at the end of the novel, the confusion in "Aparna glanced about the room. While the young girl had been talking to her, Aparna and Rashmi had disappeared" (233) dissipates the carefully built up tension in this climactic scene.

But there is more to *Snapshots* than cynical and slipshod journalese. The novel gets its title, of course, from the snapshots of a shared past that the six women of the story—Aparna, Rashmi, Swati, Reema, Surekha and Noor—are to bring to their reunion, and which, or so says the glamorous singer-actress Swati, who has so meticulously planned things out, will help them to remember and to catch up with each other. The snapshots thus link the characters together as they also link their past to their present; static souvenirs themselves, they set off a trail of memories that had lain hidden beneath the surface of everyday existence. Dé here uses the popular literary technique of exploring the lives of individuals within a closed environment for a brief period of time from shifting points of view, so that there is no one protagonist, and the different stories of the different characters make up a mosaic that represents the novelist's vision of life. This is, for instance, Arthur Hailey's particular forte, as seen in novels like *Hotel* and *Airport*; this is also, and more frequently, the basis of many significant films, such as *Grand Hotel*, the landmark film of the late twenties, or the more recent *Aranyer Din Ratri* and *Shakha-Proshakha* by Satyajit Ray. Shobha Dé began her literary career, after all, as a film journalist with the USP of colloquial gossip-mongering.

Not surprisingly, the novel reads like a film that depends largely on montage—itself resembling a series of snapshots significantly juxtaposed against one another—and editing for its effects. It is here that the interest of *Snapshots* lies: its technique of narration. In her earlier novels, Dé has generally followed the more traditional linear mode, occasionally branching out into the archetypal feminine cyclic narration; *Snapshots* marks a definite change in her technique, and, consequently, a change in her vision of life. For, as Mark Schorer has pointed out, technique is no "external machination; a mechanical affair, but a deep and primary operation; not only that technique *contains* intellectual and moral implications, but that it *discovers* them."[2] Not only is the meaning of the novel conveyed through its technique; the technique *is* the meaning, so that understanding the one is to discover the other. In Marshall McLuhan's famous formulas, "the medium is the message." McLuhan was, of course, speaking of communications technology, and *Snapshots* is a novel, and as a literary product should be beyond the scope of what is known in popular parlance as "the media." But literature itself is a communication of experience, which is the primary function of the media too. Indeed, even society, observes Raymond Williams, is "a form of communication, through which experience is described, shared, modified and preserved."[3]

Dé's choice of the cinematic technique is not just to popularize her novel and bring it into the tradition of the fiction of the media but an attempt to communicate a vision of life. This technique can be summed up in Evelyn Waugh's comments on Graham Greene: "It is as though, out of an infinite length of film, sequences had been cut which, assembled, comprise an experience which is the reader's alone without any correspondence to the experience of the protagonist. The writer has become director and producer."[4] Like Green, indeed, Dé owes much to the two techniques mentioned above, montage and editing, both of which, incidentally, have a snapshot-like effect. Greene has defined montage as "the production of a concept or sensation through the mutual impact of other conceptions or sensations; in its structural aspect, the juxtaposition of shots, series and sequences in such a way as to produce this impact";[5] and Sergei Eisenstein describes its effect in these terms: "By what, then, is montage characterized? . . . The collision. By the conflict of two pieces in opposition to each other. By conflict. By collision."[6] Pudovkin's explanation of film editing is similar: "The film is not *shot*, but *built*, built up from the separate strips of celluloid that are its raw material."[7] Though there are fundamental differences between Eisenstein's notion of intellectual montage and Pudovkin's belief in cuts and transitions, both are concerned with the importance of introducing discontinuity into linear narrative, to indicate the emotional contrast and equivalence and the simultaneity of corresponding events and characters and to suggest what anchors a series of images to a motif or an *idee fixe*. In *Snapshots,* the influence of film editing is seen particularly in the use of cross-cuts, contrast cuts, dissolves, flashbacks, and the occasional substitute image, while the shifting point of view achieves a multiple viewpoint that gives the novel a feeling of synchronicity, so that in the end the experience of one becomes a metaphor for life and society as a whole.

The novel consists of fourteen chapters, each divided into a number of sections separated from one another by cuts, so that each section is as if it were complete in itself, and each chapter a montage of snapshots, the entire novel being linked together by the transitional device of the thematic montage. A brief look at the two opening chapters will indicate how Dé works. Chapter 1 opens with the attention-riveting statement: "Prem liked to make love in public places." (1) But the point of view is not Prem's but Aparna's; this is in fact the only chapter in the novel that begins with a sentence about someone who is never at any point a centre of consciousness, and its purpose here is obvious: its immediate soft-porn appeal for the casual reader—say, the traveller at the railway station bookstall—that might tempt him (and perhaps her too) to go through the book.

But it serves another function as well. This chapter and part of the next is devoted to Aparna. By beginning with a statement about what Aparna thinks are her sexual partner's likes, it makes clear that it is not she but the man who is in control of the situation. Aparna may be the successful career woman, but she is always at the mercy of the predatory male who wishes to use women. It is Prem who always takes the initiative and the upper hand in their sexual relationship, although he may be her employee; she goes along with him, not, of course, because she is forced to but because he does give her a pleasure she had never known before, even though "she didn't even *like* Prem." (4) Prem has thus helped her to know herself better: "Did women 'need' sex? Aparna had always scoffed at the notion. No, she'd say, women need love. And caring. And tenderness. Prem had stood all these ideas on their head." (5) Aparna has learnt to look beyond the "shame" (6) that is so much a part of middle-class Indian upbringing and to accept pleasure without guilt.

This is the reality behind all the other women characters in the play as well: successful in all the roles they have assumed as adults, they are failures emotionally, and each turns to activities and relationships that enables her to give vent to her hidden frustrations. Each one of the women is trapped by a patriarchal society and her own social conditioning into a situation from which there is no escape except through a subterranean defiance of societal expectations. If Reema uses her husband's money to buy her all the fancy things that can help her to satisfy her ego, and engages in an affair with her brother-in-law to satisfy herself sexually—here too it is the aggressive male who makes the first move—Surekha in her middle-class environment makes do with a lesbian relationship with an old school friend, in which she is the aggressor and which, therefore, continues the old pattern of exploitation of the psychologically weak prevalent everywhere in such a society. Indeed, Reema's treatment of her daughter indicates that women themselves concur in their own victimization. She believes that Shonali has a boyfriend, but she indulges the girl, even though she knows the Shonali must have an arranged marriage; she does not realize that she is thereby forcing her daughter in her own unhappy mould, in which her adolescent sexual experimentation had led to an aborted pregnancy, an early and loveless marriage, a meaningless existence.

Similarly, Rashmi's endless succession of relationships gives her no satisfaction, nor security; in each one of them she is the loser. She thinks: "The trick was to get them hooked. Become an incurable habit in their petty, self-obsessed lives, get them so beholden that they thought they couldn't live without you—or more accurately—without the service only *you* could provide. . . . She was honest; and, as she had found out, men didn't like honest women. They preferred flirts and flatterers. Even manipulators. They felt more comfortable with them." (49) All that men want, she realizes, is power. This is what Champabai, the madam of a brothel, had warned her; powerlessness makes women put up not just with physical abuse but with "something even worse—humiliation and insult." (43) Indeed, her insatiable thirst for sex is a kind of revenge, a compensation for her own weakness, and an expression of her need to have the kind of power that man has. (215) She is happy that her son at least will escape that fate of the woman (213)—thus reinforcing the age-old patriarchal belief in double standards.

Noor is more completely the victim than any of her school friends. The product of a loveless marriage herself, where both her parents were always engrossed in their own extra-marital affairs, she is brought up by an elderly maid, who cannot prevent either her unsuitable friendship with the unscrupulous and exploitative Swati nor, perhaps even worse, her incestuous relationship with her younger brother. After an unfortunate accident, following which her boyfriend has managed to make a new life for himself, the already emotionally scarred Noor becomes physically and mentally handicapped too. At the time of the reunion, she is busy with research—into what nobody knows—that is a kind of compensation for her. Women's lives remain the same, whether inside or outside marriage, whether they are mothers or childless; they are all equally without hope.

Swati, apparently, is no victim but a survivor. A mixture of Pamela Bordes and the "superbitch" of the American television soap operas, Swati is the "vamp," the term that Sandra Gilbert and Susan Gubar have used to describe certain women writers and critics, who represents the "rebelliously . . . anti-hierachical impulses that have been repressed but not erased by patriarchal culture. . . . The vamp is glamorous, an address in a kind of guerrilla theatre, but the drama of seduction and betrayal that she enacts in her foray against patriarchal structures may end up being as seductively treacherous to women as to men."[8] Swati thus hovers between Positions Three and Two of Margaret Atwood's hierarchy of Basic Victim Positions,[9] whose rebellion, paradoxically, turns into a reinforcement of the same patriarchal ways to victory—through exploitation of others—that she herself had suffered from. In the end she screams at her erstwhile friends, whom she has been using even now to further her own ends: "Do you think I don't know how much all of you despise me? But you know what? I think you're jealous. You with your bleak little mediocre lives. Playing safe and yet cheating, sneaking on the side. . . . I think I'm far more ethical, yes, ethical, than the lot of you. . . . Look where I am and look where you are. Nowhere." (210) Indeed, even the men, the exploiters and the users, can be destroyed by the system: Balbir and Nawaz are evidence enough that patriarchy destroys even its own proteges, so that they believe they have won only because they have managed to exist in a meaningless emotional and moral vacuum. No relationship is fulfilling in Shobha Dé's world, least of all the sexual, through material prosperity may be attainable.

And it is the structure that is the medium and the message of her story. Thus the first four sections of Chapter 1 deal in considerable detail with Aparna's physical sensations in sexual activities only to juxtapose them with her own awareness of how her pleasure is out of character and her own loveless personal life. Then comes Reema's lunch invitation that calls up the past so insistently that she accepts it, more out of curiosity, and perhaps as an attempt at self-assertion, than anything else.

The next chapter begins with a statement about Reema; each of the next few chapters begins, in fact, with a sentence about the character who is to be a parallel centre of consciousness in the story. Swati's suggestion that all her friends bring to the reunion "snapshots . . .

Mementoes of their innocent pasts" (13) takes Reema through the past and her present: from her parents' house to her efforts to keep young and trim to her husband's unattractiveness to Swati's sophisticated appearance in newspaper photographs—all of which make her turn for reassurance to her five-carat diamond ring, which for her has become a sign that she need not feel inferior to anyone else. The section ends, significantly, with a glimpse of Reema's marriage: she spends her time sloppily watching a teenage love story on a video film, the cold glint of her solitaire mocking her loneliness, in her posh new flat so carefully done up to impress guests.

There is a cut to Aparna at the office, busy and successful, but contrasting immediately with her memories of her times with Rohit, both before and during their marriage, and her sense of loss and betrayal when he had walked out of her life. Her thoughts and memories swing back and forth without regard to chronology. This is of course typical of the way in which the human mind works (as Virginia Woolf pointed out in "Modern Fiction") but it is also characteristic of Dé's technique here, to enable her to indicate that the individual can never free herself from her past, and that there is in fact no dividing line between past, present and future.

Chapter 6 builds up the tension as it presents Reema's preparations for the party, which begins in the next chapter as the camera focusses on one character after another as each woman enters and the guests begin to catch up with each other, and with themselves, so that the reader/observer of the scene realizes how their lives have entwined themselves around each other's and how each version of their shared experiences varies from the others'. The only moment of discomfort at this stage when Noor suddenly starts screaming, like an animal in pain, when the champagne corks pop: the moment of celebration is in reality a moment to relive the pain of the past and realize the pain of the present and the fact that there is no relief, no end to it, except in death, which is the option that Noor is to choose. Her scream now is thus a foreshadowing of what is to happen in the succeeding chapters, as the facade of easy camaraderie is ripped down by reminiscence and reality. Aparna might declare, towards the end of the party, that she does not want "to rake up stuff I'd rather forget," and that she has "changed," but, as Swati tells her, "We're all schoolgirls playing adult games. . . . Nobody changes. Not that much." (181) The unscrupulous 'bugging' of private gossip that she employs for her own gains is thus of a piece with her earlier betrayals. Nothing changes for anyone.

It is this reality that the structure of the novel conveys, by its constant shifts in time and points of view and by the constant use of montage and cuts rather than the linear flow of straightforward narration. Individuals might act and intersect, but they lead separate lives, in which, ultimately, there can be no progression, but merely a reiteration and a recapitulation of the past. Alfred Hitchcock once described his method in terms that closely resemble Dé's way of working:

> You gradually build up the psychological situation, piece by piece, using the camera to emphasize first one detail, then another. . . . And you can do this [drawing the audience right inside the situation] only by breaking the action up into details and cutting from one to the other, so that each detail is forced in turn on the attention of the audience and reveals its psychological meaning.[10]

Graham Greene had complained that Hitchcock "Very perfunctorily . . . builds up to these tricky situations and then drops them; they mean nothing: they lead to nothing."[11] But this is precisely what Dé wishes to communicate: that so much sound and fury at the end, the cathartic release of primeval instincts and emotions, Noor's suicide, lead to nothing. Life continues its meaningless circle and individuals have no way of stepping outside or achieving anything; things must and will as they always have, and there is no hope at the end. In the words of Adrienne Rich in her significantly titled "Snapshots of a Daughter-in-Law"[12]:

> Two handsome women, gripped in argument,
> each proud, acute, subtle, I hear scream
> across the cut glass and majolica
> like Furies cornered from their prey;
> The argument *ad feminam*, all the old knives
> that have rusted in my back, I drive in yours,
> *ma semblance, ma soeur!*

Shobha Dé's medium is her message, and her title says it all.

NOTES

1. *Snapshots* (New Delhi: Penguin, 1995).
2. "Technique as Discovery," *20th Century Literary Criticism: A Reader*, ed. David Lodge (London: Longman, 1989), p. 391.
3. *Communications* (Harmondsworth: Penguin, 1966), p. 18.
4. "Felix Culpa?" *Commonweal*, XLVIII (July 16, 1948), p. 323.
5. *Spectator*, CLV (September 27, 1935), p. 472.
6. *Film Form*, quoted by Audrey Nelson Slate in her unpublished doctoral dissertation, "Technique and Form in the Novels of Graham Greene," University of Wisconsin, 1960, p. 92.
7. Qtd. Slate, p. 91.
8. "The Mirror and the Vamp," *The Future of Literary Theory*, ed. Ralph Cohen (NY: Routledge and Kegan Paul), pp. 145-54.
9. *Survival: A Thematic Guide to Canadian Literature* (Toronto: Anansi, 1972), pp. 37-38. In Position Three, says Atwood, you "acknowledge the fact that you are a victim but . . . refuse to accept the assumption that the role is inevitable," but "if you become locked into your anger and fail to change your situation, you might well find yourself back in Position Two," in which you acknowledge your victimization but accept it as inevitable.
10. In *Footnotes to the Film*, ed. Charles Davey (London: Dickson, 1937), p. 8.
11. *Spectator*, CLVI (May 15, 1936), p. 879.
12. *Adrienne's Rich's Poetry*, ed. Barbara Charlesworth Gelpi and Albert Gelpi (NY: Norton, 1975), p. 13.

The Equation of Power in *Snapshots*

MADHUMALATI ADHIKARI

The social scenario of today has compelled the Indian English women writers to explore the possibilities of female existence beyond the simplistically dualistic conflict of good and evil. Though the archetypal roles of women as mothers, wives, daughters and the 'other' woman continues to haunt the imaginations of these writers yet the strength and the weaknesses of the female sex are now viewed as problems arising from cultural, racial, sexual, economic, ideological, political and gender specific confrontations. The historical context reveals that man, the controller of power, dominates over woman, the prototype of powerlessness. In Shobha De's novels, this standard equation has often been radically altered and women with increased awareness of gender roles and gender identity have emerged as serious contenders of power politics. This attitude is not exclusive to De only but world over, women fiction writers have developed strategies to project the images of women as proficient manipulators of the power game. The Canadian fiction writer Margaret Atwood (*The Handmaid's Tale*), the Afro-American novelist Alice Walker (*The Color Purple*), Shashi Deshpande (*A Matter of Time*) and many others have highlighted the principles of female empowerment through inscriptions that emphasize the ideological and physical struggle of women for reclaiming and redefining the female self.

The State and economic disability are not the only powers that oppress women. Arbitrary sex roles, cultural roles and work roles re-inforce each other to create a vicious chain of subversive activity. Through literature the chronicler of society, we can look for the "clue to how we live, how we have been living, how we have been led to imagine ourselves . . . and therefore live—afresh."[1] The evolutionary changes recorded through the "Feminine, Feminist and Female"[2] phase have either imitated man's intellectual achievements or registered protest or moved to the sphere of self-discovery. Through this quest journey, female consciousness has excavated the truth that the desire for power is very close to her heart despite perilous consequences. The battle between the sexes, overtly or covertly, is as old as creation and today, the connotations have diversified. Power and powerlessness has been identified with success and failure, knowledge and ignorance, superiority and inferiority, gender and sexual discrimination. The precarious balance of power is uncovered through day-to-day, major and minor interactions. The female characters of Shobha De participate actively in this game of power to manipulate, transform and create new traditions and archetypes for their redefinition.

Hannah More in *Coelebs in Search of a Wife* (1808) describes the chief female protagonist as a model of young woman because "she enlivens without *dazzling* and entertains without *overpowering*. Contended to please she has no ambition to shine."[3] Dazzling, ambitious and overpowering women spell danger for men in society. Docile and mute women are safe and thus they are encouraged to lead a subordinate life. Jane Austen, aware of the preferences of society, records her objections obliquely: "A woman especially if she has the misfortune of knowing anything, should conceal it as well as she can . . . imbecility in women is a great enhancement of their personal charm."[4] Sita in the *Ramayana*, nowhere, is praised for her discriminating powers. She becomes the symbol of an obstinate, ignorant woman who sends Rama on the dangerous mission of capturing the *Swarnamriga*. Knowledge and discretion, two significant components of power, rarely become attributes of women. Happy with their imbecility, they remain unconsciously in the periphery while men enthrone themselves in the centre.

Adulthood for males and females have different connotations. In patriarchal literature, the hidden gender norms of society interpret female development quite differently. For a female protagonist, adulthood implies "dependent, submissive and non-adult"[5] behaviour pattern. Thus the positive images of the "good woman," in effect are not worth applauding. Since "speech is knowledge"[6] and knowledge is power, women are conveniently tutored to think that silence is the golden path for decent women. De has surely and definitely revolted against this traditional approach. Her protagonists are vocal. Other Indian women writers have remained more restricted than Shobha De in this sphere.

The other dimension of adulthood is the emergence of "sexuality." "Female sexuality," in traditional literature is inscribed as "more a danger than power" but "male sexuality is power."[7] In this context, the meaning of "female growing up" is quite different from "male adulthood." Here again, De very categorically has decided to become unconventional. In her novels, one is confronted with a celebration of "female sexuality." Her characters and themes project the female need for power and De goes on to suggest that in urban society, the demand for women power has become an integral part of female sensibility.

The concept of motherhood conceived by male imagination restricts woman's quest for wholeness. Motherhood is equated with mother earth; one who should surrender, serve and remain perpetually crushed. Patriarchy is "a symbolic male principle" and is the "power of the father."[8] Motherhood gains strength, ideologically, from the elevated myth of Mother Goddess but in all practicality, it demands the sacrifice of all ambition, liberty and identity for the sake of a happy family life. Feminist and womanist writers have learnt to handle the problem efficiently. The feminists believe in the offensive method and like Meridian, Fast Mary, Louvine of Alice Walker's *Meridian* reject all metaphorical and factual concepts of motherhood. Womanist writers on the other hand manipulate the delicate issue intelligently and inscribe a story that narrates the tale of the mother and the woman authentically. Shobha De deliberately ignores the sanctity of motherhood as prescribed by man, in *Snapshots.* Anita Desai ignores the institutionalized concept of motherhood as a necessity for woman's all-round development. Power and motherhood are treated as opposing forces. It is interesting to note that all novels authored by male and female writers can be analyzed as documents of power struggle. Outspoken Shobha De rightly observes: "Eventually every relationship is a power struggle either on an overt or subliminal level. Control over the situation has been a male prerogative over the centuries. Women's destinies have been determined largely in that context alone. It is time they were made aware of their potential and power. Man will have to come to terms with woman power."[9]

Woman, a victim of man's consumerism, is methodically exiled from the world of power. Power-mad male regime cannot tolerate woman's power to communicate, hope and become autonomous.[10] Thus, there is a conscious effort to dilute these inspiring characteristics in woman's nature. Not to be defeated by these manoeuverings, women writers have redefined and revised the "gender role" by projecting the female power as something natural. Shobha De in *Snapshots* has made her female characters more powerful than their male counterparts. Males are nothing but peripheral; they fail to control women either with their sexuality or ideological precepts. Shobha De's women are empowered by female sexuality. They exert "control, domination and influence" on others which are the defining characteristics of "power."[11] The question of partnership between man-woman is ruled out. Often tactical retreats are carried out to prepare for the future attack and the final victory. The means and methods of each character are different but the aim is common. Once, to become a heroine, women had to surrender "all that gratifies the love of power"[12] but today, in the world created by Shobha De, this very love grants them the status of the heroine. The equation of power is heavily loaded in favour of the female characters in *Snapshots*. Their game is dangerous and unethical but who cares? Bursting with self-confidence, they often stoop very low to conquer but that is the picture that Shobha De is keen to project.

The images of women, radically altered by the modern feminist writers, illustrate exploitation carried out not by males but females. In fact, the power-madness has trapped the females of the modern society. Shobha De's *Snapshots* projects an urban society where men stand on the periphery and women battle for power and supremacy. The power-hungry female characters of the novel fly at each other's throat, invent schemes to control and dominate over the weaknesses of their so-called friends. Through the album of their life, Shobha De projects the elaborated or expanded challenges, predicaments and values of these actors, often shocking and disgusting. The novel emblematizes woman-power at its worst.

The novel *Snapshots* unveils the life of six "girls of Santa Maria High School, leading predictable mundane lives of domesticity and imagined bliss."[13] Through foreseeable roles of mothers and wives, they had drifted to their respective world of routine marriage and divorce. Swati, one of the girls now residing in London, had been asked to write a 'bold and meaty' (222) serial on urban women. She plans a meeting with her school-time friends, Reema and others like Aparna, Surekha, Rashmi and Noor, despite their dislike for Swati decide to join the party because since their school days Swati always had "some kind of power over" others. All that she was to do was to "snap her fingers" and the rest of them "jumped." (181) Undoubtedly, Swati is the most powerful female who demonstrates her control over males and females alike. In this cat and mouse game, the mouse is caught and at times, the cat is also defeated. The power constantly vacillates between the cat and the mouse. Since Swati is financially and socially more powerful, Reema uses the weapon of the weak and subdues Swati temporarily by hitting her below the belt: "Poor Swati. Must be awful to be childless. No?" (89) The relation between woman's power and motherhood had been established way back by patriarchy for personal gains. Women manipulated by social norms wound and insult each other. The process invariably diminishes female power.

It is not uncommon to see that individuals gain power by revealing the dark facts of their opponents' lives and blackmailing them for their personal gains. Noor, the nervous and weak girl of the group, in this very manner exerts pressure on the more powerful members of this drama. Shobha De has visualized "changed power equations"[14] which males find difficult to accept. Even the attitudes towards the prostitutes have changed. The women of the brothels are no longer the discarded, pitied and the isolated lot. They can claim like Champa Bai: "we are here to satisfy their lust not for sex but for power." (43) Thus unconsciously, Champa Bai emphasizes the theory of French feminists that woman's sexuality wields power. Male over-confidence misguides them to believe that they are the masters of female sexuality.

Relationships in brothels are unlicensed but sanctioned relationship, a product of marriage, is no better. As Rashmi comments that mediocre women use "sex as bait but the shrewd women hold their men and keep them enslaved." (49) Out-spoken Swati claims, "We rejoice in our sexuality . . . we do not suppress it, we don't dismiss it. . . . Sex does not threaten us." (165) This psychology definitely reduces man's power over women. Men, because of their sexual dominance, have always felt like "conquerors" (93) and their sexual exploits have been their "conquests." (207) Woman's subordinate role in the power game has been radically altered by De. Modern, urban, self-sufficient, economically independent and confident women of Shobha De have transformed themselves from "commodities" to "identities." It is realized by Balbir in *Snapshots* when he asks the six women of the novel, "Do you fuck because you enjoy fucking? or is it power play." (162)

Marriage "a patriarchal enclosure"[15] can no longer hold woman down. Marriage and motherhood, symbols of parental authority and power, are diffused by Shobha De through Rashmi, an unwed mother; Swati and Aparna are divorcees and yet sufficiently powerful to reject the sexuality of men. Swati may marry on her own terms but for Aparna husband is an "awful" (24) and "dirty" word; Reema uses her husband for her material comfort. (14) The sanctity of marriage prescribed especially for woman is conveniently diluted by Shobha De's women. Reema enjoys a relationship with her brother-in-law; Noor's mother is man-crazy, Surekha has a more satisfying relationship with a woman; Swati considers man to be a commodity that she can acquire from the open market. The basic issues and values of life have been totally transformed by these ladies. Man's loss has been woman's gain. With the awakening of the power consciousness, sexuality and economic independence, new sensibilities have been included in woman's personality. Power grabbing through ethical and non-ethical means, no longer remains to be the right of man. Woman, like her counterpart, has realized the truth that all is fair in love and war. Power has ceased to remain a personal property of patriarchy. It is only Rashmi who remains physically and emotionally violated by male intrusion. Her family life, a consequence of male power, has been deeply affected. In the novel, she is the only one, who despite her rebellion, remains a victim.

The analysis clearly indicates that Shobha De, like all feminist writers, is deeply concerned with the alignment of power that exerts physical, political, economic and social control over woman to fragment her. In different novels, Shobha De has suggested different methods and means to fight discriminations of various kinds that ultimately make woman powerless. Aasha Rani of *Starry Nights* fights her battle with some degree of propriety. Karuna of *Socialite Evenings* constructs a convincing case to project woman's power. Her life-style, modelling methods and her shocking journalistic essays may go against the conventional norms of Indian society, but she proves her point that it is only power that matters. In *Snapshots*, the six friends disregard male power totally by negating the norms of traditional female behaviour prescribed by patriarchy. In fact, they establish that the things men can do, women can do better. Being strong physically and intellectually, they hold the reins of power firmly in their hands. Shobha De very rarely allows her female protagonists to become powerless creatures.

In her novels, it becomes increasingly evident that man's power-status is fragile and his position can be destabilized consciously. His loss of power is undeniably visible through his incapability to dwarf, maim or victimize women for his personal gains. The females of *Snapshots* create their own moulds and music.

NOTES

1. Adrienne Rich, 'When We Dead Awaken: Writing as Revision,' *Lies, Secrets and Silence* (New York: W.W. Norton, 1979), p. 35.
2. Elaine Showalter, "The Female Tradition," *A Literature of Their Own: British Women from Bronte to Lessing* in *Feminism: An Anthology of Literary Theory and Criticism*, ed. Robyn R. Warhol and Diana Price Herndl (N. Brunswick, NJ: Rutgers University Press, 1991), p. 274.
3. Hannah More, *Coelebs in Search of a Wife* (Caddell and Davies, 1798), p. 186. Emphasis added.
4. Jane Austen, *Northanger Abbey* (Dent, 1910), p. 199.
5. Annis Pratt, *The Archetypal Patterns in Women's Fiction* (Bloomington: Indiana University Press, 1981), p. 16.
6. Barbara T. Christian, *Black Feminist Criticism: Perspectives on Black Women Writers* (New York: Pergamon, 1985), p. xi.
7. Patricia Meyer Spacks, *The Female Imagination* (New York: Avon, 1975), p. 200.
8. Sheila Rowbotham. "The Trouble with Patriarchy," *The Women Question*, ed. Mary Evans (Oxford: Fontana Paperbacks), p. 74.
9. Shobha De, *Shooting from the Hip: Selected Writing* (New Delhi: UBS, 1994), pp. 112-13.
10. Margaret Atwood, *Second Words, Selected Critical Prose* (Toronto: Anansi, 1982), p. 145.
11. Berenice Caroll, "Peace Research: The Cult of Power," *Journal of Conflict Resolution*, 16 (December 1972), p. 585.
12. Sarah Ellis, *The Wives of England: Their Relative Duties, Domestic Influence and Social Obligation* (New York: E. Walker, 1843), p. 26.
13. Shobha De, *Snapshots* (New Delhi: Penguin, 1995).
14. Shobha De, "Sex in the Time of Stress," in Khushwant Singh and Shobha De, ed., *Uncertain Liaisons: Sex, Strife and Togetherness in Urban India* (New Delhi: Viking, 1993), p. 6.
15. Annis Pratt, p. 37.

Second Thoughts: A Slice of Urban Life

ALKA SAXENA

Shobha De has enjoyed being in the limelight as a stunning model, editor, columnist and of course as a saucy and bitchy novelist, for the last almost thirty years. She created a furore in the world of fiction with her bizarre and murky best-sellers. She has been called the Jackie Collins of India, a label she does not want to be associated with. She wants to be an author in her own right. Shobha De has thrived on controversies. She has survived controversies as well. This aspect did not have adverse affects on her popularity. On the contrary, her critics were surprised and sore to hear that *Starry Nights* was recently prescribed as a text-book in Bombay University. But we should remember that *Starry Nights*, her second novel, was already on the prescribed reading list in a British University, before it formed a part of a paper on Popular Culture for third year B.A. English students at Bombay University in 1995-96.

From *Socialite Evenings* to *Second Thoughts*, Shobha De has certainly evolved as a sensitive writer. It has been alleged that in her novels there is little insight into human nature and there is very little effort made to probe her characters, their motivations and feelings. *Second Thoughts*, her seventh novel, sets aside these allegations. A departure from her earlier novels, it is a bitter-sweet love story for the Nineties. The high society world, which was the familiar background of her earlier novels, has been replaced by the middle-class society. *Second Thoughts* evokes no conflicts. With this novel, her critics will have to think twice before labelling her the evergreen 'Queen of Pornography.'

Second Thoughts deals with a young middle-class Bengali girl, born and bred in Calcutta, who makes an arranged matrimony alliance, with a Bombay-based, foreign-returned Bengali. Maya, the young bride, is more fascinated and in love with Bombay than at the prospect of having married Ranjan. Once she lands in Bombay, after the marriage, her disillusionment begins. She realizes that despite Ranjan's stay abroad, he is very traditional and above all, an insensitive husband. The agony of Maya, who feels trapped in matrimony is the central theme of the novel.

The prologue, extremely well written, opens with Maya's first visit to Bombay on a sultry May evening, which subtly conveys the gloom that will set in when she will finally settle there, with her future husband Ranjan. Marriage ushers glamour, fascination and freedom for most young girls, but once the ceremony is over, the dreams come crashing down and it is with a lot of bitterness that they face the harsher unknown realities. Maya was fascinated by "Bombay but was taken aback when she sensed that Bombay smelt of desperation and deceit."[1] Desperation and deceit become the key words of her life when she becomes a part of Bombay. It is in desperation that she deceives Ranjan, just a few years after marriage. But ironically, at the end of the novel, we see that she has only deceived herself. While Maya is still recoiling in horror at the platform, she almost trips over a dead man. Still unable to overcome her shock, she looks in disbelief as people continue to pass by, without being bothered by the presence of the corpse on the stuffy and slimy platform. Little does she infer that on coming to Bombay her enthusiasm would be stifled, as Ranjan would hardly acknowledge her presence. She too would be reduced to a 'dead' Maya. When she met Ranjan, she was more excited at the prospect of settling in Bombay—the city of her dreams. "Marrying Ranjan would make her a part of it immediately—Maya knew she'd be bonded with Bombay forever." (12)

At the first meeting with Ranjan and his mother Mrs. Malik, Maya is tutored on the expectations of the Malik family very explicitly. Chitra, Maya's mother, drops a hint that her daughter is eager to pursue a career later in life. But from Mrs. Malik's expression, it is evident that she does not approve of working women. Ranjan agrees with his mother's views and declares: "I am earning well enough to support a wife and family. I believe it is a woman's duty to run a good home." (11) He then turns to Maya and asks her in a challenging voice if she agrees with him. Maya is taken off-guard, and before she can say anything, her uncle intervenes, "In any Indian family, the husband's comforts always come first. Everything else follows." (11) Later, on their way home, even Chitra consoles Maya by saying that the issue of taking up a job can be sorted out later. "Let them first say 'yes.' Then we can bring it up. And now stop chattering uselessly." (13) At that very moment Maya sees a group of young girls, clad in short skirts, chatting animatedly at a bus-stop. Again, the fascination for Bombay is aroused in her heart. Although her first impression of Bombay is positively hostile but as she looks at the neon-lit shops she is too eager to be a part of the city, whose "spell she had fallen under quickly. Too quickly." (14) On second thoughts, when she sees the city throbbing with life, she quickly forgets the deceit and desperation that she smells first when she steps at Victoria Terminus. It is on second thoughts of her relationship with Ranjan that she almost overcomes the guilt of meeting Nikhil, her college-going neighbour. It is with these subtle indications that the prologue ends and Maya is quite confident that Bombay would be her eventual home. "Marrying Ranjan was like marrying Bombay, and she thought she was the luckiest girl in the locality, who had bagged a foreign-educated Bombay based groom." (195) Lost in these thoughts, Maya finds herself in Bombay, for good.

Shobha De's novels are a slice of urban life. They deal with contemporary issues. In this context, *Second Thoughts* is a realistic representation of the psyche of the traditional Indian men and women. Although they claim to be the proud products of the twenty-first century, but deep down they still cherish and nourish the age-old norms and traditions. In that much familiar pattern, the status of men and women has hardly undergone any change. As individuals, they may have progressed but in the institution of marriage, the man is still the lord and master and a woman has to abide by his whims and fancies whether she likes it or not. In *Unveiling India*, Anees Jung has given a twentieth-century portrait of a man and a wife of rural India. But to quite a large extent it represents its counterparts in urban India too. Anees Jung writes of a man and a woman who are seated in a cart parked on a desert track. The cart rests on two massive dunlop tyres. The husband is 'the archetype of a male, the kind the woman of the desert prays for during Gangaur. She is hidden behind a burning yellow veil. It lends her mystery, conforms to the archetype of a woman, one who veils her bounty, expresses it only as a wife and mother. "Yes, she is my wife," he nods in a matter-of-fact manner. In his tone there is contentment that borders on smugness. She is his wife, not his better half. While he talks, she stays silent, quiescent behind the veil.[2] Anees Jung points out that all that has changed in the frame are the wheels of the cart—they are no longer made of wood. The farmer has definitely changed his wheels but not the culture of his mind.

The same mental culture can be seen in *Second Thoughts*. Ranjan has studied abroad, lived in Bombay, but as far as his wife is concerned he imposes restrictions on her movements. She is not free to go anywhere in the city. She cannot feel free to live in the house as she would wish to. The STD facility on phone is locked for her. Shobha De captures the middle class psyche by exposing various facets of Ranjan—his attitude to hold on tight to the purse strings so as to control his woman, his lectures on wifely duties, his complete control even on the use of the air-conditioner.

Both Maya and Ranjan are strongly influenced by the traditional orthodoxy of their respective parents. Mrs. Malik is rich and apparently seems quite modern and smart. Ranjan too has been brought up in a modern city, yet when it comes to making the choice of a bride, he agrees for an arranged marriage. Mrs. Malik too has a very clear picture of her future daughter-in-law. Maya is often hurt by Ranjan's indifferent attitude and wonders why he did not pick up a Bengali girl from Bombay. Mrs. Malik was an influential lady and she could have chosen for her son a girl born and bred in Bombay. Once Maya had spoken to Ranjan on this issue and he had sharply replied: "Oh no, no. These Bombay Bengalis are different, they've lost their cultural identity. Their roots are not in our tradition. My mother wouldn't have been able to adjust to someone like that." (115-16) And when Maya wants to know about his choice, he says that he had left it all to his mother. Whenever Ranjan speaks about Maya's parents, it is sans respect. The sarcastic tone and contempt is evidently a trait he has inherited from his mother. Maya knows that Ranjan can dare to speak in such a manner because he feels superior in some way to her and her background. It leaves Maya hurt and hot tears well up in her eyes. She clearly remembers Mrs. Malik comment once, "If you ask me, it's always wiser to get a girl from a socially inferior background. . . . A wealthier wife spells doom. The husband loses all control over her and she ends up having the upper hand. Such a marriage can never work which is why we were so careful while selecting the right candidate for Ranjan." (231) The irony is that while Mrs. Malik thinks that she has made the right choice in Maya, the relationship never develops satisfactorily.

A careful study of Chitra, Maya's mother, reveals the traditional outlook of a girl's mother in Indian society, particularly the middle-class. Maya is keen to complete her studies but Chitra realizes that a foreign returned boy, available for only two weeks, would get "snapped before you and I can blink our eyes." (3) She is acutely worried about Maya's slightly dark complexion. It is a cause of great concern to her. She chooses a yellow saree (a colour that Maya hates), so that it makes her look fairer. She knows that the Maliks are very fair and as is the general Indian attitude, they certainly would not like a dark daughter-in-law. When Mrs. Malik lays down the rules and explains tersely that girls can only be moulded if they stop thinking of their parents's home as their own, Chitra agrees with her without any qualms. She seems to have understood this very well as can be seen by the following comment, "I believe in the same thing myself. A girl has to cut the cord of her family quickly and identify with her in-laws. The sooner she does this, the better." (222)

Chitra issues the standard instructions to Maya that marriage involves sacrifice which has to be undertaken by the woman. Maya reflects much on this later and feels that probably her mother had uttered these words: "Perhaps she was pointing to the disaster of her own marriage and telling me how I could avoid the same pitfalls." (253) Thus, in the minds of Maya and Ranjan, the specific, set rules were hammered much before they got married. It is the pressure of this deep rooted system of thinking on the one hand and the exposure to the modern system of education, the influence of the contemporary social trends in their peer group, on the other, that they both find it difficult to maintain an equilibrium.

The well-planned and chosen match is in fact a mismatch, much to disgust of the young couple. Ranjan has a certain mental picture of a wife and Maya has to conform to it—no lapses are to be permitted. Maya's longing for adventure and romance often suffers a setback. Her desires are rudely snapped and dissolved by sharp-edged words like, "There are certain rules. You have to abide by them whether you like them or not." (83) Ranjan's contribution to the 'contract' of marriage is over the day he decides to make Maya his wife. Maya sometimes wants to retaliate but "the silent scream struck somewhere in her throat, unable to push its way out." (259) Ranjan's responsibility towards Maya is nothing beyond providing her financial support, a decent house and four square meals a day. "As far as he was concerned, he had redeemed his pledge." (263) It is upto Maya to accept or reject it. Ranjan is completely indifferent to Maya's emotional desires. And it is this detached attitude of Ranjan that hurts Maya immensely. Ranjan constantly reminds Maya of her duties as a married woman. He is hardly aware of her presence in "his home." Maya notes very sadly in the twelfth chapter of the novel as Ranjan refers to 'me' and 'my home.' Maya cannot feel a sense of belonging. She experiences utter neglect. She can never gain the confidence and sense of belonging to be able to call the house her own. She sadly admits: "It was never a home. My home. Our home always 'the house'—impersonal, distant, cold." (227) No matter how much she was brain-washed by her mother, mother-in-law or Ranjan—for her—"Home continued to be Calcutta. My parental home." (227)

Ranjan is not able to relate with Maya because of his mother's over-indulgence in their personal married life. Ranjan does not resent her interference. On the contrary he is too eager to discuss his domestic matters with her as a religious routine. He is in awe of his mother. During the first meeting, Chitra observes that Ranjan is a very dutiful and loving son. It is very true—Ranjan is only that. He fails to be a dutiful and loving husband. Duty not only means to provide food, home and money, it also includes a certain amount of respect and affection for one's spouse. Sex is a "complicated issue" (257) in their married life. "Their clumsy-sex honeymoon at a depressing hotel in Mahabaleshwar" (48) points clearly that their initial experience was unsatisfactory. Maya feels that perhaps she was too inhibited or too uptight. Later she discovers to her surprise that "It was Ranjan who was all that." (48) Ranjan has a genuine lack of interest in Maya. With coldness in this respect too, Maya is worried about her non-pregnancy. She is quite sure that if Ranjan continues to maintain a stiffness in sex affairs, she would in all probability be childless. She more or less reconciles herself to the fact that she would never bear children. This is a sensitive issue. Failure in this aggravates her sense of loneliness.

She has no sex-life at all with Ranjan. She is happy with the physical demonstration of affection by Ranjan. She enjoys being held, stroked and kissed but she also knows that "this wasn't at all what married life was meant to be." (257) Ranjan's lack of sex drive makes her feel guilty of harbouring such thoughts. When Ranjan returns from Calcutta after ten days, Maya shyly snuggles up to him and caresses him but, he jumps back "as though he had received an electric shock. He had lain trembling in bed for a long time, his breathing heavy, his eyes screwed shut." (259) As a dismayed and lonely Maya puts her head wearily on the pillow, Ranjan starts snoring—not at all aware of the pain he has caused to Maya. Their relationship is not only a failure at the sexual level but even otherwise their temperaments are different and they lack compatibility.

Their marriage is only one year old but monotony heavily erodes it. With Ranjan's non-communicative attitude, Maya sulks in the kitchen. That is the only place in the house "which had become symbolic of her refuge." (39) Whether it is the excitement of the first monsoon shower or the tingling spell of slightly wintry weather, it fails to arouse Ranjan. Maya's excitement and high spirits on such occassions look ridiculous to Ranjan. He brings down her elevated spirits by sharply rebuking, "Why cannot you be still. You know? Just still. You are always so restless, it's tiring to watch." (39)

They never do anything together, be it an outing, watch popular hit comedies, go to eating places or to the beach. While a lot of exciting things take place around Maya, Ranjan is immersed in the evening newspaper. It leaves Maya longing, "If only he'd be more enthusiastic about sharing his city with me." (97) It troubles her to see that Ranjan refuses to share a single aspect of his life with her. She wonders whether he considers her his rival, or does not have enough faith in her. Once she dares ask him and Ranjan replies without taking his eyes off the T.V. screen: "Of course I trust you but my mother is my mother. I have known her longer than you. These things take time." (205) Under the same roof, they live as strangers. The following excerpt from tenth chapter throws light on the emptiness of their relationship. "Hot weekday afternoons were to be suffered silently and stoically with just the whirr of noisy ceiling fan to stir the warm air around." (100) Regarding the air conditioner in their room, there exists a tacit understanding that it would be switched on only after dinner, for a short while, so that the room is cooled sufficiently. It runs on the weekend afternoons when Ranjan is occupying the room. Ranjan only speaks to her about economising on family budget and minutely goes over the weekly budget.

Often, in the course of such lectures, he asks Maya to learn something from his mother and follow her.

Ranjan loves Maya only as one would love a pet in the house. Even when Ranjan reaches out for Maya, "It was a gesture devoid of any passion. An impersonal friendly sort of gesture which always left me feeling like a well-trained dog being rewarded for his good behaviour." (251) Their life in the bedroom is settled in a routine—they could have been brothers or sisters or flatmates. Occasionally she does get a brotherly peck from Ranjan. Maya really does not know who would qualify as Ranjan's kind of woman apart from his mother. She draws this conclusion because Ranjan tells her about his unsuccessful involvement with a few girls in America. Ranjan confides in a broken voice that it was very difficult for him to get into a relationship with any woman: "'I tried,' he said miserably. And repeated it again, 'I tried Maya. But it didn't work.'" (52)

Maya is constantly depressed because of her crippling loneliness. There is no one in Bombay with whom she can share her miseries. She pities herself for doing nothing in a city that is not her own. There is no one with whom she can giggle and gossip or confess her problems. She feels useless. The feeling of being unwanted gnaws her. She sulks: "Nobody needed me, absolutely nobody. My parents no longer thought I belong to them. My husband belonged to his mother. It was unlikely that I would bear children who would belong to me. And I did not have a single true friend to call my own." (266-67)

But when Nikhil Verma comes into her life, he brings a new meaning of existence for her. Her dreams and desires once again surface and she suddenly sees the spectacular rainbow stretch across the sky. Maya wants to express her joy and happiness. She wants to be free, alive, reckless and go mad with joy. She expresses her newfound joy: "I wanted my insides to perform a wild dance while a mangy camel sauntered down the beach carrying me atop." (74) With Ranjan she has only seen the closed door of her house and the iron bars of the windows. Now she comes face to face with the Bombay she has craved for. She wants to flirt with the other Bombay. She is in search of adventure and she indulges in it now. With Ranjan she has learnt to curb her feelings. If she ever saw pictures of exotic resorts in magazines, she just shut her eyes and placed herself in the azure blue of the pool or the inviting mountains, but now she gets the chance to feel the tingling excitement in reality.

The outing at the beach with Nikhil is one she has craved for ever since she came to Bombay. Her feet were eager to run and explore every square and every inch of Bombay. When Ranjan is away on a business trip, Maya feels free as a bird and allows her spirits to soar.

Amidst all this enjoyment, she also feels scared by the pangs of guilt that she is betraying Ranjan. But she tries to overcome this guilt and resolves to live in the present "refused to deny myself this single right" (178) of going on the enchanting sea beach with Nikhil. She realises that it is very wrong for a married woman to go out with a man, specially if her husband does not know about it. But in the heart of her hearts, she wants to justify that she has not done anything wrong. "Is it a sin to want to go out and breathe the air?" For this question she has no answer except that "I can only say that I was helpless and wanted to go out with you very desperately." (195)

Maya's sporadic longings bring an unbearable sadness in her. She knows that her dreams would not be fulfilled with either Ranjan or Nikhil. The rainbow is only a distant dream. But these breaks, the dreams "served as a safety valve" (152) or else her mind would have exploded. With Nikhil in her life, Maya's entire being is sensitized. She feels her spirits lifted 'ridiculously.' In her longing for Nikhil, she does not imagine having a sexual relationship with him. She likes having Nikhil around her. She feels good with him, that is what makes the difference. Nikhil is full of life and cares for her. He realises that she is lonely and wants to make her feel good. As compared to Nikhil, Ranjan is more stiff, he is conscious of his movements and speech. Ranjan is not natural. Maya admits that "By temperament I was not cut for domesticity." (121) And when she is confined within the four walls of the so-called home she begins to wilt like her indoor plants. The ficus and dresnia had accompanied her from Calcutta and in the new environment of Bombay they had withered away. But soon Maya understands the redefined needs of the plants and makes the necessary adjustments—less watering, more sun and lots of fresh air. But is there anyone to bring to life her withered frame? To understand her redefined needs?

It is only Nikhil who encourages her to do something spontaneous in her life. He asks her to "stop pretending to be someone you want the world to believe you are." (171) He coaxes her to get real and act real. He points at the futility of suffering silently. His constant words of encouragement make her a little bold. Earlier she had rebelled but that was done silently. Like when she had once defiantly left the phone ringing. She knew that it was a call from Ranjan but her reaction was: "I heard him ring off finally and felt triumphant as though I had defied his edict and got away with my little rebellion." (100) Sometimes she gets a "perverse thrill" when she walks into the bed room while Ranjan is engaged in a phone call to his mother. She feels thrilled to have "ruined his concentration" (102) by her unwanted presence. But gradually she dares to become bolder than this. The initial guilt of allowing Nikhil to visit her, later gives way and makes her confident to deal with either Ranjan or her mother-in-law if they happen to arrive. Although the choice exists in the form of Nikhil, Maya knows she cannot do anything as she "felt home-bound." Once again the traditional upbringing makes her uneasy and unsure. She is caught in a complex situation, where she cannot detach herself from Ranjan, "a man for whom she didn't feel very much except a feeble attraction." (162) And Nikhil's charisma is a pull tugging her in the opposite direction. With a little encouragement from Nikhil, she is prepared to say good-bye to her "uninspiring life without the slight regret." (171) She feels sorry for Ranjan and herself. She knows he had married to satisfy his mother, Mrs. Malik, and she had married him to get away from Calcutta and also from her family from whom she never got the emotional support. She never feels a sense of belonging with her parents, as their own relations are strained. She explains: "Now here we were locked together in a relationship that did not satisfy either of us. He obviously longed to be on his own, leading the life he had become so accustomed to as a student and then as a promising bank executive living by himself. And I longed for the perfect romantic companion—if such a creature existed at all outside my imagination." (252)

The encouragement from Nikhil comes very soon. One day Maya finds Nikhil at the door with a bouquet of pink carnations. It is his birthday and fortunately for him Maya is alone in the house. Mrs. Malik suffers a heart attack and Ranjan leaves early that morning to attend to his mother. Nikhil wants to celebrate that day in a special manner. Before Maya can say anything Nikhil's mouth covers hers with a kiss. "It was a kiss that involved Nikhil's entire being. A kiss so focused, so complete" (268) Maya surrenders herself to its soft urgency. Her entire being becomes alive to Nikhil's touch. She "felt free. Lunatic. Wonderful." (268) As she desperately wants to swallow Nikhil and suck him into her womb and make him hers, she can smell the earth "as its dryness disappeared and it gradually softened, moistened by the skies as they opened up to release its trapped fragrance." (270) Life had just become worth living for her when Ranjan returns from the hospital. Maya is still "raw and shaking from having had a man inside." (277) Her body is still "tingling from having been brought to life so acutely." (277) With Ranjan back, she feels that she is becoming a corpse once again.

Maya's mother-in-law is brought home. Hence, for the next ten days she hardly gets any time for herself. While Maya longs to meet Nikhil, Mrs. Malik seeks her son's attention. And she receives overwhelming filial devotion. Ranjan is capable of giving only that kind of love. When Maya is in low spirits she thinks of the "magic of those glorious moments and nothing else mattered." (283) She just waits for the appropriate time to proclaim her decision. She knows that Ranjan would resent but she is quite sure that her decision would come as something of a relief to a man who really did not need marriage, romance or sex. (283)

It is at this juncture that Shobha De throws light on the reality of the people who fall in Nikhil's category; again a typical attitude of people who belong to his class. Nikhil, too, seems to have pre-conceived notions of marriage. He is a product of the modern generation, a man who does not mind taking one-night-stands with frustrated married women. But when it comes to marriage, it is an arranged one. Nikhil's mother Pushpa breaks the news to Maya, about her son's engagement, with obvious pride. While Maya is dreaming of the glorious relationship that she would have with Nikhil, he is already in Delhi wooing his would-be-bride. Not that Maya is unaware of Nikhil's liaisons with other married women but perhaps with the satisfaction she gets in his presence, she does not give much weightage to this aspect. Nikhil takes her once that his diary is crammed with the travel schedules of various husbands and he is always hooked up with bored housewives. Nikhil takes advantage of the limitations and weaknesses of lonely ladies and Maya is just an addition to his endless list. For him, such relations are only a stop-gap arrangement before the formal, recognised nuptial.

Maya's dream world shatters again. She knows she has no choice but to operate in the stifling atmosphere of her arranged marriage. "Two uncool people stuck together in unholy matrimony" (200) are left and Nikhil is out of the picture. Maya is "left alone to wallow in her misery." (165) The brief adventure, magic and romance is all over very abruptly. Maya stands motionless and speechless. Her mind goes blank. There is a total blackout. Ranjan's angry voice brings her back to the familiar world of sorrow and loneliness. As usual, Ranjan compares her with his mother. Maya has forgotten about the chicken soup and it has boiled and burnt. While she is stupefied after Pushpa leaves, Mrs. Malik smells it despite her illness. This is enough to irritate Ranjan who expects Maya to be a docile housewife who is supposed to discharge her household duties and not waste her time in idle gossip. At that moment, Maya perfectly fits into the slot of 'lonely lady.' How ironic indeed, that the song Nikhil has composed for her, is not a source of consolation, but it labels Maya a lonely lady for ever. After a breezy affair with Nikhil, Maya would have to spend the rest of her life, sometimes clad in her mother-in-law's discarded sarees and dance to the tune of her rigidly conservative husband. Nothing would have been more irksome. When the lonely lady enters the kitchen and looks at the spilled soup—the thick white chalky mucous like liquid looks so familiar and funny to her. She feels that it is "like a baby's puke or cogulated snot, or something I had been before somewhere, not so long ago." (289) That she has come to terms with her monotonous married life is evident from the closing lines of the novel: "The more I stared at the spilled soup, the funnier I found it. I knew I would have to make it again from scratch. So what? I had all the time in the world now." (289)

Twentieth century has seen the emergence of many women writers. Stories have been presented from the women's point of view. The long silence is broken and the anguish of women is expressed. But no matter how loudly or strongly this issue is raised, the picture is still grim. Although the woman wishes to take a bold step, but because of certain values instilled right from childhood, she feels a peculiar sense of guilt, if she breaks the preset norms. Behind the exterior of glamour and glitter, the reality is extremely bitter. The glamour vanishes at the stroke of midnight, very abruptly and rudely. One has to learn to live with the stark realities of life. For those who have been taught to conform to the traditions, it is difficult to snap the pious cord that binds them in matrimony. Freedom is permitted in a very restricted manner; it is the ancient story of sacrifice and adjustment that a woman is destined to. Sooner or later she learns to adjust, as there is no other alternative, if she needs to live a respectful life. Maya, too, accepts to remain enveloped in the loneliness and sadness. On second thoughts, she learns to survive the sultriness of not only Bombay, but also of her marriage.

NOTES

1. Shobha De, *Second Thoughts* (New Delhi: Penguin, 1996), p. 1.
2. Anees Jung, *Unveiling India* (New Delhi: Penguin, 1987), p. 47.

Maya: Another Eve in *Second Thoughts*

G.D. BARCHE

The myth of Fall has been time and again adapted by creative writers to view and review the factors destabilizing human life. This myth in brief is as follows: God created the Garden of Eden with all comforts and joys for Adam and Eve except one injunction that they will not eat the fruit of one particular tree. Then Satan as Serpent enters the Garden. He takes Eve to the forbidden tree and makes her eat the fruit. Thus falls Eve. Outwardly it is a simple biblical story offering the moral that disobedience to God is sin and vice versa. But then this is one side of it. There are other dimensions, too. For instance, Eve was caught in a situation which made her life mechanical, stagnant, devoid of any initiative or challenge. At this critical juncture, the serpent appeared as a catalytic agent and showed her a way out. Eve grabbed this opportunity and formulated her Fall. And hence the questions: Should Eve be blamed for eating the forbidden fruit? Was she really guilty? Should one roll and rust in stagnancy and sterility or chase up new channels of life? And a host of other questions.

The story of *Second Thoughts* by Shobha De goes very close to the biblical story stated above. Here too we have triangles and tribulations. Maya is an attractive young girl with her 'skin tone as warm rich, golden brown, like sunlight dancing on the Hooghly,' 'gleaming jet, black hair' and 'large, dark eyes.' (4) She is trained as a Textile Designer. (155) She has had the dream of 'becoming a journalist and changing the world. (141) She hails from an educated middle class family from Calcutta. Ranjan is equally handsome and ambitious. He has 'thick dark hair, the intense large eyes,' 'strong chest and shoulders.' (51) He has a degree from America and holds a good post in a Bank. He owns a small but beautiful flat on the fourth floor of a building in Bombay. His mother is like God to him, In their first arranged interview, Maya 'liked him and he liked her. That is how they got married.' (191) Ranjan's mother is also quite satisfied as she says, 'I think we have made right choice in Maya.' (232) So was the impression of Maya as she thought, 'marrying Ranjan was like marrying Bombay. I thought I was the luckiest girl in my locality." (195)

Thus according to the worldly norms, everything is fine and flawless. After marriage, Maya has a comfortable decent house to live in, four square meals a day, no shortage of money, fine treatment from her husband, and 'all the time in the world to just loll around in bed, if she wants to.' (262) And yet she is not satisfied. She has no contentment. Like Eve she turns rebellious and finally allows even the marriage bond to blow up. And hence the questions: What makes her feel empty amidst plenty? Why does she rebel and proceed to violate the social moral laws?

A close and careful study of the novel helps us see the Eve-like miserable condition of Maya. Maya, a green girl, too inhibited, too inexperienced, too uptight, and at twenty three with only one 'kissing boy friend' behind (48) and no one to turn for help or guidance at present, finds herself 'abandoned and horribly isolated.' (161) She is sandwiched between Ranjan and Nikhil. Ranjan is her husband. He is twenty-eight years old, physically well built, handsome, foreign educated, modern, confident and who 'had never known another woman.' (48) But then he is a failure in making love. Besides, he is parasitic. On the other hand, Nikhil, her lover, a college boy, is 'good looking, confident, sporty, cocky, flirtatious, lazy, spoilt and quite irresistible.' (329) Unlike Ranjan, he is 'always hungry always.' (54) This can be shown as under:

Satan-like experienced and tactful	Eve-like innocent and green	Adam-like plain and pious but parasitic	God-like loving but indifferent
Nikhil →	Maya →	Ranjan →	Mrs. Malik
Lover →	Beloved/Wife →	Husband/Son →	Mother
Eden Garden with all comforts except the problem of 'forbidden fruit.' So is Ranjan's flat with all comforts but missing "something."			

So finally, Maya finds herself placed in her Eden Garden, i,e., 'a small, neat, soulless flat' (163) in a Bombay suburb with all material comforts. But then she realizes that her marriage was a midsummer night's dream. Soon she starts receiving shock after shock, jolt after jolt of opposite nature from the two channels, viz., her husband Ranjan and the lover Nikhil. Let us examine both in some detail.

As their married life sets sailing, Maya realizes that theirs was a mis-marriage. Ranjan had married her either to satisfy his mother or something within him, and she had married him to get away from Calcutta and a family with whom she did't "really feel a sense of belonging." (252) She also feels that they were locked together in a relationship that did not satisfy either of them. Ranjan longs to be on his own leading the life of 'a promising bank executive' and she longs for the 'perfect romantic companion.' So neither of them is 'cool' but the areas of their warmth are different. Hence, it can be said that 'two uncool people stuck together in unholy matrimony.' (200)

Maya in her quieter movements also realizes that if her 'marriage was to work' 'to make a go of it' (253) it is she who is to try harder. As for Ranjan, he considered his contract to be over on the day he decided to make Maya 'his wife.' That act alone had redeemed him for life. (253) Actually Maya's first entry into the Bombay city was ominous. The moment she got off the train, and took a few tentative steps forward, she almost 'tripped over a figure: it was a man and he was dead.' (1) This may be taken as an indication of what life she is going to have ahead. Soon after marriage, she starts facing a series of shocks and short-circuits.

Maya experiences first such shock during their four day clumsy sex honeymoon at a depressing hotel in Mahabaleshwar, a hill resort near Bombay. There she learns from him on enquiry that he slept with other women, he tried, but 'it didn't work.' (52) As he says: 'But the love making that followed was always a let down' or 'I have tried to make friends with them . . . but it has never worked.' (50) In another situation, she is in a love-making mood, but then he asks her to wait and says: 'I am not ready yet Maya. . . . You will have to be patient. It is going to take time. I can't. I just can't.' (53) This puzzles her beyond measure. On another occasion, she decides to take initiative and try her luck with him. She tries to snuggle upto him and caress him as they lay in the bed. But then Ranjan recoils—jumping back as though he had received an electric shock. He kept trembling in bed for a long time breathing heavily and asked her to 'stop behaving like a cheap woman. A prostitute.' (259) To Ranjan such a love-making mood is 'a very negative attitude,' a matter of 'big laugh,' a sort of 'nonsense.' (261) He considers eating, sleeping, doing office duties, attending social obligations, etc., enough for a successful life. On the other hand, Maya strongly feels 'missing something' without exactly knowing 'what that something was.' (258) However, the fact remains that this 'something' is the fact that she had 'no sex life at all,' 'had never experienced an orgasm,' and had realized that she would 'never bear children.' (257)

Maya's tragedy is that she is treated like a figure made of 'alabaster' and not of 'flesh and blood' before marriage by her mother and after marriage by her husband. When she was a small girl, her mother made her very self-conscious about her nakedness and changing contours. On reaching puberty, her mother had slapped her forehead to show as if 'a catastrophe had descended.' And after this 'event,' her parents stopped 'hugging or caressing her.' Then the mother had told Maya that she had become a 'young lady' and that she should not 'allow anybody to come close to her,' or 'be touched anywhere,' etc. And one day Maya heard her mother saying: 'I have no worries where Maya is concerned. She is not like other girls. She is very pure and unspoiled.' (259) But then Maya wondered whether she was really so. She had had time when she had felt stirring between her legs and squeezed pillow held by her knees to suppress the urge. After marriage, her husband expected her to be content with a decent house, four square meals, enough money and plenty of time to loll. (262-63) As for sex, Ranjan did not consider it 'important to anybody.' According to him if one's mind is busy and one keeps oneself active, there cannot be time 'to worry about sex.' (257) He wants Maya to be busy with other things and forget sex. This shocks Maya greatly.

Perhaps she would have overcome the sex factor if she had been satisfied in other respects. On the contrary, Ranjan poohpoohs even her genuine suggestions and problems. For instance, once she asks Ranjan why they cannot go out together at least on weekends, so that she could 'explore Bombay.' At this Ranjan snubs her, labelling such a demand as childish and admonishes her that life is not a picnic and that a married woman should learn 'to deal with responsibilities.' (27)

On another occasion, she suggests to have a part-time 'good cook so that she can' find a job 'as she has a degree in textile designing.' (28) Ranjan totally turns down this proposal, telling her that Bombay is like New York or London and that she is misfit to work here and above all 'Mummy won't like it.' As Adam didn't allow Eve to go alone away from him so does Ranjan, pointing to the lurking danger. Then she has nights when Ranjan enjoys 'deep sleep,' while she 'lay awake wondering how to induce sleep as a lack of physical exercise combined with mental lethargy had dulled her senses.' (31)

One night Maya very sincerely puts up her problem thus: 'Ranjan, I have been so lonely . . . all alone in a city that is not mine. In a house I don't still feel I belong to.' (261) Instead of understanding her problem and sharing her feelings, he gets annoyed, declares this complaint as funny and the creation of a sick mind. Once on an impulse, Maya buys a present, 'an attractive, leather-bound, handcrafted, filofax.' But the moment Ranjan sees it, he tells her that 'it was not his birthday' and that she should not 'waste money like that.' (266) Not only that, he warns her not to buy such things in future without his permission as 'everything costs money' and he 'hates waste.' This instance makes her feel 'so useless.' It strongly occurs to her that nobody needed her. Her parents no longer thought she belonged to them. Her husband belonged to his mother. And it was unlikely that she would bear children who would belong to her. (267)

Ranjan's mother obsession mortifies Maya the most. For everything, he expects Maya to make his mother as her model. For instance, one day Maya suggests that she would like to utilize her 'free time' for doing 'something good . . . constructive.' (139) Ranjan argues that housewives cannot have extra time and 'there is so much to be done around the home.' And then he tells her to 'take Ma's example,' as to how she has been busy round the clock without ever joining 'some useless classes of pottery or any other nonsense of that kind.' When Maya refers to some phone call from women, Ranjan sternly asks her to stay away from those Bombay women, as 'they have no morals.' (55) He dubs them as 'lazy, spoilt' and if she needed company or consultation, then 'call my mother. She knows Bombay inside out.' (56) Once Maya buys 'Basmati rice' which annoys Ranjan who calls it 'an extravagance' and further advises her to find out from his 'mother where she gets supplies from and buy the same brand.' (101) When

Ranjan's boss Tom comes for the special dinner and appreciates the artistic touch inside the house, Ranjan puts in saying that it is done by his mother, 'a very artistic lady.' (122) This stuns Maya, the real doer of the decoration. Regarding phone calls, Ranjan did phone Maya both from the office in Bombay or when away on the office tour, but then the content of the call used to be only either 'instructions' or 'a string of errands to run,' while Maya expected him to talk to her asking how she was, what she felt or showing at least 'a little concern.' (207) She hungered to listen to a 'soft caring sentence.' (209) On the other hand, in the case of his mother, the calls were regular, prolonged ones and full of concern. And he never allowed Maya to know the content of the nightly calls of his mother. (102)

Now this part can be concluded thus: Ranjan is the lone son of his parents. He is totally moulded and shaped by his mother. So the mother becomes his God. He fully confides in her. (205) As for worldly life, he thinks it enough to have a good job for income, a flat to live in, food to eat, and a woman as wife to take care of the household things. So after marriage he does not bother to talk to Maya about his 'childhood, his adolescence, his highs and lows,' (254) nor does he try to know from Maya about hers. In brief he is self-centred, 'self-absorbed.' (207) Of course, in the heart of his hearts, he wishes Maya well. He is generally kind to her, but this kindness is the sort people reserve for 'the physically handicapped or the abject poor.' (63) Maya does not need this. She is a young beautiful married wife, full of growing up pains. She very much wishes Ranjan to confide in her, talk to her his inner world, love her and have a feel for her. Being young and warm, she also wishes to 'step into one of the lively pubs, playing jazz' and 'sway to the music,' lose themselves a little in its carefree atmosphere, stroll along one of the many beaches, eat at road side snacks (97) and so on. She yearns for the type of freedom, the banana seller woman had. (87) In brief, as wife, she expects Ranjan to satisfy her physical and emotional needs. Ranjan doesn't do it, Nikhil does it. Nikhil is the fourth floor neighbour's son. He is a collegiate student junior to Maya by 5-6 years. He seems less interested in college lectures and studies, but very adept in fishing up females. In the first meeting itself, Maya can see 'his body language to be different' (16) and the appearance that of 'a warrior leading a victory parade.' (17) In the very first encounter, he 'looked straight into Maya's eyes and smiled' (18) and in this act alone he can see the green signal. But before proceeding ahead, he gets it confirmed by putting up the question to Maya: "Should I call you 'didi'?" And the moment Maya tells him to call her whatever he felt comfortable with, Nikhil can see his path open, destination clear and no 'competition' as such. He starts his moves slowly but steadily in the desired direction. As for Maya, she finds herself painfully aware of her divided state: "But Nikhil most definitely affected me and one part of me did not 'approve.' This was ridiculous—a newly married woman day-dreaming about a neighbour's son. Disgusting. And shameful." (32) But then Nikhil's well-planned efforts and tricks, Ranjan's continued self-centred thoughts and actions, and Maya's unfulfilled genuine needs finally make Maya give in to Nikhil's net.

Nikhil's first trick is to offer a cassette of his songs to Maya requesting her to allow him to listen to it on her cassette player. Initially, Maya doesn't entertain this request, but on knowing that it contains songs about her, she gets pleased and agrees 'to listen to it later . . . tomorrow.' (75) Maya who was constantly neglected, humiliated and hurt, now for the first time finds herself being praised and honoured as the song in the cassette is about her. The thought that somebody bothered for her, saw some good in her, stirs her greatly. Later she does listen to the cassette, likes it, and even conveys it to Nikhil; 'I loved your song.' (110) Thus Nikhil's first effort proves promising.

One day Nikhil spots Maya outside the building and grabs the opportunity by making an offer; 'come on,' 'I will treat you to some . . .' (90) When she refuses to go with him, he argues his best. However, Maya finally tells him that her husband would not like it and so she cannot accompany him. Next time, he finds her being pestered by the postman, Nikhil steps up like a hero and sets the postman right by making him deliver the letter. Then he enters the house with her and proposes to help her by doing her household work as he has 'no problem about washing, cleaning, dusting, polishing.' (109) But Maya requests him to go as it was not proper 'for a young man to be alone like this with a married woman.' (110) On another occasion he phones Maya and extends his offer to help her. Noting her nervous state, he tells her that there is no point in suffering silently and that she should 'come off it. Act real. Get real.' (105) The phone talk works and she collects courage to tell him that she would like to talk to him again. (106)

Nikhil's first big break-through occurs when her husband is away on 'a five star ten day official trip.' In the absence of Ranjan, Maya 'experienced a strange emptiness.' (160) But at the same time, instead of missing him, she has relief and feels free of pressure, approval seeking, being judged, watched, corrected, scolded, nagged, pushed, instructed. (163) She wonders what she was doing there in a city that was not her own and with a man for whom she didn't feel very much except 'a feeble affection.' A long inward debate continues, pushing her in 'a slough of despair.' (164) Against this background, one morning Nikhil drops in and proposes for 'a ride': 'Let us get out of here. Come on. Be daring. Do something spontaneous for once in life.' (170) But Maya makes it clear: 'listen, Nikhil . . . whether it is in Calcutta or Bombay, a married woman is not supposed to meet other men. That is all.' (169) But Nikhil coolly argues that he is simply a friend and he has come and proposed her for a ride simply because he genuinely likes her and he has liked her since the day they first met (171) Thus he darts argument after argument like Satan and stirs her self-confidence. In these moments, Maya seriously screens her marriage, her decision to move to Bombay, her cowardice at not asserting herself vis-a-vis Ranjan, her giving up a career, etc. And after a prolonged inward talk, she agrees for the ride. He takes her to Malabar Hill, then to Naaz Cafe, Marine Drive, etc. Nikhil does not forget to use the weapon of flattery. In the hotel he says: 'that is nice. You are smiling with your eyes. It suits you, Maya . . . You are beautiful. Believe it.' (175) Through his soft, slow, skilful, well-calculated measures, Nikhil succeeds in carving a niche in Maya's heart.

On another morning, Nikhil calls on her and proposes for a movie, but Maya turns it down. (197) However, here also we notice that she refuses to go not because she did not want to but because she was afraid of 'neighbours, servants and watchmen.' (198) Nikhil's efforts finally bear fruit when one morning he calls on Maya with flowers announcing his birthday. And then without giving her any time for thinking or reaction, he pulls her into his embrace and stops not till he accomplishes the act of love making 'painlessly, smoothly, gently.' (270) Of course, even in the process of love making, Maya remains conscious of the guilt, an inevitable result of tradition and culture. She keeps her eyes shut to be free from 'any responsibility' of the act or prove her 'innocence' later. (169) After the act of love making, Maya, like Eve, becomes cunning and tricky. This is evident when Ranjan asks her about the flowers. Maya tells him that those flowers were for the mother. When he asks why she did not attend the phone, she says that she was out to buy flowers for the mother. (175) Thus, the fall is complete entailing the same age-old questions.

Shobha De has thus reproduced and restructured the myth of Fall. The forces and factors behind the Fall have also been examined. However, it can be considered from one more angle stated by Maharshi Patanjali, a great ancient Indian thinker. According to him, *Klesas* cause man's fall and suffering. They are five in number: 'Avidya asmita raga dvesa abhinivesah klesah.'[2] Of the five, only 'avidya' and 'abhinivesa' are relevant in the present context. According to Patanjali, 'anitya asuci dukha anatmasu nitya suci sukha atmakhyatih avidya.' (107) That is, to mistake the transience for permanence, the impure for the pure, pain for pleasure and non existent self for self. Maya and Nikhil suffer from 'avidya.' Maya mistakes non-existent self for self. The main source of her sorrow is the feeling that nobody, nothing belongs to her. (266) Nikhil mistakes pain for pleasure. He thinks that sensual pleasures alone are real and so he diverts all his efforts to have those pleasures. As for Ranjan, he suffers from 'abhinivesa' which is defined as 'swarasvahi vidusah api tatha arudhah abhinivesah.'[3] This means to develop a mono-directional thinking. For instance, Ranjan thinks that what he knows and does, that alone is true and important.

This long discussion can finally be closed with a brief comment that Shobha De's maturity, insightfulness, alertness and ambivalence have reached new heights in the present novel. This we see particularly with regard to projecting the psyche of an Indian married woman who is caught and crushed between the nature-culture wheels on the one hand, and pulled apart by the centrifugal acts of Ranjan, her husband and those of centripetal of Nikhil, her lover, on the other.

NOTES

1. Shobha De, *Second Thoughts* (Penguin: New Delhi, 1996)
2. B.K.S. Iyengar, *Light on the Yoga Sutras of Patanjali* (New Delhi: Harper Collins, 1993), p. 105.
3. *Ibid.*, p. 110.

Second Thoughts: A Critique

JAYDIPSINH DODIYA

Second Thoughts[1] is Shobha De's masterpiece. The narrator of the novel is the female-protagonist, Maya. The prologue is in the third person but the subsequent chapters of the novel are in the first person. In *Second Thoughts*, Shobha De vividly presents an "explosive tale of love and betrayal" at the surface level and the "hollowness and hypocrisy" lurking behind Indian traditional marriages at the deeper level. Thus the novel focuses on the hollowness of Indian marriage.

Maya is the central character in the novel. She is a very attractive young girl with her 'skin tone as warm rich, golden brown, like sunlight dancing on the Hooghly,' 'gleaming jet, black hair' and 'large, dark eyes.' (4) Maya, trained as a Textile Designer, is a charming young girl. Earlier she wanted to become a leading journalist. She belongs to an educated middle class family from Calcutta. She marries Ranjan who is equally handsome and ambitious. He has 'thick dark hair, the intense large eyes,' 'strong chest and shoulders.' (51) He has a degree from America and has been employed as a Bank Executive. He has a small but beautiful flat on the fourth floor in Bombay. In their first arranged meeting, Maya and Ranjan like each other. Then they decide to get married. Ranjan has great respect for his mother who is quite happy with her son's wife. She says, "I think we have made right choice in Maya." (252) So was the impression of Maya who thought that marrying Ranjan was like marrying Bombay: "I thought I was the luckiest girl in my locality." As the story advances we realize that both Maya and Ranjan were not made for each other. In other words, it was not a right decision as far as their so-called marriage is concerned. It disturbs their domestic harmony considerably.

Some of the reasons for the failure of their marriage can be roughly tabulated as follows. Maya has almost all the material facilities to enjoy life after marriage. But she is not happy in the true sense of the term. She has no contentment at all. She feels that her husband Ranjan is unable to cater to her basic needs. Ranjan is very cold from sexual point of view. Maya thinks that she will bear no child in future. This is the reason why she feels empty amidst plenty.

Maya's husband worships his mother like Goddess and he begins to neglect Maya day by day. In fact it is Ranjan's mother obsession that mortifies Maya most. Her husband wants that she should follow his mother as an ideal woman. When Ranjan's boss Tom comes for the special dinner and appreciates the artistic touch inside the house, Ranjan says that the credit goes to his mother, 'a very artistic lady'. These words of Ranjan upset Maya, the real doer of the decoration. Ranjan is not honest enough to appreciate the artistic talent of his wife.

Maya experiences so much shock instead of pleasure during their four-day clumsy honeymoon at a depressing hotel in Mahabaleshwar, a hill resort near Bombay. Strangely enough, she comes to know from him on enquiry that he shared bed with other women, he tried, but 'it didn't work'. At this stage, Maya is in a love-making mood but Ranjan asks her to wait and says, 'I am not ready yet Maya. . . . You will have to be patient. It is going to take time. I can't. I just can't.' (55) When Maya tries to force him, he recoils—jumping back as though he had received an electric shock. He keeps trembling in bed for a long time breathing heavily and asks her to stop behaving like 'a cheap woman. A prostitute.' (259) This incident helps readers understand Maya's plight sympathetically. Maya as the wife of Ranjan is not able to enjoy the conjugal bliss in the true sense of the term.

Maya needs someone to love her. She turns to Nikhil for the purpose. Nikhil, a college boy, is 'good looking, confident, sporty, cocky, flirtatious, lazy, spoilt and quite irresistible.' (22) Unlike Ranjan he is 'hungry always.' (54) In fact Maya is not a cheap woman. She is really good at heart. But she is helpless and circumstances compel her to change her mind. Maya fully realizes that her wedding with Ranjan was a blunder on her part.

Ranjan tries to restrain Maya's freedom. She is not allowed to mix with other women of Bombay. She is not allowed to do any job. No educated woman of Maya's calibre can tolerate this sort of nonsense. This is also one of the factors behind the conflict between Maya and

Ranjan. Ranjan and Maya are incompatible with each other. Every sensual advance from Maya's side meets with a prosaic, practical and hard response. She admits: "tonight I wanted to behave like a cheap woman. . . . I was not getting any sleep . . . the old ache between the legs was bothering me. I reached out for Ranjan, put my arm across his shoulders. [But] I could feel his body stiffening, resisting." (259-60) Asha Khare rightly observes: "The story depicts over-bearing female characters and weak male characters. It exposes the male ego, social pretences, and public facades. It is a tale of two cities, Bombay and Calcutta, which contains vivid descriptions of the two with details of food and dresses. Sexual overtones, the chief characteristic of Shobha De's work are over-riding throughout the novel."

Thus Shobha De's *Second Thoughts* throws light on the traditional marriage in Indian society in which woman has to suffer a lot . Maya's silent cry for true companionship for herself always remains unheard. The hollowness of such marriages is evident even in the case of Maya's parents, who "hardly ever talked to each other" and even their "quarrels or heated arguments were out of question." (70) Maya's own case is far more pitiable. She and her husband are not made for each other. She painfully realizes,

> Now here we were, locked together in a relationship that didn't satisfy either of us. He very obviously longed to be on his own, leading the life he had become so accustomed to as a student, and then as a promising bank executive living by himself. And I longed for the perfect romantic companion. (252)

Some literary critics have justified Maya's affair with Nikhil. When Ranjan is of no use for her, she has no other way out. Even the title *Second Thoughts* is also quite suggestive as far as the protagonist's affair with Nikhil is concerned. The novel also reveals that Shobha De's exploration of new horizons is really wonderful.

NOTES

1. Shobha De, *Second Thoughts* (New Delhi: Penguin, 1996).
2. Asha Khare, "The Text and Context in Shobha De's *Second Thoughts*."

Variations of Betrayal in *Small Betrayals*

MADHUMALATI ADHIKARI

Shobha De's dubious backdoor entry into the hallowed hall of literature, enabled her to plunge effortlessly into the world of commercial novel writing. Initially, having launched herself as a gossip columnist, she remained unconcerned about the ethical consequences; she was content to paint life through the details of fornication. Inspired by worldly aspirations, she engrossed herself in authoring pot-boilers and not classics; her devotions were towards Lakshmi and not Saraswati. The success story of Shobha De as a commercial writer is evident from the comment of David Davidar, the publisher, editor of Penguin Books: "You can either have good reviews or good sales."[1]

The superstitious streak in De has compelled her to search for titles that begin with 'S,' the first alphabet of her first name: *Socialite Evenings, Strange Obsession, Starry Nights, Sisters, Snapshots* and *Small Betrayals*. The magazines that she had founded or edited like *Stardust* and *Society*, also fit into the same design. It cannot be mere coincidence.

Despite a facile prose and the immensely readable quality of her fiction, Shobha De is condemned for the pornographic ingredients in her fiction. A.G. Khan's very strong criticism, "In fact I would regard her entire acrobatics as an attempt to reduce 'fiction' to 'fuction,'"[2] is partially, if not entirely, true. I would like to stress in this paper that De in her latest publication *Small Betrayals* (1995), a collection of short stories, has matured from 'fuction' to 'frictions' of life. She has viewed the conflicts and contradictions of human existence from multiple angles. Impossible stances of copulations and perverted sexual acts have been shifted to periphery. Her plots have liberated themselves from the questionable support of these shocking episodes. The short stories have either managed to overcome the obscenities or its significance has been reduced to nothingness. Why this metamorphosis? Undeniably, De, now seasoned, has realized that to grasp and project the complex meanings of life, one cannot remain riveted to the primordial sexual relationships only. To be accepted as a serious writer, one must rise above the surface frictions of emotions, passions and intellect in human beings.

A collection of short stories is normally popular because it presents different snapshots of life; variety is its speciality. Not many authors have attempted to weave different artistic webs around a single theme. James Joyce's *Dubliners* is one of the finest examples of the rare practice. De in *Small Betrayals*, has managed to repeat the feat quite favourably. She has explored the average experiences of betrayal in its infinite variety and reached the core of uncertainties and complexities of life that never dissolve and resolve completely. The stories of this collection are not of equal merit. Either the male or the female point of view is normally projected but occasionally, both the views are juxtaposed. One is pleasantly surprised by De's clinical interpretation of human nature. All the stories narrated in the third person, introduce rapid remodulation of circumstances to explode illusions and establish reality. In "The Motorcycle," "The Fair One," "The Bar Man" and "The Fern Lady," De is more interested in exploring the consciousness of the male protagonist than in narrating his deeds. The complex personalities, the emotions of the character demand patient, minute and unsentimental power of analysis that De possesses abundantly as an observer. "The Decision," "Voices," "The Trip," "Lines," "Dewali," "Flowers," "Late Arrival," emphasize upon obscure, unpredictable and often inexplicable impulses of women. "Repeat Performance" and "Bindi," dissimilar to other stories, apprehend reality through the disintegrating social forces that often give birth to maladjustments, distress and complexes in mortals.

"Repeat Performance" is a story of an alienated couple, Ashish and Ambika. They live together because it is bothersome to change the routine. In an interview, Ambika comments: "He has his priorities and I have mine. . . . We believe in giving each other plenty of space."[3] The space is so wide that there is no attachment between the two. At times, she wishes him to die. (133) In her sterile life, she nurtures a "hope," a hope of better communication and friendship with her licentious actor-husband. Repeated betrayal of trust fossilizes the distance. Ambika can only laugh hysterically, when she is informed by Ashish that he is suffering from some terminal disease. She cannot feel for her husband. Conditions and equations have altered for her. Ashish commits suicide and repeats the performance often acted on the stage but this time, without any accolade. The interest of the story lies in the contradictory meanings of artificiality, deception, frustration, loneliness in the tinsel town, viewed from different points of view.

'Flowers' describes the emotional and stereotyped wait of an enamoured but oft-betrayed wife for her callous and perfidious husband. A compelling question demands our attention. "Is the wife blissfully, unaware or is it conscious unawareness?" De has made the over-worked plot interesting by narrating it from the point of view of the mother, Mrs. Gokhale. She watches helplessly as life from her daughter's body drains out. The materialistic attitude of the nurse and the apathetic disposition of the husband frames the tragedy of life. Curiously enough, the psychic dwarfing takes place in the mother and the reader; the wife remains quite free from it. De the feminist, etches an archetypal condition of women that Margaret Atwood describes as "basic victim position," where one denies the fact that one is a victim.[4] De has drawn a distinction between the conventions to which people are usually oriented and the real meaning of living. 'The Repeat Performance' and 'Flowers' outline the disharmony in a conjugal life: one reflecting rebellion and the other conformity.

Focal to De's presentation in "Late Arrival" is the thrust on the plight of a girl-child, a classic example of neglect. She is betrayed by her family and the middle aged professor who exploits her sexually: "As his hands continued to explore the contours of her body . . . Amla . . . wondered which one to blame for her own rotten destiny." (185) Her precarious existence presents the archetypical narrative pattern of the hunter and the hunted, pursuit and forced submission, accompanied by images of suffocation, dwarfing and degradation. The predictable catastrophe, the perennial dilemma of woman "the rape trauma archetype"[5] impoverishes the excellence of the story. Amla's world remains unexciting because of her creator's unimaginative perception. Even in her inferiority, she fails to exercise autonomy.

"The Motorcycle," outlines the unfulfilled expectations of a young couple confined and rooted in their respective cultures. Pesi Agboatwallah, much against the wishes of his tradition bound parents, marries a Hindu girl, Mohini. The glamour of her liberated ways wanes within the first day of their married life, "Pesi Agboatwallah had made a major blunder" and embittered Mohini flings back, "I thought you were different . . . that's why I married you." (21) De should be given due credit for etching the ethos of the Parsee culture though it is not her primary concern. Her intention is to reconstruct the tragedy of life through the confrontation of two cultures, both destroying and not nourishing. Pesi and Mohini become victims of trifling cultural rituals.

Mr. Godbole's erotic fantasy about his Parsee neighbour in "The Fair One" is not the cause but the effect of his wife's temporary rejection of his sexual needs. The over-worked wife's frigidity, makes him feel alienated, unwanted and distanced from his regular bearings. To overcome the feeling of neglect, he indulges in aphrodisiac reveries, a process of wish-fulfilment. Godbole's behaviour has Freudian overtones though there is no inkling of "egoistic and ambitious wishes"[6] asserting itself. His wife's return to the role of Rambha, settles everything happily. Despite the alluring lady's presence in the opposite flat, Godbole contentedly "turned the lights out and went back to his bed. It was warm and welcoming. The light across the compound . . . had nothing to do with him." (37) Shobha De in this story skims over the details of imaginative or real erotic behaviour; it is treated as something secondary. Her emphasis is on the repercussions of sexual starvation. She never wishes to judge her creatures and yet there is a suggestion of man's vulnerability and woman's power.

The pathetic cravings of Dheeraj, a successful advertising executive, for a satisfying companionship in "The Fern Lady," and the maddening loneliness of Santosh, "the swashbuckling, sought-after, upwardly mobile" (87) hero of the past of "The Bar Man," are the inevitable conditions of modern-day existence. Dheeraj betrayed by his ex-wife and present wife, searches in vain for friendship and rapport in the mysterious Fern Lady and Santosh once successful of the woman whom he had loved in the past. She disowns him completely: "A woman giggled, glanced disinterestedly at Santosh and said, 'It's nothing . . . Don't worry. He is not anyone we know.'" (98) Indeed, a clearly focused body of meaning appears to be, "Men were such gullible dolts when it came to sex." (96) De very adroitly demolishes the archetypal image of man as the dominant gender and uncovers his Achilles' heel. Physical realities have deep significance for De and she, by asserting woman's sexual supremacy, again alters the norm.

In most of the stories, De has either presented the male's or the female's point of view but in "Bindi," she has juxtaposed the plight of a young couple, Sushma and Asif, entrapped in a politically volatile atmosphere of Bombay. After the riots, the mutual suspicion fanned by parents, friends, colleagues, servants and neighbours, interferes with their normal conjugal life. The seed of distrust planted by the obscurantists, ultimately, fractures marital relationships. In a way, Sushma and Asif betray each other's trust. The Bindi becomes the symbol of revolt and assertion. Here, neither the wife nor the husband is either the victim or the vanquisher; both are the scapegoats of different but rigid religious faiths. De's magnifying glass focuses on the betrayed human race. The desire for responsible selfhood for the achievement of authenticity is thwarted by religious dogmatism. Interestingly, the story obliterates the role of Eros. The absence of rational humanism is the cause of conflict.

"Voices," "The Decision," "Lines" and "Dewali" concretize the meaning of "wholeness" in women. Masculine culture translates the story of women into an ambiguous and devaluated symbol. Women are to be used; they are the handmaids of man; their search for identity is frustrated either by a harsh or a soft treatment. Against this run-of-the-mill portraits, De conceptualizes women as the repositories of power and authenticity in "The Decision" and "Dewali." Manisha the protagonist of "The Decision," takes a feminist stance that can be condemned by a traditionalist. The story frames a marital discord that fundamentally springs from rebellious Manisha who demands equity in marriage. In feminist fiction, more often than not, the institution of marriage is a patriarchal enclosure,[7] wherein woman's needs and opinions are habitually neglected. Manisha's loving but ambitious husband desires to migrate to America, the dream-world. Manisha, content with her bank job, opposes the move, "I never wanted to go, remember?" (45) "He should have thought of my feelings. My life. My priorities." (52) She feels betrayed because Mohan disregards her feelings and desires. Her decision is, "I am not going," (51) even if it means divorce. Her mother cannot convince her about her wrong decision. She refuses to lead a trapped existence like her mother who was forced to live with the detestable husband because she had been imprecated by this man. Since Manisha was the symbol of her bondage, she hated her;

the younger daughter was her "revenge on that wretched drunk" (56) whom she adored. Manisha foresees her caged condition in her mother and decides to take a more decent and civilized step. De hints at Manisha's future dilemma, "She began filling up cartons with things he'd left behind" (58) but she wondered if she could really get rid of Mohan's things. "She touched her stomach, something told her there was life inside." (58) She decides to handle the problem later. The open-ended story leaves much space for the conjectures of the reader. Will she or won't she learn something from her mother's example? The story handles complex psychological problems rooted in the fixed roles of women predetermined in the system. She declines to plant her frustration on her off-spring as her mother had done. Her decision, independent and non-conformist in nature, establishes Manisha's desire for self-determination. De creates Manisha through a negative dialectics and yet, the identity is positive.

If a woman's desire to defy her "decorative function" is remotely suggested in "The Decision," a variation of the same theme is more aggressively asserted in "Dewali." It too paints a picture of conjugal disharmony, the result of subversive elements in gender norms. Following the feminist trend in women writers, it closes with a defiant and optimistic mood of the protagonist, Kalindi. The story is narrated backwards and begins with, "It was going to be a bleak Diwali for Kalindi." (137) Slowly the story is unfolded before the reader. Kalindi's husband Suresh, a top-ranking marketing man hopes to make his wife an "enterpreneur" and reach "the top." (140) "The image of the well adjusted happy couple," (140) important for both of them, is nurtured carefully. But her business success atrophies the marital bliss and becomes the perennial cause of Suresh's resentment. Initially secure in his superiority, he would often comment, "'Women must be self-sufficient.' And yet, when Kalindi's small business took off and she began spending more time outside the house, Suresh's resentment had become vocal and obvious." (143) Provoked continuously by his ill-temper, one day, she flings back, "I am sick of you bullying, sick of your rudeness, sick of your threats, sick of your accusation." (145) It is not a straightforward equation of thwarted ambitions. For Kalindi, Suresh's induction is a form of betrayal. Despite her husband's "indifference," (146) Kalindi experiences the delight of "wholeness." The dark mood prevailing on the Dewali day cannot crush Kalindi's recently acquired self-confidence, "There was a light shining *within*—the flame steady and strong. And Kalindi was no longer afraid." (147, emphasis added) The image of the steady flame of light establishes beyond doubt Kalindi's autonomous position. The battle between the sexes for supremacy confirms her victory but the muted echoes are not congenial. De's message is clear: women of substance have to face irreconcilable alternatives for self-definition. Matrimony is projected as a negative institution. Our protagonist scribbles in her planner, "Marriage is the ugliest compromise in the world." (146) A parallel to Kalindi's scarring and circumscribing, an archetypal pattern, is to be found in female *Bildungsroman*.

"Voices" analyzes the complex mother-daughter relationship. It mirrors a conflict, seemingly restricted to a woman's world but factually, the problem is universal in nature. In this, De is neither interested in adultery nor in any form of female exploitation but a very subtle form of betrayal of love that is just suggested. De must be congratulated for creating a typical Maharashtrian ethos. Mangalabai, a famous singer of yester-years, takes great pride in her elder daughter Sumantai "an outstanding classical singer" (1) and patronizes her younger daughter Manik, "only an housewife." (1) The mother feels betrayed when Sumantai refuses to sing for her mother's seventy-fifth birthday celebrations. Manik is asked to sing and she agrees even though she is aware of her artistic imperfections. Dramatic events (maybe planned by Mangalabai) alter the colour of the function. Manik to collect her confidence states, "I'll do it, I'll sing for aie." (6) Her unadulterated love for her mother is quite evident. The programme is inaugurated by Mangalabai's emotional speech and while closing her lecture she invites Manik to join her on the dais, "I now invite my beloved daughter Manik to join me on the stage. . . . I have discovered something today about her and about myself that is more precious than any public performance. I have discovered a daughter's love for her mother." (8) Her final words indicate that the function is over and Manik is saved from the ordeal of singing. While leaving the hall, she speaks briefly to her younger daughter, "You'll realize one day that I did it for you to spare your public humiliation." (8) Sumantai's betrayal makes the mother aware of Manik's love and respect for her but despite this educative experience, she is not cured of her superciliousness. It is not mere maternal love that forestalls Manik's mediocre performance; it is an intelligent measure to circumvent her personal humiliation at Manik's failure. De lays stress on the traditional and modern roles of woman and also dares to project the tarnished picture of a mother. As a realist, she offers a snapshot of the darker sides of human nature and as an idealist, she remains concerned about the ethical angle.

"Lines," the most remarkable story of the collection, narrates the tale of Simran's unequal battle with the lines on her face that are out to destroy her beauty and youth. She is "still" beautiful with the aid of bottled lotions and "natural kitchen cosmetics." People are shocked by her narcissistic tendency and the inevitable question is voiced by a spokesman of the patriarchal society, "But mother, why do you want to look beautiful all the time? You are a widow—what difference is it going to make?" (111) Woman, a "possession" of man, traditionally, is supposed to become indifferent to physical beauty, if he is absent. A beauty conscious widow is considered to be evil. Simran, through her conviction, challenges the stereotyped image of woman. To her, beauty makes "the difference between being alive . . . and dead." (112) She neither nurtures nor preserves her beautiful body for others; it is for personal satisfaction. Simran's detachment towards men in general is not disintegrating but revitalizing. She remains "mesmerized" by her body, "such beauty, such perfection, such bliss." (123) By underlining Simran's personal absorption, De explodes the myth that woman's identity exists largely as being-for-others rather than being-for-herself. She challenges the dominant social constructions of identity and gender. Simran's experience is equated with 'bliss.' It cannot emerge from selfish gratification. She dislodges the males from her world and monitors personal freedom, power and all kinds of human relationships. Her inner space remains unscathed. Despite being a woman, the impossible is made possible. De's feminist viewpoint is translated unequivocally through this story.

Shobha De's present collection of short stories dedicated to her critics, challenges them to condemn her on routine charges. Unmistakably, she rises above the circumscribed and pornographic view of life. The external details do not over-shadow the exhilarating possibilities of the unplumbed consciousness. The distasteful and superfluous details of sexual acrobatics have been either erased or muted as De has realized that in literary practice, "the body of her writing and not the writing of her body," is ultimately important. It is dangerous to put any body at the centre of the search for male or female identity. Such misdirected explorations can lead one to damaging misconceptions. In this collection, De has concretized varied dimensions of male-female relationships, often tortured and tormented. Jaundiced gender perceptions have not blurred her vision. Demanding questions have been raised and answered; primitive instinctive conflicts pushed to the periphery have given way to the eroding and fragmenting frictions of human life. The institution of marriage has been viewed from the male and female angle. De has established that the realization of selfhood is a problematic experience for man as well as woman. She pinpoints strategic moments of betrayal when self-knowledge vanishes into ignorance. Her sensitive portrayal of life neutralizes the effect of derogatory criticism.

NOTES

1. Sunil Sethi, "De In, De Out," *Seminar*, No. 384, 1991, p. 40.
2. A.G. Khan, "Shobha De 'Vatsyayani,'" *Fiction of the Nineties*, ed. Veena Noble Das and R.K. Dhawan (New Delhi: Prestige, 1994), p. 47.
3. Shobha De, *Small Betrayals* (New Delhi: UBS, 1995), p. 129.
4. Margaret Atwood, *Survival: A Thematic Guide to Canadian Literature* (Toronto: Anansi, 1972), p. 36.
5. Annis Pratt, *Archetypal Patterns in Women's Fiction* (Bloomington: Indiana University Press, 1981), p. 5.
6. Sigmund Freud, "The Relation of the Poet to Day Dreaming," *On Creativity and the Unconscious*, trans. I.F. Grant Duff (NY: Harper, 1958), p. 44.
7. Pratt, p. 46.
8. Nancy K. Miller, "Women's Autobiography in France: For a Dialectic Identification," *Women and Language in Literature and Society*, ed. Sally Macnell, Ginet Ruth Borkar and Nelly Furman (NY: Praeger, 1980), p. 27.

Reflections on *Shooting from the Hip*

K.V. SURENDRAN

"From a very early age, perhaps the age of five or six, I knew that when I grew up I should be a writer. Between the ages of about seventeen and twenty-four I tried to abandon this idea, but I did so with the consciousness that I was outraging my true nature and that sooner or later I should have to settle down and write books." This is how George Orwell begins his famous essay "Why I Write." The essay concludes as follows: "And looking back through my work, I see that it is invariably where I lacked a political purpose that I wrote lifeless books and was betrayed into purple passages, sentences without meaning, decorative adjectives and humbug generally."[1]

The immediate provocation to quote Orwell is the "Why I Write" of Shobha De which is prefixed to her selected writings entitled *Shooting from the Hip*. In the author's note to the volume, she remarks that "over twenty years of writing lies carelessly stuffed into countless plastic bags in different cupboards and corners"[2] of her home. She says that the initial excitement of an enthusiasm for seeing her name in print lasted for the first three months or so: "It was during this all-too-short period that I actually took the time and trouble to maintain some semblance of order by filing my published pieces neatly." (xi) In "Why I Write," De observes that she writes because she loves writing: "I write because I like the feel of paper under my ball-point pen. Writing is pure sex. I like to see a blank sheet fill up. I like to think while my fingers move. I like the way words jump around inside my head impatiently like they can't wait to pop out and be born." (2) Like Orwell, De does not speak about "the power of facing unpleasant facts" but she is versatile in her writings and touches upon different areas like politics, media, food, festivals, films, books, people, travelogues and a lot more.

In this paper, an attempt is made to have a bird's eye view of her volume *Shooting from the Hip* which consists of fourteen major titles which are 'Politics,' 'Media,' 'Profiles,' 'Gender Issues,' 'India and Her People,' 'Festivals and Religion,' 'Bombay,' 'Travel,' 'Food,' 'Shobha in Retrospect,' 'On Being a Writer, a Columinst and a Media Person,' 'Of Books and Reviews,' '"Phirang" Film Reviews,' 'Miscellany' and 'Sushila's Secret,' De's first short story.

The first section which is on politics has five essays in it. The opening essay is titled "Angana Vastrams, ahoy," where her target is P.V. Narasimha Rao, the former prime minister of India. She remarks that "the nation must be assured a plentiful supply of angavastrams if we are to get anywhere at all." (6)

In her next essay, "Quit, and Quickly Too," she criticizes the 'desis with a phoren-fixation.' According to her there are some who get into fifth-rate American universities and frown at everything that is Indian when they come back. "They acquire accents at the airport. Then come back one summer later and find everything 'dirty' and 'noisy.' . . . They only drink mineral water. . . . They refer to hoardings as 'billboards.' And bring their favourite brand of toilet paper with them. . . . They deserve to clean their own toilets 'back home.'" (10)

In her essay "An Unequal Exchange," De chooses to laugh at the new economic policies initiated by Dr. Manmohan Singh, the former finance minister. The budget presentation is a major event both in the eyes of the government and the ordinary tax-payer. The effect of the budget will be reflected in the prices of the commodities in a society which has already turned market-oriented. That is why we find observations like "My shampoos will cost less and I'll finally be able to buy a micro-oven" (11) in the novel. The tendency of an average Indian to blindly believe whatever is given on the TV is laughed at by the author. "I believe what I see on TV and according to Montek Singh Ahluwalia," (12) the effect of the TV on the society is tremendous and it is the market which decides what a person should buy or not buy. "For most of us what really counts is that washing machines will cost less. So will video recorders. If I'm lucky I'll be able to buy a new car." (13)

In the essay "Billet-Doux to Bill," De laughs at the Indian intellectuals. She also attacks the leftists, especially the Marxists and remarks that "the marxist machine in our country functions differently from anywhere else in the world." (18-19) The next target is paper presentations: "In case you'd like me to present a paper on the subject just give me a shout from the White House. No problem. Anything for an old friend. First class fare, of course. And accommodation in a five-star hotel." (19)

In her first essay "Rhapsody in black'n'white" in the section on 'Media,' De makes interesting observations on the way newspapers work. What specially appeals to her is the "cabins" which play an important role in the lives of *The Times of India* employees: "A person's worth was judged by his 'cabin-status'—no cabin meant he or she was a nobody. Cabins were jealously guarded. There was a fierce atmosphere that separated the have from the have-nots." (25) The employees occupying the cabins enjoy all kinds of facilities. They have a bell to summon the peon seated on a stool outside their cabins, an intercom to get the secretary in etc.

In "Independent Opinion," De is critical of the attitude of the Indians. She makes a reference to the announcement on board an aircraft and hastens to add that Indian Airlines or Vayudoot don't bother about greeting the passengers. If they do, "they sound surly and mechanical." (29) According to her, the worst sin a journalist can commit is to admit his or her weakness. She thinks that we Indians sepecialise in laughing at others, never at ourselves.

De talks about double standards in journalism in her essay "Martyr or Traitor." It begins with a query: "Does the sacking of an editor warrant front page coverage in a national paper?" (32) She is of the view that editors of competitive dailies seem to think so. The reference is to the dismissal of Arun Shourie, the noted journalist. She is of the opinion that once a person is down, the whole community will come out openly against him with all sorts of allegations. "All those who chose silence for so many years will suddenly develop overnight vociferousness and attack the man who is now seen as an intolerable bigot. One can almost hear the invectives—fascist, hypocrite, pamphleteer, psychotic, megalomaniac . . . and worst of all, a traitor—someone out to wreck the unity of India by shoving his own narrow-minded politics down his readers' throats while attempting to overthrow an elected government." (33)

In "More Indian than Most Indians," the Indian English is made fun of more than anything else. The typical Indian way of addressing people as "saar," use of progressive tense even when verbs of perception are used and also the general tendency to use this tense form, the unbearable pronunciation of certain words ('gorrment,' for example) the use of the unenglish phrase "goodname," the Indian way of referring to one's wife as "Mrs.," mixing of codes in speech ("Shubhkaamna," for example), ungrammatical constructions ("why you accepted it?") etc. all come under attack in this beautiful piece.

"The Vulnerable Vernacular" is an essay where De criticizes the "Angrez" complex which Bombay suffers from. According to her, "a cub-reporter from any old English language publication is given immediate access whereas an editor with years of experience and a proven track record belonging to 'Lingo Press' is denied the courtesy of even a phone interview at times." (38) She closes the essay narrating her own experience where she received a call around 10.30 p.m. with a request for an instant telephonic interview for her magazine. Eventhough her daughter told her to call back the next morning at a decent hour, she never did it. That is the Indian way of doing things.

The section "Profiles" has fourteen essays where De tells us about personalities who made their mark in different areas. The first one in the series is on the noted journalist and writer Khushwant Singh. Gender issue comes in a small way in her discussion on Khushwant Singh where she says that men are "O.K. provided they can be kept in their place" (44) which according to her is easier said than done. She is full of praise for Khushwant Singh: "One can accuse him of several things, but one thing you can be sure of—with him the word boredom becomes extinct. He has one of the liveliest, naughtiest, funniest minds in the business." (44) He is described as a shy, unconfident individual looking for constant reassurance. At the same time he is a great performer. He is not a shrewd and calculating man. But he has "concentrated on cultivating a particularly unpalatable image of himself as a free leader, boozer and womanizer." (45)

Vikram Seth is another person for whom De has great admiration: "I like him instantly. But then . . . so does everybody who meets him. I comment on his T.V. chat show appearance." (49) De found out that they had something in common: "My sympathies were entirely with him. I'd discovered by then that Vikram Seth and I have at least one big thing in common—we both need 10 hours of sleep. Maybe more." (50)

Ramnath Goenka of the Indian Express Group fascinated De for different reasons. "Mr. Goenka was known to be particularly adept at recalling every employee's salary down to the last paisa. He also used to keep an eye on expense accounts." (52) He was one who trusted and respected few people. "As far as he was concerned, a person either fitted into his game-plan for a specific purpose or he didn't. If the latter, he became irrelevant, insignificant and virtually non-existent overnight. But if he sensed even potential future use, the taps were turned on and charm dripped with each word." (53)

The world famous cartoonist R.K. Laxman appears in De's essay "A very unusual 'Common Man'": "Laxman wouldn't be Laxman without his prickliness, vitriol and arrogance. He doesn't suffer fools lightly and makes his impatience with them most obvious." (56) De describes him as a very hardworking type of man who does not even spare his Sundays. She observes that his cartoons are sold like hot cakes and collectors queue up for his prized cows. He is one who travels extensively and she concludes the portrait by maintaining that he has earned a permanent and well-deserved place in history.

Maqbool Fida Husain who has been in news for his controversial painting of Goddess Saraswati is described as 'the Quintessential Sensualist' in the essay of the same title. According to De when the history of contemporary art in India gets written, "one solitary name will stand out from the rest and that will be M.F. Husain's." (61) She is sure that his art will live on while mediocrity fades away into "ignominious oblivion." De regards Husain a true genius who is receptive, sensitive and responsive and who will live in the empire of the senses—"reacting to colour, sound, taste, touch and smell." (60)

De is full of appreciation for the business giant J.R.D. Tata. Tata who was honoured with Bharat Ratna by the Govt. of India, according to De, had a dream for a free way connecting the narrow, loosely linked islands that make up Bombay to the mainland. "He pursued the plan for ten long years, through the Antulay regime and later, taking up the issue with no less a person than Indira Gandhi, who was the Prime Minister then." (64) However, he was shocked to discover that the project was being stalled at the highest level. She concludes her essay by observing that what amazed her much was "the unmistakable gleam in his eyes as he stared" (65) at her midriff.

Film actress Rekha, who according to De is committed to herself, is nothing short of a "terrific bore." De doesn't know Rekha personally and she has no regrets about it. "The one time I had met her was when she'd been on the fringes of the film world. She'd struck me as a giddy headed, loud, coarse and empty teenager. She was far from attractive at that point and one wouldn't have given her more than a couple of years in the business as a C-grade actress." (67) It is not De's concern whether Rekha is a fantastic actress or not: "I can't comment on that since I haven't watched too many of her movies." (68)

De considers Amitabh Bachchan, "a superstar in Retirement" to be "a well-bred, well-mannered, polished corporate executive." (69) The Bofors cloud has made the superstar's position untenable and De suspects that all is not well with him vis-a-vis the Bofors gun deal. "Mr. Bachchan may have India at his feet. But the old ghosts have yet to be exorcised. He may have been exonerated by the Prime Minister. But somewhere, past guilts still remain." (72) There was no change in her impression about the filmstar in spite of the meeting that she had with him.

The article "Killer on the Prowl" begins with a discussion of Imran Khan's affair with Zeenat Aman which was once the top story of the "gossip circuit." She says that Imran, as is well known, is "an unbearable, arrogant so-and-so." (75) Imran, De says, has a vast fan-following in India, but unlike Kapil Dev, he is hardly one to be kind or even polite to his admirers. She concludes the note with the remark that "Imran at 40 can continue his winning streak with women, confident that all he has to do is shrug and they'll come running. Some men have all the luck. And all the looks, too." (76)

She had a couple of meetings with Gavaskar but her impression about him is not very high. She thinks that he is fit to be a political leader. "He would have made a splendid neta, or may be it's an ambassadorial posting he's after? A great idea, especially if it's Pakistan. Tea and sympathy from Naqaz Sharif. And countless fans too." (60) De remembers that Sunil isn't an easy subject to interview. However, she does not ignore the strengths of Gavaskar. She considers him one of the world's greatest cricketers. "He combines great intelligence with focused concentration and a single-mindedness of purpose that's most intimidating to ordinary mortals." (78)

In her article on Pamella Bordes, De tries to talk about a woman who according to her "desperately seeks herself." De says that "it is easy to see why people fall in lust with Pamella Bordes. In pin-up photographs, or high-gloss fashion-spreads. In person, the bawdy Ms. Bordes turns out to be a harmless-looking hatti katti Punjab di putri. . . . But the first impression is of a waif-like, slightly lost young woman desperately seeking herself." (80)

Benazir Bhutto who is described as the "daughter of the Yeast" comes in for close evaluation where one can read a lot of things between the lines. The comparison is mostly with that of the Indian scenario and leaders. De says that Benazir "won't be silly enough to rope in school/college/jail friends to fill key slots. She will not handover the country's affairs to a PIA pilot or an aging matinee idol from the Paki screen." (88) She further notes that Benazir's oratory extends well beyond "the hume dekhna hai . . . level of mundanity" (89) which will certainly ring a bell.

Asha Bhonsle, who is known for her professionalism is discussed in "Life Begins at 60." De says Bhonsle is the holder of innumerable records that go well beyond computing. The voices of Lata and Asha have surpassed all the others which have come and gone. "When and if the history of commercial music in India ever gets written, it is their names that shall be emblazoned in letters of gold. Perhaps Lata's will have a sprinkling of diamonds—but then, she is Asha's senior in more ways than merely chronological." (93) She concludes the essay by saying that "only Asha springs eternal."

The last piece in the series is on Germaine Greer whose identification with the women's movement, according to De, was total. She chooses to laugh at the spokespersons of women's lib who she refers to as "libbers." "While earnest women parroted Manhattan-style slogans and refused to shave their armpits, the men reacted with horror and scorn." (94-95) Greer is said to have been deeply affected by India and the plight of the average Indian woman when she came to Bombay. Greer, according to De, is not an average woman and she is vulnerable on all fronts.

There are five essays on Gender issues. The opening one is on Miss India contest. De disapproves of what goes in the name of Miss India contest. She says that "there is something almost comical" about the entire concept. She has "often wondered about the kind of young girl who enters such a contest. She is, in fact, telling the world that she thinks she is beautiful." (101) Her main complaint is that the manner in which local beauty contests are held is a poor imitation of the multi-million-dollar super productions abroad.

Money is De's concern in her essay "Don't Bank on Your Men." She observes: "The point of this piece is not whether money-talk should be the second language after one's mother tongue, but that women should damn well get down to it and understand what the money game is all about." (104-5) She says that money matters are managed by women in many of the households. She has also heard a wife being referred to as "the finance minister" in the family. She regrets that women do not take major money decisions by themselves.

The essay "The Mirage of Womancipation" calls for a situation where "men will have to come to terms with woman power." (113) This, according to her, is not the voice of naive female optimism but the voice of reason and logic. She believes that another alternative does not exist any longer. Women should no more be complacent and placid and they should start asserting themselves. Says De: "Shakti needs to be harnessed, directed and exploited for the furtherance of overall, human development." (112)

We very often hear the remark "women are women's worst enemies." De takes a contrary view and thus have her title "Women Are My Best Friends." She says that her most enduring relationships have been with women, starting with her mother and sisters. "I have also enjoyed warm, supportive friendships going back to more than twenty years with women I have grown up with." (115) She says that she has opted for female colleagues and has also been partial to members of her own sex in other social and professional interactions. She sums up the piece with this observation: "A woman's best friends are undoubtedly diamonds but there is enough room for other women too." (116)

Homosexuality is the topic of discussion in her essay "Of Friends, Gaily." She opens the piece with the remark that most of the men she is friends with are gay. "Very often, while walking down the street with one of my gay friends, I hear sniggers or even cat-calls and hooting followed by shouts of 'hijra' or 'Chhakka.'" (117-18) She is surprised to see that most foreign men regard India as a haven for homosexuals. According to her, "maintaining even the most normal of normal man-woman relationships is among the toughest enterprises in the world. It is an effort that requires extraordinary skill and patience." (121) The homosexuals are a group of people who are damned, hounded, cast aside, pitied and rejected. The gays need a little more sympathy and affection from the society, which is the message she tries to convey.

The section "India and Her People" also contains five essays of which the first one is titled "Oh, To Be a Court Clerk." Basically, she talks about the things that happen to a person in a decadent city. A meaningless case going on in one of the courts is the worst among them. The bad things, according to her, are hitting by a bus, stranded during a morcha, going without milk/vegetables/fruits and other essential items due to transport strike.

"Muppies" is an essay where De talks about Maharashtrian Yuppies. She says that when Maharashtrian Yuppies are shown relaxing at home it is always with *India Today* or some other English language magazine. "Muppies love to eat out, especially on Sundays when the wife refuses to enter the kitchen to touch the food processor." (130) They have discovered pizzas and fast food and the muppy mothers constantly complain that their children have become impossibly demanding. Holidays at a hill station are a Muppy must. Muppy mothers no longer wear their hair in a traditional bun. The final observation on the muppies is that the ultimate Muppy dream is to become a puppy, because a Muppy believes that it's the puppies who get the most out of life.

De finds that the Maharashtrians are a little touchy. This she realized specially when she got her article on "Muppies" published. She was attacked for having "massacred" her own community. In her article "Maharashtrians—Touchy, Touchy" she gives two reasons why she chose Maharashtrians. "We live in Maharashtra and secondly, it is the one community I know best." (134) She describes an amusing encounter which she had with a couple, which makes interesting reading: "We were at some sort of a reception when a young Maharashtrian couple came up and the man introduced himself. The two of them epitomised the Muppy Syndrome and yet, they haven't identified themselves in the piece. . . . Even physically, they suited the Muppy description, and I'm certain if I'd probed a little about their lifestyle it would have conformed to the general Muppy picture." (134-35)

"The Convertible Culture" is one where De says that the foreign fixation of the Indians has slowly started changing. "Our phoren-obsessed people are encountering more and more interest in everything desi, while they are busy clearing the counters in fancy stores abroad."

(136) However, when it comes to electronic gadgets, watches etc. it is a different story altogether: "It will be a long, long time before the average Indian can completely shake off the foreign fixation where electronic gadgets, watches and the like are concerned." (138)

The last piece in the series "Beautiful Land, Ugly People" tells us about the timeless beauty of the country and the ugly people who are its occupants. She is specially critical of the "avaricious, grotesque politicians." On a second thought she feels that the politicians are not to be blamed: "When we talk of the 'ugly politicians' aren't we being hypocritical and unfair? How did these ugly people get there in the first place? Why should we blame them? We should blame ourselves—first and last. For, it is we who have put them there." (141) Indians have become notorious for bribing and the politicians are not to be blamed for this. "From school admissions for your toddler, to licences for industry, the rampant practice of greasing eager, outstretched palms, has become so commonplace as to go entirely unnoticed. Are politicians to blame? No, we are." (142)

"Festivals and Religion" has five essays in it. The first one "Festivals without Faith" tells us how the festivals have lost their old glory. "With each passing year, I regret that most festivals have been reduced to a happy childhood memory." (148) Mothers are not ready to take pains and they don't even want to prepare the dishes at home. Everything is readily available in the market and the proprietor of the ancient eateries claim: "Our dishes are just like home-cooked ones." (151)

The essay "A Dekko at Dhakai" is on the travelling saree salesmen from Dhaka who make long journey to Bombay. Somehow the customers fall a prey to their designs. "While counting the notes they tell you what a bargain you have got. 'In Calcutta the same sarees will be a thousand rupees costlier. We get ours straight from the weavers . . . no middlemen . . . best selection.'" (153) Her conclusion is as follows: "All is fair in love and saree selling." (154)

"Ganapati Babba—forgive us!" Speaks about the changing trends in the way Ganapati festival is celebrated. "With each passing year one can keep a track of fresh trends on the fashion and film scenes by watching the hordes dancing vigorously before Bombay's best-loved deity." (157) To add to the glamour Disco Kings appear and "Ganapati himself is rigged out like a sophisticated walkie-talkie doll, and moves to keep time with the insistent drum-beat." (159) Even priests have changed. In the place of potbellied pundits in frayed silk dhotis and grimy sacred threads, the modern-day versions roar up on a fire-engine red Honda, wearing faded jeans.

"Writing in the New" is a dig at the Doordarshan authorities who make the audience suffer by compelling them watch programmes which are nothing short of bores. In this connection, De asks a couple of pertinent questions: "Do we have to suffer while relatives of Bombay Kendra producers pretend they are a specially invited audience and ask asinine questions? And where do they dig up those fossils from?" (160)

The last essay "Come, Buy My Mystic Merchandise" is about "emissaries of God." According to De, "the biggest con business in our country continues to be the godmen and godwomen enterprise." (163) What surprises her is the entry of the female counterparts in the "guru game." "With flowing tresses, blood-red bindis, virgin-white sarees, these buxom matrons encourage their male devotees to massage their legs, kiss their feet and clutch their clammy hands, in search of eternal truth, through 'magnetic vibrations.'" (163)

The series on "Bombay" begins with the essay "Bombay—The Juicy Mango." The picture of Bombay that she delineates is that of a bitch: "Bombay is the ultimate burlesque bitch—garish, enticing, carnal and brittle. Bombay is also like the gaudy film billboards that are splashed across its face—it promises a lot and delivers very little." (169) One finds exhilaration, apathy and cruelty compatibly blended in Bombay.

In her essay "Mumbai Meri Hai," De says that it's fun being a Bombay person. She talks of all kinds of 'funs' like "unshaven film stars and virginal sex-symbols," "culture clubs and club culture," "white-washed sheriffs and colourless mayors," "man-mountain CMs and diminutive governors," "Roading tigers" (Bal Thackeray) "Gang-land wars" (Dawoodmia and pals), "Black cat security and daylight burglaries" and so on. Naturally, there shouldn't be a case for a dull moment!

Theatre is the focus of De's article "what, no Chekov?" According to her, "Bombay has a theatre crowd like Delhi has its sammelanwallahs." (175) The audience-profile, she says, was undergoing a change. Bombay has changed a lot and "once upon a time there was a pretty seaside city called Bombay," (178) says De in her essay "The Bubble that Burst." In the next essay "Bombay—Blasts and All," she observes that "Bombay was no Beirut, even if it is very fashionable to say so." (183) She is sad that riots, bombs, arson and killings are contributing in a nontrivial way to spoil the charm of Bombay.

The section on "Travel" has four essays in it. In the first essay "Strange Places, New Faces," she says that "true salvation lies in travel." (187) Travelling offers her a succession of sublime moments like life itself. In "The City of Little Joy," De talks about Delhi where she says "to be fair to that city, even a dump has its attractions." (192) From Delhi, it is to Madras and in this essay ("Madras Musings") she talks of her impressions of Madras. She has before her "the salwar-kameez generation," the Iyengars, doctors, the frequently used phrase "It seems," the Madras Marina, Cho Ramaswamy, Sridevi, Khushboo (a Bombay reject), Rajnikant and a host of other persons and things. The last essay "Bon jour Paris" is mostly on her Paris experience. She talks about the expensive laundries, beedies, exotic Indian food, chicken, 'mixed cuisines,' etc. in this essay. "But at the end of the short holiday, even my finicky palate had turned adventurous and didn't rebel too much while tentatively sampling duckling or rabbit or even strange looking *hors d'oeuvres* in a Vietnamese or Russian restaurant." (208)

The next section "Food," which has four articles, begins with the essay "What Bombay Needs are More Ghati Eateries." She observes that what Bombay needs in the eatery department are more ghati restaurants. The next essay ("The Editor Who Would Be Chef") tells us how she got the man with the second most important job in the country to cook in her kitchen. The person under reference is Dileep Padgaonkar. "Weight and Watch," the next essay asks the questions, "if you eat so much—how come you don't put on weight? Where does it all go?" etc. The last essay in the series which makes interesting reading is full of references to political leaders, actors and cricketers. According to De, one of the five-hundred and thirty-nine Tirupati cooks was in search of celebrity mouths to feed. The cook, it seems, has told her that Sonia Gandhi's favourite was "An (A)methi paratha with very little ghee." The Bofors Bun was Ambitabh Bachchan's favourite and Gavaskar would like to have Pilaf Pakistani as a must on his menu.

Section X of the collection is titled "Shobha in Retrospect." The first essay in the series is "Confessions of a Fame-Junkie." She has her reveries which help her make it through the night: "No cherished dream, no golden goal, just the deep-seated assurance that one day I'd get to control a fleet of taxis with a riveting declaration on the dashboard." (232) The next essay ("Flashbacks in Colour and Black and White") is mostly about Zeenat Aman and Phyllis Mendes: "I met her on her triumphant return to this doubting city and was relieved to discover the same old Phyllis, someone who could laugh at herself and say, 'I know back home in India, people will still point out to me and say, 'Chhee Kitni Kaali.' 'But in Paris they call me beautiful.''" (237) In the essay "Presley Yesterday, Lennon Today," De appears to become a little emotional. "The fact that I can't fluently read or write an Indian language, even my mother tongue, depresses me no end." (242) She wishes that she had courage and perseverance to do something about it. "Shobha Ko Gussa Kyoon Aata Hai," De says that her GUSSA is reserved for herself. "I feel angry about being angry. I feel angry about writing columns like this one." (246)

"On Being a Writer, a Columnist and a Media Person" has four essays. In "A Hard De's Write," she narrates how a day has frequent interruptions and she is made "to squeeze in forty minutes of reasonably interrupted writing." (251) "Sense and Nonsense" is an essay where De hopes that some day she will "receive the one response that will reassure her that someone somewhere has read something that has made sense (or nonsense) on some level." (257) The essay "Reviewers Reviewed" is about erring book reviewers. "Is Seminar a Dirty Word" is a piece where De laughs at seminars and seminarists. "Like Doordarshan panelists (mainly out-of-job editors and self-styled political analysts), seminarists too belong to an informal, cosy club." (261)

"Of Books and Reviews" is a section where there are four essays. The first one "Diana" says that the Diana books are like the princess herself—light, bright and trite. At the same time she observes: "while Diana, the manipulative, scheming, insecure, neurotic, selfish vixen dominates Campbell's book, Morton's princess emerges as the misunderstood martyr having to put up with a straying callous husband while presenting an ever-smiling facade to the watching world." (272) Khushwant Singh reappears in the essay "The Importance of Being Khushwant." According to De, his book *Not a Nice Man to Know* "establishes the importance of being Khushwant—it doesn't matter what he churns out or when." (274) "An Unsuitable Gift" is on top sellers and how salespersons manage their sales with offers and prizes. The last piece in the series is entitled "Write—And Be Hanged." She has titles like "Nature Books," "Medical Tomes," "Children's Books," "Films," "Poetry" etc. She says that the most important thing is money and "the bottom line is what counts even for intellectuals who wish to break rules." (280)

The section "'Phirang' Film Reviews" has as its first essay "Blame It on the Movies." She talks about "Heat and Dust" and "Octopussy," the India-based films she saw in Paris and London. She says that so many foreign film companies have suddenly decoded to use India as their locale. "One would prefer to be optimistic and believe that by projecting India in the distorted fashion, they might be indirectly giving a boost to the tourist trade." (287) Her essay "Salaam Gimmicks" parodies "Salaam Bombay" where she frowns at the view of a self-styled intellectual: "After Ray's *Pather Panchali*, this is the most important films ever made by an Indian." (288) In "Oh Boy! No Joy!" she talks about the film *The City of Joy*. She says that the human spirit finally triumphs in a rousing finale.

The penultimate section entitled "Miscellany" begins with "The Crayon Boy" which talks about Moti Singh, the Gurkha's son. He was good at painting and he would create huge posters using bits of Kite paper, paint, strips of gold and silver from mango baskets, discarded fabric and any material he could lay his hands on. "How dumb can you get?" is about a mother and a son, a mother who would thrust leather-bound classics under his nose, but nothing worked. In "Poetic Musings," De says that ghazals make her giggle. She has tried all kinds of poetry which includes erotic Sanskrit poems translated into English, Oriya love poetry and so on. Also, she herself is a poet who waits for a publisher to sign her on. The piece "Carry On, Truckers" has in it De drawing our attention to the havoc caused by truck owners. The strike ultimately leads to non-availability of milk, sugar, bread etc. and ultimately causes untold misery to ordinary people.

The collection ends with the story "Sushila's Secret." It is about a married woman Sushila who has an affair with Mr. Deshpande, her boss. She goes to Pune with her boss for an official tour and as expected, he makes advances to her in the hotel room. She is a little confused and wonders: "If all men were basically the same and they did it more or less the same way and said more or less the same things—then why do women have affairs? Why not stick to just one fellow?"

(317) She takes her mangalsutra out of her purse and wears it again. "I was feeling happy. And relieved. As if some big mystery had been solved for me. In a way, I suppose it had. I knew I wasn't missing anything. Not really. Next time with Milind would be easy. And the next. And next." (318)

To sum up, *Shooting from the Hip* is an excellent collection of essays—plus a short story—where Shobha De is at her best in her observation and analysis of persons and events. Her greatest strength is that she can see things and persons most dispassionately. She boldly responds to situations around her even when political bigwigs are involved. Whether it is media or politics she is unconcerned about the consequences of the observations she makes. She can be very unkind when she writes about people who she doesn't like whether it is Rekha or Bachchan. At the same time, there is absolutely no constraint when she describes people of her liking. She can be critical of her own sex when it comes to unrealistic approaches as regards gender issues. She has her own likes and dislikes of cities like Bombay, Delhi, Madras and Paris. On her observations on travel, food and films she is straightforward and original. Finally, De is at her best as a short story writer, as is evident from her story "Sushila's Secret."

NOTES

1. George Orwell, "Why I Write," *Selections from George Orwell*, ed. R. Sundararaju (Madras: Orient Longman, 1971), pp. 1 and 9.
2 Shobha De, *Shooting from the Hip* (New Delhi: UBS, 1994), p. xi.

6

Generation Gap in *Selective Memory: Stories from My Life*

N.P. SINGH

The publication of *Selective Memory* (Penguin Books, 1998) has been a momentous event of the year. Shobha De has always been in news due to her novels which have depicted with candour and sarcasm the glamour, boredom and crazy fun-saturated life of the socialites of Bombay, the metropolis of dreamers, seekers and achievers. She has also been in news due to her association with modelling and film journalism, especially of the kind found in *Stardust*. *Selective Memory* is, however, not a chronological autobiography of Shobha De. It is an imaginative recreation of her past and the present and encompasses graphically both her career blues and the tangles of her family life. The writer has dedicated *Stories from My Life*, subtitle of her memoirs, to Lord Ganesh. Her words of dedication are an index of her candour, "To Lord Ganesh from whom there can be no secrets, and my beloved family, from whom I've still kept a few."

What Shobha De says in her dedication to Lord Ganesh is also reflected in the "Epilogue" of her memoirs. She has written her memoirs in order to let the reader have a glimpse of her journey of life. Her intention has not been to reveal everything to shock and titillate the reader but only to share those memories which she is ready to share. It would be appropriate to convey the writer's literary credo in her own words, "*Selective Memory*, as the title itself suggests provides an overview of the journey. I've experienced much in these years, met a great number of interesting people, raised a large family, tried hard to lead an integrated life. Today, I am prepared to provide a peep into the past without indulging in a voyeuristic catharsis." (526) She also makes it clear that "Nobody in India has succeeded in writing a real honest to goodness, no holds-barred autobiography." (528) In other words, those readers who have a preconceived image of Shobha De as an audacious, no-nonsense, utterly liberated woman of post-independence generation out to shock and titillate would, perhaps be, astonished—even shocked—on confronting the truth as portrayed in *Selective Memory*: "The woman you meet in *Selective Memory* may not be the woman you think you know." (528) One can safely affirm that Shobha De's memoirs, *Stories from My Life*, are preoccupied less with the myth as projected by the media and more with the reality that Shobha De actually embodies, that is a daring daughter, a wife, and a worried mother. Even if she has not revealed all the secrets of her hectic, colourful life, an unbiased reading of *Stories from My Life* gives us an authentic picture of a middle class, Maharashtrian Bombay-wali. The daring daughter of the opening chapters is gradually transformed into a distracted mother who is bluntly told by her eldest son that she is too old to visit New York's hottest new clubs. One can discern a generation gap embedded in the text of the narrative from the beginning to the end.

While "Prologue" depicts the circumstances under which Shobha De began the writing of her memoirs, it is the chapter "Glancing Back" that recounts her birth in a typical, middle class Maharashtrian family in Satara. Her arrival in a family that already had two daughters makes both her mother and maternal grandmother unhappy. The writer's comment on her birth is quite revealing, "My birth could not possibly have been a day of celebration for the family especially since my maternal grandmother was around to remind everybody that a third daughter had arrived as an additional liability and it had been rather reckless of my parents to have gone in for a fourth child with no guarantee that it would be male." (12) In spite of the initial reaction of her mother and maternal grandmother, the child was brought up in a happy atmosphere and her father declared her lucky for the family. Her father got a job in Delhi and the stay in the metropolis liberated the family from the constricted notions of a small town in Maharashtra. When her father was transferred to Bombay, and from the suburb of Ghatkopar to a flat opposite Churchgate station in Bombay, the process of liberation was accelerated. In spite of the change in the family environment, her father continued to thunder, "Character building, youth is meant for character building." (30) Shobha De, however, loved the kind of life she lived in the most fashionable part of Bombay, "I loved my new home. More than the area. This was downtown Mumbai—fashionable, affluent and sexy." (20)

There is no wonder that Shobha De began her career in modelling. It was an occupation that gave her some money and a sense of independence. She had told her mother about it but she did not have the guts to reveal it to her father. Shobha De's observation on her patriarchal father's reaction is significant and revealing, "As soon as I came clean about my modelling to the rest of the family, all hell broke loose. My mother was caught in the cross-fire instantly. 'Who allowed her to accept these shows?' My father thundered. It was my mother's turn to take the rap and mutter softly, 'It isn't as bad as you imagine. She hasn't done anything wrong . . . the people she's working with are quite decent.' My father didn't wish to listen. He wasn't ready to be convinced. And that's how it stayed even five years later. He disapproved. Period. He didn't want his daughter to be in a field he considered cheap and disreputable." (40) Her father would have liked his pet daughter to become a doctor, a lawyer or an engineer but she was different. Her aim was radically different, "But I sure as hell didn't want to be a doctor, lawyer or engineer. I didn't want to be anything at all, except a happy, carefree young person." (42)

In spite of her father's strong reaction, Shobha De's modelling continued. Her face appeared on the cover of two of the leading women's magazines, *Femina* and *Eve's Weekly.* She also got a chance to work as a model along with Zeenat Aman. She was also featured in *Vogue.* It is true that modelling gave her an exposure to the world of glamour and advertising, both national and international, but it didn't satisfy her fully. In spite of spending five years of youth as a model, Shobha De's assessment is blunt and harsh, "No matter what they say, modelling was and remains a thinly-disguised cattle show." (72) There is no wonder that even Shobha De's eldest daughter, Radhika, didn't like her mother as a model. The writer's description of her daughter's response is as following: "Recently my eldest daughter Radhika came home waving a calendar dating back to 68, which featured three exceptionally garish photographs of mine. It had been found by her then boy friend while spring-cleaning—the textile mill that had commissioned the shoot belonged to his father. We pored over the horrendous pictures which had me clad in ugly, gaudy outfits, my hair teased into an unnaturally large bouffant, the eyes painted peacock blue, the lips outlined in plastic pink. Arundhati turned to me and said, 'Mother, you look so much better now.' She said it with complete sincerity and I hugged her gratefully." (79) It is interesting to know that while Shobha De's father couldn't make her realize the shallowness and vulgarity of modelling, her daughters did succeed in making her aware that modelling led to a sort of commodification of women and stripped them of their natural dignity and poise. Her career as a model came to an abrupt end soon. She had gone to meet a friend at Creative Unit, a modest advertising agency. As she was chatting with her friend Shilpa Shah, a question was hurled at her: "Can you write?" (84) It was a question that changed her life and gave her a new vocation. Shobha De sums up the new situation in these words, "But later that afternoon, the girl who pranced out on the busy road was someone who'd just chucked up a modelling career and got herself a brand-new job as a trainee copy writer. The salary? Three hundred and fifty rupees. It was a turning point." (89)

From copy editing to editing *Stardust* didn't take much time. Nari Hira, the boss of Creative Unit asked Shobha De if she would like to do magazine writing. She told him that she knew nothing either about film stars or film industry. His reply was straightforward, "You don't have to know too much about the film industry. I'm looking for someone who can write provocatively, interview the stars, put various columns together. I'm sure you'll be able to do it." (98) The first piece that she wrote for *Stardust* in October 1971 was, 'Is Rajesh Khanna secretly married?' The inaugural issue was sold out within a week. The popularity and success of *Stardust* made Shobha De aware of the glamour, boredom, bitching and scandal-mongering that enveloped the life of popular film stars. In chapters entitled "Blazing Trails" and "Shining Through" there are interesting anecdotes about Rekha, Shatrughan Sinha, Kabir Bedi, Zeenat Aman and Sanjeev Kumar. Her assessment of Sanjeev Kumar would definitely shock millions of his admirers, "Rustic, ill-mannered and uncouth is what I found the late Sanjeev Kumar." (115) Her observation on film stars in general is also sarcastic and bitter, "It is a well-known fact that stars are amongst the stringest and meanest of people. The more money they make, the faster and tighter their fists close." (128) In spite of Shobha De's aversion to film stars in general, her encounters with Jaya Bachchan, Zeenat Aman and Parveen Babi were far more genial and friendly. Her description of Parveen Babi's beauty is quite generous and glowing, "Easily the most beautiful actress I came across during my magazine years was Parveen Babi. I can see her now as clearly as the first time, over twenty years ago, when she floated into my line of vision dressed in a soft white Grecian-style gown in floaty chiffon. Ravishing is an understatement." (153)

Stardust became the number one film magazine and as its editor Shobha De became a sort of celebrity herself. She was, however, too much of an individualist to rest on her laurels. Disturbing questions came to her mind, "Listen. You can do this on your own. Why work for somebody else? Go on. Float your own magazine. Do it now." (201-2) She was also advised, "You have to shed your middle class attitudes. Take risks." (202) She started her own magazine, *Celebrity*. She found it difficult to look after the financial side of the venture. She had other problems as well. She had interviewed Simranjit Singh Mann for *Celebrity* and as Mann was accused of being a part of the conspiracy to murder Indira Gandhi, the publisher Shobha De was named "Accused number two in a case of treason against the state of India." (207) It was a most difficult and critical time in Shobha De's life. In a chapter entitled "Flying Solo" she has described with candour the crises in her life, "The next couple of years were difficult, very difficult. I had never been in such a situation before. Nothing, but nothing was going right—financially or emotionally. My marriage was breaking up. The magazine I had started, *Celebrity*, was facing all sorts of problems. For the first time in my adult life I felt alone, alienated and isolated." (203)

Shobha De, however, survived the multiple crises of her life. She had a call from Penguin Books India which was on the look out for new writers. Shobha De began with hesitation, "But I've never written a book before," (315) but eventually she was persuaded to write her first book. She completed the book and it was titled *Socialite Evenings*. The book was attacked by critics but was read by readers. Shobha De's comment on her first novel is quite revealing, "Why did *Socialite Evenings* generate so much heat, I now wonder. It was innocuously written—no explicit sex scenes. No foul language. Could it have been the theme itself? That a woman could walk out of a perfectly secure marriage out of boredom? Karuna, the main protagonist, is not a bitch, if anything she is far too sensible and controlled. But she's the one who recognized her marriage for what it is—empty." (330) Although Shobha De was hurt by the critics's vehement attack on her first novel, but it did something positive as well, "One thing did change however, I had discovered the joy of writing fiction." (327) Beginning with modelling, talking up copy editing and switching on to writing and editing *Stardust*, eventually Shobha De discovered her true vocation, that is writing fiction which found millions of readers all over India and abroad. Her second novel, *Starry Nights*, followed which made her notorious due to her "deliberate use of choice Hindi epithets and the descriptive sex scenes." (332) It was, perhaps, *Starry Nights* that gave Shobha De the image of a pornographic writer and at a literary meet a gentleman asked her, "Madam, is it true that women in India do not experience real pleasure . . . you know what I mean . . . and that they fool their husbands by pretending? What, according to you, is the percentage of ladies who . . . who . . . experience real pleasure? I wanted to fling the plate of fragrant biryani at his smug face. Just who the hell did he imagine I was—a sexologist with statistics at my finger-tips? Someone who'd conducted a study on female orgasms?" (368)

The image of being a pornographer, however, stuck. At times she wondered how her children would look upon her. She also wondered how her husband Dileep would react to her notorious image. She was reassured by the fact that Dileep always stood by her and her children were, perhaps, too small then to react. While Shobha De rationalized to herself that if she could be so critical of others, the critics also had a right to examine her trenchantly. Her confession is touching indeed, "My rational self accepted the argument, but emotionally I was shattered." (363) It was, however, the tact and insight of her husband that gave her the strength to bear the critics' attack. There is no wonder that Shobha De brings out frankly the difficult situation in which her husband was placed: "Dilip would always make light of the whole thing, and successfully blunted the edge of the unrelenting attacks. When I look back, it couldn't have been easy for him—husband of a woman the entire critic's community had dubbed a pornographer." (363-64) At times, she received nasty mail and obscene calls but she learnt to bear them with equanimity and poise. It was the support of her family, her husband, father and children that gave her the strength to bear the infamy of being a pornographer. Her old father might not have approved his young daughter's choice of modelling as a career but he did respect her as a writer who could portray man-woman relationship with utmost candour. Recently he rang up his daughter at 11 p.m. one night to say, "I've been unable to find an answer to something that has been troubling me. Maybe you'll be able to throw some light on it. I've noticed that in surveys about sexual attitudes, it's always the men who are asked questions on frequency—how many times a week? A month? A year? Women are rarely asked this. Why is that? I gave him a ten-minute dissertation on the subject, and he listened most attentively. 'Thank you, my dear,' he said politely. 'I have learnt a lot tonight.' That alarmed me. I hastily added, 'Baba, I am not an expert on the subject.' But he had got the answer he was looking for." (364) It is clear from a perusal of the dialogue between the father and the daughter that in spite of a generation gap that definitely existed between them, a dialogue was always possible. There was no communication gap between the father and the daughter, between an octogenarian father and a daughter in forties. In spite of the difference in age, lifestyle, and goals, both the father and the daughter seem to have an infinite hunger for life and a desire to understand life clearly, without harbouring illusions and taboos.

Subhash K. Jha has asked in *Indian Review of Books*: "Where in all this stock-taking and fire-spewing is the real Shobha De?" (16 Jan.-15 Feb. 99, p. 30) In my view the real Shobha De emerges before us in her confrontation with her father, easily the most alive character in *Selective Memory: Stories from My Life*, and also in the tangles of her personal life described so graphically in chapters like "Getting Personal" and "Feeling Great" towards the end of her memoirs. In spite of the line of communication being open between the father and the daughter, a generation gap is unmistakable in "Getting Personal" when the father tells her bluntly, "You don't live lavishly, you don't throw weekly dinner parties or wear grand clothes. What's the point of working hard, earning well and not showing it?" (403) Her friend Sunita also tells Shobha De to adorn herself with expensive clothes, jewellery and diamonds. But Shobha De's response is that of a middle class, working woman. She says, "I am and shall remain a working woman, at heart and in practice. This must disappoint my father, who has a far more aristocratic vision of life. In his view, I should be spending my days like Sunita—only more luxuriously." (404) It is evident that

Shobha De has the capacity to express diametrically opposite, contrary points of view through her open-ended, dialogic narrative. Subhash K. Jha has rightly said in *Indian Review of Books*, "Shobha De adopts a pattern of narration that is no different from her fictional mode; a flip casual tone, loads of laconic cynicism and a complete disregard for the feelings of those whom she writes about, except the immediate family and a few super-privileged friends whom she actually designs to like and appreciate." (30)

I do agree that Shobha De is at her best when she writes of her growth as a daughter, and her tension as she brings up her daughters and sons in Bombay in 80s and 90s. Her description of her mother's death and his old father's response to his wife's death (being all alone in the flat) is the most moving part of her life's story, "None of his four children was with him to share his insurmountable grief and offer solace. All of us were far too busy with our own lives, our own families, our own preoccupations, our own priorities. The woman who'd brought us into this world was lying dead on her bed, with a fragile eighty-seven-year-old man by her side in a dimly lit bedroom of a modern high-rise whose neighbours were merely familiar faces across the landing. There was no one to lighten the burden of this lonely man's sorrow." (442) This is the stark tragedy of the life of old men and women in a metropolis like Bombay. There are children, grand children but they are so busy as dreamers, seekers and achievers. The old are invisible but Shobha De's pen makes them visible and unforgettable.

Sunil Mehra's comment in *Outlook*, October 12, 1998 is not very far from truth, "Shobha De's real as when she talks of her mother's death, little sorrows, fleeting regrets, remembered happiness." (94) "Feeling Great" is a chapter in which she describes her divorce and remarriage to Dilip De. As the adage goes, truth is stranger than fiction. Her divorce came through at 11.30 a.m. and she married Dilip at 1 p.m. She was a divorcee for precisely one and a half hours. (474) Her remarriage has not been, however, a bed of roses. Shobha De has been frank in describing her second marriage, "We've had our rough moments, bumpy patches, arguments, disagreements and fights. There have been tears, accusations and recriminations. But no real regrets. The parameters of our relationship have been drawn by Dilip." (48) This remark may not be liked by ardent feminists, but this is the truth as perceived by Shobha De. There is no wonder that her children feel that she is too traditional, too middle-class to be a really modern, liberated woman of the 90s. In the last but one chapter, "Taking Stock" Shobha De confesses frankly that she has learnt much from her children who have been utterly candid in their comments, "There have been several such incidents involving our children. Each time I learned a new and refreshing 'truth.' They helped me change, re-evaluate my worn attitudes, reassess my rigid positions on issues that concern us all. I feel thankful to them for having pointed out my mistakes." (488)

While in "Prologue" Shobha De tells us how she was persuaded to write *Selective Memory: Stories from My Life*, in "Epilogue" she sums up her life in terms of Frank Sinatra's popular song, "My Way." She listens to the song and has a realization, "I felt naked. I felt good. . . . Frank Sinatra was on his last bars. I hummed along with him. His way, huh? And mine too. Yes, most definitely mine too." (531) Shobha De has the courage to live in her own way. A multi-dimensional life, full of joys and sorrows—and insights as well.

Selective Memory: Celebrity Memoirs

URBASHI BARAT

> This was the journey he remembered. The actual journey may have been quite different, but the actual journey has no interest for education. The memory was all that mattered.
>
> Henry Adams, *The Education of Henry Adams*

Shobha De begins *Selective Memory*[1] with a Prologue in which she describes how she was persuaded to write her autobiography by David Davidar of Penguin India now that she was nearing the "mid-point age" of fifty, the time for "stock-taking" and "flashback." (2) As Shobha De began the task of "put[ting her] life on line" the "exhilaration of forced remembering" empowered her to rediscover her past, which she had "lost touch with" "in[her] preoccupation with the present" (11) and to understand how, and how much, she had changed and grown through the years. But in her Epilogue, where she sums up the implications of her "overview of a journey," (527) she makes it quite clear that she has not given her readers India's first "real honest-to-goodness, no-holds-barred autobiography," a "'bare-all-dare-all' shocker." She has been completely honest as far as "perceptions and feeling," "emotions and textures" go, but she has also deliberately and carefully chosen what she reveals of her past, which means that much has been left out which she would not like to share with others. (527-28)

Very obvious omissions include, among other things, accounts of her first marriage and divorce, her relationships with men and the pain they have obviously caused her (her novels as much as the tongue-in-cheek *Surviving Men* are clear evidence of this), and above all any explanations of how a young girl from a traditional middle class Maharashtrian family managed to become a supermodel of her time and achieved celebrity status so early, without the knowledge and consent of her parents, especially her suspicious and dominating father. Not that she does not refer to the process of her growth, but that is all there is, the references to what she has had to overcome rather than a remembering and a retelling. There is thus considerable glossing and sugar-coating over past distress and pain, and Shobha De usually emerges as an often misunderstood and frequently holier-than-thou protagonist of the apologia of an intrepid survivor. The reader might, indeed, be forgiven for occasionally wondering whether "Selective Amnesia" would have been a more appropriate title for the work.

Shobha De's title continues, in fact, to cause a few ripples of amusement. But then memory is always selective: one cannot, after all, remember everything. Besides, as Freud has suggested, forgetting is often intentional, a kind of self-protective repression of the unacceptable and the painful; this seems to be behind Shobha De's declaration, "it is my conscious decision to exercise control over those aspects of my life I'm not ready to make public," (527) rather than her professed desire to keep "private" whatever is "precious" to her. She might state that she regards the conventional "agonizing[ly] detail[ed]" autobiography as boring (228), an indulgence in "a voyeuristic catharsis," or "the worst kind of narcissism," (527) and has therefore chosen to write differently, but it is noticeable that her silence is most eloquent when it covers moments of pain, humiliation and defeat, such moments that everyone must experience, especially someone who is clearly so sensitive and who has so obviously learnt to survive the hard way.

Shobha De's focus on only certain aspects of her life is also quite in the tradition of autobiography, which imposes form on the shapeless, disorganized, and frequently fractured series of events in a person's life by selecting, shaping and remoulding experience in order to understand and (re)interpret the past. There is often, accordingly, very little difference between an autobiographical novel like Shobha De's *Socialite Evenings*[2] and autobiography itself, like her *Selective Memory*, in fact, as a Bildungsroman/Kunstlerroman. Shobha De's novel traces the growth of the protagonist much as biography/autobiography sets out to do, and as Barthes points out, an autobiography is "really a novel that does not speak its name"[3]: it is as much fiction as novel proper.

Since it involves a creative retelling of fact, the autobiographical perspective "has to do with taking oneself up and bringing oneself to language."[4] As a tool for self-discovery the writer can centre him/herself from the margins of life and society through text: that is how, indeed, the novel form itself originated, as women in the seventeenth century in Europe wrote autobiographies through which they tried "to create a history from a state of flux, a flux in which they were feeling themselves in the process of becoming women within a new bourgeois society." Through writing autobiography,

> A female persona creates herself anew and calls herself into being as the protagonist of a fabulated history. As both author and narrator to her own identity, she gives birth to a heroine mythically resurrected from the ashes of patriarchy. She becomes empowered to define her subjective identity in a narrative that offers her control of a chaotic, alien, and antagonistic environment.[5]

This is what Karuna does in *Socialite Evenings*: she becomes Margaret Atwood's survivor, who can shrug off the burden of patriarchy by becoming a "creative non-victim"[6] through the act of writing out her memories. but where Karuna's liberation may be seen as having just begun, when Shobha De engages in "rememory" (Toni Morrison's phrase in *Beloved*) she has already discovered acceptance and is at peace with herself. But then not only is Shobha De older in *Selective Memory* than Karuna was in *Socialite Evenings*, in both works she is narrator/author/protagonist, who can discard the dross as she mines for gold, who can reinvent the past, (re)create her self/herself, and in controlling her world and her memories she empowers her present. As she admits in her Prologue:

> If nothing else, *Selective Memory* aided and abetted the transformation of myself. Kick-started the process, as it were. Forced me to glance over my shoulder. Look back, sift, discard, reinforce, assess, re-assess[sic], come to terms, recognize, accept—above all, accept. It was not easy. Not easy at all. But having endured the experience, I feel that much stronger. (11)

Not surprisingly, therefore, *Selective Memory* ends, like Shobha De's first novel, where it began: this circularity is not only characteristic of women's writing in general and of the first-person/Bildungsroman/Kunstlerroman in particular, it underscores the implications of a return to the past, which include, interestingly, a return also to the values of the past, evident, most obviously, in Shobha De's constant allusions to the importance of family relationships, her recognition of the way she so frequently slips into her parents' roles while dealing with her own children, and her distaste for the superficiality of the celebrity lifestyles she always describes.

Selective Memory has thus helped Shobha De understand Shobha De: it also helps the reader to understand much about the writer, why she writes the way she does of what she does. Her novels and short stories, her television serial *Swabhimaan* and her newspaper columns, are all, she admits, inspired by and based upon people, incidents, experiences and emotions in her own life. The dark side of human nature, the squalor and the evil in society and in human relationships that Shobha De explores in her fiction are, it becomes evident as she narrates her version of her life, the product of her own middle class puritanical upbringing, which has always kept her an outsider in that glittering "upper crust" world into which she has been thrust (or has thrust herself). (330-31) The rewriting of her life enables Shobha De as the narrator/author of her text to reinterpret the multitude of social and cultural codes imprinted on the personal consciousness.

Shobha De might deprecate attempts by earnest and enthusiastic researchers to find meanings in her work she had never intended (262-64), but she is nonetheless an important socio-cultural phenomenon, representing, especially through her popular fiction, the changing social mores of "middle India" (330): the middle class values of post-Independent India, in which a sound education is prized above all else and the term *professional* refers only to a doctor or an engineer, have been replaced by a colder, harsher, and more openly focused search for money, the real "aphrodisiac." (380) With all its journalistic cliches and buzz-words, its pop-psychology and pop-sociology, its frank appeal to commercial success—note the name-dropping and the descriptions of the celebrity circuit that the magazine-reading public would find fascinating—and its subtext of self-justification, *Selective Memory* deserves careful and serious study, for Shobha De's stories about her past not only form the basis of her fiction, they are a kind of metonymic projection of contemporary Indian society. She regards herself, it must be remembered, as a "social commentator." (229) and David Davidar has described her life as "an unending [newspaper] column" of social comment. (2) Thus, for example, as she talks about mother-daughter relationships in contemporary upper-class society:

> I fear for my generation of women—they really are iike danglers, neither here nor there. . . . We talk of options, opportunities and choices—sure we have them. What do we actually do with these goodies? We earn, we travel, we splurge . . . [sic] and we weep.

She looks back nostalgically to her mother's days: "Has it been worth those extra tears our mothers never felt the need to shed? . . . They slept soundly at night, they awoke feeling cheerful and fresh, they had time for themselves, time for their families, time to savour the small pleasures of life." The point, however, is that she immediately questions the veracity of this portrait: it is this that distinguishes the contemporary woman, the freedom of self-questioning:

> do I sound I'm filled with an unfulfilled longing to swap places with my mother? No, I guess I just sound like I'm growing old. Over-romanticizing my mother's reality. Maybe she wasn't all that blissed out. Maybe she did resent not having had a more exciting, fulfilling existence. (414)

In most cases, of course, the self-examination is not so open or conscious; it is tentative and subversive, for it makes its presence felt through her silences, her refusal to reveal her hidden self. If Shobha De's gaps, her silences, are compared with the intricate network of self-revelation in Kamala Das's *My Story*, the way they subvert Shobha De's certainties becomes evident.

Shobha De's remarks about how each of her novels originated are also of considerable social/sociological interest. For instance, she points out that her picture of the *haut monde* in *Socialite Evenings* is no Indianized version of Beverley Hills but an entirely accurate if merciless exposure of Bombay "high society." (330) Similarly, *Starry Nights* "is the accumulation of countless images and memories gathered during [her] *Stardust* period" (331):

> The grime and grit of the movie world was represented in all its squalor, but so was my own contempt, which came through clearly in the narrative. I made no attempt to hide it. Every bit of the revulsion I'd always harboured against the film industry poured out on the pages—it was a dirty business I was dealing with and I had no desire to sanitize it.

That is why she used the kind of language and the explicit sex scenes that caused "major shock waves" among readers when it was first published: this was the first time that an Indian woman wrote in this manner, and it was difficult to accept. (331) Shobha De believes, obviously, that she was writing the truth as she saw it, in the only way it could be expressed, and not because it ensured quick sales and a glamorous notoriety with which, however, she is only too often and easily identified.

As interesting, especially in the light of present developments in Indian publishing of writing in English, is her description of the marketing strategies adopted by her publishers and publicists, without which, evidently, few Indian novelists in English can be sold—or read—today. In any case, Shobha De's writing is undeniably market-based: she was perhaps the first journalist to make respectable that unique form of expression called Hinglish in affectionate derision, which was to become soon a great literary success as the postcolonial Indian empire writing back. But in her need to write and be read easily and quickly, she is frequently slipshod and often so informal as to be tacky and meaningless and superficial: her fondness for the epithet *lousy*, for instance, that she can apply to everything. But she also has the true instinct for knowing what sells; like Jackie Collins, whom she always dislikes being compared to, Shobha De is extremely readable, as "racy, gossipy, chatty and shocking" (99) as *Stardust*, and as successful. But, in spite of all the sleaze and the slime that she portrays, in spite of producing pulp fiction that only too often titillates rather than entertains, she is, paradoxically enough, a serious writer with her clear-eyed honest appraisal of human relationships and her overriding concern for human values—even though she may not realize that this is what emerges in her fiction. In *Selective Memory*, however, she is conscious of other commitment to these values. Consequently, it is not only about her understanding of her self, it is also about the way in which social and cultural conditions form personality and about whether the self, if it can be known at all, can be known through writing.

At this point a caveat must be entered. *Selective Memory* is, strictly speaking, not an autobiography but a memoir. The preposition in its sub-title, *Stories from My Life*, makes this clear: it is not *My Story*, as Kamala Das might put it, not *My Days*, as R.K. Narayan might put it, nor even *A Sort of Life*, as Graham Greene might put it, but stories—note the plural form—*from,* not *of* Shobha De's life, and where an autobiography is the story *of* a life, memoirs are stories *from* a life. William Zinsser explains the difference: "Unlike autobiography, which moves in a dutiful line from birth to fame, omitting nothing significant, memoir assumes the life a corner of his or her life that was unusually vivid or intense . . . or that was framed by unique events. By narrowing the lens, the writer achieves a focus that is a window into a life."[7] Interestingly enough, Shobha De herself uses the same image when she writes in her Epilogue of her technique in *Selective Memory*: "A window opens, but often the light only falls on a few specific artifacts inside." (527)

When Shobha De narrates her life in *Selective Memory*, accordingly, there is little of the continuous chronological flow associated with biography/autobiography; she omits, sums up, condenses, comments about, large chunks of her life rather than re-creates it for her reader, who is often left dangling, wondering what had happened and how it had happened, and what led to what. A temporality is of course characteristic of both autobiography and memoir; both are "committed to a vertical thrust from consciousness down into the unconscious rather than to a horizontal thrust from the present into the past."[8] In traditional autobiography, which is based on a belief that the writer is in conscious control over the subject—as Shobha De declares she is (527)—and which consists of what Olney calls "recapitulation and recall," (1047) the gaps in time and space are usually unnoticed by the reader, so that the narrative seems like a seamless continuity. In memoir, however, "The interior life is in constant vertical motion: consciousness runs up and down the scales every hour like a slide trombone. It dreams down below; it notices up above and it notices itself, too, and its own alertness."[9]

Women's autobiographical texts, being consciously or unconsciously gender-driven, resist the authoritarianism of autobiography proper, and align themselves to the discontinuity of memoir: witness, for instance, Virginia Woolf's *Moments of Being*. Shobha De, whose entire career is one of rebellion against patriarchy, from her choice of profession/s and her relationships to her language and her attempts to "write the body," might accept the authority of authorship in her belief that she is in control of her matter and her medium but in *Selective Memory* her construction of her selfhood is subverted by the way she has "chosen to carve up [her] life into those segments [she has] no reservations about revealing and serving up to readers." (527) Thus the self that should lie at the centre of autobiography is here decentred, as it were, for in memoir the text the writer fashions inevitably moves from the "interior landscape—one brain's own idiosyncratic topography" to the "vast setting of our common history,"[10] and in so doing also moves away from the writer him/herself. In *Selective Memory*, in Annie Dillard's description of memoir: "The personal pronoun can be the subject of the verb: 'I see this, I did that.' But not the object of the verb: 'I analyze me, I discuss me, I describe me, I quote me.'" (67)

Not only does Shobha De omit sensitive topics as memoir-writers do, very often in the process she also leaves out herself. *Selective Memory* is a record of De's achievements, her views on life, society and human relationships as they have been shaped through the years, but they do not always add up to total a round sum. This fractured selfhood emerges especially at the end of her Epilogue, when she tries to sum up herself through her memories, and finds that she cannot find her own words to do so. She turns, instead, to the popular Frank Sinatra song "I did it my way," to epitomize what she has gone through to survive, like "all those individuals who'd chosen to stick their necks out for different reasons at different times, and paid the price for doing so." Neither the voice, nor the story, nor the self, is uniquely and solely her own. She has always thought of herself "as someone who dared."

> Dared what? Thankfully, I wasn't asked or I'd have been stumped for an answer.

For her twelve-year-old daughter, however, Shobha De is a "traditional" person. This dichotomy within herself—the demon within, as she puts it—can never be resolved, and as she learns to accept it, "I felt naked. I felt good." (531)

The number of pages Shobha De devotes to the modelling scene of her times, to how *Stardust, Society* and *Celebrity* came into being, to comments about changing social relationships, and above all to her impressions of the celebrities she has met and observed with a keen unforgiving eye, from Nari Hira and M.F. Husain to Kajol, all darlings of media-driven popular curiosity, points to the nature of her focus: she may begin, of course, with herself, but very soon she turns the light away from herself. Not, of course, that *Selective Memory* is social history; it is a carefully structured literary endeavour in which she tries to make her memories discover a pattern where none really exists. She turns the spotlight only on certain selected incidents, but very often what she illuminates are only, in her own words, "artefacts," (527) the memorabilia and the bric-a-brac of a past artfully arranged to simulate a life and a persona, not a steady stream of vignettes from a lived life that create the persona. Obviously, therefore, she has found it difficult to "chapterize" her life. (528) The fourteen chapters into which the work is divided have each a title that uses popular catchwords about successful development, phrases that, moreover, begin with a present participle that invariably suggest that the process described is a continuing one: "Glancing Back," "Walking Tall," "Cutting Loose," "Blazing Trails," and so on. But how much of that growth is really shown, much less examined? Each chapter can in fact stand on its own, with its own collection of anecdotes, instead of marking a stage in emotional and psychological or intellectual development; each is a closed text.

Selective Memory is basically the memoirs of a celebrity who prefers, interestingly, to concentrate on other celebrities. Shobha De might "cringe" at the label of celebrity usually attached to her—"Everybody and anybody is loosely described as a 'celebrity' these days, especially if that person has no known profession, talent or gift" (223)—but she has to admit that she is well-known enough (and attractive and rich enough!) to be regarded as one by her public. Except for *Second Thoughts*, all her novels, many if not most of her newspaper columns, and her three forays into magazine editing (*Stardust* and *Society*, both of which she was the first editor, and her own short-lived enterprise, *Celebrity*, an Indian version of the popular American magazine *People*) are, or have been, about the rich and famous, the glittering superficiality of their public lives and the dark shows that cloud their private ones; they often seem specifically designed, in fact, to satisfy middle class prurient inquisitiveness about the so-called beautiful people and whether they can indeed be brought down to earth. No doubt the celebrity syndrome has also been responsible for turning *Selective Memory* into memoir rather than autobiography. Behind it, after all, lies, Shobha De notes, Davidar's words to her: "You have the ability to pick out that one characteristic that defines an individual, and bury it in amber. Tap into it. Use it—and you've got your book." (4)

In her search for the defining moment of each celebrity she talks about, Shobha De has avoided revealing her own. She agrees, of course, that "'celebrity'" (230) is a difficult state and that she has managed to survive "the 'fame thing'" by "never tak[ing] it (or [her]self) seriously," (231) and admits candidly—this is De's special virtue, her ability to be honest about whatever little she does expose of herself:

> I suppose I am guilty of participating in the celebrity trip. I don't always adore the people whose homes I visit. I do talk about them behind their backs. I know they don't like me just as I don't like them. That's life in any competitive city. I've reached a stage when I'm so switched off, . . . I really don't give a damn. . . . [In] the jungle I inhabit, . . . it's each one for himself or herself. (290)

Shobha De has always been a private person, perhaps not quite the kind of person to engage in the kind of self-revelation associated with autobiography. But some of the best parts of *Selective Memory* deal not with celebrities but with the few personal moments Shobha De agrees to share with her readers: her relationship with her children and stepchild in "Getting Personal," and her accounts of what writing means to her. One of these deserves to be reproduced, for it explains why Shobha De continues to be read and enjoyed even by those who are uncomfortable with her kind of journalese:

> For a woman, a book in progress is like a secret lover she has to hide from her family. Steal time to go back to. Dream about. Luxuriate in. Fantasize about. It's a guilty secret she can't share with anybody. There is a sense of regret—you can't make love

> to a book or talk to it. And yet, the secret thrill of each encounter provides a high. The book makes you feel desirable, sexy, beautiful, interesting. It's better than the best sex. (2)

Here, ultimately, is where the appeal of *Selective Memory* lies: its ability to convey the excitement and the obsession of creation and creativity.

NOTES

1. Shobha De, *Selective Memory: Stories from My Life* (New Delhi: Penguin, 1998).
2. Shobha De *Socialite Evenings* (New Delhi: Penguin, 1989).
3. Gloria L. Cronin, "Fundamental Views and Feminist Dilemmas: Elizabeth Dewberry Vaughn's *Many Things Have Happened Since He Died* and *Break the Heat of Me*," in Melvin J. Friedman and Ben Siegel, ed., *Tradition, Voices, and Dreams: The American Novel since the 1960s* (Newark: University of Delaware Press, 1996), pp. 254-78.
4. Janet Varner Gunn, qtd. in Shari Benstock, "Authorizing the Autobiographical," *Feminisms: An Anthology of Literary Theory and Criticism*, ed. Robyn R. Warhol and Diana Price Herndl (N. Brunswick, NJ: Rutgers University Press, 1991), p. 1041.
5. Suzette A. Henke, "Women's Life-Writing and the Minority Voice: Maya Angelou, Maxine Hong Kingston, and Alice Walker," in Friedman and Siegel, p. 211.
6. Margaret Atwood, *Survival: A Thematic Guide to Canadian Literature* (Toronto: House of Anansi Press, 1972), pp. 40-42.
7. William Zinsser, "Writing and Remembering: A Memoir and an Introduction." in Zinsser, ed., *Inventing the Truth: The Art and Craft of Memoir* (Boston: Houghton Mifflin, 1987), p. 21.
8. James Olney, qtd. in Benstock, p. 1040.
9. Annie Dillard, "To Fashion a Text," in Zinsser, p. 57.
10. *Ibid.*, p. 56.

Shobha De on Shobha De: Autobiographic Strategies in *Selective Memory*

CHITTARANJAN MISRA

Shobha De's autobiography is written at a time in her life that is appropriate to take stock of things as anybody would feel at fifty. But taking stock and looking back for a novelist and a journalist like Shobha De is special. For the fact that she has two modes of writing—fictive and the other basically related to documenting facts—in command. Being both creative and critical at the same time, Shobha De has acquired an enviable fluency as a writer whose own life story for that matter becomes no less gripping than fiction, no less interesting than a profile sketch of newsmakers in columns of glossy journals.

In this epic first person narrative, she talks about the art of autobiography like a self-conscious narrator. A woman who thinks of her existence as consumed by the act of writing for years comes to confront for the first time the feeling of her own mortality while embarking upon writing about herself. Reconstructing oneself from the memories of a myriad echoes and images is a different kind of experience. It makes one aware of changes and transformation that take place in one's attitude. In the 'Prologue,' she writes:

> If nothing else, *Selective Memory* aided and abetted the transformation. Kick-started the process, as it were forced me to glance over my shoulder. Look back, sift, discard, reinforce, assess, reassess, come to terms, recognize, accept—above all, accept. It was not easy. Not easy at all. But having endured the experience, I feel that much stronger. It wasn't as painful as I'd imagined. I didn't suffer. It's the exhilaration of forced remembering that I'll cherish. In my preoccupation with the present I'd lost touch with

> my past. The book served as an excuse, an alibi and a prod. There was no escape.[1]

There are such passages where she tries at baring the devices of the genre to expose the challenges. While doing this, she indirectly hints at the areas selectively hidden through the bulky frame of *Selective Memory* having sixteen sections.

The autobiographer reconstructs the images of the self lost in the irrevocable past. The images are not only different from and contradictory to one another as mental constructs of the autobiographer but often shaped by the society, imposed and established by the collective entity outside her. And yet all images fuse into a narrator continuously entering into and struggling out of various personae through time. That makes the autobiographer obliged to concentrate on patches of memory involving selection and elimination. Human memory is sometimes unreliable, wistful and recollection of past itself is selective at the natural, involuntary level. But when it comes to the art of putting them together through language as a non-fiction prose the selection of things recalled is conscious, artful, schematized and subjective. Shobha De is a conscious narrator restructuring the contexts of the images of herself as a model, a columnist, a novelist addressing the vast audience of Indian English writing. She, too, in the same manner, portrays public figures (from the world of politics, film and art) she has come across in her life in an unconventional manner mixing her indulgence for and disapproval of them. In addition to all these, she states her views in a straightforward manner on kinds of relationship on both personal and impersonal levels. This ranges from highly artificial relationship among people of high society coming together in parties and banquets in star hotels to the private relationship between two people following a divorce or marriage. For Shobha De, life is a becoming and the ever changing process is captured through the titles of different chapters like "Glancing Back," "Walking Tall," "Cutting Loose," "Blazing Trails," "Shining Through," "Sitting Pretty," "Flying Solo," "Naming, Names," "Writing On," "Getting Ahead," "Moving Images," "Getting Personal," "Feeling Great," and "Taking Stock." The nomenclature offers unity to the sequence of ever-changing thoughts and action. The expression of this sense of continuity and change seems more effective through a cluster of mostly gerunds. Shobha De is very careful in naming things—all her books from the first novel *Socialite Evenings* to *Selective Memory* start with the letter 'S.'

Selective Memory is written when the author turns fifty and coincidentally the country commemorates fifty years of independence. The story of Shobha De's life is the story of the New Woman of independent India. Her self-identification is described in the new ideology. Her combat against the fixed identity of the docile, tortured and conformist woman of pre-independence period turns out to be an individual protest as much as it is a product of influence of the new pace, the invasion of the western culture. The career chosen by Shobha De cannot be seen as totally personal but as happening to her in different ways. The memoir renders vividly what she has done and what has been done to her by this new context. She is not interested in the old and the ancient but wants to be immersed in present moment experience:

> Ruins don't interest me. I have no feel for history. There is nothing romantic about fossils; give me a busy bazaar bursting with activity, a street-side cafe, a theatre, crowds, people, chaos, noise. And give me the new foods to excite the palate. New textures, new smells, new columns. (152)

No wonder, the spell of the new world and its paradigm associated with avenues to power and glamour have effected and shaped the lives of people like Shobha De who are intellectually open to the world and do not believe in taboos. Exposed to public school snobbery from childhood and associated with friends some of whom preferred "Sartre and Satyajit Ray for breakfast, Camus and Kamaladevi Chattopadhyaya for lunch, Nietzsche and Nirad C. Choudhuri for dinner" (3) through "a haze of marijuana and rum," (34) Shobha De faced a problem of choice like the existentialists: "I wanted direction. A strong firm guide to lead me through the tunnel and show me the light." (89) And while searching for that—she waited for happy accidents. She states: "I've always waited for happy accidents. So far, they've always happened. Almost on cue." (89)

Even after writing for twenty-eight years, she thinks of the experience as a transitory phase before moving onto her real vocation. But she does not know exactly as to what could that 'real vocation' be. Writing came to her as one of so many alternatives she could follow:

"I have not *chosen*. Writing has happened to me. Like so many other, very important, wonderful, unexpected things in my life." (382)

Selective Memory is not a nostalgic chronicle of the autobiographer but an account of a "critical revisiting." Talking about the days when she was a champion athlete, a thirty-year-old basketball player, she feels different; she visualizes this young image with complete detachment: "Like an old movie starring someone familiar. It's hard to think of that person as a young one." (25) She looks critically at her achievement in the field of modelling. Apart from fame what modelling has offered her that mattered was 'a certain level of self-awareness' that was of great help in later years. She has cherished her media image as a celebrity no doubt, but at the same time, "there have been occasions when I haven't enjoyed being Shobha De, the public personae," (251) she confesses. Rising upto public expectation is not an easy thing. She is critical about her self-image but the attempts at methodical self-promotion she is asked about is treated by her as professionalism. She writes highly about the way she was raised up culturally in her family and has a high sense of etiquette. She is critical about the 'vulgar, pelvis-gyrating' dancing youngmen of today and is particularly reluctant to accept the stubble-faced, earring wearing youngmen in tattered jeans easily. She operates more or less in the same fashionable society they belong to.

Shobha De has depicted in brief the personality traits of many celebrated actors and actresses. Their off-stage behind the personae images are revealing. She praises all that is positive in them but does not spare any for the defects she has observed in them. For example:

> Waheeda Rahman didn't ever have star quality (exactly like Jaya Bachchan) but she did captivate hearts with her on-screen personae. (186)
>
> Rustic, ill-mannered and uncouth is what I found the late Sanjeev Kumar. (115)
>
> Rekha has the voice of an illiterate washer woman. (114)
>
> Amitabh and Rajesh don't have friends—only docile devotees, and obsequious hangers-on. (121)

In the two chapters "Blazing Trails" and "Shining Through," she deals with movie stars mostly reminiscent of the manner of writing for *Star-*

dust. In another chapter "Flying Solo" she speaks about other celebrities she came across in connection with her working for *Society* and her other magazine *Celebrity.* She writes abut M.F. Husain's "Madhuri fixation" as a trick for self-promotion. In the chapter "Naming Names," she talks about Sunil Gavaskar, Kiran Bedi, Asha Bhonsle, Stevan Seagal, V.S. Naipaul, Morarji Desai, Imran Khan and a great many from India and abroad. She is critical about Naipaul's carrying an air of being one of the world's greatest living writers and Kiran Bedi's media-friendly dynamism as a mastery over "the art of playing to the gallery" for a future in politics. The verifiability of these critical observations and assumptions may be related to the commonly shared contexts outside the text. It calls into question Shobha De's positioning of herself in a culture she as a writer tries to condemn and transcend.

Shobha De has scaled heights of success as an Indian woman 'breaking through rigid barriers.' She has been featured in different international journals like *Vogue, Asia Week, The Times* and *Newsweek.* She has epitomized in her and her novels the face of the new woman of India. Her individualistic views on social aspects of life in *Surviving Men* and *Socialite Evenings*, her emphasis on sex in *Starry Nights*, the depiction of the new woman in *Sisters* and other works are dealt at length by Shobha De herself in the autobiography. Writing about her own writing she has contributed to the making of *Selective Memory* a 'writerly text.'

The chapter 'Getting Personal' offers a different taste of reading as there is more of the Indian self of Shobha De. Vividly she describes the death of her mother. She also narrates her meeting Dilip De (her second husband) for the first time as a destined moment after her first marriage ended in a divorce. She tries to fit these and other incidents in this chapter as a sequence of destined occurrences and tries to come to terms with life (a conventional Indian approach).

One very important aspect of the autobiography is Shobha De's handling of language as signifying her gender consciousness. There is an attempt at demolishing the male ego while writing about males. Instead of submitting to the general male-centric view of woman as merely erotic objects she in a novel discovers males as insecure who "feel terribly threatened by self-suffficient women."[2] The same feminist views here depict males through an animal imagery associating the power and option of taming the animals with women. She refers to a man in disapproval: "The man was a dog. A rabid one. I didn't see myself as a lamp-post." (97) Similar utterances are there in her fiction (that can be read as concealed autobiography) like *Socialite Evenings* where "Ritu confesses to Karuna the lesson that men, like dogs, could be conditioned through reward and punishment."[3] Shobha De narrates in great detail her experience of pregnancy, labour and childbirth unique to women and inaccessible to men. She considers 'giving birth' as the most significant moment of her life: "One that I would cherish till my last breath. Too precious to dilute through conversations . . . even thought." (497)

Shobha De is very careful about words and their order. She says: "I've always found words very seductive. If they're arranged in a startlingly original way." (311) Both chatty and distant, she verbally re-enacts scenes and situations. Her innovative flair for using words can be easily guessed from a few pairing like 'fluff and frippery' (295), 'grime and grit' (332), 'festooned with flowers' (491), 'pegs and pakoras' (296), 'pariahs and parasites' (336) and 'pulped and pulverized' (269).

Shobha De belongs to the postcolonial Indian women writers who according to Lakshmisree Banerjee have "outgrown their earlier plagiaristic and assimilative modes, which mainly seemed to be an extension of male literature or established forms of such writings. Indian women, writing in English today, are an urbane, sophisticated and intellectually alert lot with a proper English education; hence they have become more innovative, experimental, confessional and realistic than they were ever before, their creative effects being largely fresh and experience based."[4] Shobha De's *Selective Memory* can be analyzed against this perspective.

What Shobha De has written about Shobha De should not be taken as a kind of narcissism by thinking more of what she has not written about herself. Even Roland Barthes who declared death of the author in favour of the birth of the reader and autonomy of text wrote his fragmentary 'autobiography' *Roland Barthes by Roland Barthes* (1977). But he prescribed in the book's epigraph: it should be considered as if spoken by a character in a novel.[5]

In Shobha De's *Selective Memory*, there is a detachment in the treatment of her past images and one never complains of any tyranny of subjectivity. Shobha De is both subjective and objective in writing her autobiography, giving a picture of fifty years of her life, 'as confused as the nation itself, without any 'strong message to deliver.' She has only tried to mix up the individual artist with the social commentator as an aggregate entity. She has tasted the narcotic called fame by choosing to tread a 'less-peopled pathway' and has honestly and candidly put the experiences in five hundred and thirty one printed pages of a Penguin Book. *Selective Memory* certainly is something more than an 'overview of a journey.'

NOTES

1. Shobha De, *Selective Memory: Stories from My Life* (New Delhi: Penguin, 1998), p. 11.
2. Shobha De, *Socialite Evenings* (New Delhi: Penguin Books, 1990).
3. Soumyajit Samanta, "Against Marginalisation of Indian Women: A Feminist Reading of Shobha De's *Socialite Evenings*," *Feminism and Indian English Fiction*, ed. P.M. Nayak (Bareilly: PBD, 1996), p. 81.
4. Lakshmisree Banerjee, "Indian Women's Voices: The Post Colonial and Post Modernist Era," *The Commonwealth Review*, Vol. VII, No. 2, 1995-96, p. 128.
5. Christopher Norris, "Roots: Structuralism and New Criticism," *Deconstruction: Theory and Practice* (Routledge: London & New York 1993), p. 11.

Selective Memory: A Study in Autobiography

P.S. KASTURE

A well-written life is almost as rare as a well-spent one.

Carlyle

With a few exceptions, man generally dotes on himself. In spite of the awareness of human mortality, he is ever engaged in perpetuating his memory. Sculpture, painting, carving, photography point to the same human desire. They are biographies in some sense. Human mind leaped ahead. Man perhaps thought of creating his own life as a novel and perhaps the most truthful account of his life, and autobiography was born. Autobiography is a form of biography, with a significant basic difference. In a biography, the writer recreates the truth of another life. An autobiographer, on the other hand, tries to discover his own self.

Autobiography is the truthful record of the writer's own life presented in such a way that it attracts the attention of the reader and gives him aesthetic pleasure. *Encyclopaedia Britannica* defines autobiography as "the account of an individual human life written by the subject himself."[1] *The Universal Dictionary of the English Language* describes autobiography thus: "Art and practice of writing a narrative of one's own life."[2] To *Webster,* autobiography is "a written account of one's own life."[3]

Encyclopaedia Britannica, *Universal Dictionary* and *Webster* emphasize the main thrust of the attempt but do not signify the extent of the concept. To D.G. Naik, "The details of any given life, therefore, when accommodated in a story or narrative inevitably take a shape or form in literary terminology is called the form of autobiography."[4] The columns of *Encyclopaedia Britannica* while describing biography remark, "Unlike history it deals with the individual; unlike fiction it records a life that actually has been lived. At the same time the biographer shares with the historian a concern for truth and he shares with the novelist the ambition to create a work of art." (636) The idea of the distinction between biography and history is modern. It is doubtful whether any writer of antiquity, even Plutarch, clearly perceived its possible existence as an independent branch of literature. They considered the writing of a man's life as an opportunity of celebrating in his person certain definite moral qualities. The true concept of biography, as a faithful portrait of a soul in its adventure through life is very modern. With great advance in psychology, to descend deep into the recesses of human heart, to find perennial sources of human thoughts, feelings, hidden motives and springs of action is at once the problem and joy of a good biographer and also of an autobiographer. A scrupulous and relentless selection and artistic arrangement of the selected material is the primary function of an autobiographer. An ideal autobiography can then be defined as a review of one's life, to recreate his self, done with a sense of detachment. The values of various genres of literature constantly change so that it is difficult to fit an art-form in a static definition. Autobiography, as an art-form, is no exception.

The present paper is an attempt to assess Shobha De's *Selective Memory: Stories from My Life* as her autobiography.

II

A work of art is often shaped according to the implicit basic motive. Autobiographies are written with various aims. As many minds, so many aims and forms. Some write for their own amusement, for enjoying time, to impress others with their great victories, to share joys and sorrows with others, to discover oneself. For some, autobiography is a medium of the song of his life. Rousseau titled his autobiography as *Confessions*. Autobiographies also spring from social and political consciousness. They reflect and comment upon the contemporary life. Most often a man is in a mood of writing autobiography when he becomes conscious of his end. Somewhere the self, bound by various relations, feels the loss of his personality, or feels disoriented as he is no more the centre of his dear one's life. This hurt-self once again gets lost in the memories of his past.

"Who should write autobiography?" is one of the pertinent questions under study. The canvas of autobiography, as an art-form, is so vast that anybody and everybody can handle it and it is shaped according to the personality of the writer. Autobiography is interesting only if the life concerned is worth narrating. For writing autobiography, life must have form, melody and colour of its own.

"When to write autobiography?" is a debatable point. Writing autobiography is related not to the age, but to the attitude. When man has courage to face his mind nakedly, when nothing is yet to be achieved, when he is past caring ego-drives, he writes about his life. Autobiographies written at the mid-point of life are regarded more successful. The aim of such autobiographies differs from that of the old good-bye ones. The new one tries to look back not only at the dead part of his life, but attempts to understand his self that will have its bearing on his future too. Such autobiographies are more honest and bear a truthful mirror to life because of their detached point of view. This attempt of the author to give a coherent shape and meaning to his past also makes the reader introvert in the search of his self.

In *Selective Memory,* Shobha De commemorates her experience of turning fifty. Though David Davidar phoned her to write her autobiography "now that you are about to turn fifty,"[5] she was not sure about the right time. Perhaps old age (seventy) is best as "It's all behind you. Good times and bad. You want to chronicle it before memory itself fades"; or perhaps, twenty is the best as "It's all ahead of you." (1) Initially she felt she hated mid-points and she was scared to make up, invent and rub out. But when David asked her to think of writing as much a part of her routine as life has been, she got it. She catches this moment in its entirety very graphically:

> 'Think of it as a column. A really long one. That's what your life has been for twenty-five years—an unending column,' David.
>
> Has it? Just that? A column?
>
> Maybe.
>
> And then I started to think. Fifty. Funny, I didn't feel it. Fifty. Such finality in that word. Fifty. Stock-taking time. Fifty. Flashback time. Ugh. Fifty. Wow. I repeated fifty, fifty times over. It had to sink in. Register. I needed that sense of fifty to fix it.— And did I want to write the damn book?

> I guess I did.
>
> 'Please go away,' I pleaded with the unwritten manuscript, even as I prepared to write it.
>
> 'Leave me alone,' I beseeched as images exploded in my head. I knew what it was leading up to. (2)

At the 1998 Winter Olympics, while she watched the sole Indian representative Shiva Keshvan preparing for the luge—his special event, she envisioned herself down the narrow memory path and felt the necessity of expression as things were not under her control, just "lie back and enjoy the ride." (4)

Though *Selective Memory* was not an easy book to write, it wasn't that tough either. Once she put her foot into it, she enjoyed herself. She was not bound or troubled by any notes, dates, diaries, clippings. She was lured by those mostly colourful and generally pleasant "myriad echoes and images." (4) She perceives turning fifty has given her the right perspective of detached acceptance: "At fifty, nothing is at stake. Nothing and nobody matters all that much—not even old adversaries. Enmity itself gets diluted. Poison disappears. Co-existence becomes the key. People cease to affect you with the same intensity." (4)

III

Autobiography does not need wings of imagination like a fiction, sharp intellect or deep study like a scientific book, or hard work like biography or history. In addition, involvement necessary for the creation of a good work of art can never be found better in any other work than autobiography. It is the man alone who can really tell the truth about himself. Dr. Johnson's words seem appropriate, "Every man's life may be best written by himself."[6] So autobiography seems to be a very easy form of art, but this is not so. Autobiography is a form of literature that appears to be easy but is most difficult to handle.

Truthful narration, detachment, centrality of self, selection and presentation of events are some of the salient features of an ideal autobiography.[7] It is more probable to lose their balance rather than to effect it because it is difficult to tell the truth. The process of narrating truth is hindered by the loss of memory, natural human awkwardness, and love of self.

Truth in autobiography is different from the historical or the fictional truth. In it there is no flight of imagination, nor is there a sweeping generalization. Though it is presented through the eye of an individual, it is expected not to be limited or personal, but the 'naked, unblushing truth.' This ideal was enunciated by Othello long ago.

> Speak of me as I am; nothing extenuate,
> Nor set down ought in malice. (V.ii.349-50)

An autobiography to be true to its own nature should not merely show the man in brilliant colours and in triumphant moments, but must also show his trouble, anger, grief and exhaustion. The whites and the blacks, the virtues and vices should mingle in natural relief and harmony. A man's failure is his autobiographer's gain because failure is more human than success, therefore, more interesting. It is hoped that things are presented with honesty, that lapses are presented with equal transparency as are strong points. To look at the self with dispassionate equanimity needs a great ability and courage. To confess one's faults publicly, ego-drives are to be left aside.

Shobha De is able, in general, to effect this balance, thus, making her narration highly interesting. She narrates her experiences honestly, without any sham pose. When her father got transferred from Delhi to Bombay again, she records her feeling of home-coming, though she confesses her utter inability to explain any obvious reason—upbringing, social circle, fond memory, food-habit, special liking.

> I felt we were finally going 'home.' This was rather surprising. Our upbringing had not been fiercely 'Maharashtrian.' Anything but. I did not know a single Marathi-speaking person. . . . By now, I was speaking more Hindi than Marathi, more English than Hindi. I had never tasted bhel puri. . . . I had no recollection of having seen the sea . . . the only mangoes I'd enjoyed were langdas not aapoos (Alphonso); double-decker buses were associated with the London of picture postcards, not Mumbai. And yet . . . and yet . . . we were going home. (18)

While talking about her modelling adventure, she points out areas of innovation and improvisation. Most models agreed to pose for them even though no money was offered, because it not only gave them fun but offered a great deal of exposure. Such pictures gave the photographers and models enough scope to experiment with lighting, make-up, hair styles and looks. Still Shobha De is quite conscious that the main inspiration came from foreign fashion magazines and photographic journals: "we stole shamelessly. There was nothing 'original' about our fashion spreads—all we did was pore over *Vogue*, *Elle*, *Harper's* and *Queen* and copy like crazy." (45)

Detached attitude is an essential quality of a good autobiography. According to Harold Nicolson, autobiography requires "Scientific autopsy and rigorous postmortem."[9] Keeping aside social inhibitions Shobha De courageously presents total pictures of many contemporary celebrities. Her bluntness speaks for her comprehensive understanding and truthful narration. When Shatrughan Sinha strode in the Cat House with his chamchas, and tried to impress her with his broad Bihari accent and crude manner, she saw through him. She was not at all taken aback by his loudmouth behaviour: "he went ahead and made a complete fool of himself—even though the man is not a fool at all. It was his lack of exposure, the absence of sophistication and the mistaken belief that this sort of posturing was making us all go weak in the knees." (109) She so simply punctured his over-estimated image when he pompously tried to offer a ride home.

> A dull green Mercedes Benz was parked along the pavement.
> He pointed and said, 'That's my car.'
> There were no audible gasps. 'How are you going home?'
> 'Like I do every day—I walk.'
> 'Why don't you come with me in my Mercedes?'
> 'No, thank you. I need the exercise.'
> He almost wept. (109)

This razor's edge is counter-balanced by her genuine contrastive pictures. "Some seem to carry the load of fame more easily than others—Ruszard Kapuscinski, the Polish writer, for one." (274) Naipaul is hard to ignore. He is quite conscious of his own importance in the world and makes others acknowledge it. Shabbily dressed and stooped Kapuscinski, on the other hand, was so meek and unobtrusive that he was not noticed at all. "But when he spoke, it was his genuine humility and humanity," that shone forth. (275)

Shobha De's encounter with Kishori Amonkar once again indicates that De's attempt is not to molest a person but to go beyond the celebrated image to discover the real self behind. She candidly confesses, "In Kishori Amonkar's case, I wasn't exactly bad, just slightly wicked. Perhaps not even that. My sin was that I'd passed a profile in *Celebrity* that was less than referential. It was written by a woman whose viewpoint I respected." (248) The writer was a bit naughty in the introductory remarks but Kishori's 'monumental ego' furiously summoned Shobha De to her residence when the interview appeared in *Celebrity*. Shobha tried to calm her but she would have none of it. Shobha tried to ask Kishori Amonkar whether she wanted to object for factual incorrectness or misquotation. Amonkar's 'vanity was pricked' because 'the cheek of that girl' dared to refer to her actual age.

Shobha De decided to go over and assure her that she looked no more than thirty. Kishori verbally attacked Shobha De very ruthlessly, "I had heard you were a very beautiful woman . . . but look at you . . . you resemble a TB patient." (249) Nonplussed with Shobha De's calm smile, Kishori Amonkar again taunted her. Shobha De merely smiled and told her how wonderful she was looking. With great skill Shobha De unveils Kishori Amonkar's hurt ego and without comment exposes her puffed vanity that dwarfs her own person.

> 'You are so right, obviously my writer was mistaken,' I said quietly. 'But how old are you really?'
>
> Kishori paused, 'Fifty-seven.'
>
> 'So why are you upset if she mentioned that?'
>
> 'Because I don't look it,' she all but roared. (249)

Shobha De's perceptive observations subtly testify to her deep understanding of hidden recesses of human psyche.

> Once she'd gotten that out of her system, she seemed to calm down. (249)
>
> She was so childlike, in both her hurt and enthusiasm. (250)

When Kishori Amonkar seemed to be convinced that Shobha De was consumptive, Shobha De didn't have the heart to correct her. Kishori

Amonkar prepared sweet sheera and lovingly forced her to eat it. The concluding remark stands out with its deep understanding and genial humour.

> "It's good for you," she chucked like a mother hen, "go on, eat it up and I'll give you some more."
>
> Believe me, V.C. Shukla's threat seemed kinder at that moment. I'd have preferred a public hanging at Flora Fountain to this. Kishori had had her revenge after all—and it couldn't have been sweeter. (250)

Shobha De's success as an auobiographer lies in her capacity to look at her own self with equal candidness and sharpness. Even though she is regarded as one of the successful models, she voices her awareness of her lack of contemporary value-scales in the field.

> I didn't see myself as a sleek, sexy, soignee creature of collective fantasy. If anything, I kept wondering what the hell I was doing in that business, when I didn't possess what I thought where the prerequisites for such a high-visibility job; I wasn't in love with myself, and I didn't believe I was particularly effective on stage, wracked as I was with self-consciousness and self-doubt. (50-51)

In the complex where Shobha De lives, she is often visited by school kids who need a quick essay, points for debate, headlines for a project, missing words from a crossword, even ad copy for their mothers' leaflets for 'short cookery summer courses.' She writes all that she is asked to 'obediently and think nothing of it.' Not even when the young shopkeeper in the arcade door does not approve of the many names she has submitted to him for his to-be-opened man's boutique. He regretfully rejects her brilliant suggestions, but invites her for opening it. She faces no ego problem, but when her daughter doubts her capacity, the mother in her feels deeply hurt.

> My ego can handle it. But when my daughter's sixth-grade teacher rejects 'her' assignment—a poster for a blood donation campaign, saying 'it doesn't make sense,' I feel crushed. And terribly hurt. Not because the teacher has told her it isn't good enough but

because my daughter had started to think so too. So I smile a small smile and say 'It's okay, darling. We'll try harder the next time.' And I really do. (301)

After establishing herself as the best-selling author, Shobha De recalls her first experience of writing a book with blunt frankness. With self-searching attitude she views herself reliving those moments. With the transparency of mind she not only convinces the reader of the candidness of her stand, but also retraces the author in making: "One telephone call. That's it. Just one, single telephone call it was that led to the journey I'm still on." (313) She liked the approach—businesslike, friendly enough, but not familiar. David Davidar, the editor-publisher and CEO of Penguin Books India, was on the lookout for new writers. She said he'd read "My columns over the years and strongly believed there was a book in there somewhere." (314) Her initial response was not at all positive. It was his belief, but not hers. She listened but not too carefully. She was not at all focused or particularly interested because of her pregnancy. Reading her columns, David had the impression that she had "the pulse of the city." As there was no good book that had captured that aspect, she could be 'the right person.' He told her briefly about himself. She listened vaguely, her mind elsewhere. She started lamely, hoping to end the meeting: "But I've never written a book before." She made it clear that a book about Bombay didn't excite her at all. "David had another immediate opinion—make it fiction." She felt the business tedious. To relieve herself, she cheerfully promised that she would think about it. David agreed and said that he would be back in a month's time.

She promptly forgot all about him and her tentative assurance that she would work on something. Exactly after a month the call came: 'have you got the outline?' She panicked. She felt like a penitent school girl who hadn't worked on her vacation assignment. She stammered and then fibbed, 'Yes, I've got it.' David would be coming in an hour to take a look. She feared that she would be exposed for 'the cheap little fibber.' That would be too humiliating. She had to produce something—anything. She pulled out the pad and started scribbling. She graphically presents those moments conveying the spontaneity of her creative impulse. "So many years later, I can still recall the rush I experienced during those few minutes, as the outline for *Socialite Eve-*

nings took shape on the lined pages of a cheap pad. I cannot explain even now where the story emerged from, but as I began to write it down, I felt a sense of urgency to record it all before it went away . . . disappeared altogether." (316) At that stage she was too preoccupied with impending motherhood to bother about the possibility of a brand-new career option. (317) And yet, she felt uneasy and self-conscious at being judged by a much younger man. She still wonders why did she submit herself to such a test. She waited for the verdict with no hope. David pushed his glasses further up the bridge of his nose and said 'Right.' She did not understand its meaning but dared not asked him to clarify.

She candidly confesses her initial difficulty. She didn't have the slightest notion of how to go about writing a book, nor did she know writers to whom she could ask. Her mind was beset with contrasting doubts. Was a real writer supposed to know instinctively how it's done? Maybe she wasn't a real writer. She didn't have a clue. Of course, there was no going back. She tried to shun off the tension thinking that she didn't need that. Instead of concentrating on her coming child, she was foolishly agonizing herself over 'some stupid book.' She spent a week feeling hostile and resentful, but 'the book wouldn't disappear from my mental radar.' She very much wanted to write it and be free, but she did not know how to. 'I needed a guide, a guru, someone to hold my hand and take me through the paces . . . just show the way.' She decided to make a call to Delhi. Came the answer and she continued with her work.

> 'Shobha . . . there's nothing to it. you have a good story—just tell it. And don't worry about the format. You write it as it emerges. The chapters will fall into place as you go along. And you'll know the book has ended when your story is finished. Good luck. Happy writing.'
>
> And that was basically it. I was flying solo. . . . Once the process got underway, I couldn't stop. . . . I'd often heard authors saying glibly, 'oh . . . the story just wrote itself.' Well, that was precisely what was happening to me too. . . . A feeling of enormous relief swept over me as I wrote the final sentence. 'Send it across,' said David. I did that. (320-22)

Along with narrating how she wrote her first book *Socialite Evenings*, she refers to various problems a writer faces. She realized her feverish pace as her natural rhythm. Whether she was satisfied with that creative exercise, she candidly confesses that because of the nearness and newness of the experience she didn't know. She only knew that she had actually done it. It was 'accomplishment enough' for her mind. She also knew that if she could do it once, she'd do it again. 'Nothing else counted. Not even David's verdict.' She never thought of possible rejection of the manuscript. Without any sham pose she acknowledges, 'I believe it was my ignorance rather than self-confidence at work here.' So simply she talks about her great virtue of detachment that came naturally to her because she has never been a narcissist. "It was at this stage that I discovered something funny about myself—once the book was over and done with, I felt completely disconnected from its fate. The book was then on its own—free falling or scaling heights, all by itself. There was no emotional attachment left." (324)

IV

The real beauty of an autobiography is constituted in the image of the self that emerges through the writing. So 'self' must be placed at the central position. Man being a social creature, his life-story must include many other individuals, without any threat to his centrality. Roy Pascal opines, "In the autobiography proper attention is focused on the self."[10] At times, too many events and characters push the self aside. If the writer is not able to focus his self, the book loses its importance as an autobiography.

In *Selective Memory,* Shobha De is successful in keeping constant focus on her self without violating the sanctity of other selves. They are not her shadows, but live men in their own right, rightly viewed in her life-story, from her point of view.

At the very outset of the book, Shobha De gives a touching account of a deeply moving moment she shared with her father. There is no towering father-figure, but a loving father who wants to share the joy of the moment saving it from the oncoming tide of mortality. One month before her fiftieth birthday, Shobha De received a phone call from her father, "suppressed excitement in his voice, a strange sense of urgency, secrecy. 'My dear . . . can you come and see me today?'" (6) Shobha De was mildly irritated because of interruption. She was pressed by the dead-lines. But he was unwilling to wait. She then promised that she would visit him at lunch time. She failed due to her work. Close to 2 p.m. he phoned again and insisted her immediate coming at least for fifteen minutes. "Don't disappoint me. And don't be late." On her arrival he told her, "I want to give you your fiftieth birthday present today." In spite of her entreaties of denial, it was his decision.

> In case . . . in case . . . something happens to me . . . I wouldn't want the gift to lie unclaimed. . . . It has a special significance. . . . But if for any reason I am no more, this gift will lose its charm. You were born in free India. You will not know what that moment of freedom meant to people of my generation. So, don't argue with me. Take it. And keep it safely. (7)

He mischievously asked her to guess what was inside. When she gave up, he took back the envelope, opened it carefully and removed a small neat packet which he handed over to her. It was from the Government of India mint. A gold coin commemorating fifty years of independence. 'Beautiful and so appropriate.' She took the coin and stared at it for a long time.

> It looked like a miniature sun on my palm. I was far too moved by the gesture to say anything. It really was perfect, even in its execution. . . . There was nothing ostentatious about the coin. And I could only marvel at my father's imagination. Another man might have handed over a sum of money and said, 'Buy yourself something.' But here we were, sharing such a deeply moving moment—and I couldn't think of a thing to say, not even 'thank you.' . . . Finally, I bent down and touched his feet. (8)

Still her father emerges as an independent live figure through various incidents and narrative flashes. Unfortunately, for her mother, Shobha De was not the second son she'd prayed for, but a third daughter and an additional liability. Her maternal grandmother was greatly displeased and her mother distressed. But her father declared her 'lucky' for the family. (13) His middle-class Maharashtrian male domineering traits are revealed through a constant strain between the father and the daughter. Her narration not only captures a post moment in isolation, but as one more encounter that shaped her life. The first ambitious canvas Shobha De painted did not meet with her father's approval. It was a nude. Embarrassed and shocked by its position on the second-floor balcony, he ordered it to be removed and admonished, 'Paint flowers, trees, birds, mountains, scenic themes. Not these types of vulgar, shameless pictures.' Shobha De's last remark about that episode highlights her mastery in characterization. 'I got the message. I stopped painting.' (26) Father wanted Shobha to study hard and secure success in competitive examinations like his other children. He often scolded her, "It's your attitude. You have the aptitude and grasp. But no application. How can you excel with such a lackadaisical approach?" (35) Shobha De candidly admits she couldn't because she didn't want to. When her sisters visit her father's house, he makes clear to them: "So long as you are staying under my roof, you are my responsibility . . . and answerable to me. This is my house, you must abide by my rules." (415) Her father, a man with different value-scales, but true to them as she is to her own.

Keeping the centrality of her own self, Shobha De has successfully created a galaxy of brilliant portraits in her life-story—some remarkable for shaping her life, others interesting in their own right as character studies e.g. her mother, Nari Hira, Mahesh Bhatt, Sunil Gavaskar, Zeenat Aman. But this is not so in the case of Sudhir and even Dilip De. Even though no malice is sensed, there are scanty references to Sudhir. Dilip De is also introduced as a person at quite a late stage of the book. Of course, she is able to recall her first visit to De's house in all details. 'I haven't forgotten a single word' is a rightful claim. Her honest touching narration about Dilip De highlights Mr. De's sincerity, directness, intuitive sense of understanding, calm conviction and consequent confident behaviour.

Shobha De was awarded the Reuters Fellowship for the year and was given a few days to decide whether or not she was going to accept it. She was in a fix. She didn't want to leave her children. And yet she knew that was her big opportunity, perhaps the last one. If she didn't grab it, she'd have to be satisfied with a familiar rut. She felt miserable.

> I was restless and bored. Demoralized and depressed. . . . I was

> wracked with self-doubt and guilt. . . . I would lose the love of my children. My family would disown and despise me. . . . My flight . . . was at dawn on 16 August. I met Dilip on the night of the 11th. It was a meeting that altered my life—and gave me the answer I was so desperately looking for. (465-66)

Too embarrassed to follow her hosts into a stranger's residence, Shobha De lingered at the door. When she looked up 'a well-built man in his forties' was walking towards her. Dilip De. "Please . . . do come in, welcome, welcome. This is quite an occasion," he said, not bothering to hide his delight. (467) She followed him into a large living room where she saw many familiar faces. She noticed his strong Bengali accent. When he asked her about a drink, she stiffly refused. Undeterred, he added, 'How about champagne?' She smiled. 'Why not? I never say no to champage.' (467) She had always scoffed at words like 'destiny' 'karma' 'pre-ordained'—but she hadn't found a more convincing explanation for that unusual encounter. Both of them were not looking for a mate. 'And yet, he was certain about our entwined fates and he didn't take more than a few minutes to tell me so. His manner was amazingly direct and sure. 'So . . . . when can I meet your parents? Tomorrow? . . . The man was serious. Very serious. Like I said, Dilip recognized something—something very deep and precious—intuitively, instinctively.' When she expressed her shock regarding the non-concern of the guests about the two little children sleeping trustingly on their father's bed, he said, 'They are used to it . . . now that I am alone. My children often sleep in the room with me.' That sentence said it all. Next evening Dilip talked a lot. The narration was impassioned and honest sounding. Here is a man saying, 'This is me. This is my life. Take it or leave it. But mainly—take it.' . . . It was Hariprasad Chaurasia who helped me to make that fateful decision." Dilip and Shobha De met her father and his brother at the concert. Dilip handled the situation properly. 'He was respectful but not deferential.' (473)

Shobha De's happy matrimonial life with Dilip De is reflected throughout the book. But their first encounter is the only instant in the book when Dilip is presented with all his individual traits. At other points Dilip is 'my husband' and his contribution is only narrated.

Dilip would always make light of the whole thing, and success-

> fully blunted the edge of the unrelenting attacks. . . . And if some tried a cheap shot in my presence, he deflected it cleverly but always with a broad smile. Had he reacted any differently, I doubt that I would have found the motivation or even the courage to carry on. (363-64)
>
> The parameters of our relationship have been drawn by Dilip. Initially I chafed at some of them. Now I know it was his more mature, more experienced voice redefining marriage for me. (480)

Then she goes on talking about what marriage meant to her: "Marriage to me connotes commitment and surrender. Merging with, blending, overlapping, combining. It is a symbiotic relationship where one feeds on the other, depends on the other, needs the other." (481) She is grateful that she met Dilip and glad that she listened to her heart and stayed.

A natural question comes up—what was her response to marriage when she married Sudhir? This leads to a basic question regarding autobiography. "All memory is selective," (527) claims Shobha De. Autobiography is a review of a life. *Selective Memory*, as the title itself suggests, "provides an overview of a journey." (527) As it is not a historical chronicle, the writer has to select and artistically arrange the significant events from his life. Banal repetitions are to be omitted. The narratives are 'stories' from a life but presented with detached acceptance of life. The image of the self presented is total only if the self is looked at nakedly, without any reservation, from all significant turning modes in life. Shobha De has established not only in her fictions but even in *Selective Memory* her superb mastery over characterization. So the problem of no lines in the picture of Sudhir and not sufficient dark ones in the case of Dilip De does not originate from Shobha De's inability as an artist but from her claim to privacy or secrecy as an artist.

> I have chosen to carve up my life into those segments I have no reservations about revealing and serving up to readers. It isn't lapses in memory I'm hiding behind. Rather, it is my conscious decision to exercise control over those aspects of my life I'm not ready to make public. Those that are precious and private to me. It's all about 'readiness,' isn't it? Some people can do it (reveal all) without any reservations and even fewer regrets. I cannot. And have no desire to. (527)

If *Selective Memory* is to be regarded as a fictional autobiography then the 'fictional' nature of the work surely allows such an uncontrolled freedom to the writer. But if the book is to be regarded as a pure/non-fictional autobiography, such a claim to control life under focus is doubtful and debatable. It's not a question of readiness, but of the tenets of an art-form.

V

An autobiographer can begin his life-story from any point, not necessarily from birth. He is free to choose his starting point, but he has to effect a judicious choice in the selection of events. Regarding the choice of events, Andre Maurois says, "A biographer or autobiographer is obliged to omit from his narrative, the commonplace of daily life and to limit himself almost exclusively to salient events, actions and traits. The writing and the reading of the bulky volumes otherwise required would be alike impossible."[11] The significance of an event is judged not from general point cf view, but from the point of view of the autobiographer. A small and casual event that contributes to building his character is of immense significance and should find place in his life-story.

Shobha De has evidenced a great mastery in selecting and weaving a chain of such events that have shaped her mind and have contributed to her development. "If nothing else, *Selective Memory* aided and abetted the transformation, kick-started the process, as it were. Forced me to glance over my shoulder. Look back, sift, discard, reinforce, assess, re-assess, come to terms, recognize, accept—above all, accept." (11) She remembers the past in all its colours and significance. Even the location also contributes to the course one's life takes and the choices one makes. When they shifted to a smart area of Bombay, the old Queen's road, 'This was downtown Mumbai—fashionable, affluent and sexy. . . . I had found my kind of environment, my kind of people, my kind of fun.' (20)

She narrates the stories of men who have shaped her life significantly. On a wet gloomy morning in mid-1970, Shobha De entered the cabin of Shilpa Shah in Creative Unit, a modest size ad agency. Shobha De was busy with her modelling. Shilpa asked her, 'can you write?' Of course, she can, how good, don't know. Shilpa was looking for someone to do her work—copy writing during her maternity leave. Her boss, Nari Hira, asked Shobha De to see him but with a cutting remark, "He said he needs someone who's willing to work hard. Someone who can write . . . not a glamour doll." (85) Shilpa insisted 'go prove him wrong' and Shobha De also agreed as she had nothing to lose.

Nari Hira was no fat, bald, smelly Sindhi, but had movie-star good looks. He aggressively asked her, 'can you write?' She was annoyed by the question and resented the tone. He gave a copy test for three products and went away for lunch. She was not eager for getting a job but faced the moment with 'why not?' attitude. He looked through her effort. 'Expressionless. I was beyond caring.' He ordered for the second test. She wanted to revolt. 'But something about the way I was ordered to do the second on-the-spot test kept me stuck to the chair. I can't explain it.' (88) She was angry and mad. She handed him the sheet indifferently. Her self-searching attitude makes Shobha De see through her past reactions.

> I didn't want the job anyway . . . or did I? I was fed up with modelling. . . . I was twenty-two. Restless. Directionless. Drifting along . . . I wanted to do something. I wanted someone to tell me exactly what. . . . Nari was that person. Though Nari did not know or intend playing that role. Maybe . . . by happy accident that one casually uttered . . . question . . . changed the direction of my life for me, gave me my future vocation. Another identity. A new future. (88-89)

As Shobha De feels 'very contained and complete within the family fold,' (409) in the stories of her life crucial moments and relations find ample space. Each experience traces her developing self. In Ranadip and Radhika, Shobha sees their mother far more clearly than she can see herself. She is no longer agonized by this fact, doesn't feel it to be her defeat. She accepts the triumph of nature over nurture not with resignation but with calm acceptance. "Instead I remember how bravely she'd defended me in a hostile classroom when I was asked to give a presentation on popular culture to seniors majoring in English literature at her college. . . . She'd sat through my hour-long lecture with her head held high, unflinching in her support." (486)

Not only the choice, but Shobha De's presentation of the events is also very effective. Her expression and her mature understanding of human mind are artistically fused together. "Asha knows exactly which buttons to press, how hard and for how long. That is her strength." (244) When Asha Bhonsale became the surprise winner in the first channel V awards, she knew she challenged not just youth, but an entire life style. "As she simpered on stage while clutching her award, she 'blurted' out mock-innocently that she was stumped for words since the place was full of 'little, little kids in little, little clothes.' The reference wasn't missed on the crowd. . . . It roared its approval and she knew she'd won over a brand-new constituency with that one, well thought-out remark." (245)

VI

Though portrayal of self is the prime function of autobiography, man is not an isolated island. Man and society are so interweaved together that in every life-story, society is always a live presence. D.G. Naik perceptively remarks, "Certain autobiographies enable us to know the history of certain periods in a far better way than the actual books of history." (42)

Shobha De's childhood memories recreate middle-class Maharashtrian family of that time with all its marked characteristics. The triumphant cries of 'Mulga' (boy), 'Mulga' and the scornful references to poor Raosaheb's 'Mulgi' (girl) indicate the traditional tendency to celebrate the birth of a male child and regard a female child as a liability to the family. Shobha De presents this situation so tellingly. When her brother Ashok was born, the elder sister Mandakini had an auspicious kumkum hand impression imprinted on her back. When Shobha De was born, her elder sister Kunda also expected the same celebration but met with a withering snap from their maternal grandmother: "What? you want kumkum on your back? Go and fetch some cow-dung instead. Do you realize there are three daughters in the family now? Three, weren't two enough?" (13)

In equally forthright manner, Shobha De relates her experiences in modelling. As an insider, she regarded the fashion world to be 'fake, unnatural and comical.' (39) To her, fashion shows were nothing but entertaining 'tamashas.' (51) Ramp modelling was something she forced herself to do, but photographic modelling really interested her. Still she was not particularly proud of what she was doing. She felt embarrassed and ashamed of the job description—the mention of the 'm-word.' (53) Through her adventures with *Stardust, Society* and *Celebrity,* she bluntly exposes the world of glamour "brash, affluent and ambitious" with their "hi-jinks, follies and neuroses." Even the criminal world does not escape her unsparing eye and comic sense of paradox.

> 'Nobody from Pakistan can perform in India unless Hajibhai or I clear the visit,' she bragged. 'Crawford Market falls at his feet, darling. Every shopkeeper there garlands us when we go. We've done so much for them.' Rukhsana continued. Crawford Market was infested with smugglers and unofficial money changers. The funny thing about her boasts was that every word was probably true. And to think the enormous, covered market was located right opposite one of Bombay's largest police stations. (200)

Simranjit Singh Mann's interview published in her magazine *Celebrity* highlights contemporary complex political situation. She did not know Mann was on the 'Most Wanted' list as the main person accused of plotting against the government, the master-mind behind Mrs. Indira Gandhi's assassination. She published the piece for two reasons, "to oblige Olga, my journalist friend, and because I enjoyed meeting controversial, kinky people." (208) The situation in Punjab was violent and volatile. Mann had formed his own political party. He was regarded as a 'martyr to Sikh cause.' Shobha De was dragged into the mess "only because of bad timing—the *Celebrity* interview with Mann was his sole interview in print besides being the last one published before his dramatic disappearance. The cops wanted to establish some sort of a link." (209) Shobha De was named accused number two in a case of treason against the State of India. Just then the government fell. Chandra Shekhar, as P.M., released all political prisoners. Shobha De delivered Arundhati and Mann went back as a hero to Punjab and contested the next election successfully.

She has "no quarrel with changing mores, changing definitions. Every generation feels morally obliged to register its horror at falling standards." (226) She is painfully aware of filthy lure of the present young generation for glamour and publicity. Of course, she is conscious that in such an undisguisedly materialistic environment, all other values lose their meaning. Everybody wants to be famous in these 'celebrity-driven' times: 'we are rapidly becoming a nation of fame-junkies.' (227)

VII

Through the chain of small events interwoven intricately, a successful autobiographer goes beyond the tiny details and presents a total vision of the true self who plays the various roles. In *Selective Memory* there is no dichotomy between the private and the public, but a happy intermingling of the two aspects, each enriching the texture of the other. Shobha De is able to discover a developing feminine mind that helped her to scale heights in various fields of public life as a super model, a magazine editor, columnist, social commentator, TV scriptwriter, celebrity journalist and best-selling author.

Shobha De begins her life-story in right mood of 'sweet acceptance.' (10) She doesn't like to interpret this change as a sign of mellowing which implies fiery youth to be an immature stage. To her, this is a natural phenomenon of change that occurs with advancing age. She has no nostalgia to hanker after her earlier images, but has readiness to accept her new identity.

> Mellow? who needs Mellow? I am not 'nice,' you dumb clucks. Nor mellow. Merely older. I can't be a brat at fifty. It's obscene. Fortunately a few remnants of that other woman are still intact. I found myself squaring my shoulders, sticking my chin out and thinking, 'so what? I've changed, I'm entitled to. Those who're looking for the familiar me will just have to settle for this one—or lump it. For, this one is here to stay. And frankly, I'm rather enjoying being her.' (10-11)

Because of the independent functioning mind and blunt courage to assert her self, Shobha De is often regarded as a rebel. She doesn't agree with her social image as a 'rebel,' a controversial personality. 'Journalists often ask me whether I was a rebel. And I hotly deny ever having been one.' (31) She doesn't remember going through 'angry, defiant, rebellious outbursts.' She was often baffled by adult reactions to actions which seemed to her 'perfectly acceptable' and 'very reasonable.' 'It's true I'd sulk, but overt displays of rebellion were not my style.' (31) The real question is not of style, but of mental make-up. She views rebel only in negative colours. 'The image I harbour of a rebel is a negative one. Of a person who determinedly shatters known rules of conduct and upsets everybody around by being impossible and obstinate.' (32) But rebel is an open-eneded concept—not only negative. Rebel is 'one who resents and resists authority.'[12] In this definition, the expression may be open or indirect. His refusal to adhere to the established norms is a reaction to the already set action of pressurizing. Independence of mind is the basis of a rebel. This is exactly what Shobha De has done throughout her life. 'Maybe I didn't conform to norms laid down by those in authority.' (31) It is equally true that she has never been an iconoclast. She was not a rude or difficult child. She didn't set out to break rules or shock anybody deliberately. Her honest assessment of her stand truly speaks for herself. "I did what came naturally to me without worrying too much about the consequences." (31)

Shobha De claims, "I was not a careerist. So many years later, I still don't consider myself one." (90) Surely, she is not a person whose chief interest is personal advancement in her profession. She worked in various fields but never ran after anything madly. Her career 'happened' in unexpected ways. With each change she tries to discover new identity for her 'self.' Her multi-faceted personality happily constitutes such diverse images—a dashing media person, a best-selling controversial writer and a woman doting on her family. She has faced each moment naturally as a woman discovering her natural feminine identity. It is significant that her response to writing as a creative activity is characteristically feminine. "For a woman, a book in progress is like a secret lover she has to hide from her family. Steal time to go back to. Dream about. Luxuriate in. Fantasize about. . . . The book makes you feel desirable, sexy, beautiful, interesting. It's better than the best sex." (2)

Of course, she is not a feminist. Even though her life took unexpected turns and she always carved a way out for her in her own way, she has 'nothing to prove.' She does not long for anything grand. Even her writing is not in conflict with her daily routine. "As for writing—it will always be there, in one form, or another. . . . I used to think I would be paralysed without a pen to wield. Not so. There is life after and beyond writing." (400) She willingly compromises with life, but her options are neither forced compulsions for her, nor meek submissions before any authority. They are her choices. She is not 'traditional' in the sense her mother was. Through *Selective Memory* emerges a woman who has loved, laughed, cried, lived life fully, not in a shy way but with daring, in her own way. She may not be female Frank Sinatra, but she is Shobha De. She is able to discover herself. "This is my reality. I have chosen it!" (384) *Selective Memory: Stories from My Life* is an honest record of this eternal search for self, "The makeover isn't over yet. But the book is." (11)

NOTES

1. *Encyclopedia Britannica* (1768; London: William Benton, 1973), Vol. 2, p. 854.
2. *The Universal Dictionary of the English Language*, Comp. Henry Cecil Wyld (Hertfordshire: Wordsworth, 1989), p. 67.
3. *The New Lexicon Webster's Dictionary of the English Language* (rev. ed. 1972; New York: Lexicon, 1987), p. 64.
4. D.G. Naik, *Art of Autobiography* (Poona: Vidarbha Marathwada Book Company, 1962), p. 44.
5. Shobha De, *Selective Memory: Stories from My Life* (New Delhi: Penguin India, 1998), p. 1.
6. James Boswell, *The Life of Samuel Johnson* (London: Henry Frowde, 1904), Vol. 1, p. 1.
7. Vimal Bhalerao, *Aadhunik Marathi Vangmayatil Sriyanehi Atmacharitre, Ek Abhyasa* (Nagpur: Sahitya Prasar Kendra, 1986), p. 19.
8. William Shakespeare, *Othello*, ed. K.N. Khandelwal (Agra: Laxmi Narain Agarwal), p. 164.
9. Harold Nicolson, *The Development of English Biography* (London: The Hogarth Press, 1947).
10. Roy Pascal, *Design and Truth in Autobiography* (London: Routledge and Kegan Paul, 1962), p. 41.
11. Andre Maurois, *Aspects of Biography* (Cambridge: Cambridge Univ. Press, 1929), p. 141.
12. *Chambers's Twentieth Century Dictionary*, ed. William Geddie (rev. ed. 1969; rpt. Bombay: Allied, 1970), p. 919.

Selective Memory: A Reflective Response

NIRMALA C. PRAKASH

An autobiography, other than being the specimen of a distinguished literary genre, provides abundant scope to know the person behind the writer closely. It opens a window into the many-sided personality of the writer. This kind of knowledge, though not a pre-condition for interpreting literay texts, certainly proves gainful to the reader/critic in terms of adding new dimensions to the interpretation of the works of the author.

There has been a pretty long tradition of writing autobiographies in India as evidenced by, to quote a few, *The Story of My Experiments with Truth* by Mahatma Gandhi, *An Autobiography* by Jawaharlal Nehru *Autobiography of a Native Alien* by Zulfikar Ghose and of course what C.D. Narasimaiah calls "that unreadable" *Autobiography of an Unknown Indian* by Nirad Chaudhuri. If it were great men like Gandhi and Nehru who propagated the tradition of writing autobiographies, women writers of the Indian Literary scene too have shown extraordinary courage by demolishing the socially imposed fortress of feminine inhibitions and dwelling publicly upon the experiences and responses of their private life. *With No Regrets* by Krishna Hutheesingh, *My Story* by Kamala Das and *Prison and Chocolate* by Nayantara Sahgal are some of the noteworthy examples. Shobha De too, by writing *Selective Memory*, has chosen to embark upon a bold adventure even while carrying forward the tradition of writing autobiographies.

Selective Memory subtitled as "Stories from My Life" is a heartening change for the readers of Shobha De. It gives them an ample opportunity to know this popular fiction writer, well-known newspaper columnist and glamorous personality more intimately. The book has, in my opinion, also added in great measure to the literary stature of the author herself. I say so because Shobha De has never been considered a serious writer. She has either been dismissed or, at best, discussed among literary circles as a female counterpart of Khushwant Singh, who, as even discernible readers of literature know, enjoys the reputation of being peerless in handling certain themes in his very own inimitable and titillatingly distinct style.

Partly her own writings and to some extent media have projected Shobha De as a glamorous person who is a keen observer of upper-class life of cosmopolitan cities (particularly Mumbai) but lacks commitment to the social cause. This kind of public and literary image does not augur well for Shobha De, the person, either. But *Selective Memory* has worked wonders in favour of Shobha De, the person as well as Shobha De, the writer. After reading this book one is bound to shake off the image of the writer who could inhabit only the fringe of literary canvas. There also emerges the image of a person who is deeply conventional and devoted and tries to play every role assigned by life or circumstances to perfection, has immense capacity to judge people impersonally and possesses a mischievous charm to disarm people even while appearing to be modest. Here is a new Shobha De, at least I feel so, having gone through the book closely.

The author seems to be conscious of the tremendous responsibility involved in handling this particular genre. She seems to make amends for being peripheral and merely titillating in some of her earlier works. In *Selective Memory*, she puts across her experiences and responses in a convincing manner so as to form a unified literary whole.

Theorists of the autobiographical genre frequently use the metaphor of mirror to drive home the similarities between the creation and the creator, or the writing and the writer. Employing the same metaphor, Georges Gusdorf writes in his highly acclaimed essay "Conditions and Limits of Autobiography," "Autobiography is the mirror in which the individual reflects his own image." (1956:33) In the 'Prologue,' Shobha De gives a candid account of recreating her image in form of an autobiography at a mid-point of her life as she writes:

> I thought people wrote their memoirs at seventy. Nice number, seventy. It's all behind you. Good times and bad. You want to chronicle it before memory itself fades. People also write their memoirs at twenty. Nice number again. Twenty. It's all ahead of you. Good and bad. You can't wait to get it all down before

> life itself hurtles past and memories seem redundant.
> 'Fifty is in between.' . . . Fifty is so . . . non-committal and boring. I hate mid-points. (1)

Transparency is the watchword in autobiographical writings. To quote W.B. Yeats, "there is more enterprise in walking naked." However, transparency is not to be viewed in isolation. It does reflect the individual, but the individual is viewed against the prevailing social norms. Shobha De, while rediscovering her individual self turns reflective and evinces a high level of social consciousness:

> The image I harbor of a rebel is a negative one. Of a person who determinedly shatters known rules of conduct and upsets everybody around by being impossible and obstinate. I did swim against the tide but while I was doing so, my own sights were on getting to the other shore, not on the turbulence I may have been learning in my wake. (32)
> The fact that I was nowhere as clever as my siblings did not cause me any anxiety. I didn't lose sleep over my average report cards. I didn't envy those who did far better. Nor did I feel inferior by comparison. Perhaps had I shown a little shame, remorse or contrition, my father would have felt less hostile. It didn't occur to me to pretend or make promises I had no intention of keeping. (33)

Reflection on the past can be an amalgamation of the sweet sour memories when viewed in a mature perspective. The writer might in the process probe into his/her experiences afresh and gain new insights. Shobha De's reflections upon her past from the days of a struggling model to a successful career girl who rarely cared for the social embarrassment faced by her parents bespeak of her rediscovered sensibility. 'Walking Tall' and 'Cutting Loose' serve as reminiscences of these feelings wherein she writes:

> My father did express strong disapproval over my pose, outfit and brief interview for *Femina*—understandably so. I was clad in a smart blouse . . . made out of handmade paper . . . staring goggly-eyed at a paper parrot, while the blurb inside quoted me

> saying my sole ambition in life was to get married and have lots of children. Oh well, I guess I've fulfilled that all right. But my father was disappointed and disgusted by my lack of drive (42)

Shobha De is capable of looking at people and her own relationship with them dispassionately. This is symptomatic of the capacity to develop an inward eye to look within one's own self critically. 'Blazing Trails' and 'Shining Through' account for Shobha De's close communion as a film journalist with film stars and other social celebrities.

Her reminiscences of the celebrity world are unprejudiced and well balanced. However, she does not fail to observe the film stars' cherished desire of being always surrounded by the celebrity halo. Their lives are, by and large, spurred by an unbridled desire for name and fame, as she writes: "Initially I'd find it strange that the same people whose lives we'd ripped apart, whose sentiments we'd often hurt, whose reputations we'd shredded, were ready to extend party invitations and grant interviews to the staffers they were supposed to be at war with." (117)

Shobha De raises a very pertinent question here, "How could anyone forgive so easily?" And Dharmendra is singled out as an exception who could dare "to break the cozy pact between maligned stars and reporters." (118) As one goes on to read, one finds the author harnessing inimitable courage to use not-so-complimentary terms for people who are still bracketed as celebrities in the Indian society.

The conventional self of Shobha De frequently commands and moulds her feelings. Attitudes for her have to measure up to social values when adopting a didactic tone. Shobha De writes about two successful young stars who were

> ill-mannered, self-absorbed and unsophisticated enough to chatter idiotically through other people's speeches . . . that they were arrogant enough to keep several senior citizens waiting, that they didn't have the grace to apologize for coming late and worse, nobody had taught them better or given them lessons in basic etiquette. (163)

This, however, is not a sweeping remark to dismiss the entire younger generation of stars. Madhuri Dixit receives a clean chit for her sagaciously balanced professional and personal life.

Since an autobiography deals with the vicissitudes of one's own life, the writer might show a tendency to deliberately indulge in details so as to win sympathy or to present a holistic picture of the self. It requires maturity of vision to ride over such temptations. Shobha De, while dwelling upon the memories of hard days when she was almost jobless, penniless, does not show signs of self-pity or self-dramatization. On the contrary, one comes across a woman of tremendous grit who was prepared to fight her way out. However, she does not forget to express her gratitude towards Nari Hira for his immense support during the thick and thin of her life. Sunil Gavaskar too is placed on the same pedestal for his sincerity as a friend and honestly pragmatic as well as level-headed attitude towards life.

All writers of autobiographies are faced with a complex problem. They have to strike a balance between revelation and concealment, between openness and secrecy. Shobha De seems to know her job well. In 'Getting Personal' she delineates certain bitter experiences of her personal life such as her first marriage leading to divorce. But the revelations are far from being scandalous: at no point she elaborates upon the unpalatable realities that might have led to hurt feelings or bruised eyes. Here, she evinces the polished style of a skilful craftswoman who is capable of hiding much more than what she reveals. However, the details are free from even a remote tinge of bitterness.

Rather one comes across a totally new side of the celebrity that Shobha De has been popularly acclaimed. One envisages a typical Indian woman who struggles hard to strike a balance between her professional and domestic front and yet comes out successfully. She exudes rare energy, warmth, care and dedication, particularly, as a mother who manages to snatch time for school meetings too. "My life was crowded with family and I preferred it that way." (409) One also notices here her capacity to have fun at her own cost when she observes other young mothers in school and considers them fit enough to be her daughters. Rare sense of humour, indeed.

The warm, conventional and thoughtful aide of Shobha De's personality is further revealed when she recalls the details of the last moments of her mother's life. One discovers a dedicated daughter who is prepared to sacrifice everything for the happiness of her parents.

And, then, a thought to spare on her own generation. One certainly needs a treasure house of experiences to ponder over life in such a philosophical vein:

> I fear for my generation of women—they really are like daughters, neither here nor there. They definitely don't want to be like their mothers and they definitely want to switch places with their daughters (what for, I ask you?). We talk of options, opportunites and choices—sure we have them. What do we do actually with these goodies? We earn, we travel, we splurge . . . and we weep. (414)

Finally *Selective Memory* serves as a mirror to reflect the author's own life and also a lamp which lights others's ways through the thick and thin of her experiences. It proves beyond doubt the coming of mellowing age of the author who has every reason to feel "better about myself, so comfortable in my skin, never as much at peace." (10)

To conclude, I quote her own reassuring words, "whispered behind my back or uttered sweetly to my face; know something? You've mellowed. Really you. It's so nice." (10) No traces of vainglory. Mellowed you have indeed, Shobha De, both in style and perception, and gained in stature.

Contributors

MADHUMALATI ADHIKARI	Maharani Durgavati Univ. Jabalpur
NEENA ARORA	H.P. University Shimla.
URBASHI BARAT	Maharani Durgavati Univ Jabalpur
G.D. BARCHE	S.S.V.P.S. Arts & MFMA Commerce College. Dhule
GITA BARUA	Institute of Tibetan Studies. Varanasi
INDIRA BHATT	C.U. Shah Science College Ahmedabad
SUBHASH CHANDRA	S.B.S. College University of Delhi
SANDHYARANI DASH	V.N. College Jajpur
R.K. DHAWAN	S.B.S. College University of Delhi
JAYDIPSINH DODIYA	Saurashtra University Rajkot
P.S. KASTURE	R.D.G. College for Women Akola
GAJENDRA KUMAR	Rajendra College Chapra
SANJAY KUMAR	M.K. Saboo P.G. College Pilani
SUDHIR KUMAR	Punjab University Chandigarh
PUSHP LATA	Languages Department FDI. BITS. Pilani

CHITTARANJAN MISRA
S.C.S. College
Puri

ALESSANDRO MONTI
University of Torino
Italy

PRAMOD NAYAR
Kuvempu University
Shimoga

PRABHAT K. PANDEYA
B.H.U.
Varanasi

R.S. PATHAK
Dr. H.S. Gour University
Sagar

NIRMALA C. PRAKASH
Karnataka State Open Univ.
Mysore

SHEELA SWAROOPA RANI
S.P. Mahila University
Tirupati

BHARGAVI P. RAO
Osmania University
Hyderabad

E. SATYANARAYANA
Univ. Arts & Sc. College
Kakatiya Univ., Warangal

ALKA SAXENA
D.A.V. College
Kanpur

SARBANI SEN
Formerly at Modern College
Pune

SHARAD SHRIVASTAVA
M.L. Sukhadia University
Udaipur

N.P. SINGH
Rajdhani College
University of Delhi

K.V. SURENDRAN
Kannur University
Palayad, Thalassery

S.P. SWAIN
Municipal College
Rourkela

NEELAM TIKKHA
Nagpur University
Nagpur

NISHA TRIVEDI
Govt. Girls School
Bilaspur

INNA WALTER
Osmania University
Hyderabad